D0731897

WORKERS' COMPENSATION AND EMPLOYEE PROTECTION LAWS
IN A NUTSHELL

Fifth Edition

By

JACK B. HOOD

Former Adjunct Professor of Law
University of Georgia School of Law

BENJAMIN A. HARDY, JR.

Associate Professor
Jacksonville State University

HAROLD S. LEWIS, JR.

Walter F. George Professor of Law
Mercer University School of Law

A Thomson Reuters business

Mat #41144040

Nutshell Series, In a Nutshell and the Nutshell Logo are trademarks registered in the U.S. Patent and Trademark Office.

COPYRIGHT © 1984, 1990 WEST PUBLISHING CO.
© West a Thomson business, 1999, 2005
© 2011 Thomson Reuters

    610 Opperman Drive
    St. Paul, MN 55123
    1–800–313–9378

Printed in the United States of America

ISBN: 978–0–314–27532–5

TO

Our wives and families:
Wife, Pat Hood; daughters Sara and Laura Hood;
and Laura's son, Walkin E. Cleage
Wife, Linda Hardy; and son, Andy Hardy
Wife, Leslie Lewis; daughter, Carmen Miller, and
her children Isabel and Gabriel

PREFACE

Our purpose in writing this Nutshell is to provide an overview of the laws affecting employees in the workplace. It is our hope that the sections on workers' compensation and employment discrimination will provide both students and lawyers with insight into the most common questions in the fields. Only brief summaries have been attempted in the chapters and sections dealing with other employee protection laws because the subject areas were too large for a more detailed explanation in a Nutshell book.

It should be noted that one hundred years ago, in 1911, Wisconsin enacted the first constitutional workers' compensation law on the state level in the United States. Since then many changes have occurred in social legislation, but workers' compensation has remained a central part of the employee-employer legal relationship. It appears that workers' compensation will retain that important role for the foreseeable future. An excellent and comprehensive treatment of workers' compensation is to be found in Larsons' multi-volume treatise on the subject, and we have given some useful citations to that work at relevant points. We have also given numerous cites to Modern Workers Compensation (Westlaw database MWC) and to West's Workers' Compensation Guide (Westlaw database WCGD).

The following Nutshells also may be useful in the study of employee rights and protections: Barron and Dienes' Constitutional Law in a Nutshell (Westlaw database CONLAW–NS); Colker's Federal Disability Law in a Nutshell (Westlaw database FEDDISABL–NS); Collins' Section 1983 Litigation in a Nutshell (Westlaw database SEC1983–NS); Conison's Employee Benefit Plans in a Nutshell (Westlaw database EMPBENPLN–NS); Covington and Decker's Employment Law in a Nutshell (Westlaw database EMPLAW–NS); Frolik and Kaplan's Elder Law in a Nutshell (Westlaw database ELDERLAW–NS); Leslie's Labor Law in a Nutshell (Westlaw database LABLAW–NS); Maraist and Galligan's Admiralty in a Nutshell (Westlaw database ADMIRALTY–NS); Nolan's Labor and Employment Arbitration in a Nutshell (Westlaw database EMPARB–NS); Player's Federal Law of Employment Discrimination in a Nutshell (Westlaw database EMPDISCR–NS); and Weissbrodt's and Danielson's Immigration Law and Procedure in a Nutshell (Westlaw database IMLPRO–NS).

Citations to legislation, cases, materials, websites, works, and/or treatises have been added in most of the chapters and sections so that one can further pursue the specific topics and issues more easily.

We would like to acknowledge and thank our research assistant and University of Virginia Law School student, Lauren A. Simpson, of Birmingham,

PREFACE

Alabama. We further acknowledge and thank Louis H. Higgins, Editor in Chief of West Academic Publishing in Eagan, Minnesota. We also express our appreciation to the law libraries at Mercer University, Cumberland School of Law of Samford University, and the University of Alabama.

JACK B. HOOD

BENJAMIN A. HARDY, JR.

HAROLD S. LEWIS, JR.

June 1, 2011
Birmingham, Alabama

OUTLINE

PART 2. THE LAW OF WORKERS' COMPENSATION

TABLE OF CASES

References are to Pages

A

B

C

D

E

F

G

H

K

L

M

N

O

P

Q

R

S

T

U

V

W

Y

Z

—

WORKERS' COMPENSATION AND EMPLOYEE PROTECTION LAWS
IN A NUTSHELL

Fifth Edition

PART 1

HISTORICAL BACKGROUND OF COMPENSATION LEGISLATION

CHAPTER 1

EMPLOYMENT RELATED ACTIONS AND LEGISLATION

A. EMPLOYEE COMMON–LAW REMEDIES

The common law imposed a number of duties on employers for the protection of their employees, and an action existed for the breach of these duties; however, as a practical matter, the common law failed to provide adequate remedies for such injuries and deaths. The common-law duties imposed upon the master were as follows:

(1) to provide a safe place to work;

(2) to provide safe appliances, tools, and equipment;

(3) to give warnings of dangers of which the employee might reasonably be expected to remain in ignorance;

(4) to provide a sufficient number of fit, trained, or suitable fellow servants to perform assigned tasks; and

(5) to promulgate and enforce rules relating to employee conduct that would make the work safe.

1

Employee remedies based upon a breach of the foregoing duties were restricted by the "unholy trinity" of common-law defenses: (1) fellow-servant doctrine; (2) contributory negligence; and (3) assumption of risk. See *Prosser and Keeton on Torts* § 80 (5th ed. 1984).

1. FELLOW–SERVANT DOCTRINE

Unless there was an express contract, the rule at common law was that a master was not liable to a servant for injuries due to the negligence of a fellow servant. *Priestley v. Fowler*, (1837) 150 Eng. Rep. 1030 (Exch.); see *Murray v. South Carolina Rail Road Co.*, 26 S.C.L. 385 (1 McMul.) (1841). The doctrine provided that the negligence of a co-employee was not to be imputed to the master; of course, the injured employee, for what it was worth, could still sue a co-employee. The fellow-servant rule was not founded in abstract or natural justice, and the rule was an exception to the rule of agency and the general rule that a master was responsible for injuries caused to third persons by the negligence of servants who were acting within the scope of their employment. In support of the fellow-servant doctrine, it was said that the negligence of a fellow servant was one of the risks incident to employment, and the risk was assumed by the servant as an implied term of the employment contract. Public policy in support of the doctrine was to the effect that the rule would make servants careful and watchful with regard to each other, thus promoting greater care in the performance of their duties.

The harshness of the fellow-servant doctrine was lessened by the recognition of certain exceptions. For example, servants who did not have a common master and who were not engaged in the same enterprise were not barred from recovery by the fellow-servant rules. Furthermore, if they were employed in different departments of the same enterprise, the employees were not generally to be treated as fellow servants. The most important exception involved the negligence of a "vice-principal" because the fellow-servant bar did not apply to the vice-principal. One approach required that the vice-principal be a supervisory employee, representing the employer in his duty toward the employee. The vice-principal exception has been held to apply to any servant, as opposed to just superior servants. The key inquiry aimed at an employer's liability was whether a servant (the alleged vice-principal) owed an obligation to the injured employee to meet the common-law duties of the employer. In order for the master to be liable, these duties were viewed as being non-delegable. The vice-principal exception was subject to an important qualification: It was not applicable to those incidental dangers that arose out of the operational details of a fellow servant's work. No duty was owed by the master with regard to these risks. See generally J.D. Lee & B. Lindahl, 4 *Modern Tort Law: Liability and Litigation* § 43:9—Master–Servant Relationship—Defenses—Fellow Servant Doctrine (2d ed. 2008).

In modern times, the fellow-servant doctrine has been abolished or severely limited in most jurisdictions by legislation under the workers' compensation acts or by judicial decision. (See *Glass v. City of Chattanooga*, 858 S.W.2d 312, 315 (Tenn. 1993) ("The fellow servant rule was created by judicial fiat and we now declare its demise. It is a rule that has largely been displaced by enactment of the Workers' Compensation statutes and under present conditions serves no useful purpose in the work place."); *Buckley v. City of New York*, 437 N.E.2d 1088 (N.Y. 1982)).

2. CONTRIBUTORY NEGLIGENCE

An employee or servant was required to exercise reasonable care for his own safety, and his failure to use the precautions that ordinary prudence required barred any recovery under the contributory negligence defense. Exceptions existed on the basis of the last clear chance doctrine and in situations in which the master's conduct was willful or wanton. As a result of the doctrine's harshness, statutes sometimes abrogated the defense and statutorily imposed requirements for worker safety, placing certain servants in a special, protected category. In some jurisdictions, comparative negligence statutes aided employees. In others, the courts adopted comparative fault principles. See *Carroll v. Whitney*, 29 S.W.3d 14, 17–18 (Tenn. 2000) (history of change to comparative negligence); but see *Williams v. Delta Int'l Machinery Corp.*, 619 So.2d 1330 (Ala. 1993) (retaining contributory negligence and rejecting comparative fault principles).

3. ASSUMPTION OF RISK

The assumption of risk defense was grounded in the notion that the servant or employee had voluntarily agreed to assume the dangers normally and ordinarily incident to the work. Risks that a mature worker was presumed to know were covered, regardless of whether one had actual knowledge. The employee further assumed such extraordinary and abnormal risks of which he had knowledge and appreciation. Assumption of risk was customarily based upon contract theory, as opposed to contributory negligence, which was based upon tort theory. Contributory negligence involved the notion of fault and a breach of duty to one's self, whereas assumption of risk could exist in the absence of fault because of its contractual nature. Employees or servants did not assume those risks growing out of the negligence of the master or of a vice-principal. Generally, risks arising out of the non-delegable duties doctrine were not viewed as the ordinary sort of risks that one could assume; these were treated as extraordinary risks that one did not assume. It should be kept in mind that recovery could still be barred by one's contributory negligence. See *Jenkins v. Union Pac. R.R. Co.*, 22 F.3d 206, 210–11 (9th Cir. 1994) (discussion of history of assumption of risk, the statutory abolition in FELA cases, and the interplay of the FELA's modified contributory negligence principles with comparative fault).

In summary, the foregoing "unholy trinity" may be explained in large part on the basis of the highly individualistic attitude of the common-law courts and society's desire to encourage industrial expansion and development by lessening the financial costs upon industry for industrial injuries and deaths. See R. Epstein, *The Historical Origins and Economic Structure of Workers' Compensation Law*, 16 Ga. L. Rev. 775 (1982); see generally W. Dodd, *Administration of Workmen's Compensation* § 7 (1936); S. Horovitz, *Injury and Death Under Workmen's Compensation Laws* (1944); *Prosser & Keeton on Torts* § 80 (5th ed. 1984).

B. EMPLOYERS' LIABILITY ACTS

Employers' liability acts came into being in response to rising industrial injury and death rates in the 19th century, and in response to dissatisfaction with the common-law remedies available to employees. For example, in 1855, the State of Georgia enacted a statute making railroads liable to employees and others for negligence in situations previously barred by the fellow-servant defense. By 1908, almost every American jurisdiction had passed similar legislation. In that year, Congress placed interstate railroad employees under an employers' liability act system and later extended this coverage to seamen. The state and federal acts generally barred the use of the fellow-servant rule, substituted comparative negligence for pure contributory negligence, and later barred the use of the assumption of risk defense. These employers' liability laws were, however, soon found to be unsatisfactory for several reasons: Workers or their survivors had to bring lawsuits for damages; the employers' defenses, while considerably weakened, still made it difficult for workers to prosecute their cases; the outcomes of the cases were always uncertain; actions were costly to bring and were lengthy; and cases produced ill-will between the employers and employees and posed a constant threat to job security. See generally A. Larson & L. Larson, 1 *Larson's Workers' Compensation Law* ch. 2—Historical Development of Workers' Compensation (Rev. ed. 2000). For a view on the role of insurance in the historical development of this area, see J. Witt, *Toward a New History of American Accident Law: Classical Tort Law and the Cooperative First–Party Insurance Movement*, 114 Harv. L. Rev. 690 (2001).

C. EUROPEAN COMPENSATION LEGISLATION

The historical origins of modern workers' compensation legislation may be found first in Germany, and then in Great Britain. Philosophers and politicians, especially socialists, were of great influence in the development of European compensation legislation, which later influenced the development of similar compensation legislation in the United States.

1. GERMANY

The German influence began in 1838 with the enactment of an employers' liability act that was applicable to railroads. In 1873, Germany extended coverage to workers in factories, mines, and quarries. In 1884, Germany enacted a compulsory system of accident insurance, regarded as the first true workers' compensation act, that covered all employees engaged in manufacturing, mining, and transportation. Similar workers' compensation laws were enacted in Austria in 1887, Norway in 1894, Finland in 1895, and Great Britain in 1897.

2. GREAT BRITAIN

The Workmen's Compensation Act of 1897 provided the prototype and was the forerunner of the majority of compensation acts passed in the early 1900s in the United States. The Act contained important limitations: Only hazardous employments were covered; there were no insurance provisions; and the employer bore the complete burden of compensation benefit costs. The statute also gave rise to the key phrase, "arising out of and in the course of employment," which is generally found today in compensation statutes in the United States. The British legislation differed from the German in several respects: The German statutes attempted to provide broader coverage in the area of social insurance and to provide a more complete compensation system, while the British Act gave a workman only moderate recovery, with the cost being borne by the employer as an expense of doing business.

D. STATE COMPENSATION ACTS

In the early years of the 20th century, there was a gradual recognition that the common-law remedies of employees injured or killed on the job were filled with inequities. The states were slow, however, to adopt workers' compensation laws, and initial attempts to do so faced legal and political opposition. Early compensation legislation was very limited and legislators exercised great caution in replacing the common-law recovery system. While it is beyond the scope of this work to address the various attempts of the states to enact compensation legislation, a sampling is necessary for historical appreciation of workers' compensation legislation in the United States. See R. Epstein, *The Historical Origins and Economic Structure of Workers' Compensation Law*, 16 Ga. L. Rev. 775 (1982); see generally W. Dodd, *Administration of Workmen's Compensation* § 7 (1936); S. Horovitz, *Injury and Death Under Workmen's Compensation Laws* (1944); A. Larson & L. Larson, 1 *Larson's Workers' Compensation Law* ch. 2—Historical Development of Workers' Compensation (Rev. ed. 2000); *Prosser and Keeton on Torts* § 80 (5th ed. 1984).

1. MARYLAND

In 1902, Maryland passed the first workers' compensation act in the United States. It applied to death cases only, and provided coverage to a limited number of workers. This act was declared unconstitutional in *Franklin v. United Railways & Electric Co.*, 2 Baltimore City Reports 309 (1904), however, because it was held to deprive the parties of the right to jury trial and was said to be violative of the separation of powers doctrine (an insurance commissioner, under the executive branch, was performing judicial functions). In 1910, Maryland enacted a voluntary workers' compensation statute, but apathy by employers and employees rendered the legislation ineffective.

The current Maryland workers' compensation law contains the following features:

ADMINISTRATION

State agency—Workers' Compensation Commission.

Notice and filing requirements—Notice within 10 days of injury or 30 days of death; injury claims filed with Commission within 60 days (excusable to two years) and death claims filed within 18 months.

Waiting period for income benefits—three days with retroactive benefits for disability longer than two weeks.

Second injury fund—Subsequent Injury Fund.

COVERAGE

Compulsory—Compulsory for all private employments and public state, county, and agency employments, including minors; elective for sole proprietors and partners; corporate officers with 20% shareholding may reject; other special exceptions for certain domestics, casual workers, farm laborers, and others.

Injuries, deaths, and occupational diseases—Must arise out of and in the course of employment (including frostbite and sunstroke caused by a weather condition).

INSURANCE

Compulsory—State fund with private, individual, and limited group self-insurance permitted.

Penalties for failure to insure—Fines and/or imprisonment; penalty on award; employer's defenses to suit abrogated.

Uninsured Employers' Fund—Pays compensation awards in case of uninsured employers.

Insurance costs—For 2010, $1.63 per $100 of payroll; compared to costs in other states and the District of Columbia, ranks 42nd highest in the nation.

BENEFITS

Income disability benefits—Total disability (permanent and temporary) set at 66 2/3% of worker's average weekly wage (AWW), subject to maximum and minimum; partial disability (scheduled injuries) subject to duration limits and to maximums and minimums calculated using AWW; disfigurement covered.

Income benefits to spouse and children or partial dependents for death—Set at 66 2/3% of worker's AWW, subject to maximum and minimum and conditional time limitations; burial expense allowance subject to $5,000 maximum.

Medical benefits—All hospital, physician, surgical, nursing, and related costs; worker can choose physician but employer can recommend.

Rehabilitation—Loss of compensation for worker's unreasonable refusal once referred for rehabilitation.

STATUTE

Md. Code Ann., Lab. & Empl. § 9–101 *et seq.* (West 2010) (The Workers' Compensation Act includes the Employer's Liability Act).

See generally 4 *Modern Workers Compensation* ch. 321— Statutory Comparison Table (1998); U.S. Chamber of Commerce, *2010 Analysis of Workers' Compensation Laws*; *Workers' Compensation Guide* ch.7—State Laws (2008).

2. MONTANA

In 1909, Montana enacted a compulsory workers' compensation statute, which was designed for employees in the coal industry. Employers and employees alike were required to contribute to a state fund, and a covered employee or his beneficiaries could elect to sue at law or receive compensation from the fund; however, workers could not receive the benefits of both. This legislation was declared unconstitutional in *Cunningham v. Northwestern Improvement Co.*, 119 P. 554 (Mont. 1911), because it was held that employers were denied equal protection of the laws, in that there was the potential for double liability (employers had to contribute to the state compensation fund and additionally were open to suit if an employee or beneficiary so elected).

The current Montana workers' compensation law contains the following features:

ADMINISTRATION

State agency—Department of Labor and Industry.

Notice and filing requirements—Employee must give notice within 30 days unless employer has actual knowledge. Injury and death claims must be filed within 12 months of accident; occupational disease claims must be filed within 12 months of when worker knew or should have known that condition resulted from occupational disease. Claim filing is through the Workers' Compensation Court with direct appeals to the Montana Supreme Court.

Waiting period for income benefits—32 hours or four days of wage loss, whichever is less; eligible for compensation on day 5.

Second injury fund—Insurer pays for first 104 weeks and the fund pays thereafter.

COVERAGE

Compulsory—Unless exempt, coverage is compulsory for all private and public employments, including minors. Exempt employments include domestics, casual workers, certain salespersons, newspaper carriers, licensed foster parents, barbers, licensed horse trainers and jockeys, religious organizations, and others; voluntary coverage is permitted for exempt employments, however. Elective coverage is available for partners, sole proprietors, corporate officers, and certain volunteers.

Injuries, deaths, and occupational diseases—Must arise out of and in the course of employment.

INSURANCE

Compulsory—State fund with private, individual, and limited group self-insurance permitted.

Penalties for failure to insure—Employer's defenses to suit abrogated; assessment of double the amount of unpaid premium.

Uninsured Employers' Fund—Pays compensation awards in case of uninsured employers.

Insurance costs—For 2010, $3.33 per $100 of payroll; compared to costs in other states and the District of Columbia, ranks highest in the nation.

BENEFITS

Income disability benefits—Total disability (permanent and temporary) set at 66 2/3% of worker's average weekly wage (AWW), subject to maximum of 100% of state's average weekly wage and offset by Social Security; partial disability (no scheduled injuries) subject to duration limits and to maximums calculated using the state AWW and reference to AMA Guides; disfigurement covered up to $2,500 for serious face, head, and neck disfigurements.

Income benefits to spouse and children or partial dependents for death—Set at 66 2/3% of worker's AWW, subject to maximum and conditional time limitations; burial expense allowance subject to $4,000 maximum.

Medical benefits—All hospital, physician, surgical, nursing, and related costs; worker can choose physician; after first visit, worker pays $25 for each subsequent emergency room visit unless directed by insurer; after 60 consecutive months of non-use, medical benefits terminate.

Rehabilitation—Allowed for a maximum of 104 weeks with rehabilitation plan to be completed in 26 weeks.

STATUTE

Mont. Code Ann. § 39–71–101 *et seq.*

See generally 4 *Modern Workers Compensation* ch. 321— Statutory Comparison Table (1998); U.S. Chamber of Commerce, *2010 Analysis of Workers' Compensation Laws*; *Workers' Compensation Guide* ch.7—State Laws (2008).

3. MASSACHUSETTS

In 1908, Massachusetts passed a voluntary workers' compensation statute in an effort to avoid some of the theoretical constitutional problems concerning mandatory compensation acts. As a result of the voluntary nature of the act, both employers and employees had no incentive to commit themselves to the scheme, and thus, the Massachusetts act proved to be ineffective.

The current Massachusetts workers' compensation law contains the following features:

ADMINISTRATION

State agency—Division of Industrial Accidents.

Notice and filing requirements—Employee must notify insurer as soon as practicable in writing; this may be excused. Injury and death claims must be filed within four years of knowledge of injury's relationship to employment or within four years after death.

Waiting period for income benefits—Five days with retroactive benefits to date of injury if disability lasts longer than 21 days; if disability lasts between 5 and 21 days, benefits are paid from the sixth day.

Second injury fund—Employer pays for first 104 weeks, and the fund reimburses employer for 75% of benefits thereafter.

COVERAGE

Compulsory—Compulsory for all private and state employments, including minors. Elective coverage for all counties, cities, and districts with the power to tax. Elective coverage for partners, sole proprietors, and corporate officers and directors with at least 25% stock ownerships. Elective coverage for casual, seasonal, or domestics employed less than 16 hours per week. Exempt are masters and seamen in interstate commerce covered by federal laws, commission-paid real estate and non-retail salespersons, independent taxi drivers, athletes with contracts that have disability pay provisions, and certain owners and managers of dwelling houses. Police and firefighters are indemnified by their municipalities.

Injuries, deaths, and occupational diseases—Must arise out of employment.

INSURANCE

Compulsory—Private, individual, and limited group self-insurance permitted.

Penalties for failure to insure—Fines and/or jail; employer's defenses to suit abrogated; employer subject to stop work order; double compensation for injuries caused by employer's serious and willful misconduct; civil penalties also available.

Uninsured Employers' Fund—Workers' Compensation Trust Fund.

Insurance costs—For 2010, $1.54 per $100 of payroll; compared to costs in other states and the District of Columbia, ranks 44th highest in the nation.

BENEFITS

Income disability benefits—Temporary total disability set at 60% of worker's average weekly wage (AWW), subject to maximum and minimum and duration of 156 weeks; total disability (permanent and total) set at 66 2/3% of worker's AWW, subject to maximum and minimum; benefits are offset by pensions, unemployment compensation, and Social Security; partial disability set at 60% of the difference between worker's AWW before and after injury, subject to maximum of 75% of state average weekly wage (AWW) or 66 2/3%, whichever is less, for a duration of 260 weeks, which can be extended to 520 weeks; disfigurement covered up to an additional $15,000, provided that purely scar-based disfigurement awards are for the face, neck, and hands only.

Income benefits to spouse and children or partial dependents for death—Set at 66 2/3% of worker's AWW, subject to maximum and minimum and conditional time limitations; burial expense allowance subject to $4,000 maximum.

Medical benefits—All hospital, physician, surgical, nursing, and related costs; worker can choose physician.

Rehabilitation—Allowed for a maximum of 104 weeks; compensation can be suspended for refusal to participate in rehabilitation.

STATUTE

Mass. Gen. Laws Ann. ch. 152, § 1 *et seq.* (West 2010) (The Workers' Compensation Act does not include the Employer's Liability Act, which is located in Mass. Gen. Laws Ann. ch. 153, § 1 *et seq.* (West 2010), which, with certain limitations, applies to injured or killed workers and employers not covered by the Workers' Compensation Act.)

See generally 4 *Modern Workers Compensation* ch. 321—Statutory Comparison Table (1998); U.S. Chamber of Commerce, *2010 Analysis of Workers' Compensation Laws*; *Workers' Compensation Guide* ch. 7—State Laws (2008).

4. NEW YORK

In 1909, a commission on Employers' Liability was created (popularly known as the "Wainwright Commission") in New

York. Its purpose was to inquire into the liabilities of employers to employees for industrial accidents, and to compare and study efficiencies, costs, justice, merits, and defects in the laws of the other industrial states and countries. The Commission reported that the current common-law system with its employers' liability act exceptions provided insufficient compensation, was wasteful in terms of resources, caused unsatisfactory delays, and was essentially antagonistic in nature. The Commission proposed two statutes in light of constitutional problems. One proposal was aimed at employers and employees when especially dangerous employments were involved. The other statute was designed as an elective statute to cover employments outside of the especially dangerous work categories. In 1910, both the compulsory and voluntary acts were passed. Predictably, the voluntary statute suffered from employer indifference, and the compulsory statute was declared unconstitutional in *Ives v. South Buffalo Railway*, 94 N.E. 431 (N.Y. 1911). Employers were viewed as having been denied due process under both the state and federal constitutions in that employers' property, i.e., money, was taken without consent and without fault.

In 1913, New York amended its constitution to permit the enactment of a compulsory workers' compensation statute, and in 1914, the New York legislature passed a compulsory workers' compensation law that applied only to hazardous employments. In *Jensen v. Southern Pacific Co.*, 109 N.E. 600 (N.Y. 1915), the New York Court of Appeals upheld the statute as a valid exercise of police power. As might be expected, thereafter, mandatory coverage was extended and broadened in New York.

The current New York workers' compensation law contains the following features:

ADMINISTRATION

State agency—Workers' Compensation Board.

Notice and filing requirements—Notice in writing must be given to employer within 30 days of injury or death; this may be excused. Claims must be filed within two years of accident or death. For occupational disease claims, notice must be given to employer within two years of disablement or date claimant knew or should have known of relation to employment; claim must be filed within two years of disablement, death, or date claimant knew or should have known of relation to employment.

Waiting period for income benefits—Seven days with retroactive payments of benefits for disabilities longer than 14 days.

Second injury fund—The Special Injury Disability Fund does not permit new claims for reimbursement after July 1, 2007, and no claims for reimbursement can be filed after July 1, 2010.

COVERAGE

Compulsory—Compulsory for all private and state employments, including minors. Coverage is compulsory for state subdivisions and municipalities for workers engaged in hazardous employments (listed in statute); coverage is voluntary for workers engaged in non-hazardous employments. Coverage is compulsory for public school teachers, except those employed by New York City, and public school aides, including those employed by New York City. Coverage is compulsory for some state volunteer workers, domestics employed 40 or more hours per week by the same employer, and farm workers whose employers paid $1,200 or more for farm labor in the preceding year. Elective coverage is allowed for partners, self-employed persons, sole shareholder/officers, two sole shareholders/officers, and executive officers of religious, charitable, educational, or veterans' organizations. Exempt employments include certain farm laborers; domestics; casual laborers; clergy; charity and educational workers; workers covered by federal compensation laws; minor babysitters; owner-operators of taxicabs; employees of foreign governments; New York City sanitation workers, firefighters, and police officers; and commission-paid real estate, insurance, and stockbroker salespersons. Coverage is voluntary for all exempt employments. There are also two special compensation funds directed to special employment situations: (1) the New York Jockey Injury Compensation Fund and (2) the New York Black Car Operators' Injury Compensation Fund.

Injuries, deaths, and occupational diseases—Must arise out of and in the course of employment.

INSURANCE

Compulsory—State fund with private, individual, and limited group self-insurance permitted.

Penalties for failure to insure—Fines and/or criminal (misdemeanor or felony depending on number of employees) penalties or both; employer's defenses to suit abrogated; employer's business may be enjoined; and additional fines are also available.

Uninsured Employers' Fund—Uninsured Employers' Fund (U.E.F.)

Aggregate Trust Fund—Following permanent disability awards or death awards extending over two years, the Board may require or permit the employer to pay into this fund the present value of future payments under the award. For some scheduled injures and death benefits, the payment is mandatory. In either case, once the payment is made, the employer and insurer are discharged from further payment obligations.

Insurance costs—For 2010, $2.34 per $100 of payroll; compared to costs in other states and the District of Columbia, ranks 13th highest in the nation.

BENEFITS

Income disability benefits—Total disability (permanent and temporary) set at 66 2/3% of worker's average weekly wage (AWW), subject to maximum; permanent partial disabilities from the schedule set at 66 2/3% of worker's AWW, subject to maximum, and duration limits from 15 to 312 weeks as established by the schedule; permanent partial disabilities for unscheduled injuries set at 66 2/3% of the difference between worker's AWW before and after injury and subject to maximum. The Disability Benefit Law (N.Y. Workers' Comp. Law §§ 200–242 (McKinney 2010)) also provides benefits for non-occupational injuries and diseases; this specifically includes pregnancy, even though pregnancy is not a disability; administration is by the Workers' Compensation Board. Supplemental benefits may be awarded to claimants with older awards whose benefits have not kept up with inflation and become inadequate as wage loss replacement; employers may seek reimbursement from the Reopened Case Fund or the Special Fund.

Income benefits to spouse and children or partial dependents for death—Set at 66 2/3% of worker's AWW, subject to maximum and conditional time limitations; some Social Security benefits may be offset; burial expense allowance subject to $5,000 maximum for funerals north of Rockland County and subject to $6,000 maximum for funerals south of Rockland County.

Medical benefits—All hospital, physician, surgical, nursing, and related costs; worker must choose physician from a state list.

Rehabilitation—For vocational rehabilitation maintenance, up to $30 per week is allowed.

STATUTE

N.Y. Workers' Comp. Law § 1 *et seq.* (McKinney 2010) (For injuries and deaths not covered by the New York Workers' Compensation Law, the New York Employers' Liability Act applies.)

See generally 4 *Modern Workers Compensation* ch. 321—Statutory Comparison Table (1998); U.S. Chamber of Commerce, *2010 Analysis of Workers' Compensation Laws*; *Workers' Compensation Guide* ch. 7—State Laws (2008).

5. CALIFORNIA

In 1911, California passed the Roseberry Act, which created its first workers' compensation laws, and in 1917, the Workman's Compensation, Insurance and Safety Act was enacted. Subsequent amendments were frequent in the 1900s, and included the 1937 provisions that consolidated workers' compensation into the state's Labor Code. Important amendments to the Labor Code were made with the passage of the Workers' Compensation Reform Act of 1989, and several important subsequent amendments were also enacted in the 1990s. See generally Cal. Lab. Code § 3200 *et seq.* (West 2010); *Mathews v. Workmen's Comp. App. Bd.*, 493 P.2d 1165 (Cal. 1972); *Grossmont Hosp. v. Workers' Comp. Appeals Bd.*, 69 Cal. Rptr.2d 842 (App. 1997).

In 2004, new reform legislation was passed at the urging of business groups and the California Chamber of Commerce because of perceived high insurance costs and low benefits. Among other items, the reform legislation attempted to increase benefits for workers with severe permanent disabilities, decrease benefits for minor permanent injuries, cap temporary disability benefits for most injuries at two years, remove subjective factors in physician-determined impairment ratings, require physicians to employ national standards in impairment determinations, encourage reinstatement of injured employees, and give employers a better ability to apportion liability by requiring physicians to address causation issues in their disability evaluations and by requiring employees to disclose all prior physical impairments and permanent disabilities.

The foregoing reforms, aimed primarily at benefit eligibility restrictions and medical cost containment, have not had a uniform impact on the rising costs of insurance. The California state fund premiums have increased significantly since 2004, while workers' compensation insurers have been refused rate increases by the Insurance Commissioner. California accounts for approximately 20% of all disability benefits paid in the United States, and therefore, the political and economic realities of the current economic downturn continue to place workers' compensation policy at the forefront of debate in California.

The current California workers' compensation law contains the following features:

ADMINISTRATION

State agency—Division of Workers' Compensation.

Notice and filing requirements—Notice in writing must be given to employer within 30 days of injury or death; this may be excused. Claims for disability or death must be filed within one year of injury or death. Claims for occupational disease must be filed within one year of injury, death, or last payment; further, no death claims can be made more than 240 weeks after injury, except for death claims related to asbestosis, which must be brought within one year of death.

Waiting period for income benefits—Three days with retroactive benefits paid after 14 days; waiting period is terminated by hospitalization.

Second injury fund—Employer pays only for disability resulting from second injury; fund pays for injuries that add to preexisting disabilities that result in a combined permanent disability of at least 70%; second injury must account for 35% unless disability resulted from a major member with the second injury being to the opposite member, and which further resulted in a disability of 5% or more.

COVERAGE

Compulsory—Compulsory for all private and state employments (except clerks and deputies working without pay), including minors. Compulsory coverage for workers in regional occupational centers, programs, or school districts offering training to pupils outside attendance area. Volunteer workers have coverage if the appropriate recreation and park district, school district, sheriff's reserve locality, or public agency adopts resolutions of coverage; court may also adopt a resolution of coverage for juvenile rehabilitation workers. Elective coverage is allowed for partners and private corporation officers, and for directors who are sole shareholders. Excepted from coverage are employer-sponsored bowling teams; watchmen for non-industrial establishments; certain law enforcement officers; certain sports officials; student athletes and uncompensated athletes; certain owner-builder participants in non-profit mutual self-help programs; domestics who work less than 52 hours or earn less than $100 per 90–day period; domestics employed by a parent, spouse, or child; charity workers and volunteers at camps operated by non-profit organizations, or which receive aid or sustenance only from religious, charitable, or relief organizations; or workers at ski lift facilities. For all excepted workers, coverage is voluntary. Employers are not liable for workers injured or killed during off-duty recreational, social, or athletic activities.

Injuries, deaths, and occupational diseases—Must arise out of and in the course of employment.

INSURANCE

Compulsory—State fund with private, individual, and limited group self-insurance permitted.

Penalties for failure to insure—Fines (up to double the premium but not less than $10,000) and/or criminal (misdemeanor—less than one year) penalties; cost of investigation; employer's defenses to suit abrogated and employer presumed negligent; and additional penalties also available for subsequent convictions.

Uninsured Employers' Fund—Uninsured Employers Benefits Trust Fund.

Insurance costs—For 2010, $2.68 per $100 of payroll; compared to costs in other states and the District of Columbia, ranks 5th highest in the nation.

BENEFITS

Income disability benefits—Temporary disability set at 66 2/3% of worker's average weekly wage (AWW), subject to maximum and duration requirements with automatic cost of living after two years; maximum aggregate disability payments and periods apply. Permanent disability set at 66 2/3% of worker's AWW and dependent on permanent disability rating; reference should be made to the "Schedule of Rating Permanent Disabilities" adopted and prepared by the Administrative Director. Compensation can be increased by 50% for serious, willful misconduct by employer. Temporary partial disability set at 66 2/3% of wage loss during disability period, as reduced by unemployment compensation and extended duration benefits received during the same time frame. Permanent partial disability set at 66 2/3% of worker's AWW and dependent on disability rating; reference should be made to the "Schedule of Rating Permanent Disabilities"; amount is reduced by unemployment compensation and extended duration benefits received during the same time frame. Depending upon extent of injured worker's permanent disability, a worker who does not return to work within 60 days of the close of the temporary disability period will receive a supplemental job displacement benefit in the form of a voucher to be used for vocational rehabilitation purposes (i.e., retraining or skill enhancement) at state-approved or accredited schools.

Income benefits to spouse and children or partial dependents for death—For two total dependents, regardless of the number of partial dependents, $290,000; for one total dependent and no partial dependents, $250,000; for no total dependents and one or more partial dependents, eight times the amount of annual support for partial dependents, but not more than $250,000; for three or more total dependents, regardless of the number of partial dependents, $320,000. Death benefits are paid in installments in the same manner and amounts as temporary total disability at 66 2/3% of worker's AWW, subject to a weekly minimum of $224. Benefits for a child expire at age 18, or at death if child remains mentally incapacitated. The maximum burial allowance is $5,000.

Medical benefits—All hospital, physician, surgical, nursing, and related costs; worker must choose physician after 30 days; worker can choose physician from date of injury if worker has a pre-designated provider; and worker has the right to change physician at any time, but one time only.

Rehabilitation—Repealed in 2003.

STATUTE

Cal. Lab. Code § 110 *et seq.*; § 3200 *et seq.* (West 2010)

See generally 4 *Modern Workers Compensation* ch. 321— Statutory Comparison Table (1998); U.S. Chamber of Commerce, *2010 Analysis of Workers' Compensation Laws*; *Workers' Compensation Guide* ch. 7—State Laws (2008).

6. FLORIDA

By 1920, most states had adopted some form of workers' compensation legislation. (The last state to adopt a compensation act was Mississippi in 1949.) In 1935, the State of Florida enacted its first workers' compensation act, which was elective in theory. The development of the law in this area in Florida is typical of its development in the United States. For example, from 1935 forward, practically every session of the Florida legislature amended the compensation act.

In 1978, the Florida legislature initiated a study of the problems because of its concern over excessive awards and a backlog of claims. In 1979, the legislature enacted a Workers' Compensation Reform Act, which "re-established the centrality of the wage-loss principle," and represented a departure from the development in many other jurisdictions. The wage-loss theory in Florida attempted to provide that awards should not be based on the medical nature of the injury alone but should focus on the economic impact of the injury. Florida's wage-loss approach was designed to avoid compensating a worker for an injury per se, or basing an award on conjecture as to the future course of a specific injury; instead, its goal was to provide compensation for an employee's economic losses as they arise. See B. Abberger & G. Granoff, *Legislative Overview: The Florida Workers' Compensation Act, 1979,* 4 Nova L.J. 91 (1980). The state used this approach in an advertising effort to attract new industry.

By 1993, however, wage loss was eliminated and replaced by impairment income and supplemental benefits. See generally

T. Watson & M. Valen, *A Historic View of Workers' Compensation Reform in Florida*, 21 Fla. St. U. L. Rev. 501 (1993). In 2003, another major reform brought further changes to permanent total disabilities, permanent total supplements, permanent partial benefits, and the elimination of supplemental benefits. The Florida experience exemplifies the continuing political battles fought in legislatures between employees in the workforce and employers and insurance carriers. See generally P. McGinley, 10 West's Fla. Prac., Workers' Comp. With Forms §§ 28:1–20 (2009–2010 ed.).

The current Florida workers' compensation law contains the following features:

ADMINISTRATION

State agency—Department of Financial Services, Division of Workers' Compensation.

Notice and filing requirements—Notice must be given to employer within 30 days of injury, death, or first knowledge; this may be excused. Claims for injury or death must be filed within two years of knowledge of relationship of injury or death to employment, or one year from the last payment, which may be excused. Claims for occupational disease must be filed within one year of the date the worker should have known of the existence of the occupational disease but not more than seven years from the last injurious exposure, except for asbestosis and mesothelioma related to asbestos exposure, which may be filed one year from the date of first disablement after diagnosis. In death cases from occupational disease, in situations where the cause of action was not barred during the worker's life, a claim must be filed within one year of death.

Waiting period for income benefits—Seven days with retroactive benefits for disabilities beyond 21 days.

Second injury fund—The Special Disability Trust Fund reimburses employer for 50% of compensation paid over $10,000; there is also a preferred worker reimbursement program.

COVERAGE

Compulsory—Compulsory for all private employers of four or more workers (one or more if in the construction industry), including minors. Compulsory for all state and political subdivisions. Coverage is elective for partners and sole proprietors that are not in the construction industry. Coverage is elective for corporate officers, but construction employers may only elect exemption for up to three officers. Excepted employments that are eligible for voluntary coverage include independent contractors not engaged in construction industry; domestics; casual workers; 12 or fewer seasonal or five or fewer regular farm laborers; motor vehicle owner-operators engaged in written contracts with motor carriers; professional athletes; certain inmates; court-ordered laborers; volunteers (except government entities); Medicaid-enrolled clients excluded from the definition of employment; licensed real estate agents solely on commissions; sports officials for interscholastic sports events or public entity or private non-profit-organization-sponsored sports events; bands, orchestras, and musical and theatrical performers, including disc jockeys, performing at licensed premises as independent contractors; non-employee exercise riders who do not work for a single horse farm or breeder, who are compensated for riding on a case-by-case basis; and taxicab, limousine, or other passenger for-hire drivers operating under written agreements with companies that provide dispatch, marketing, insurance, communication, or other services under which the drivers and any fees or charges are not conditioned upon, or expressed as a proportion of, fare revenues.

Injuries, deaths, and occupational diseases—Must arise out of and in the course of employment.

INSURANCE

Compulsory—Private carrier, individual, and group self-insurance permitted.

Penalties for failure to insure—Fine, with maximum the greater of $1,000 or the amount employer would have paid for coverage in the preceding three years for failure to produce proof of insurance; subsequent violations within five years punishable as a felony; employer can be precluded from work and subject to $1,000 per day fine for violation of the stop work order.

Uninsured Employers' Fund—Florida Insurance Guaranty Association, Inc.

Insurance costs—For 2010, $1.70 per $100 of payroll; compared to costs in other states and the District of Columbia, ranks 40th highest in the nation.

BENEFITS

Income disability benefits—Temporary total disability set at 66 2/3/% of worker's average weekly wage (AWW), subject to maximum and minimum, for 104 weeks; for a temporary total disability resulting from the loss of an arm, leg, hand, or foot, from the loss of sight in both eyes, or for a worker who has been rendered paraplegic, paraparetic, quadriplegic, or quadriparetic is set at 80% of worker's AWW for up to six months, subject to a maximum weekly compensation rate of $700. Permanent total disability is set at 66 2/3% of worker's AWW, subject to maximum and minimum, with a supplement equal to 3% of worker's AWW on the date of injury multiplied times the calendar years since worker's date of injury; permanent total disability continues until the age of 75, unless worker is not eligible for Social Security. Temporary partial disability is set at 80% of the difference between 80% of worker's AWW and the salary, wages, and other remuneration worker is able to earn post-injury, up to an amount equal to 66 2/3% of worker's AWW at the time of injury, all limited to 104 weeks. Permanent partial disability is set subject to an impairment rating and paid biweekly at 75% of worker's average weekly temporary total disability benefit subject to a maximum and minimum. All benefits are subject to offsets for Social Security and unemployment insurance.

Income benefits to spouse and children or partial dependents for death—For spouse only, benefit rate is set at 50% of worker's AWW; for one child only, rate is 33 1/3% of worker's AWW; for multiple children only, rate is 33 1/3% per child of worker's AWW; for spouse and children, rate is 66 2/3% of worker's AWW; for dependent parents, rate is 25% each of worker's AWW; for dependent siblings or grandchildren, rate is 15% each of worker's AWW; all of the foregoing are subject to maximum and minimum weekly payments. Also, the following time limits apply: for spouse, lifetime, but not to exceed $150,000; a lump sum of 26 weeks of compensation at 50% of worker's AWW is payable upon remarriage; children to age 18 unless physically or mentally disabled; children to age 22 if full-time students; parents, for the continuance of dependency. Spouses are also entitled to 80 semester hours at a community college or 1,800 hours of training at a vocational-technical school. The maximum burial allowance is $7,500.

Medical benefits—All hospital, physician, surgical, nursing, and related costs; worker must choose physician from list provided by employer; after maximum medical improvement, worker has $10 co-pay for all medical services except emergency care.

Rehabilitation—Private rehabilitation costs are voluntary; fund pays for evaluations of training and education and provides reasonable board, lodging, and travel if more than 50 miles from home. Carriers may pay for 26 to 52 weeks of rehabilitation; if carriers voluntarily provide rehabilitation for more than 180 days, or spend more than $2,500, they are required to discontinue reemployment services and refer the worker to the Department of Financial Services, Division of Workers' Compensation. A refusal to accept rehabilitation results in a worker's forfeiture of benefits and compensation.

STATUTE

Fla. Stat. Ann. § 440.01 *et seq.* (West 2010)

See generally 4 *Modern Workers Compensation* ch. 321—Statutory Comparison Table (1998); U.S. Chamber of Commerce, *2010 Analysis of Workers' Compensation Laws; Workers' Compensation Guide* ch. 7—State Laws (2008).

7. TEXAS

In 1913, Texas enacted elective workers' compensation laws that allowed employers to choose whether to offer workers benefits. This was due in part to the fact that many courts at the time were holding mandatory workers' compensation statutes unconstitutional as a violation of due process. The Texas Industrial Accident Board was created in 1917 and administered the workers' compensation laws until 1989. A Joint Select Committee on Workers' Compensation Insurance was created by the Texas legislature in 1987, and its activities resulted in the passage of the 1989 Workers' Compensation Act. A new benefit system was established along with a new administering agency called the Texas Workers' Compensation Commission (TWCC), which replaced the Texas Industrial Accident Board.

In 2005, the TWCC was eliminated and replaced by the Texas Department of Insurance, Division of Workers' Compensation, which is overseen by a Commissioner of Workers' Compensation, who is appointed by the governor. Also created was the Office of Injured Employee Counsel (OIEC), which is overseen by a Public Counsel, also appointed by the governor. The Public Counsel represents workers' interests in the rule-making process and coordinates the use of ombudsmen in disputed administrative proceedings.

Today, Texas remains the only state in which workers' compensation is elective by private employers, but it should be noted that workers' compensation must be provided by public employers and by any private employers who enter into a building or construction contract with a governmental entity. For employers electing to be without workers' compensation coverage, workers can bring common-law actions with the employers' defenses of fellow servant, contributory negligence, and assumption of risk barred; however, the defenses of intoxication and intentional act to bring injury are preserved. Tex. Lab. Code Ann. § 406.033 (West 2009).

A worker's right to bring common-law actions against the employer is also preserved if notice is given at the time of hire, but the right of action is subject to all common-law defenses. Tex. Lab. Code Ann. § 406.034 (West 2009). While workers' compensation coverage is elective or voluntary for employers, they are required to notify all workers of the existence of coverage. Tex. Lab. Code Ann. §§ 406.002, 406.004 (West 2009).

The current Texas workers' compensation law contains the following features:

ADMINISTRATION

State agency—Texas Department of Insurance, Division of Workers' Compensation.

Notice and filing requirements—Notice must be given to employer within 30 days of occurrence of injury or when worker knew or should have known relation of disease to employment; this may be excused. Claims must be filed one year after occurrence of injury or when worker knew or should have known of relation of disease to employment, or death; this may be excused.

Waiting period for income benefits—Seven days with retroactive benefits paid after 14 days.

Second injury fund—Subsequent Injury Fund allows employer to pay only benefits for second injury, and the fund pays the balance for lifetime duration.

COVERAGE

Elective—Coverage is elective for all private employments, with the exception of contractors on public construction or building projects; such contractors who are partners, sole proprietors, and corporate officers with at least 24% equity in the business remain entitled to elective coverage. All state employees are provided coverage by the state, and all political subdivisions may provide coverage for their workers. Exceptions to coverage include workers covered by federal laws; domestics or casual workers employed incidental to personal residence; migrant workers; seasonal workers employed on truck farms, orchards, or vineyards, or employed by employer with payroll under $25,000; other farm and ranch workers employed by employer with payroll under $25,000 or employing fewer than three workers. Voluntary coverage is available to all of the foregoing excepted non-federal employments. Elective coverage is also allowed for commission-paid real estate salespersons and brokers. Certain professional athletes under contract must elect benefits under their contract or under the workers' compensation laws. Minors are covered. Farm and ranch operators may elect to cover themselves, family members, partners, and corporate officers. Elective coverage is also available to volunteer emergency services organizations that are not a part of a political subdivision.

Injuries, deaths, and occupational diseases—Must arise out of and in the course and scope of employment.

INSURANCE

Elective—Private carrier and self-insurance permitted for private employers and public entities; also, group self-insurance permitted for private employers.

Penalties for failure to insure—Employer's defenses to suit abrogated.

Uninsured Employers' Fund—Texas Certified Self–Insurer Guaranty Association.

Insurance costs—For 2010, $2.38 per $100 of payroll; compared to costs in other states and the District of Columbia, ranks 12th highest in the nation.

BENEFITS

Income disability benefits—Temporary total disability set at 70% of worker's average weekly wage (AWW), if earnings are over $8.50 per hour, for 104 weeks (may be extended in cases of spinal surgery) or maximum medical improvement, whichever is sooner, subject to state's minimum of 15% of state's average weekly wage and maximum of 100% of state's average weekly wage. Permanent total is 75% of worker's AWW if earnings are over $8.50 per hour for 401 weeks, or for life for certain specified injuries, subject to state's minimum of 15% of state's average weekly wage and maximum of 100% of state's average weekly wage. Permanent partial disability (schedule injuries) is set at 70% of worker's AWW, not to exceed 70% of state's average weekly wage for specific number of weeks (three weeks per percentage point using the American Medical Association (AMA) Guides to the Evaluation of Permanent

Impairment), depending upon the severity of disability, subject to state's minimum of 15% of state's average weekly wage and maximum of 100% of state's average weekly wage. Supplemental benefits are possible when impairment benefits expire, depending in part on whether the remaining impairment rating is greater than 15.

Income benefits to spouse and children or partial dependents for death—For spouse only, benefit rate is set at 75% of worker's AWW; for one child only, rate is 75% of worker's AWW; for multiple children only, rate is 75% of worker's AWW; for spouse and children, rate is 75% of worker's AWW; all of the foregoing are subject to maximum of 100% of state's average weekly wage and minimum of 15% of the state's average weekly wage. Also, the following time limits apply: for spouse, lifetime or remarriage (two-year lump sum on remarriage); children, death or age 18 unless physically or mentally disabled or because of a reason other than a physical or mental disability, the date of the expiration of 364 weeks of death benefit payments; also, children to age 25 if full-time students. The maximum burial allowance is $6,000.

Medical benefits—All hospital, physician, surgical, nursing, and related costs; worker must choose physician from list provided by employer who participates in a healthcare network; otherwise, worker chooses from a Division-approved list; one change of physician is allowed with approval of the Division.

Rehabilitation—No fund is established, and insurer furnishes necessary rehabilitation services; worker may be referred to the Department of Assistive and Rehabilitative Services with a recommendation for vocational rehabilitation services; also, insurer may pay for a private provider of vocational rehabilitation services. A worker who refuses services loses entitlement to supplemental income benefits.

STATUTE

Tex. Lab. Code Ann. § 406.001 *et seq.* (West 2009)

See generally 4 *Modern Workers Compensation* ch. 321—Statutory Comparison Table (1998); U.S. Chamber of Commerce, *2010 Analysis of Workers' Compensation Laws; Workers' Compensation Guide* ch. 7—State Laws (2008).

8. ILLINOIS

In 1909, a mine fire killed 259 workers in Cherry, Illinois. This disaster led directly to the creation of a commission by a special session of the legislature to study compensation for industrial accidents and make recommendations. The first compensation law, enacted in 1912, applied only to hazardous industries and was elective by most employers and workers, either of which could opt out. The courts promptly declared the law invalid. In 1913, a new compensation law was enacted and upheld. Due to a high volume of court claims filed, an Industrial Board was created to manage the claims process and decide disputed cases. In 1917, the legislature mandated coverage for extra-hazardous employments and renamed the Board as the Industrial Commission under the Department of Labor. The Commission was made its own agency in 1957, and was taken out from under the Department of Labor.

Major changes to the workers' compensation laws were enacted in 1975, due in part to the 84 recommendations of the National Commission on State Workmen's Compensation Laws, which had been established in 1972 under the federal Occupational Safety and Health Act (OSHA). In 1989, a Workers' Compensation Advisory Board was created to help the Commission formulate goals and polices.

In 1995, the legislature repealed the 1907 Structural Work Act, which had allowed workers injured in construction accidents to make claims for compensation in both the civil courts and under the workers' compensation laws. In 2003, the legislature established an independent source of funding for the Commission, and in 2005, the Commission's name was changed to the Illinois Workers' Compensation Commission.

The current Illinois workers' compensation law contains the following features:

ADMINISTRATION

State agency—Illinois Workers' Compensation Commission.

Notice and filing requirements—Notice must be given to employer within 45 days of injury or 90 days after a worker knows or suspects excessive exposure to radiation. Claims must be filed within three years after injury or death or within two years after last payment, whichever is later. For asbestosis and radiation injury claims, they must be filed within 25 years after last exposure; for death, claims must be filed within three years after death or two years after last payment, whichever is later.

Waiting period for income benefits—Three days for temporary total disability only; benefits paid from the fourth to the fourteenth day and retroactively to the first day if disability is longer than two weeks.

Second injury fund—The Second Injury Fund allows employer to pay only benefits for second injury, and the fund pays for the difference between the second injury and permanent total disability.

COVERAGE

Compulsory—Compulsory for private employments, including minors. Compulsory for all public employments except police and firefighters in cities over 200,000 in population (firefighters to the extent of burn-related disfigurement). Partners and sole proprietors have elective coverage. Certain persons providing services on a commission basis in sales or real estate are exempt from coverage. Voluntary coverage exists for exempted or excluded employments.

Injuries, deaths, and occupational diseases—Must arise out of and in the course of employment.

INSURANCE

Compulsory—Private, individual, and group self-insurance permitted.

Penalties for failure to insure—Fines of up to $1,000 per day for each violation with a maximum of $50,000 per project or contract under which work in violation is performed; employer subject to suit by workers.

Uninsured Employers' Fund—Group Workers' Compensation Pool Insolvency Fund.

Insurance costs—For 2010, $3.05 per $100 of payroll; compared to costs in other states and the District of Columbia, ranks 3rd highest in the nation.

BENEFITS

Income disability benefits—Temporary total disability set at 66 2/3% of worker's average weekly wage (AWW), subject to maximum of 133 1/3% of state's average weekly wage and minimum of 66 2/3% of the sum of the federal minimum wage under the Fair Labor Standards Act, or Illinois minimum wage under the Minimum Wage Law, whichever is more, multiplied by 40 hours, and increased by 10% for each spouse and child, not to exceed 100% of the total minimum wage calculation or worker's AWW, whichever is less; time limit is length of disability. Permanent total disability set at 66 2/3% of worker's AWW, subject to maximum of 133 1/3% of state's average weekly wage and minimum of 66 2/3% of the sum of the federal minimum wage under the Fair Labor Standards Act, or Illinois minimum wage under the Minimum Wage Law, whichever is more, multiplied by 40 hours, and increased by 10% for each spouse and child, not to exceed 100% of the total minimum wage calculation or worker's average weekly wage (AWW), whichever is less; time limit is the length of disability. Serious and permanent disfigurement disability set at 60% of worker's AWW, subject to maximum of 133 1/3% of state's average weekly wage and minimum of 66 2/3% of the sum of the federal minimum wage under the Fair Labor Standards Act, or Illinois minimum wage under the Minimum Wage Law, whichever is more, multiplied by 40 hours, and increased by 10% for each spouse and child, not to exceed 100% of the total minimum wage calculation or worker's AWW, whichever is less; time limit is 162 weeks. Permanent partial disability set at 66 2/3% of the difference between worker's AWW at the time of accident and worker's AWW after the accident, subject to maximum of 100% of state's average weekly wage and minimum of 66 2/3% of the sum of the federal minimum wage under the Fair Labor Standards Act, or Illinois minimum wage under the Minimum Wage Law, whichever is more, multiplied by 40 hours, and increased by 10% for each spouse and child, not to exceed 100% of the total minimum wage calculation or worker's AWW, whichever is less; time limit is length of disability or according to the schedule for certain injuries, or 500 weeks if worker is able to pursue usual work duties. For certain other permanent partial serious injuries, benefits may be in addition to compensation for temporary total disability at 60% of worker's AWW for that percentage of 500 weeks that the partial disability resulting from the injury bears to total disability.

Income benefits to spouse and children or partial dependents for death—For spouse only, benefit rate is set at 66 2/3% of worker's AWW; for one child only, rate is 66 2/3% of worker's AWW; for multiple children only, rate is 66 2/3% of worker's AWW; for dependent parents, rate is 66 2/3% of worker's AWW; for spouse and children, rate is 66 2/3% of worker's AWW; all of the foregoing are subject to maximum of 133 1/3% of state's average weekly wage and minimum of 66 2/3% of the sum of the federal minimum wage under the Fair Labor Standards Act, or Illinois minimum wage under the Minimum Wage Law, whichever is more, multiplied by 40 hours, and increased by 10% for spouse and each child, not to exceed 100% of the total minimum wage calculation or worker's AWW, whichever is less. Maximum benefit is $500,000 or 25 years of compensation, whichever is greater. Also, the following time limits apply: for spouse, lifetime or remarriage (two-year lump sum on remarriage, if no children); children, age 18 unless physically or mentally disabled, then for the duration of incapacity; also, children to age 25 if full-time students; for surviving children under 18, benefits continue for at least six years; for parents, benefits for life. The maximum burial allowance is $8,000.

Medical benefits—All hospital, physician, surgical, nursing, and related costs; worker may choose physician without restriction; in addition, worker and employer may agree to limit selection to employer's panel of four physicians.

Rehabilitation—No fund established, but rehabilitation must be provided as necessary by employer or insurer.

STATUTE

820 Ill. Comp. Stat. Ann. 305/1 *et seq.* (West 2010)

See generally 4 *Modern Workers Compensation* ch. 321— Statutory Comparison Table (1998); U.S. Chamber of Commerce, *2010 Analysis of Workers' Compensation Laws*; *Workers' Compensation Guide* ch. 7—State Laws (2008).

9.　OHIO

In 1911, Ohio enacted its first workers' compensation law, which was elective or voluntary. The law sought to encourage compensation coverage by removing common-law defenses from all employers who refused acceptance and by removing common-law negligence suits for injured workers who might also refuse acceptance. The Ohio courts upheld the law as a valid exercise of the police powers and further held that neither the state nor U.S. constitutions were an impediment to the enactment. Most employers, however, rejected coverage.

In 1912, Ohio amended its state constitution to authorize workers' compensation legislation. Ohio Const. art. II, § 35. Among other provisions, the constitutional amendment authorized the legislature to create a state compensation fund for the payment of workers' benefits and require contributions to the fund from employers. Ohio maintains an exclusive or monopolistic workers' compensation fund to this day.

Originally, an Industrial Commission adjudicated claims and administered the fund, but in 1955, the Bureau of Workers' Compensation (BWC) was created for fund administration purposes. A reorganization of the Commission and the Bureau occurred in 1989 and again in 1993.

In 1992, the Ohio courts held that there was an intentional tort exception to the exclusive remedy provisions of the workers' compensation laws. *Blankenship v. Cincinnati Milacron Chemicals, Inc.*, 433 N.E.2d 572 (Ohio 1982), reinstated, 707 N.E.2d 1107 (Ohio 1999). In response, in 1993, the legislature enacted an employment intentional tort statute, which benefited employers who were paying compensation to workers and being sued at the same time for intentional torts. The Ohio courts struck down the legislation, however, and the battle between the legislature and the courts on this issue has continued to the present.

Certain important legislative changes occurred in 1995, including the abolition of the Workers' Compensation Board, which had responsibilities over the fund, its investments, and its management. It was replace by a Workers' Compensation Oversight Commission, which appointed an Administrator to assume the same financial duties. A fund investment scandal involving rare coins came to light in 2005, dubbed "Coingate," and in 2007, a Board of Directors and three working committees replaced the Oversight Commission.

Today, Ohio maintains the largest exclusive state fund in the United States, with a reported $22 billion in assets under management.

The current Ohio workers' compensation law contains the following features:

ADMINISTRATION

State agency—Bureau of Workers' Compensation and Industrial Commission.

Notice and filing requirements—No notice is required except to self-insurers. Claims must be filed within two years of injury or death. Occupational disease claims must be filed within two years of disability or six months of diagnosis, whichever is longer, or within two years of death.

Waiting period for income benefits—Seven days with retroactive benefits after two weeks of disability.

Second injury fund—Reserve from state fund allows employer to pay only benefits for second injury; reserve pays for the difference between the second injury and temporary total disability, permanent total disability, or disabilities from the schedule.

COVERAGE

Compulsory—Coverage is compulsory for all private and public employments, including minors. Exempt from coverage are casual workers and domestics paid less than $160 by one employer in any calendar quarter, and certain religious sect employers, who are allowed to apply for an exemption. Elective coverage is available for officers of family farms, ordained or licensed ministers, individuals incorporated as corporations, sole proprietors, and partners.

Injuries, deaths, and occupational diseases—Must be in the course of and arise out of employment.

INSURANCE

Compulsory—State fund participation required but individual self-insurance permitted. The private insurance industry is precluded from state fund competition by way of the workers' compensation law voiding all contracts that might insure or indemnify employers against losses or liabilities arising out of the payment of workers' benefits for injury, death, or occupational disease.

Penalties for failure to insure—Minor misdemeanor, but if willful, second-degree misdemeanor; employer's defenses to suit abrogated; employer's business can be enjoined.

Uninsured Employers' Fund—Self–Insuring Employer's Guaranty Fund.

Insurance costs—For 2010, $2.24 per $100 of payroll; compared to costs in other states and the District of Columbia, ranks 17th highest in the nation.

BENEFITS

Income disability benefits—Temporary total disability set at 72% of worker's average weekly wage (AWW) for first 12 weeks with receipt of Social Security retirement offsetting to 66 2/3% of worker's AWW; benefit after 12 weeks is 66 2/3% of worker's AWW; maximum for first 12 weeks is the lesser of

100% of the state average weekly wage or 100% of worker's net take-home pay; after 12 weeks, maximum is 66 2/3% of state average weekly wage; minimum weekly benefit is 33 1/3% of state average weekly wage or actual wage if less; time limit is length of disability, but an examination is required after 200 weeks of benefits. Permanent total disability set at 66 2/3% of worker's AWW; maximum is 66 2/3% of state average weekly wage from the date of injury; minimum is 50% of state average weekly wage or worker's actual wage, if less; time limit is life. Permanent partial disability set according to schedule at 100% of state average weekly wage for 10 to 225 weeks, depending on severity, with a maximum of 100% of state average weekly wage; unscheduled permanent partial disability set at 66 2/3% of worker's AWW, not to exceed 33 1/3% of state average weekly wage for up to 200 weeks, depending upon severity of disability. For serious facial or head disfigurement that may impair employability, an award of up to $10,000 can be made.

Income benefits to spouse and children or partial dependents for death—For spouse only, benefit rate is set at 66 2/3% of worker's AWW; for one child only, rate is 66 2/3% of worker's AWW; for multiple children only, rate is 66 2/3% of worker's AWW; for spouse and children, rate is 66 2/3% of worker's AWW; all of the foregoing are subject to maximum of 100% of state's average weekly wage and minimum of 50% of the state's average weekly wage. Also, the following time limits apply: for spouse, lifetime or remarriage (two-year lump sum on remarriage); children, age 18 unless physically or mentally disabled, then for the duration of incapacity; also, children to age 25 if full-time students. The maximum burial allowance is $5,500.

Medical benefits—All hospital, physician, surgical, nursing, and related costs; worker may choose physician.

Rehabilitation—A surplus fund or a self-insurer making direct payments provide rehabilitation benefits, which include: living maintenance payments in place of temporary total benefits from up to six months in the aggregate, with extension possible; maximum benefits for the first 12 weeks is lesser of 100% of state average weekly wage or 100% of employee's net take-home pay, then 66 2/3% of state average weekly wage, with a minimum of 50% of state average weekly wage (AWW); for a worker successfully completing rehabilitation program, who suffers a wage loss compared to the wage the worker received at the time of injury, then the benefit is 66 2/3% of the difference in worker's AWW before and after injury up to maximum of 100% of the state AWW for 200 weeks, which is reduced by the number of weeks in which the worker receives temporary disability benefit payments.

STATUTE

Ohio Rev. Code Ann. § 4123.01 *et seq.* (West 2010)

See generally 4 *Modern Workers Compensation* ch. 321—Statutory Comparison Table (1998); U.S. Chamber of Commerce, *2010 Analysis of Workers' Compensation Laws*; *Workers' Compensation Guide* ch. 7—State Laws (2008).

10. ALABAMA

The Alabama Workmen's Compensation Act was first enacted in 1919, and it was based upon similar laws passed in Minnesota. In fact, Minnesota construction is persuasive in Alabama courts. See *Eley v. Brunner–Lay Southern Corp.*, 266 So.2d 276 (Ala. 1972). Claims are filed in the Circuit Courts, not with the Alabama Department of Industrial Relations, which has other administrative responsibilities under the Act.

Alabama has no state constitutional provision that specifically authorizes workers' compensation legislation, and the elective nature of the early laws created constitutional problems later when the legislature tried to abolish co-employee liability in 1975. *Grantham v. Denke*, 359 So.2d 785 (Ala. 1978); see generally T. Moore, 1 *Alabama Workers' Compensation* § 3:3—Constitutionality of Elective Compensation Act; § 3:4—Constitutionality of Compulsory Coverage (2010). The Act remains elective in character, though it is compulsory in fact.

The current Alabama workers' compensation law contains the following features:

ADMINISTRATION

State agency—Department of Industrial Relations.

Notice and filing requirements—Notice must be given to employer within five days of accident; excusable for 90 days. Claims for disability must be filed within two years of accident or last payment. Claims for death must be filed within two years of death or last payment. Claims for disability due to occupational disease, pneumoconiosis, or radiation must be filed within two years of last exposure; date of injury for last exposure purposes involving pneumoconiosis and radiation requires exposure in at least 12 of the last 60 months prior to exposure. Disability claims for radiation must be filed within one year of a worker's knowledge of relation to employment but no more than three years from last exposure. Death claims for radiation must be filed within one year of death.

Waiting period for income benefits—Three days, but retroactive benefits are paid after 21 days.

Second injury fund—Second Injury Fund abolished.

COVERAGE

Compulsory—Compulsory coverage for all private employers with five or more employees, including minor. Compulsory coverage for all counties and municipalities with populations greater than 2,000 but less than 250,000; also, coverage for certain school systems and institutions. Employees of the state, its agencies, and departments are not covered and must seek relief from the State Board of Adjustment or through special casualty insurance maintained to provide benefits equivalent to workers' compensation. Partners are not covered and corporate officers may reject coverage. Exempt from coverage are employers who regularly employ fewer than five workers in any one business; domestics; farm laborers; casual workers; licensed real estate agents; product demonstrators; and municipalities having a population of less than 2,000 or greater than 250,000. Voluntary coverage is available for employers who regularly employ fewer than five workers in any one business; domestics; farmers; volunteer fire departments and rescue squads; and municipalities with populations of less than 2,000.

Injuries, deaths, and occupational diseases—Must arise out of and in the course of employment.

INSURANCE

Compulsory—Private insurance, individual, and group self-insurance are permitted.

Penalties for failure to insure—Misdemeanor and fine of not less than $100 and not more than $1,000; civil penalties of not more than $100 per day and double compensation; employer's defenses to suit abrogated.

Uninsured Employers' Fund—Alabama Workmen's Compensation Self–Insures Guarantee Association.

Insurance costs—For 2010, $2.45 per $100 of payroll; compared to costs in other states and the District of Columbia, ranks 10th highest in the nation.

BENEFITS

Income disability benefits—Temporary total and permanent total disability set at 66 2/3% of workers' average weekly earnings (AWE), subject to a maximum of 100% of state average weekly wage on the date of injury, and a minimum of 27 1/2% of the state average weekly wage, or actual wage if less. Partial disability set at 66 2/3% of the difference between worker's AWE at the time of injury and AWE worker is able to earn in worker's partially disabled condition, payable up to 300 weeks for temporary partial disability and up to 400 weeks for permanent partial disability, depending on the severity of the disability, as shown by the schedule or otherwise, subject to a maximum of up to the lesser of $220 per week or 100% of the average weekly wage. Disfigurement disability set at 66 2/3% or worker's AWE, not to exceed 100 weeks.

Income benefits to spouse and children or partial dependents for death—For spouse only or one dependent, benefit rate is set at 50% of worker's AWE, subject to a maximum of 100% of the state average weekly wage at the time of accident and minimum of 27 1/2% of the state average weekly wage or actual wage, if less; for two or more dependents, rate is set at 66 2/3% of worker's AWE, subject to a maximum of 100% of the state average weekly wage at the time of accident and minimum of 27 1/2% of the state average weekly wage or actual wage, if less. Partial dependents are entitled to a portion of the benefits. If there are no dependents, then a lump sum of $7,500 is paid to the estate. Maximum period of benefits is 500 weeks and benefits to spouse end upon death or remarriage, but if spouse remarries and deceased worker had another dependent, then the unpaid balance is paid to the dependent.

Medical benefits—All hospital, physician, surgical, nursing, and related costs; employer initially chooses physician; worker can choose second physician from a panel of four chosen by employer.

Rehabilitation—Employer or insurer must provide upon request of vocational rehabilitation specialist or physician for restoration to gainful employment. Refusal of rehabilitation results in loss of compensation during the period of refusal.

STATUTE

Ala. Code § 25–5–1 *et seq.* (2010)

See generally 4 *Modern Workers Compensation* ch. 321—Statutory Comparison Table (1998); U.S. Chamber of Commerce, *2010 Analysis of Workers' Compensation Laws*; *Workers' Compensation Guide* ch. 7—State Laws (2008).

E. FEDERAL LEGISLATION

There are a variety of federal acts designed to provide compensation or recovery for certain employees injured or killed on the job. Additionally, there has been federal legislation aimed at the regulation of safety practices, labor standards, discrimination, Social Security benefits, etc. and which may affect employees' rights in the workplace. Provided below is a brief history and introduction of the more important federal acts providing compensation or recovery; other employee protection laws will be addressed in Part III.

1. FEDERAL EMPLOYEES' COMPENSATION ACT

In 1908, Congress enacted a workers' compensation act for a limited group of federal employees, and in 1916, it expanded the coverage to all civil employees of the United States government without regard to the hazards of their employment. An extensive revision of the FECA was undertaken in 1949, and today, the FECA, 5 U.S.C.A. § 8101 *et seq.* (West 2010), is considered to be one of the most liberal workers' compensation acts in existence, and provides coverage for federal employees and their dependents for death or disability resulting from personal injury "sustained in the performance of duty." Congressional appropriations finance all administrative and benefit costs, thus making the government a self-insurer. The Secretary of Labor supervises administrative claims procedures through the Office of Workers' Compensation Programs. The Employees' Compensation Appeals Board reviews appeals from final decisions.

When an employee is covered by the FECA, all other rights against the government are barred. See *Noble v. United States*, 216 F.3d 1229 (11th Cir. 2000) (exclusive remedy case). Third-party actions may be commenced when appropriate, and there may be an election of civil service retirement benefits (assuming eligibility), as opposed to compensation benefits. The Supreme Court, in *Westfall v. Erwin*, 484 U.S. 292 (1988), indicated that co-employee liability was possible in FECA situations; however, Congress legislatively overruled *Westfall* by enacting the Federal Employees Liability Reform and Tort Compensation Act of 1988 (28 U.S.C.A. § 2679 (West 2010)). The FECA's exclusive liability provision does not directly preclude third-party indemnity actions against the United States. *Lockheed Aircraft Corp. v. United States*, 460 U.S. 190 (1983). See generally H. Graham, *Federal Employees Compensation Act Practice Guide* (2d. ed. 2008); 1 *West's Federal Administrative Practice* §§ 1001–1090 (2010); U.S. Department of Labor, Federal Workers' Compensation Program, http://www.dol.gov/compliance/topics/benefits-comp-fed.htm.

Members of the armed forces of the United States are not covered by the FECA; however, analogous legislation does provide them with disability compensation and death benefits. 10 U.S.C.A. §§ 1201–1222, 1471–1491; 38 U.S.C.A. § 301 *et seq.* (West 2010). Coverage is allowed in cases of service-connected disability or death. The military scheme requires a line of duty determination to be made in each case, and either the particular branch of service and/or the Veterans Administration provides the machinery for the claims process and supervision. See generally 6 *West's Federal Administrative Practice* §§ 6571–6637 (2010).

It should be noted that the *Feres* doctrine precludes servicemen's recoveries under the Federal Tort Claims Act against the United States for injury, death, or loss "incident to service." *Feres v. United States*, 340 U.S. 135 (1950). Furthermore, service personnel cannot generally maintain damage actions against superior officers for violation of constitutional rights. *Chappell v. Wallace*, 462 U.S. 296 (1983).

It should also be noted that the Prison Industries Fund, 18 U.S.C. § 4126, provides an exclusive remedy for federal prisoners. See *Vander v. U.S. Department of Justice*, 268 F.3d 661 (9th Cir. 2001) (fund held exclusive remedy for prisoner who made claim under the Federal Tort Claims Act for delay in medical treatment). In some circumstances, federal prisoners can have valid constitutional tort claims for ill treatment. See, e.g., *Magluta v. Samples*, 375 F.3d 1269 (11th Cir. 2004) (prisoner could sue Bureau of Prisons employees for unlawful solitary confinement). See generally M. Mushlin, 1 *Rights of Prisoners* § 4:1 *et seq.* (4th ed. 2009).

2. FEDERAL EMPLOYERS' LIABILITY ACT

In 1906, Congress passed the first Federal Employers' Liability Act, but the United States Supreme Court held the Act unconstitutional because it infringed upon state rights in that the Act applied to intrastate as well as interstate commerce. *Howard v. Illinois Cent. R.R.*, 207 U.S. 463 (1908). This first FELA was held constitutional, however, as far as the District of Columbia and the territories of the United States were concerned. *El Paso & Northeastern Ry. v. Gutierrez*, 215 U.S. 87 (1909). In 1908, Congress enacted a second FELA, which applied to common carriers engaged in interstate commerce only. It is this second FELA statute that remains effective to this day and is codified at 45 U.S.C.A. §§ 51–60 (West 2010).

The FELA is not a true workers' compensation act, for it requires an employee to prove negligence, even though the burden of proving that negligence has been greatly liberalized by the courts. *CSX Transp., Inc. v. McBride*, ___ U.S. ___, 131 S.Ct. 2630 (2011) (a railroad worker need only demonstrate that the railroad's negligence played a part, no matter how small, in bringing about the injury). At the time of its passage, the FELA was considered the most progressive of the various employers' liability acts in existence; comparative fault replaced contributory negligence and the fellow-servant rule was abolished completely. In 1939, Congress amended the act with an eye toward the elimination of the assumption of risk defense. Subsequent court decisions make it clear that there is no assumption of inherent risks based upon the risk of ordinary railroading; nor can there be assumption of risk for obvious dangers knowingly encountered by the railroad employee, but of course, comparative fault may come into play. See generally 1 *Modern Workers Compensation* § 106:51.1— Railroad Employees (1998); Transportation Research Board, *Compensating Injured Railroad Workers Under the Federal Employer's Liability Act: Special Report 241* (1994); M. Griffith, *The Vindication of a National Public Policy Under the Federal Employers' Liability Act*, 18 Law & Contemp. Probs. 160 (1953).

In recent times, some have advocated that the FELA should be repealed and replaced with traditional workers' compensation systems. See generally T. Baker, *Why Congress Should Replace the Federal Employers' Liability Act of 1908*, 29 Harv. J. on Legis. 79 (1992); V. Schwartz & L. Mahshigian, *The Federal Employers' Liability Act, a Bane for Workers, a Bust for Railroads, a Boon for Lawyers*, 23 San Diego L. Rev. 1 (1986).

One should note that the Safety Appliance Act and the Boiler Inspection Act impose absolute and mandatory duties upon the defendant carriers, which can provide the basis for liability under the FELA. The traditional common-law tort compensatory approach is taken toward personal injury damages under the FELA, but the Supreme Court has remained receptive to new claims, especially in the emotional distress area. *CSX Transp., Inc. v. Hensley*, ___ U.S. ___, 129 S.Ct. 2139 (2009) (fear of cancer jury instructions required as a part of pain and suffering in asbestos cases); *Norfolk & Western Ry. Co. v. Ayers*, 538 U.S. 135 (2003) (mental anguish damages resulting from fear of cancer can be recovered under FELA by railroad worker suffering from actionable injury asbestosis caused by work-related exposure to asbestos); *Atchison, Topeka & Santa Fe Ry. Co. v. Buell*, 480 U.S. 557 (1987); see also *Consolidated Rail Corp. v. Gottshall*, 512 U.S. 532 (1994) (fear of cancer). In death cases, a pecuniary loss approach is employed for beneficiaries. Most courts have held that punitive damages are not recoverable. Actions may be filed in state or federal courts; if filed in state court, an action cannot be removed to federal court.

3. THE JONES ACT

Historically, under the general maritime law, seamen were allowed maintenance and cure, which consisted of subsistence, medical care, and unearned wages, but they had no effective negligence remedy. At the turn of the 20th century, the Supreme Court began fashioning the doctrine of unseaworthiness, which provided a proper cause of action but a limited remedy for seamen. See *The Osceola*, 189 U.S. 158 (1903). Because of concern for the welfare of seamen, Congress enacted the Seamen's Act of 1915, which abolished the fellow-servant defense, but this legislation was effectively nullified in *Chelentis v. Luckenbach S.S. Co.*, 247 U.S. 372 (1918).

In 1920, Congress passed the Merchant Marine Act of 1920, commonly known as the Jones Act. It provided seamen with the same negligence remedy that is available to railroad employees under the Federal Employers Liability Act. 46 U.S.C.A. §§ 30104–30105 (West 2010). Both state and federal courts may entertain these actions, and comparative negligence applies. In the 1940s, the Supreme Court transformed the unseaworthiness doctrine into an effective liability basis for recoveries by seamen. The doctrine essentially imposes liability without fault on the part of a shipowner who fails to provide a safe and seaworthy vessel.

The determination of a worker's status as a seaman is of critical importance. *Stewart v. Dutra Constr. Co.*, 543 U.S. 481 (2005) (a floating work platform being used as a dredge to excavate a tunnel in Boston Harbor was a vessel in navigation for Jones Act purposes); *Chandris, Inc. v. Latsis*, 515 U.S. 347 (1995); see *Harbor Tug & Barge Co. v. Papai*, 520 U.S. 548 (1997).

Thus, today, once a person is classified as a seaman, he may join actions for maintenance and cure, Jones Act negligence, and unseaworthiness in order to obtain compensation for his personal injuries. *Fitzgerald v. United States Lines Co.*, 374 U.S. 16 (1963).

In 2009, the Supreme Court indicated that punitive damages have long been an accepted remedy under general maritime law and that nothing in the Jones Act altered this understanding; therefore, punitive damages for the willful and wanton disregard of the maintenance and cure obligation are available as a matter of general maritime law. *Atlantic Sounding Co., Inc. v. Townsend*, 557 U.S. ___, 129 S.Ct. 2561 (2009).

See generally R. Force, *Admiralty & Maritime Law* (2004); R. Force & M. Norris, *The Law of Maritime Personal Injuries* (5th ed. 2010); R. Force & M. Norris, *The Law of Seamen* (5th ed. 2010); T. Schoenbaum, *Admiralty and Maritime Law* (4th ed. 2009).

Sometimes, there can be an overlap between seamen's rights to recovery under the aforementioned theories and the various state workers' compensation laws. This area has been called a "twilight zone" of coverage. See Ch. 9, C., *infra*.

In *Miles v. Apex Marine Corp.*, 498 U.S. 19 (1990), the Supreme Court recognized that seamen have a general maritime law cause of action for wrongful death. This action is generally limited to pecuniary damages. The Death on the High Seas Act of 1920, 46 U.S.C.A. §§ 761–767 (West 2010), is generally applicable beyond one marine league from shore, but seamen's damages are pecuniary in nature, regardless of whether they are sought under the Jones Act, general maritime law, or the Death on the High Seas Act. See also *Dooley v. Korean Air Lines Co., Ltd.*, 524 U.S. 116 (1998). As a result of the *Miles* decision, lower courts have generally held that seamen can only recover for general and special damages in claims for personal injuries. See generally T. Schoenbaum, *Admiralty and Maritime Law* § 6–14—Survival and Wrongful Death (4th ed. 2009).

It should be noted that the penalty wage statute, 46 U.S.C.A. §§ 10313(f)–(i), 10501(b)–(d) (West 2010), permits an action for delayed payment of wages. In appropriate circumstances, this action may be joined with other seamen's remedies. *Griffin v. Oceanic Contractors, Inc.*, 458 U.S. 564 (1982). See generally T. Schoenbaum, *Admiralty and Maritime Law* § 6–4—Wages (4th ed. 2009).

4. LONGSHORE AND HARBOR WORKERS' COMPENSATION ACT

In 1927, Congress enacted a national workers' compensation statute for the benefit of longshoremen and other persons engaged in maritime employment on navigable waters. The Longshoremen's and Harbor Workers' Compensation Act (hereinafter "LHWCA") was prompted by the case of *Southern Pacific Co. v. Jensen*, 244 U.S. 205 (1917), which had nullified a New York workers' compensation statute as applied to longshoremen. See generally R. Force, *Deconstructing Jensen: Admiralty and Federalism in the Twenty–First Century*, 32 J. Mar. L. & Com. 517 (2001). Coverage under the 1927 legislation was said to exist only if the accident occurred on navigable waters, *Nacirema Operating Co. v. Johnson*, 396 U.S. 212 (1969), and the fact that a worker's employment was maritime in nature was not a coverage issue. *Calbeck v. Travelers Insurance Co.*, 370 U.S. 114 (1962). By decisions of the Supreme Court, covered workers were also given an unseaworthiness remedy against a vessel, *Seas Shipping Co. v. Sieracki*, 328 U.S. 85 (1946), and the vessel owner was given an indemnity action against the stevedore employer, *Ryan Stevedoring Co. v. Pan–Atlantic Steamship Corp.*, 350 U.S. 124 (1956).

In 1972, Congress significantly amended the LHWCA. In summary, the amendments increased benefits, eliminated the unseaworthiness remedy against vessels, abolished the vessel owner's right of indemnity against stevedore employers, and instituted needed administrative changes. Most importantly, the 1972 amendments broadened coverage by using both "situs" and status for coverage. The situs test is no longer confined to navigable waters, and includes dockside workers on adjoining shore areas. See *Northeast Marine Terminal Co. v. Caputo*, 432 U.S. 249 (1977). The status test is met if a worker is engaged in "maritime employment." 33 U.S.C.A. § 902(3) (West 2010). See *Chesapeake & Ohio Ry. Co. v. Schwalb*, 493 U.S. 40 (1989). See generally R. Force and M. Norris, *The Law of Seamen* (5th ed. 2010); 1 *West's Federal Administrative Practice* § 1101 (4th ed. 2010); U.S. Department of Labor Benefits Review Board, *Longshore Deskbook*, http://www.dol.gov/brb/lsdesk.htm.

Congress amended the LHWCA in 1984, restricting coverage and changing the name of the act to the Longshore and Harbor Workers' Compensation Act, 33 U.S.C.A. § 901 *et seq.* (West 2001). All private maritime employments upon navigable waters or adjoining land areas are generally covered by the LHWCA. See *Cunningham v. Director, OWCP*, 377 F.3d 98 (1st Cir. 2004) (pipe-fabrication facility four miles from shipbuilder's main shipyard was not an "adjoining area" for coverage by LHWCA). Specifically excluded are seamen and government employees. Also excluded are clerical employees, recreation employees, temporary employees not engaged in longshore or harbor work, agricultural employees, employees on certain small commercial vessels, and employees who repair or break recreational vessels under 65 feet in length, so long as there is state workers' compensation coverage for these employees.

As might be expected, jurisdictional battles arise because claimants wish to assert seaman status, while employers prefer to claim immunity from suit under the LHWCA. Seaman status is usually a jury question. *Southwest Marine, Inc. v. Gizoni*, 502 U.S. 81 (1991). See generally J. Hillsman, *Still Lost in the Labyrinth: The Continuing Puzzle of Seaman Status*, 15 U.S.F. Mar. L.J. 49 (2003).

When there is an overlap of coverage due to state workers' compensation law, the LHWCA does not necessarily preempt. The Supreme Court's concurrent jurisdiction doctrines (sometimes applied in twilight zone cases) indicate that generally, an employee covered by both has an option. See *Sun Ship, Inc. v. Pennsylvania*, 447 U.S. 715 (1980). See Ch. 9, C., *infra*.

It should be pointed out that the receipt of LHWCA benefits does not preclude the initiation of a third-party action based upon traditional negligence concepts. 33 U.S.C.A. § 905(b) (West 2010); see *Scindia Steam Navigation Co., Ltd. v. De Los Santos*, 451 U.S. 156 (1981). Furthermore, a longshoreman can pursue a negligence remedy under the LHWCA against a vessel owner who acts as his own stevedore, despite the fact that the longshoreman has received compensation under the LHWCA from the stevedore-vessel owner, *Jones & Laughlin Steel Corp. v. Pfeifer*, 462 U.S. 523 (1983), but ship repairers' actions are barred by § 905(b).

Congress has also applied the LHWCA to employees other than longshoremen and maritime workers. The Defense Base Act applies the LHWCA to injuries or deaths of certain persons engaged in public works contracts outside the continental United States and to certain persons employed at military bases outside the United States. 42 U.S.C.A. § 1651 *et seq.* (West 2010). The War Hazards Compensation Act (42 U.S.C.A. § 1701 *et seq.* (West 2010)) provides a compensation remedy for death, injury, or detention of certain persons employed overseas by U.S. government contractors or by the United States government; benefits, disability, etc., are determined by reference to the LHWCA. Administration of these claims is accomplished under the Federal Employees' Compensation Act. Subject to certain criteria, employees of non-appropriated fund instrumentalities of the United States are also entitled to the benefits of the LHWCA. 5 U.S.C.A. §§ 8171–8172 (West 2010).

In 1928, Congress extended the substantive and procedural provisions of the LHWCA to employees in the District of

Columbia (D.C. Code §§ 36–501, 36–502 (1973)). These provisions were replaced by the District of Columbia Workers' Compensation Act. D.C. Code § 1–233 (1981); see *District of Columbia v. Greater Washington Central Labor Council, AFL–CIO*, 442 A.2d 110 (D.C. 1982). For the current workers' compensation provisions, see D.C. Code § 32–1501 *et seq.* (2001). See also, e.g., *Washington Post v. District of Columbia Dept. Emp't Serv.*, 853 A.2d 704 (D.C. 2004) (disability is an economic concept rather than a medical condition for purposes of workers' compensation).

Finally, the Outer Continental Shelf Lands Act (43 U.S.C.A. §§ 1331–1343 (West 2010)) incorporates the provisions of the LHWCA for the benefit of certain employees engaged in natural resources exploration, development, transportation, etc., outside the states' seaward boundaries on the continental shelves. See *Mills v. Director*, 877 F.2d 356 (1989); *Herb's Welding, Inc. v. Gray*, 470 U.S. 414 (1985). See generally W. Hastings, *To Avoid Drowning in the Gaps of Workers' Compensation Coverage on the Outer Continental Shelf*, 35 J. Mar. L. & Com. 35 (2004).

The U.S. Department of Labor maintains a useful website at http://www.dol.gov/owcp/dlhwc.

5. FEDERAL BLACK LUNG BENEFITS LEGISLATION

a. *Background and Scope*

The Federal Coal Mine Health and Safety Act of 1969, 30 U.S.C.A. § 801 *et seq.* (West 2010), was enacted in an effort to provide standards for safety and health for coal mines in the United States. It also provided compensation benefits for coal miners and their dependents or survivors when a miner's disability or death was the result of pneumoconiosis, otherwise known as "black lung," a chronic dust disease, which is more fully defined in the act. This act has been the subject of several important amendments: the Black Lung Benefits Act of 1972, the Black Lung Benefits Reform Act of 1977, the Black Lung Benefits Review Act of 1977, the Black Lung Benefits Revenue Act of 1981, the Black Lung Benefits Amendments of 1981, and the Consolidated Omnibus Budget Reconciliation Act of 1985. The constitutionality of federal black lung legislation was upheld in *Usery v. Turner Elkhorn Mining Co.*, 428 U.S. 1 (1976). See *Pauley v. Bethenergy Mines, Inc.*, 501 U.S. 680 (1991) (upholding rebuttal regulations).

The original federal black lung legislation attempted to place the responsibility for compensation and medical expenses on responsible mine operators whose identities could be determined, but the federal government assumed these obligations when no responsible mine operator could be determined. The federal government has employed various devices to insure the payment of black lung benefits. Reforms in 1977 created the Black Lung Disability Trust Fund, which is administered jointly by the Secretaries of Labor, Treasury, and Health and Human Services. This fund is financed primarily by excise taxes on mined coal. The Black Lung Disability Trust Fund has suffered from a chronic lack of funding, and this resulted in amendments in 1981 aimed at preserving the fund through increased excise taxes and through benefit limitations. From 1974 through 1996, over $10.7 billion in black lung payments were made to claimants. See generally U.S. Department of Labor Benefits Review Board, *Black Lung Deskbook*, http://www.dol.gov/brb/bldesk.htm; A. Larson & L. Larson, 3 *Larson's Workers' Compensation Law* ch. 54—Occupational Disease: the Black Lung Act (Rev. ed. 2000); 2 *Modern Workers Compensation* § 109:13—Lung Diseases, Generally, § 109:16—Pneumoconiosis (1998).

Originally, claims were processed by the Social Security Administration, but the Department of Labor has since assumed this responsibility, a logical adjustment in light of the fact that the Department of Labor is the responsible agency for mining health and safety. Claims filed up to July 1, 1973, continue to be under the Social Security Administration's jurisdiction, but claims filed after July 1, 1973, are administered by the Department of Labor. The Black Lung Benefits Reform Act of 1977 broadened entitlement and provided review for some previously denied claims, either by the Social Security Administration or the Department of Labor. Current claims procedures are set forth in detail in 20 C.F.R. § 410.101 *et seq.* (2011) and in 20 C.F.R. § 718.1 *et seq.* (2011). See 20 C.F.R. Parts 722, 725, 726, & 727. See generally U.S. Department of Labor website, http://www.dol.gov/compliance/guide/blklung.htm.

b. *Eligibility and Benefits*

Monthly cash benefits are payable under the federal black lung program to past and present coal miners who are totally disabled as a result of pneumoconiosis; a miner's compensation increases if there are dependents. Additionally, in miner death cases, widows, children, surviving divorced wives, parents, and siblings may receive benefits. If a widow was entitled to benefits at the time of her death, her children may receive benefits.

The basic benefit for a disabled coal miner is equal to 37 1/2% of the monthly pay of a federal employee in the Grade of GS–2, step 1, who is totally disabled. A surviving widow is paid the same benefit. Any single surviving child receives the same benefit that a surviving widow would have received, is also entitled to a full widow's benefit if a widow dies while receiving benefits. Miner's benefits and the benefits of dependents are increased based upon the number of dependents, and are reduced by state workers' compensation, unemployment compensation, state disability insurance, or excess earnings under the Social Security Act.

In order to be eligible for benefits under the federal black lung program, a coverage formula must be met. See *Mullins Coal Co. v. Director*, 484 U.S. 135 (1987). The formula requires: (1) A "miner," who is (2) "totally disabled due to pneumoconiosis." In order to qualify as a "miner," a person must have worked as an employee in a coal mine, whether underground or above ground, performing functions in extracting the coal or preparing the coal so extracted. The definition of "miner" has undergone several statutory changes since the original act, and in 1977, it was expanded to provide coverage for self-employed miners and certain others in the coal mine construction and transportation industries. See *Baker v. United States Steel Corp.*, 867 F.2d 1297 (1989) (liberal construction given to the term "miner"). Once miner status is established, a claimant must prove total disability due to pneumoconiosis. In doing so, claimants traditionally enjoyed the assistance of certain rebuttable and irrebuttable presumptions.

The 1981 amendments effectively eliminated some presumptions, but two important ones remained: (1) A miner with pneumoconiosis who was exposed for 10 or more years was rebuttably presumed to have pneumoconiosis that arose out of employment; and (2) a miner with complicated pneumoconiosis received an irrebuttable presumption of the necessary total disability, or in death cases, that death was due to the pneumoconiosis, or that total disability from pneumoconiosis existed at the time of death. See generally *Pittston Coal Group v. Sebben*, 488 U.S. 105 (1988).

The 1981 amendments also addressed the issue of proof and provided that after their effective date, the Secretary of Labor need not accept a radiologist's interpretation of chest x-rays and could consider second interpretations. Furthermore, the Secretary need not accept as binding the affidavits of interested persons who are eligible for benefits in death cases.

In 2010, the Healthcare Reform Law (Patient Protection and Affordable Care Act of 2010 ("PPACA")), Pub. L. No. 111–148, 124 Stat. 119), as amended by the Health Care Education and Affordability Reconciliation Act of 2010 ("HCERA"), Pub. L. No. 111–152, 124 Stat. 1029 (together, the Healthcare Reform Law), repealed a 1981 provision in the Black Lung Benefits Act that eliminated the presumption that a lung disease was contracted on the job; it was replaced with a presumption that a mine worker with 15 years or more of service who suffers a lung disease contracted it on the job. The new provision is retroactive to claims filed after January 1, 2005, and it will prevent most employers from claiming that a mine worker's lung problems were caused by factors other than work, in particular, smoking.

c. Procedures

Claims for black lung benefits may be filed at certain offices of the Department of Labor, Social Security district offices, or Foreign Service offices of the United States by mail or presentation. The Department of Labor's Office of Workers' Compensation supervises the claims procedures, and once a claim has been forwarded to them, a deputy commissioner conducts an initial investigation, which is designed to determine whether a claimant is eligible for benefits and whether a responsible operator exists.

Deputy commissioner decisions in contested cases are assigned to Administrative Law Judges for formal hearings in accordance with the Administrative Procedure Act. See *Pyro Mining Co. v. Slaton*, 879 F.2d 187 (6th Cir. 1989). Appeals from these hearings are lodged with the Benefits Review

Board, which may enter a final decision or remand the case either to the Administrative Law Judge or the deputy commissioner. Final decisions of the Benefits Review Board may be appealed to the U.S. Circuit Court of Appeals in the circuit where the miner was last employed.

d. Mining Safety and Health

The Federal Mine Safety Act of 1997 (Mine Act), 30 U.S.C.A. § 801 *et seq.* (West 2010), protects persons working on mine properties, and is administered by the Mine Safety and Health Administration (MSHA). Responsibility is placed upon employers for miners' safety and health, and regular inspections are required for both underground and surface mines. Miners' training requirements have been established, and dangerous mines can be closed. The Act prescribes penalties for health and safety violations, and specific health and safety regulations cover mining hazards. See generally U.S. Department of Labor website, http://www.dol.gov/compliance/laws/comp-fmsha.htm.

The Mine Improvement and New Emergency Response Act of 2006 (MINER Act) amended the Mine Act to provide enhanced safety in underground coal mines by requiring emergency response planning for the evacuation of miners who may be endangered in emergencies or, if miners cannot evacuated, provide for their maintenance and support while underground until their safety can be assured. See generally *CCH Employment Safety & Health Guide Mine Act, Regulations, Standards* (2010).

6. ENERGY EMPLOYEES

The United States government created a workers' compensation system pursuant to the Energy Employees Occupational Illness Compensation Act of 2000, Pub. L. No. 106–398, 114

Stat. 1654, and the Energy Employees Occupational Illness Compensation Amendments of 2001. The legislation provides a compensation program for employees, or their survivors, of the Department of Energy, its contractors, subcontractors, and employees of related private companies who have suffered occupational illnesses from exposure to the unique hazards associated with nuclear weapons development and testing processes. Specifically targeted are beryllium-related diseases, radiation-related cancers, silica-related diseases, special exposure cohorts, uranium miners, and other occupational diseases. The U.S. Department of Labor has primary responsibility for administering the compensation and medical benefit programs, and the Department of Energy's Office of Worker Advocacy provides the Department of Labor with medical and employment records necessary for claims. Claimants pursuing state workers' compensation benefits are also provided assistance. Ten resource centers are open near Department of Energy sites to provide further assistance to workers and their families: Hanford, Washington; Idaho Falls, Idaho; Las Vegas, Nevada; Espanola, New Mexico; Denver, Colorado; Aiken, South Carolina; Portsmouth, Ohio; Paducah, Kentucky; Oak Ridge, Tennessee; and Anchorage, Alaska.

The Department of Energy made public an initial list of facilities to be covered, including beryllium vendors, Department of Energy sites where radioactive materials were used, and facilities where atomic weapons workers may have been employed. The list includes 317 sites in 37 states, Puerto Rico, the District of Columbia, and the Marshall Islands. Claimants may be entitled to medical benefits and compensation in the amount of $150,000. Information can be obtained from the Department of Energy's website at http://www.hss.doe.gov/healthsafety/fwsp/advocacy. Similarly, information can be obtained from the Department of Labor's website at http://www.dol.gov/owcp/energy/regs/compliance/progbenefits.htm.

7. RADIATION EXPOSURE CLAIMS

In 1990, Congress enacted the Radiation Exposure Compensation Act (42 U.S.C.A. § 2210 (West 2010)), which provided for compensation to the victims of certain diseases and cancers that resulted from radiation exposure during nuclear tests or because of employment exposure to radiation in mines. On July 10, 2000, Congress enacted the Radiation Exposure Compensation Act Amendments of 2000, Pub. L. No. 106–245, 114 Stat. 501, which expanded coverage to include broader classes of claimants and additional diseases, lowered exposure requirements, and modified medical documentation requirements. There are five groups of claimants: onsite participants, downwinders, ore transporters, uranium millers, and uranium miners. Eligible miners, millers, and transporters may be entitled to compensation payments of $100,000 each. Onsite participants may be entitled to compensation payments of $75,000 each, and downwinders may be entitled to compensation payments of $50,000 each. This program is administered by the Department of Justice, and information can be obtained its website at http://www.justice.gov/civil/torts/const/reca/index.htm.

8. SEPTEMBER 11TH VICTIM
COMPENSATION FUND

In 2002, the United States government created a special compensation fund to provide a no-fault alternative to tort litigation for individuals who were physically injured or killed as a result of the aircraft hijackings and crashes on September 11, 2001. See the Air Transportation Safety and System Stabilization Act of September 22, 2001, Pub. L. No. 107–42, 115 Stat. 230, and the Victims of Terrorism Relief Act of 2001 of January 23, 2002, Pub. L. No. 107–134.

Eligibility was generally limited to (1) individuals on the planes at the time of the crashes (excluding the terrorists, of course) and (2) individuals present at the World Trade Center, the Pentagon, or the site of the crash in Pennsylvania at the time of the crashes or in the immediate aftermath of the crashes. A claimant filing for compensation under this legislation waived any right to file a civil action or be a party to a civil action in any state or federal court for damages sustained as a result of the terrorist crashes, except actions to recover collateral source obligations. Determinations of eligibility were made by a Special Master, Kenneth R. Feinberg. See 28 C. F. R. Part 104 (2010). There were two basic claims: personal injury and death. The program contained presumed economic and noneconomic losses.

The Department of Justice conducted the administration of the fund, and the last day to file a claim was December 22, 2003. The federal program became inactive on June 15, 2004, but claims processing and administrative matters for claims made continued after that date. Information about the program can still be obtained from its website at http://www.justice.gov/archive/victimcompensation.

9. SEPTEMBER 11TH FIRST RESPONDER FUND

The James Zadroga 9/11 Health and Compensation Act of 2010, Pub. L. No. 111–347, 124 Stat. 3623, provides medical benefits and compensation payments to first responders and family members who were involved in the response and clean-up of the September 11, 2001, terrorist attacks on the World Trade Center in New York City. The legislation established the World Trade Center Health Program, which conducts medical monitoring and studies of responders and their families. The World Trade Center Program Administrator is responsible for supervising the program.

F. DISABILITY COMPENSATION SYSTEMS IN THE UNITED STATES

One cannot properly understand a particular state's workers' compensation law without considering its place in the overall federal and state disability and wage-loss protection schemes and employee protection laws that presently exist in the United States. To properly advise a potential claimant, for example, attorneys must be capable of explaining the impact of Social Security, unemployment compensation, the various federal compensation coverage systems, private health and disability plans, anti-retaliation and whistleblower laws, wage and hour regulation, union benefits, no-fault insurance, employment discrimination, disability discrimination and accommodation laws, training and communication programs, state labor laws and special compensation funds, and a whole range of targets for potential third-party tort recoveries.

Generally speaking, a broad safety net of coverage exists for most workers in the United States that allows modest but fairly certain recovery for work related injuries and deaths. Non-occupational injuries and deaths are covered to an extent by Social Security and by private health and disability plans. Relief is given for short periods of unemployment by the unemployment compensation laws.

More and more federal and state compensation programs and public and private insurance plans try to coordinate benefits to prevent duplication and contain costs in the overall system of social legislation that exists in the United States. See generally A. Larson & L. Larson, 9 *Larson's Workers' Compensation Law* ch. 156—Compensation as Part of General Wage-loss System, ch. 157—Coordinating Compensation and Other Wage-loss Benefits (Rev. ed. 2000); 2 2 *Modern Workers Compensation* ch. 206—Liens, ch. 207—Offsets (1998); *Work-*

ers' Compensation Guide ch. 8—Relationship to Other Laws (2008).

In should be noted that employers have sponsored some new programs to combat rising workers' compensation and health care costs: utilization review, integrated disability management, return-to-work, and evidence-based medicine. The effectiveness of these programs depends on management styles, medical profession attitudes, and worker cooperation. See generally *Workers' Compensation Guide* ch. 7—State Laws, I. New Developments (2008).

Cost containment by employers favoring utilization review and integrated disability management methods was aided by the U.S. Supreme Court in *American Manufacturers Mutual Insurance Co. v. Sullivan*, 526 U.S. 40 (1999). Plaintiffs had brought a § 1983 civil rights action against Pennsylvania state officials, the Pennsylvania State Workers' Insurance Fund (SWIF), private insurers, and a school district, alleging that their due process rights were violated by provisions of the Pennsylvania Workers' Compensation Act that permitted suspension of benefits without notice or opportunity to be heard pursuant to utilization review process. The Court held that insurers' decisions to withhold payment for disputed medical treatment pending utilization review was not fairly attributable to the State of Pennsylvania, as required for insurers to be subjected to the constraints of the Fourteenth Amendment, and that plaintiffs did not have a property interest in having insurers pay for medical treatments prior to a determination that the treatments were reasonable and necessary.

PART 2

THE LAW OF WORKERS' COMPENSATION

CHAPTER 2

THEORIES AND POLICIES OF WORKERS' COMPENSATION

A. CONSTITUTIONAL THEORIES

Traditionally, there have been several key constitutional objections to workers' compensation legislation. Most of these objections have centered on the following constitutional issues: due process of law, equal protection, impairment of contract obligations, trial by jury, and the privileges and immunities of the citizens of the different states. Initially, many of these constitutional objections were sustained; however, most constitutional problems have fallen by the wayside, particularly with the adoption by most states of specific constitutional amendments that authorize workers' compensation legislation.

These constitutional problems are not always of just historical interest. They can be of importance to a modern-day analysis of a particular compensation scheme; for example, see *Reed v. Brunson*, 527 So.2d 102 (Ala. 1988) (statute limiting actions for personal injuries that employee, who is receiving workers' compensation benefits, can bring against fellow employee to actions for willful conduct that did not violate constitutional provisions that every person for every injury shall have remedy); *Schmill v. Liberty Northwest Ins. Corp.*, 223 P.3d 842 (Mont. 2009) (claimants' vested right to payment of past due benefits, regardless of which insurer was responsible for payment, did not violate insurer's due process rights); *State ex rel. Doersam v. Industrial Com'n of Ohio*, 533 N.E.2d 321, 323 (Ohio 1988) ("All laws, including those dealing with workers' compensation, are subject to the limitations imposed by the Equal Protection Clauses of the Ohio and United States Constitutions. Those limitations are essentially identical."); *Conaghan v. Riverfield Country Day Sch.*, 163 P.3d 557 (Okla. 2007) (language in statute restricting Workers' Compensation Court's determination of impairment and disability within the range of opinions of treating physician and independent medical examiner was constitutionally infirm under separation-of-powers doctrine and would be stricken); *Repass v. Workers' Comp. Div.*, 569 S.E.2d 162 (W. Va. 2002) (adoption of AMA Guides as the exclusive measure for disability determination conflicted with several other statutory provisions and was therefore invalid); see also *Kline v. Berg Drywall, Inc.*, 685 N.W.2d 12 (Minn. 2004) (exclusion of claimant's legal counsel in early stages of ADR process violated collective bargaining statute; constitutional issues not addressed).

1. FREEDOM OF CONTRACT

The U.S. Constitution prohibits the states from enacting laws that impair contract obligations. U.S. Const. art. 1, § 10. At one time, some workers' compensation acts were held to be violative of this general provision and of the parallel provisions sometimes found within state constitutions. The current general view is to the effect that even if a workers' compensation act impairs an existing contract obligation between an employer and employee, the impairment may nevertheless be valid because a proper exercise of the police power has occurred. The health, safety, and welfare of the people are of overriding importance. See generally 1 *Modern Workers Compensation* § 100:2—Validity (1998).

2. ELECTION

Many of the original workers' compensation acts were said to be "elective" in order to avoid the constitutional difficulties imposed by the impairment-of-contract clause. An elective compensation act could thus be said to be a part of or to be "read into" every contract of employment, and the act contained provisions for employers or employees to opt in or out. There were usually penalty provisions that encouraged coverage. Later, most elective acts were said to be presumptive; that is, the employer and employee were presumed to be covered unless they had taken specific steps in accordance with the act to avoid coverage. Many acts appear to retain their elective and contractual character because of the manner in which they were written, despite the fact that today, most state workers' compensation acts are compulsory. See generally 1 *Modern Workers Compensation* pt. 2—Compulsory/Elective Coverage (1998); *Workers' Compensation Guide* ch. 7—State Laws (2008).

The majority of states have enacted constitutional amendments that eliminate the constitutional difficulties originally posed in this area. See, e.g., Cal. Const. art. XIV, § 4. Virtually all states today have compulsory coverage for the majority of workers, but allow some exempt categories of workers to elect coverage. Any system other than a compulsory one appears to be at odds with the purposes and policies of workers' compensation. It should be recalled that when coverage fails for one reason or another, the employee must then rely upon the common-law remedies or those remedies provided by the employers' liability acts.

3. PRESUMPTIVE COVERAGE

As previously mentioned, many compensation acts were elective, thus affording the employer and employee the right to accept or reject coverage. While most acts today are compulsory in character, the few remaining elective acts can pose coverage problems. For example, an employer could refuse on the basis of costs to carry workers' compensation insurance, and some employees may not be sufficiently knowledgeable of their rights to make intelligent elections. Consequently, some of the elective acts contain presumptive coverage provisions. In other words, the acts may provide for an election, but coverage is presumed unless the employee or employer takes specific steps to preclude coverage. See generally 1 *Modern Workers Compensation* § 101:1—Generally (1998).

4. COMPULSORY COVERAGE

A majority of states employ a compulsory coverage system of workers' compensation. This has generally been accomplished by state constitutional amendments authorizing workers' compensation statutes; see *Schmidt v. Wolf Contracting Co.*, 55 N.Y.S.2d 162 (N.Y. App. Div. 1945). These state amendments grant the necessary legislative power for the enactment of workers' compensation laws, including the power to enact all reasonable and proper provisions necessary to effectuate the law and to fulfill the objectives of the constitutional provisions. Needless to say, the legislation cannot exceed whatever limitations exist in the constitutional provision. See generally 1 *Modern Workers Compensation* pt. 2—Compulsory/Elective Coverage (1998); *Workers' Compensation Guide* ch. 7—State Laws (2008).

5. EXCLUSIVENESS OF REMEDY

Regardless of whether a workers' compensation act is compulsory or elective, it generally affords the exclusive remedy for employees or dependents against employers for personal injuries, diseases, or deaths arising out of and in the course of employment. The exclusivity provision of workers' compensation acts is the keystone of all such legislation. The employee or dependents recover without regard to fault, and the employer is spared the possibility of large tort verdicts. Initial assaults on the exclusive remedy provided by workers' compensation were based on allegations of denial of due process of law. Common law and statutory actions were being abrogated along with common-law defenses. There was strong early resistance (just as there is today) to the adoption of no-fault statutory systems of compensation. Moreover, constitutional controversies surrounded meanings of employment, requirements to secure payment of compensation, and the hazardous employment classifications. Equal protection arguments were also made. For a discussion of constitutional issues, see generally *Cudahy Packing Co. v. Parramore*, 263 U.S. 418 (1923); *Arizona Employers' Liability Cases*, 250 U.S. 400 (1919); *Jensen v. Southern Pac. Co.*, 109 N.E. 600 (N.Y. 1915). Most constitutional issues have been laid to rest by state constitutional amendments and by more liberal, pragmatic, and progressive judicial decisions. See generally 1 *Modern Workers Compensation* § 102:1—Workers' Compensation as Exclusive Remedy (1998).

B. SOCIAL AND ECONOMIC POLICIES

1. EMPLOYEE–EMPLOYER "BARGAIN"

It is sometimes said that the employee and employer have entered into an "industrial bargain." The employee has given up his right to sue his employer for negligence and possibly receive a potentially greater damage award, and the employer has surrendered the common-law defenses available in negligence actions. In exchange, the employee is entitled to prompt but modest compensation for injuries (or the employee's dependents, in the case of his death) arising out of the employment relationship, regardless of fault. The employer avoids costly litigation and faces fixed and limited liability that can be covered by insurance. See generally 1 *Modern Workers Compensation* § 100:1—Replacement of Tort System (1998).

2. INDUSTRIAL BURDEN FOR INJURIES AND DEATH

An important economic and social theory underlying the workers' compensation idea is that the cost of employment-related injuries, diseases, and deaths ultimately should be borne by the purchasers' and consumers' products and services. In other words, built into the cost of any product is the employer's insurance premium for the cost of workers' compensation or the cost of self-insurance. Thus, the costs of employment-related injuries, diseases, and deaths are properly distributed throughout society. See generally A. Larson & L. Larson, 1 *Larson's Workers' Compensation Law* ch. 1—The Nature of Workers' Compensation (Rev. ed. 2000).

3. MEDICAL LOSS AND WAGE LOSS

The benefits payable vary from jurisdiction to jurisdiction. An essential inquiry to be made in each jurisdiction is whether the particular statute is based upon a medical loss theory, a wage loss theory, or both. A medical loss theory dictates, for example, that in the case of one who has lost an arm, compensation is required for the loss of that limb regardless of whether there has been an adverse impact upon earning capacity or lost wages. The wage loss theory, on the other hand, is based upon the idea that a person should be compensated for loss of wages or diminished earning capacity and not for any purely medical losses that have occurred. Most jurisdictions mix the two theories and provide compensation based upon wage and medical losses. The allocation of benefits usually involves the utilization of an injury schedule, which provides compensation for purely medical losses enumerated within. For example, one would be entitled a specific amount of weekly compensation benefits for the loss of an arm, regardless of any diminution in earning capacity. See generally 2 *Modern Workers Compensation* ch. 200—Basis for Compensation (1998).

It is worth noting that the State of Florida in recent years attempted to employ an almost pure wage loss theory. As a result, Florida reduced the costs to employers of its workers' compensation system. Florida later added a schedule (medical loss) back into its system. Recent legislative reforms based upon medical loss and wage loss theories have not always produced better or more efficient systems. Regardless of the theory chosen, workers' compensation benefits generally remain modest and have failed to keep abreast of inflation. See generally M. McCluskey, *The Illusion of Efficiency In Workers' Compensation "Reform,"* 50 Rutgers L. Rev. 657 (1998).

4. SOCIAL INSURANCE

It must be emphasized that workers' compensation in the United States is privately funded with an insurance base, whereas some countries, such as Great Britain, maintain a comprehensive social insurance system encompassing workers' compensation. Although there have been reform proposals in the United States aimed at establishing a more comprehensive national system, the American system remains a private one, grounded in insurance. Certainly, a legitimate criticism of the current system can be made because compensation allocations are made regardless of need. It would at first appear that the general public bears the costs of workers' compensation; however, the actual costs are probably borne by limited groups of consumers of particular products and services. As a result of the fact that workers' compensation is a statutory no-fault scheme, many lose sight of the relevance of tort law and its notions of culpability and fault. For example, intoxication on the job and intentional self-injuries can prevent the recovery of compensation despite the no-fault theory of the system. See generally A. Larson & L. Larson, 1 *Larson's Workers' Compensation Law* ch. 1—The Nature of Workers' Compensation (Rev. ed. 2000).

5. ECONOMIC APPRAISAL

In comparison with the tort compensation system, workers' compensation provides a more efficient economic model. For example, in the case of automobile accidents, the tort system provides recovery to victims and families of only 44% of the sums provided by the system, with the remainder of the costs consumed by the inefficiency of the system itself, i.e., court costs, lawyers' fees, insurance administration, etc. Workers' compensation ordinarily does not require lengthy and costly hearings; attorney's fees are regulated by statute, and while issues of fault do creep into compensation decisions, ordinarily compensation is assured when a work related injury or death is demonstrated, as opposed to the perils of the tort system.

In 2005, the combined state and federal workers' compensation benefits totaled $55.3 billion, and in the United States, only Social Security disability and Medicare benefits were larger. The economic impact of the state workers' compensation system, which is not federally regulated, cannot be overestimated. See generally I. Sengupta, V. Reno & J. Burton, Jr., Nat'l Acad. of Soc. Ins., *Workers' Compensation: Benefits, Coverage, and Costs, 2005* (2007).

In evaluating the workers' compensation system, however, one must consider the economic status of today's industrial worker. Wages generally have not kept up with inflation, and workers' compensation payments do not reflect current costs of living; further, the system fails to provide the amounts necessary for effective educational retraining and vocational rehabilitation. Compensation benefits simply do not reflect the degree of economic harm suffered by a worker and his family; all persons are treated in a uniform manner by the particular workers' compensation act. Additionally, there is generally no provision allowing for increases and escalations due to inflation. As a final criticism, workers' compensation benefits vary a great deal from state to state. Because of this disparity, a National Workers' Compensation Standards Act has been proposed. See Chapter 11, B., *infra*.

The U.S. Chamber of Commerce compiles annual surveys of state and federal workers' compensation law changes, which are useful in evaluating policy changes from jurisdiction to jurisdiction. Its website is http://www.uschamber.com. An abbreviated annual survey of workers' compensation and unemployment insurance laws is available from the AFL–CIO Department of Occupational Safety and Health. Its website is http://www.aflcio.org. Also, a complete legal survey of workers' compensation laws is compiled each year by the American Insurance Association, whose website is http://www.aiadc.org.

It should be noted that the terrorist acts of September 11, 2001, combined to create the most costly catastrophic events in insurance industry history. These events have had a serious economic impact on workers' compensation and other insurance. Congress stepped in and enacted the Terrorism Risk

Insurance Act of 2002 (TRIA), Pub. L. No. 107–297, §§ 101–108, 116 Stat. 2322, which stabilized the insurance markets by providing federal backstops to reimburse insurers for terrorism losses above established thresholds. Because terrorism creates risks of loss that traditionally lacked private insurability, the TRIA provides federal support and protection to private insurers who would be exposed to insurer insolvency due to terrorist attacks. The Terrorism Risk Insurance Extension Act of 2005 (TRIEA), Pub. L. No. 109–144, 119 Stat. 2660, extended the program to the end of 2007, and the Terrorism Risk Insurance Program Reauthorization Act of 2007 (TRIPRA), Pub. L. 110–160, 121 Stat. 1839, extended the program until the end of 2014. The latter legislation covers terrorist attack risks on U.S. soil from foreign and domestic terrorists. See generally Towers Perrin, *Workers' Compensation Terrorism Reinsurance Pool Feasibility Study* (2004); L. Dhooge, *A Previously Unimaginable Risk Potential: September 11 and the Insurance Industry*, 40 Am. Bus. L.J. 687 (2003); L. Reiter, *The Need for a Long–Term Federal Backstop in the Terrorism Insurance Market*, 2 Brook. J. Corp. Fin. & Com. L. 243 (2007); M. Shields, Annotation, *Recovery of Workers' Compensation for Acts of Terrorism*, 20 A.L.R.6th 729 (2006).

C. LIBERAL CONSTRUCTION OF COMPENSATION ACTS

Traditionally, it was generally said that there is to be a liberal construction of all workers' compensation acts because such legislation is remedial in nature. In fact, many workers' compensation acts have an express provision requiring liberal construction. The humane and beneficent purposes of workers' compensation legislation are certainly taken to heart by judges and compensation commissions. For example, see *Ex parte Byrom*, 895 So.2d 942 (Ala. 2004); *Pacific Emp'rs Ins.*

Co. v. Industrial Accident Comm'n, 158 P.2d 9 (Cal. 1945); *Flores v. United Air Lines, Inc.*, 757 P.2d 641 (Haw. 1988). While as a general rule workers' compensation acts are to be liberally construed, liberality of construction should not rise to the level of judicial legislation. See generally 1 *Modern Workers Compensation* § 100:4—Liberal Construction (1998).

In recent times, in an effort at cost saving, some states have backed away from the tradition of liberal construction favoring workers. These states have enacted statutes that attempt to provide neutrality of construction that favors neither the worker nor the employer. See, e.g., Fla. Stat. Ann. § 440.015 (West 2010); N.M. Stat. Ann. § 52–5–1 (West 2010).

CHAPTER 3

WORKERS' COMPENSATION AND THE LAW OF TORTS

A. COMMON LAW AND STATUTORY ACTIONS

The common-law remedies and the statutory actions provided by the various employers' liability acts form the underlying layer of law upon which a remedy can be based when the applicable workers' compensation act fails to provide coverage. Thus, common-law and statutory actions still remain significant, and are extremely important when recovery is sought against an involved third party. Third parties are not covered by the act and are not allowed to limit their liability in the same manner as an employer. Workers can sue third parties for damages, and workers' rights of action do not limit their rights to workers compensation. See generally 1 *Modern Workers Compensation* ch. 102—Remedies Against Employer, ch. 103—Remedies Against Third Persons (1998).

B. THE STRUGGLE FOR COVERAGE AND NON–COVERAGE

Workers are constantly searching for greater compensation than that provided by the applicable workers' compensation system. Whenever possible, and certainly in situations in which there has been no fault on the part of the workers, they will attempt to obtain increased recoveries through the utilization of traditional tort theories. Attorneys have certainly been creative in this area, and have made many attempts to circumvent the limitations on tort recovery imposed by workers' compensation legislation. Needless to say, because of the potential economic harm posed by large tort damages awards, employers want to ensure that workers' compensation remains as a viable shield to tort recoveries. The more important areas in which the struggle for coverage and non-coverage exists are co-employee suits, dual capacity situations, property damages, negligent inspectors, bad faith liability, products liability, negligent physicians, intentional torts, nonphysical torts, and retaliatory discharge. See generally 1 *Modern Workers Compensation* ch. 102—Remedies Against Employer, ch. 103—Remedies Against Third Persons (1998).

1.   CO–EMPLOYEES

The majority of states provide co-employees with immunity from ordinary tort liability in connection with the employer immunity provisions found in the workers' compensation acts. In a few states, however, common-law or statutory actions may be brought against all persons other than one's employer, and this would include a right against a co-employee who may have negligently injured or killed a fellow employee. The co-employee immunity that exists in the majority of states can be found in both statutes and judicial decisions. For an example of a statutory provision creating co-employee immunity, see N.Y. Workers' Comp. Law § 29(6) (McKinney 2010); for an example of a judicial decision in favor of co-employee immunity that was grounded on public policy, see *Miller v. Scott*, 339 S.W.2d 941 (Ky. 1960). Even when immunity exists, it will not be available to a co-employee in most intentional tort situations. See, e.g., *Torres v. Parkhouse Tire Serv., Inc.*, 30 P.3d 57 (Cal. 2001) (worker required to prove that co-employee acted with intent to cause injury in order to show exception to exclusive remedy rule); *Olszewski v. BMC West Corp.*, 94 P.3d

739 (Mont. 2004) (worker failed to meet burden of proof to show intentional tort exception to exclusive remedy provision). Immunity does not extend to all acts of persons who happen to be co-employees. See *Sauve v. Winfree*, 985 P.2d 997 (Alaska 1999). See generally 1 *Modern Workers Compensation* § 103:7—Coemployees (1998).

2.　DUAL CAPACITY EMPLOYERS

Despite the fact that the employer is generally immune from tort liability, the dual capacity doctrine may place an employer in a position to be sued in an alternative capacity, thus avoiding the immunity provided by a workers' compensation act. Although the majority of courts are reluctant to find a dual capacity on the part of an employer, see *Wilder v. United States*, 873 F.2d 285 (11th Cir. 1989) (noting the doctrine to be disfavored), there have been rare instances of success on the basis of dual capacity theories. See generally 1 *Modern Workers Compensation* § 102:10—Dual Persona Doctrine (1998).

One should contrast the similar dual persona doctrine, in which an employer is sometimes sued in tort by a worker because the employer has a different legal identity, usually by way of merger or successor in interest. See, e.g., *Van Bebber & Assocs., Inc. v. Cook*, 870 So.2d 150 (Fla. Dist. Ct. App. 2004) (rejecting application of dual persona exception to particular facts); *Herbolsheimer v. SMS Holding Co.*, 608 N.W.2d 487 (Mich. Ct. App. 2000) (discussion of dual capacity and dual persons concepts). See generally A. Larson & L. Larson, 6 *Larson's Workers' Compensation Law* ch. 113—Who Are "Third Persons": The Dual–Persona Doctrine (Rev. ed. 2000).

3. PROPERTY ACTIONS

It should always be remembered that the exclusive remedy provisions granting immunity to employers do not deny a worker's tort claim for any property damage. See *Superb Carpet Mills, Inc. v. Thomason*, 359 S.E.2d 370 (Ga. Ct. App. 1987) (property action allowed but no punitive damages permitted); *Haddad v. Justice*, 235 N.W.2d 159 (Mich. Ct. App. 1975). Liberal and modern views of what constitute property interests raise questions with regard to what types of actions might be maintainable against employers. See *Silkwood v. Kerr–McGee Corp.*, 667 F.2d 908, 916 (10th Cir. 1981), *rev'd on other grounds*, 464 U.S. 238 (1984) (Oklahoma's workers' compensation law does not bar employee property damage claims); *Brewer v. Monsanto Corp.*, 644 F.Supp. 1267 (M.D. Tenn. 1986) (property damage claims for nuisance by employees not barred by Tennessee's exclusive remedy provision).

4. NEGLIGENT INSPECTORS

Some jurisdictions extend the employer's immunity to insurance carriers and others that may conduct safety inspections. In other jurisdictions, however, an insurance carrier or, for example, a union or union inspector may be held liable under traditional tort concepts for the negligent performance of such an inspection. See, e.g., *Bryant v. Old Republic Ins. Co.*, 431 F.2d 1385 (6th Cir. 1970) (estates of deceased coal miners could maintain action for negligence against workers' compensation insurance carrier because carrier voluntarily engaged to undertake safety inspections but allegedly failed to do so adequately); *Nelson v. Union Wire Rope Corp.*, 199 N.E.2d 769 (Ill. 1964) (where general contractor's compensation and liability insurer gratuitously undertook to make safety inspections, which were planned, periodic, and directed to safety of project employees, duty devolved upon insurer to make such inspections with due care); see also *Coker v. Deep South Surplus of Ga., Inc.*, 574 S.E.2d 815 (Ga. Ct. App. 2002) (action against third party hired by compensation carrier to perform safety inspection allowed). See generally A. Larson & L. Larson, 6 *Larson's Workers' Compensation Law* ch. 114—Who Are "Third Persons": Insurers (Rev. ed. 2000); 1 *Modern Workers Compensation* § 103:36—Labor Unions, § 103:42—Improper Safety Devices (1998).

5. BAD FAITH

A strong policy argument for bad faith on the part of an insurance company can be made when the company intentionally fails to process an employee's legitimate claim for workers' compensation in a manner that demonstrates good faith. In most jurisdictions, the possibility exists for a successful bad faith action against either the employer or the insurance compensation carrier based upon the manner in which an employee's claim for workers' compensation benefits is administered. Thus, the potential exists for a large tort recovery even if a simple or fairly minor injury has occurred, but courts can be reluctant to impose undue burdens on insurers in this area. See *Simkins v. Great West Cas. Co.*, 831 F.2d 792 (8th Cir. 1987) (in South Dakota, a plaintiff must demonstrate an absence of a reasonable basis for denial of policy benefits and the knowledge of or reckless disregard for a reasonable basis for a denial on the part of the insurer; an insurance company will be held liable only when it intentionally denies a claim without a reasonable basis). See generally S. Ashley, *Bad Faith Actions: Liability & Damages* § 5:2—Meaning of Bad Faith in First–Party Cases (2d ed. 2010); J.D. Lee & B. Lindahl, 4 *Modern Tort Law: Liability and Litigation* § 43.38—Workers' Compensation—Third Party Actions—

Claims Against Employer's Workers' Compensation Insurer (2d ed. 2008); 1 *Modern Workers Compensation* § 103:5—Wrongful or Bad Faith Claims Processing (1998).

6. PRODUCTS LIABILITY

Perhaps the area of greatest interest for third party consideration is that of products liability. In practically every workers' compensation case when an employee has been injured by a particular product or instrumentality, attorneys should consider that deeper pocket provided by the product manufacturer. This is especially true today in light of the impact of Section 402A of the Restatement (Second) of Torts (1965) and its strict liability approach. See generally *American Law of Products Liability* (3d ed. 1997).

Furthermore, the possibility exists for a products liability action by a worker against his employer through a dual capacity theory. For example, an employee of a company manufacturing a product may be injured in the normal course of his employment through the use of that particular product. See *Schump v. Firestone Tire and Rubber Co.*, 541 N.E.2d 1040 (Ohio 1989). See generally D. Owen, M. Madden & M. Davis, 2 *Madden & Owen on Products Liability* § 19:7—Employers as Manufacturers (3d ed. 2000).

7. PHYSICIANS

Ordinarily, a physician who commits malpractice on an injured employee who is covered by workers' compensation is liable in tort to the employee, just as the physician would be to any other patient in the particular jurisdiction. See *Greenberg v. Orthosport, Inc.*, 668 N.E.2d 1012 (Ill. App. Ct. 1996) (medical malpractice claim permitted against physical therapy clinic that injured worker's neck during a return-to-work evaluation). However, workers' compensation acts providing co-employees with immunity may provide protection to a physician employed by the employer. See, e.g., *Hayes v. Marshall Field & Co.*, 115 N.E.2d 99 (Ill. App. Ct. 1953). On the other hand, a physician employee could be viewed as an independent contractor and thus subject to tort liability as a third person. See generally 1 *Modern Workers Compensation* § 103:44—Medical Malpractice Claims (1998). It should be noted that the dual capacity theory could be used to impose tort liability on an employer for the negligence of a physician employee that causes additional harm to a worker. See, e.g., *Davis v. Stover*, 362 S.E.2d 97 (Ga. Ct. App. 1987) (action allowed against physician who also happened to be a co-employee).

8. INTENTIONAL TORTS OF EMPLOYERS

Generally, there is tort liability on the part of an employer for intentional torts committed against a worker. See, e.g., *Smolarek v. Chrysler Corp.*, 879 F.2d 1326 (6th Cir. 1989) (retaliation and discrimination); *Paroline v. Unisys Corp.*, 879 F.2d 100 (4th Cir. 1989), *vacated in part*, 900 F.2d 27 (4th Cir. 1990) (sexual assault); *Childers v. Chesapeake & Potomac Tel. Co.*, 881 F.2d 1259 (4th Cir. 1989) (intentional infliction of emotional distress). Problems are posed by those difficult cases in which an employer has knowledge of a continuing dangerous condition to a worker and then knowingly fails to take appropriate action to eliminate the hazard. It is possible for the employer's conduct to be characterized as an "intentional tort" that is outside the coverage of the act. For example, see *Johns–Manville Prods. Corp. v. Contra Costa* Superior Court, 612 P.2d 948 (Cal. 1980); *Blankenship v. Cincinnati Milacron Chems., Inc.*, 433 N.E.2d 572 (Ohio 1982); but see *Kofron v. Amoco Chems. Corp.*, 441 A.2d 226

(Del. Supr. 1982). See generally A. Larson & L. Larson, 6 *Larson's Workers' Compensation Law* ch. 103—Intentional Injury by Employer or Its Agent (Rev. ed. 2000); J.D. Lee & B. Lindahl, 4 *Modern Tort Law: Liability and Litigation* § 43.29—Workers' Compensation—Exclusive Nature of Worker's Compensation Remedy Against Employer—Intentional Injuries—By Employer (2d ed. 2008).

There is a growing trend in some states to provide enhanced workers' compensation awards for intentional torts in the workplace. See generally 1 *Modern Workers Compensation* § 102:13—Intentional Torts, § 102:14—Willful Misconduct (1998). These provisions punish the employer while providing a more efficient remedy to the employee, who would otherwise have to resort to a traditional tort action with its cost, delay, and uncertainty.

Further, there is a recent trend to impose criminal responsibility for certain employer conduct that injures or kills employees. See, e.g., *Illinois v. Chicago Magnet Wire Corp.*, 534 N.E.2d 962 (Ill. 1989) (aggravated battery charged for exposing employees to hazardous substances in the workplace; no federal preemption by OSHA). These criminal proceedings can be of assistance to claimants pursuing compensation and other civil remedies.

9. NONPHYSICAL TORTS

The exclusive remedy provisions of workers' compensation acts generally do not bar what are sometimes referred to as nonphysical torts. These would include actions for false arrest or imprisonment, libel, and slander. Additionally, actions for sex, race, and handicap discrimination, etc., would not be excluded. See, e.g., *Cole v. Fair Oaks Fire Prot. Dist.*, 729 P.2d 743 (Cal. 1987); *Dorr v. C.B. Johnson, Inc.*, 660 P.2d 517 (Colo. App. 1983); *Boscaglia v. Michigan Bell Tel. Co.*, 362

N.W.2d 642 (Mich. 1984). See generally A. Larson & L. Larson, 6 *Larson's Workers' Compensation Law* ch. 104—Intentional Injury: Non–Physical–Injury–Torts (Rev. ed. 2000); 1 *Modern Workers Compensation* ch. 102—Remedies Against Employer (1998).

10. RETALIATORY DISCHARGE

Retaliatory discharge actions are permitted in most states when an employer discharges an employee for filing a workers' compensation claim. See, e.g., *Tyson Foods, Inc. v. McCollum*, 881 So.2d 976 (Ala. 2003) (retaliatory discharge claim under the workers' compensation act can be based upon a constructive discharge); *City of Moorpark v. Superior Court*, 959 P.2d 752 (Cal. 1998) (disability discrimination arising out of a workers' compensation claim could form the basis for a common-law wrongful discharge claim). *Griess v. Consolidated Freightways Corp.*, 776 P.2d 752 (Wyo. 1989) (public policy supports retaliatory discharge claim); see also *Lingle v. Norge Div. of Magic Chef, Inc.*, 486 U.S. 399 (1988) (retaliatory discharge action arising out of the filing of a workers' compensation claim is not preempted by section 301 of the Labor Management Relations Act). See generally S. Pepe & S. Dunham, *Avoiding and Defending Wrongful Discharge Claims* (2000); 1 *Modern Workers Compensation* § 102:32—Wrongful Discharge (1998).

11. RACKETEER INFLUENCED AND CORRUPT ORGANIZATIONS ACT (RICO)

Claims are possible under the federal Racketeer Influenced and Corrupt Organizations Act (RICO), 18 U.S.C.A. § 1961 *et seq.* (West 2010), against an employer, an adjusting service, and a physician alleging mail and wire fraud in a scheme to deprive workers of benefits under workers' compensation laws. See, e.g., *Brown v. Cassens Transp. Co.*, 546 F.3d 347 (6th Cir. 2008) (rejecting defendants' argument that the Michigan Workers' Compensation Act regulated the "business of insurance" as that term is utilized in the McCarran–Ferguson Act). This represents a new and developing area of the law that could have a significant impact on employers, insurers, and medical service providers. See generally *Modern Workers Compensation* § 103:6—Racketeer Influenced and Corrupt Organizations Act (RICO) (1998).

CHAPTER 4

THE EMPLOYEE–EMPLOYER RELATIONSHIP

A. EMPLOYEES AND EMPLOYERS GENERALLY

The common law defined a master as one who employed another to perform services and who controls or has a right of control over the other's conduct in performing such services. The master had to have not only the power to control, choose, and direct the servant with regard to the object to be accomplished, but also had to possess the power to control the details of the work. The common-law definitions are still of importance in establishing who is an employer and employee, but definitions provided in workers' compensation legislation are controlling. Typically, an employee for workers' compensation coverage purposes is defined as one who works for, and under the control of, another for hire. A liberal construction should be given to the definitions of employer and employee because of the objectives of workers' compensation and the need to make coverage as expansive as possible. See generally 1 *Modern Workers Compensation* § 105:1—Generally, § 106:1—Generally, § 106:2—Employee Defined (1998).

The Restatement (Third) of Agency § 7.07(3) (2006) relating to master and servant provides the basic definitions of employee and employer. The Restatement places primary emphasis on the employer's right to control the details of the work in order for a sufficient employment relationship to exist. Professor Arthur Larson has criticized this test and advocates in its place that an inquiry be directed at the nature of the claimant's work in relation to the employer's regular business. He argues that if the particular work has become a part of the cost of the product or services, then the work, and thus the employee, should be covered by compensation. Further, he indicates that the right of control test is a false one and that the independent contractor-employee classification issue can lead to unsatisfactory results. See A. Larson & L. Larson, 3 *Larson's Workers' Compensation Law* ch. 60—"Employee" Defined (Rev. ed. 2000). Despite this criticism, the traditional test of the employer/employee relationship continues, and the following factors, inter alia, are to be considered: who has assumed the direction and control of the employee; who possesses the power to hire and fire or recall, who bears responsibility for wages and compensation, in whose work the employee was engaged and for whose benefit the work was primarily being done, who furnished any equipment to be used by the employee, and who bore responsibility for the employee's working conditions.

B. EMPLOYEES

On the basis of statutes and judicial decisions, particular classes of employees are sometimes specifically included in or excluded from workers' compensation coverage. Typical employee classifications are provided hereinafter. See generally 1 *Modern Workers Compensation* pt. 5—Covered Employers/Employees/Dependents (1998).

1. CASUAL EMPLOYEES

Casual employees are sometimes excluded from workers' compensation coverage. Real difficulties exist in determining who is a casual employee because of a failure to distinguish properly between casual and non-casual employments. Determinations may be based upon the following issues: the contract of hire, the nature of the service or work to be rendered, the scope and purpose of the employment, and the duration and regularity of the service. Ordinarily, employment may be casual if it is temporary in nature and limited in purpose, or if it is incidental, accidental, or irregular. The casual classification is not determined solely by a lack of frequency or length. As might be expected, the law in this area varies greatly from jurisdiction to jurisdiction, but the majority view may well be to exclude an employment from compensation coverage only if the employment is both casual and outside of the course of the employer's business. See, e.g., *Stoica v. Pocol*, 39 P.3d 601 (Idaho 2001) (carpet layer employer's argument that claimant was a casual employee was rejected where claimant worked 30% of the time); *Riden v. Kemet Elecs. Corp.*, 437 S.E.2d 156 (S.C. App. 1993) (duct cleaner worker was not exempt from workers' compensation as a casual employee). See generally 4 *Modern Workers Compensation* § 321:4—Covered "Employees" (1998); U.S. Chamber of Commerce, *2010 Analysis of Workers' Compensation Laws*; *Workers' Compensation Guide* ch. 7—State Laws (2008).

2. AGRICULTURAL EMPLOYEES

The majority of workers' compensation acts specifically exclude agricultural and farm laborers from coverage. See *Eastway v. Eisenga*, 362 N.W.2d 684 (Mich. 1984) (exclusion of agricultural worker from compensation coverage held constitutional). Difficulties in this area exist with regard to the appropriate label; for example, one who trained a race horse was not an agricultural employee. See *Tuma v. Kosterman*, 682 P.2d 1275 (Idaho 1984). Usually, the focus is upon the substance of the employee's work as opposed to the employer's class of business. Because of the great number of workers employed in activities incidental to farm enterprises, the line between compensation coverage for ordinary employment and non-coverage for agricultural workers can be a perplexing one. For example, one employed as an agricultural worker, whose duties also include the repair of farm buildings, might not be covered; while one specially employed to repair a farm building would receive the benefits of workers' compensation coverage. See *Cannon v. Industrial Accident Comm'n*, 346 P.2d 1 (Cal. 1959). See generally 4 *Modern Workers Compensation* § 321:4—Covered "Employees" (1998); U.S. Chamber of Commerce, *2010 Analysis of Workers' Compensation Laws*; *Workers' Compensation Guide* ch. 7—State Laws (2008).

3. DOMESTIC EMPLOYEES

Most compensation acts exempt domestic and household employment from coverage. The test for domestic or household employment is generally whether the duties performed are directed at the maintenance of the home. Some jurisdictions treat domestic employees as "casual" employees; others exclude them from coverage because of the "non-business" nature of their employment, and they are excluded in other jurisdictions because of the coverage exception applicable to employers who have less than the statutorily requisite number of employees. See generally 4 *Modern Workers Compensation* § 321:4—Covered "Employees" (2010); U.S. Chamber of Commerce, *2010 Analysis of Workers' Compensation Laws*; *Workers' Compensation Guide* ch. 7—State Laws (2008). It should be noted that the 1972 Report of the National Commission on State Workmen's Compensation Laws recommended that household workers be covered at least to the extent they are covered by federal Social Security insurance.

4. LOANED EMPLOYEES

The case law addressing the issue of loaned employees is confusing and conflicting. See, e.g., *Borneman v. Corwyn Transp., Ltd.*, 580 N.W.2d 253 (Wis. 1998) (acknowledging that the question of the "loaned employee" is troublesome; driver held not to be a loaned employee for exclusive remedy purposes). The common-law rules are relevant to a determination of who is a lent employee and who occupies the status of the employee's general or special employer. The traditional test of special employment focuses on whether the employee has moved out of the control of the general employer and into the direction and control of the special employer. This inquiry is frequently made in tort cases in an effort to establish the proper employer for purposes of vicarious liability. It must be stressed that the issue in workers' compensation cases is simply the need to find an employer who can provide coverage. While in some states lent employee issues are resolved by statute, other states address the questions through case law, which may impose compensation liability on the general or special employer, or both. See generally 1 *Modern Workers Compensation* § 105:9—Borrowing and Loaning Employers, § 106:41—Loaned Employees and Staffing Agencies (1998).

5. STATE AND MUNICIPAL EMPLOYEES

State, municipal, and public agency employees may be covered by the provisions of state workers' compensation acts, or by some alternative state compensation system. Workers' compensation statutes vary considerably, and each state's act must be consulted individually in an effort to learn if a particular public employee is covered. Some of the more common issues are whether municipal corporations are "employers" under the act, and whether one is a state officer or official, and thus outside coverage, or is an employee. Generally, individuals exercising some portion of a state's sovereign power are considered officials. Police officers and firemen, in particular, have posed problems with regard to workers' compensation coverage. Generally, they are not viewed as "workmen" or "employees," and thus are not covered; however, many workers' compensation acts have special provisions covering these occupations. See generally 4 *Modern Workers Compensation* § 321:4—Covered "Employees" (1998); U.S. Chamber of Commerce, *2010 Analysis of Workers' Compensation Laws*; *Workers' Compensation Guide* ch. 7—State Laws (2008).

6.   FEDERAL EMPLOYEES

Employees and civil officers of the various branches of the United States Government or any of its wholly-owned instrumentalities who are injured or killed in the performance of their duties are provided compensation under the Federal Employee's Compensation Act, 5 U.S.C.A. § 8101 *et seq.* (West 2010). The FECA is liberally construed, administered by the Secretary of Labor, and provides federal employees with their exclusive remedy against the United States for injuries or deaths sustained in the performance of their duties. Traditional third-party liability is not disturbed. The term "employee" under the Act is defined by statute, and various classes of employees are specifically covered, while others are specifically excluded. See 5 U.S.C.A. § 8101 (West 2010). The amounts and duration of compensation payable under the Act are among the most liberal in the United States; compensation is generally based on the employee's monthly pay. Disputed claims for compensation are handled administratively under the Department of Labor. Hearings may be had and final decisions of the Secretary of Labor are subject to review by the Employees' Compensation Appeals Board within the U.S. Department of Labor. See Chapter 1, E, *supra*.

Active duty members of the U.S. military services are not covered by state compensation acts or the FECA. Rather, they are subject to special federal statutory provisions that cover injury and death sustained in the line of duty. See Chapter 1, E, *supra*.

7. PARTICIPATION OF EMPLOYEES IN ENTERPRISE

Originally, workers' compensation acts excluded executives, partners, corporate officers, and the like from coverage because they did not fall under the definition of a workman; it was felt that workers' compensation legislation was not intended to apply to these groups. Today, the fact that a claimant is a corporate officer does not generally preclude coverage. Even if an injury occurs while one is acting in a managerial capacity, one may still be considered an employee under an act. Because of stock ownership and a controlling interest, however, it is possible for one, in effect, to be the business. In these instances, there would be no coverage unless, perhaps, one could be classified as an employee on the basis of the activities one was engaged in at the time of injury (i.e., non-executive activities). This result is reached on the basis of the dual capacity doctrine (not to be confused with the dual capacity doctrine concerning an employer's potential tort liability, see Chapter 3, B.2, *supra*, which makes it possible for an executive who at the time of injury was acting as an employee rather than as an executive to recover compensation). See *Hirsch v. Hirsch Bros., Inc.*, 92 A.2d 402 (N.H. 1952). See generally 82 Am. Jur. 2d *Workers' Compensation* § 111—Partnerships; Joint Ventures (1962).

Partners are treated differently because there is no separate employer entity; partners share equal liability and possess comparable rights in management. In the absence of special legislation, partners are not considered to be employees within compensation coverage, even if they have been injured in situations in which they would have been entitled to compensation had they been employees. See generally 4 *Modern Workers Compensation* § 321:4—Covered "Employees" (1998); U.S. Chamber of Commerce, *2010 Analysis of Workers' Compensation Laws*; *Workers' Compensation Guide* ch. 7—State Laws (2008).

8.   VOLUNTEERS

One who works for another as a volunteer is not generally entitled to the benefits of workers' compensation because one is not deemed to be an employee. Under most acts, only those persons who perform a service for hire are employees, and therefore, volunteers are excluded. See generally 1 *Modern Workers Compensation* § 106:63—Volunteers, Generally (1998).

9.   ALIENS

The term "employee" in the various workers' compensation acts includes all persons who perform services for hire, including aliens. It should be pointed out, however, that some acts require that one be a state resident in order to receive workers' compensation benefits. States are not uniform in this regard, and in the absence of a provision to the contrary, it is generally said that residency is not a requirement for compensation. It should be noted that certain classes of nonresident alien dependents are often excluded from the receipt of death benefits. See *Jurado v. Popejoy Constr. Co.*, 853 P.2d 669 (Kan. 1993) (constitutional challenge); *Alvarez Martinez v. Industrial Comm'n*, 720 P.2d 416 (Utah 1986). See generally 1 *Modern Workers Compensation* § 106:9—Aliens (1998).

10. MINORS

Generally, any person may be an "employee" for the purposes of workers' compensation coverage, and one is not excluded from such coverage simply because of minority. Most states have specific provisions in their compensation acts regarding minors. In some states, minors are entitled to double compensation, and in others, minors may either opt for compensation or sue for damages. A minor's unlawful employment may itself provide a separate tort basis for liability. See Restatement (Second) of Torts § 286 cmt. e (1966). See generally 1 *Modern Workers Compensation* § 106:46—Minors (1998); 4 *Modern Workers Compensation* § 321:4—Covered "Employees" (1998); U.S. Chamber of Commerce, *2010 Analysis of Workers' Compensation Laws*; *Workers' Compensation Guide* ch. 7—State Laws (2008).

11. ILLEGAL EMPLOYMENTS

Illegally employed workers can present unique coverage problems. The difficulty usually relates to the question of whether the employment itself is prohibited by statute; for example, prostitution would be a prohibited employment in most jurisdictions, and thus, if one is employed to perform acts in violation of a penal statute, coverage would be denied. On the other hand, one who has been illegally employed still enjoys coverage when the employment contract is unlawful because of a provision relating to the legality of such an agreement; for example, laws prohibiting the employment of a minor should not interfere with coverage if a minor is injured in an otherwise lawful employment. See generally 1 *Modern Workers Compensation* § 106:3—Lawful Employment (1998).

12. INDEPENDENT CONTRACTORS

If one is classified as an independent contractor, rather than the servant or employee of another, one may lose the right to workers' compensation coverage. The independent contractor issue is one of the most frequently litigated questions in the law of workers' compensation. The Restatement (Third) of Agency §§ 7.07(3) (2006) provides the usual definition and tests utilized in this area. The most common factors considered are the right of control; the method of payment; the providing of materials, tools, or supplies; control over the work site; and the right to discharge the employee. See generally 1 *Modern Workers Compensation* § 106:31—Independent Contractors (1998).

Independent contractor decisions are often conflicting and irreconcilable. The difficulty in this area stems from attempts by the courts to resolve independent contractor issues in tort cases in which the question is one of vicarious liability. It is questionable whether an inquiry aimed at the avoidance of vicarious liability should be of any relevance to a determination of workers' compensation coverage, given the social and economic policies underlying workers' compensation legislation. See *Laurel Daily Leader, Inc. v. James*, 80 So.2d 770 (Miss. 1955); see also A. Larson & L. Larson, 3 *Larson's Workers' Compensation Law* ch. 60—"Employee" Defined (Rev. ed. 2000). Professor Arthur Larson argued that a relative nature of work test should be used because it is supported by workers' compensation theory. This test provides that any worker whose efforts are regularly and continually included in the costs of products or services should receive compensation from the manufacturer of such products or the provider of such services.

13. PROFESSIONAL EMPLOYEES

While often professionals may be viewed as independent contractors, it is possible for them in certain employment circumstances to be employees for purposes of workers' compensation coverage. For example, nurses and interns regularly employed by hospitals are generally employees and included within coverage. Additionally, it is possible for an attorney to have an employer and be an "employee" for workers' compensation coverage. See *Egan v. New York State Joint Legislative Comm.*, 158 N.Y.S.2d 47 (App. Div. 1956). See generally 1 *Modern Workers Compensation* pt. 5—Covered Employers/Employees/Dependents (1998).

14. NATIONAL GUARD MEMBERS

While not uniform, most state workers' compensation statutes cover National Guard members as state employees when performing duties for the state. When called into federal service, most National Guard members are covered by federal compensation statutes, but in a few states, there is a deduction of any federal compensation from state coverage. The federal government typically pays for compensation while National Guard members are called for routine weekend drill or two-week annual training under 32 U.S.C.A. § 502 (West 2010). See generally 1 *Modern Workers Compensation* § 106:44—Military Personnel (1998).

15. COMMISSION–PAID SALESPERSONS

Most states exempt commission-paid salespersons, typically real estate agents and commercial brokers, from the compulsory coverage provisions of their workers' compensation laws. In most jurisdictions, however, these workers are allowed to elect coverage. Each state's coverage provisions should be examined for inclusion or exempt status. When coverage is disputed, most cases turn on independent contractor issues. See generally 1 *Modern Workers Compensation* § 106:52—Real Estate Agents, § 106:54—Sales Representatives (1998); U.S. Chamber of Commerce, *2010 Analysis of Workers' Compensation Laws*; *Workers' Compensation Guide* ch. 7—State Laws (2008).

16. DRIVERS FOR HIRE

Some state workers' compensation laws exempt certain drivers for hire, taxi and limousine drivers, and the like from compulsory coverage. Elective coverage is typically available. Independent contractor issues arise when coverage is contested. See generally 1 *Modern Workers Compensation* § 106:37—Transportation Personnel, § 106:59—Taxi Drivers (1998).

17. TRAINEES

Some states have special coverage provisions for trainees, apprentices, job applicants, and the like. In situations in which there are no special coverage provisions, disputed cases will usually turn on whether there was an express or implied contact for hire; some form of payment, remuneration, or benefit; and control of the trainee's activities. See generally A. Larson & L. Larson, 3 *Larson's Workers' Compensation Law* ch. 64—Necessity for "Contract of Hire," ch. 65—Necessity for Payment (Rev. ed. 2000).

Vocational training programs exist in most states, and trainees may be covered if they are being paid while in training. Typically, student trainees without pay are not covered. Some federally funded programs have some form of federal coverage. See generally 1 *Modern Workers Compensation* § 105:22—Training and Rehabilitation Employers, § 106:62—Vocational Trainees (1998).

18. ATHLETES

In most jurisdictions, amateur athletes are not covered by workers compensation. Professional athletes are covered in some states, but other states may exclude or exempt them from coverage if their contracts for hire provide for disability payments or if they make twice the state's average weekly wage. Coverage in some states is elective. See generally 1 *Modern Workers Compensation* § 106:12—Athletic Personnel (1998).

19. STUDENTS

Some jurisdictions specifically exclude student coverage for services in exchange for tuition, room, board, and the like. Generally, students receiving no pay, benefits, or remuneration would not be afforded coverage. If factors exist showing payment, an express or implied hiring contract, and control, then student employment coverage can be established. See generally 1 *Modern Workers Compensation* § 106:58—Student Workers (1998).

20. PRISONERS

Many state jurisdictions exclude prisoner coverage for workers' compensation purposes, regardless of any work activity that prisoners might be assigned to perform at the time of accident. Some states provide coverage for work in prison industries or work release programs, but specifically disallow coverage if the injury or death arising out of an assault, riot, fight, or activity is not directly related to assigned work. See generally 1 *Modern Workers Compensation* § 106:50—Prisoners (1998).

21. RESIDENTIAL EMPLOYEES

In situations involving residential employees, the key factor for compensation coverage is whether the employer requires the employees to reside on the premises out of some business necessity or simply permits workers to reside on the premises for their own convenience as a matter of free choice. Activities that are related to a worker's duties would be covered, and a residence requirement would encompass many activities that would not be covered if the residence was furnished as a convenience for the worker. Under what is referred to as the bunkhouse rule, a worker who is required to live on employer premises usually is entitled to compensation if injured during any reasonable use of the premises. See generally A. Larson & L. Larson, 2 *Larson's Workers' Compensation Law* ch. 24—Resident Employees (Rev. ed. 2000); 2 *Modern Workers Compensation* § 112:17—Resident Employees, § 112:18—Resident Employees—For Employee's Convenience, § 112:19—Resident Employees—At Employer's Requirement (1998).

C. EMPLOYERS

Workers' compensation acts in each jurisdiction must be consulted for the definition of "employer." As in the case of "employees," the statutory definition of "employer" is the controlling one to the extent that common-law concepts of master and servant are modified. Typically, "employer" means a master or principal who employs another to perform services for hire, who controls or has the right of control of the other, and who usually pays another's wages directly. See generally 1 *Modern Workers Compensation* ch. 105—Covered Employers (2010); 4 *Modern Workers Compensation* § 321:4—Covered "Employees" (1998); U.S. Chamber of Commerce, *2010 Analysis of Workers' Compensation Laws*; *Workers' Compensation Guide* ch. 7—State Laws (2008).

Situations may arise in which an employee appears to have two employers. For example, an employer's employee may hire another without informing the hiree of the true employer's identity. Since an employer for workers' compensation coverage is usually provided on agency theories, the employee is permitted to elect a covered "employer" for compensation purposes. See *Hesse v. J.J. Oys & Co.*, 91 N.W.2d 925 (Minn. 1958).

1. MINIMUM NUMBER OF EMPLOYEES

A minority of workers' compensation acts contain provisions that mandate coverage only in situations in which an employer has a specified number of regular employees. Typical provisions of this nature would, for example, require coverage in the case of three or more employees. Minimum employee requirements are liberally construed in favor of coverage. See *Jackson v. Fly*, 60 So.2d 782 (Miss. 1952). See generally 1 *Modern Workers Compensation* § 105:6—Number of Employees (1998).

Furthermore, the usual requirement of workers "regularly" employed does not necessarily mean constant or continuous employment in order to meet the minimum threshold for coverage. See generally 4 *Modern Workers Compensation* § 321:4—Covered "Employees" (1998); U.S. Chamber of Commerce, *2010 Analysis of Workers' Compensation Laws*; *Workers' Compensation Guide* ch. 7—State Laws (2008).

2. GENERAL AND SPECIAL EMPLOYERS

General and special employer issues usually arise in loaned employee cases. The term "general employer" refers to a worker's original employer, while the term "special employer" refers to the employer to whom a worker is loaned. It is possible for one to be the employee of both at the same time, and thus seek compensation against one or both. Special employment relationships require the consent and knowledge of the employee. The basic test for determining one's employer in the loaned employee situation is deciding who had the right of control and direction over the worker at the relevant time. The pertinent factors, inter alia, include the power to fire, who paid the wages, and whose business was being furthered. See also Chapter 4, B.4, *supra*. See generally 1 *Modern Workers Compensation* § 105:9—Borrowing and Loaning Employers (1998).

3. SUBCONTRACTORS AND STATUTORY EMPLOYERS

A majority of states have provisions in their workers' compensation acts that are designed to prevent a general contractor from shielding himself from compensation liability through the use of subcontractors. These "statutory employer" or "contracting under" provisions are intended to provide protection for employees injured or killed while working for uninsured or judgment-proof subcontractors. In order to successfully maintain a compensation claim against a statutory employer, the subcontractor's employee must establish that the work that gave rise to the injury was a part of the regular business of the statutory employer. The statutory employer may also be benefited in that tort liability can be precluded. See *Black v. Cabot Petroleum Corp.*, 877 F.2d 822 (10th Cir. 1989) (exclusive remedy protection involving upstream and downstream contractors); *Kelpfer v. Joyce*, 197 F.Supp. 676 (W.D. Pa. 1961). It must be pointed out, however, that issues of primary versus secondary liability, the status of the statutory employer as guarantor or insurer under some acts, and the subcontractor's failure to carry insurance may affect third-party tort liability on the part of the statutory employer, even if he has paid workers' compensation benefits. See A. Larson & L. Larson, 4 *Larson's Workers' Compensation Law* §§ 70.01–.06 (Rev. ed. 2000). A statutory employer may possibly obtain reimbursement from a solvent subcontractor. See, e.g., N.Y. Workers' Comp. Law § 56 (McKinney 2010). See generally 1 *Modern Workers Compensation* § 103:17—Statutory Employers (1998).

4. CHARITABLE ORGANIZATIONS

Employees of charitable or nonprofit organizations may not be covered by workers' compensation in some states. Some acts expressly exclude charitable employers. Charities and nonprofit organizations may be excluded as employers because they involve employments not carried on "for pecuniary gain." In those jurisdictions that require that one be engaged "in the trade or business of the employer" in order to be covered, there are conflicting decisions with regard to the coverage of an employee of a charitable organization. The better view allows coverage. See *Smith v. Lincoln Mem'l Univ.*, 304 S.W.2d 70 (Tenn. 1957). Many states also allow for elective coverage for these workers. See generally 1 *Modern Workers Compensation* § 106:16—Charity or Nonprofit Organization Personnel (1998).

5. CONCURRENT EMPLOYERS

An employee may have more than one employer for workers' compensation purposes. These employers may be characterized as either concurrent employers or as joint employers. Several approaches have been taken toward compensation for workers injured or killed in the service of such employers. Liability may be joint, apportioned, or placed upon only one employer. In apportionment situations, employers may be required to provide compensation in proportion to the wages they paid the employee. See *Newman v. Bennett*, 512 P.2d 497 (Kan. 1973). See generally J.D. Lee & B. Lindahl, 4 *Modern Tort Law: Liability and Litigation* § 43.23—Workers' Compensation—Scope of Coverage—Covered "Employees" (2d ed. 2008); 2 *Modern Workers Compensation* § 205:21—Multiemployer Liability (1998).

6. SUCCESSIVE EMPLOYERS

It is not uncommon for an employee to have successive employers, and difficulties can arise in determining which employer is the "employer" for workers' compensation purposes. One method of determining one's responsible employer is to focus simply on the date of injury, and to view the employer at that time as the appropriate one. In those cases in which a disability or injury has resulted from successive employments, the various employers may be required to provide compensation on the basis of their contribution to such disability or injury. Some injuries and certainly death, as in tort cases, can be viewed as single and indivisible, or as incapable of apportionment, with entire liability imposed upon the employers. See generally 2 *Modern Workers Compensation* § 205:21—Multiemployer Liability (1998).

In cases of occupational disease and successive employers, the following possibilities exist: Liability is placed upon the employer in whose service the disease was contracted, liability is borne by the employer in whose employ the worker was last exposed to the disease's hazards, or liability may be apportioned among several employers. Statutory variations exist with respect to the foregoing possibilities, but given the objectives and policies of workers' compensation, there should be complete compensation for employment-related diseases whenever a solvent contributing employer exists. See generally 2 *Modern Workers Compensation* ch. 109—Diseases (1998).

7. COMMON CARRIERS AND TRANSPORTATION EMPLOYERS

In general, most states consider motor carrier businesses to be employers for workers' compensation purposes, unless driver workers have been certified as independent contractors or are otherwise deemed by state law to be independent contractors. Due to vehicle leasing arrangements, owner-operator contracts, driver supplier companies, and common carrier regulation, some jurisdictions look to an economic realities test to determine coverage issues. Special driver-for-hire rules can come into play in many jurisdictions when transportation of persons is contracted. See generally 1 *Modern Workers Compensation* § 105:23—Transportation Employers, § 106:37—Transportation Personnel, § 106:59—Taxi and Other "for Hire" Drivers, § 106:60—Truckers (1998).

CHAPTER 5

THE COVERAGE FORMULA NECESSITY FOR A "PERSONAL INJURY BY ACCIDENT ARISING OUT OF AND IN THE COURSE OF EMPLOYMENT"

A. THE COVERAGE INQUIRY

Since the inception of workers' compensation legislation in the early 1900s, there have been difficulties in fixing and defining the boundaries of coverage. Problems in this area have largely been the result of a failure to properly identify and inquire into the issue of the scope of the risk. The early cases took a tort law, proximate cause approach toward the risk inquiry. Needless to say, a fault-based risk analysis is totally incompatible with the objective and policies of workers' compensation. Subsequent decisions developed various doctrines aimed at defining the scope of the risk, e.g., the "peculiar risk" doctrine, see Chapter 5, B.1.b, *infra*.

One can best understand scope of the risk questions by reference to three broad categories of risks. First, there are definite employment-related risks, such as the loss of limb by a machinery operator; all would agree that this type of injury is within the scope of the risk of employment and covered by workers' compensation. Second, there are personal risks, such as an injury produced by an epileptic seizure while at work, but unrelated to the employment; this injury might be covered by hospital insurance, but not by workers' compensation because the injury arose from a purely personal condition and was unrelated to a risk of employment. Third, there are neutral risks, such as acts of God or random acts of violence unrelated to the employment. These risks are neutral because they bear no relation to the employment, and they cannot be classified as personal risks. Neutral risks are the cause of a great deal of conflict and confusion.

In a further effort to define the boundaries of coverage, an inquiry is made with regard to whether a sufficient relation exists between one's employment and one's injury. Factors such as time, place, and circumstances are considered; however, scope of the risk issues with concomitant confusion also arise in this context. For example, an employee traveling to and from work could be excluded from coverage because at the time of injury, the employee was not at work and was off the employer's business premises. While time, place, and circumstances may be relevant, the true question in to and from work situations may be whether the perils of such a journey should be within the scope of the risk created by one's employment, given the policies and purposes of workers' compensation.

An additional inquiry that must be made in an effort to define coverage boundaries is that of factual cause. This refers to the necessity for a factual connection between one's activities at the time of injury and the injury of which one complains; i.e., the employment in which one was allegedly engaged produced the medical complaint for which one now seeks compensation. For example, did one's employment activity contribute to or cause a heart attack that occurred while one was at work?

In summary, the principal elements directed at coverage in workers' compensation cases are:

1. scope of the risk,

2. sufficient relation to employment, and

3. factual cause.

The preceding issues arise in the context of the statutory language or coverage formula found in workers' compensation legislation. The coverage formula used in the vast majority of workers' compensation acts requires a "personal injury or death by accident arising out of and in the course of employment." The "arising out of" requirement refers to the scope of the risk issue previously discussed in this section, which will be more fully discussed hereinafter. The "in the course of" requirement refers to the sufficient relation to employment issue (time, place, and circumstances factors), which was discussed above and which will be more fully developed later. Factual causation issues will also be discussed.

The coverage formula requirements of "personal injury by accident" have posed problems in cases involving diseases, mental illnesses, and injuries to artificial limbs. Originally, injuries to artificial limbs were not considered "personal injuries," and disabilities from disease that developed over long time periods were excluded from coverage because no personal inquiry "by accident" had occurred.

It should be noted that while the coverage formula speaks in terms of "personal injury," workers' compensation legislation also provides coverage for death cases. Thus, much of what ordinarily is stated with regard to injuries is also applicable to death situations. Therefore, the analysis of various circumstances producing injuries in the following sections is also applicable when those circumstances have resulted in death. See generally A. Larson & L. Larson, 1 *Larson's Workers'*

Compensation Law ch. 4—The Categories of Risk (Rev. ed. 2000); 2 *Modern Workers Compensation* ch. 110—Employment Connection (1998).

B. THE "ARISING OUT OF" CONCEPT

One can best understand the "arising out of" concept by comparing it to the scope of the risk question asked and resolved by courts on the basis of policy considerations in tort cases. Sometimes, this issue is dealt with in tort cases through the use of proximate cause terminology. It is important to remember that this is a question of law and policy exclusively for the court, and certainly scope of the risk issues should be approached in a similar fashion in workers' compensation cases. In light of the objectives and policies of workers' compensation, it is submitted that a much broader approach should be taken toward the scope of the risk than is taken in tort cases. See generally 2 *Modern Workers Compensation* § 110:4—Arising Out of Requirement (1998).

There appear to be five basic risk doctrines employed by the courts to determine the scope of the risk.

1. THE FIVE BASIC RISK DOCTRINES

a. Proximate Cause

Originally, judges had difficulty divorcing themselves from tort law with its proximate cause and fault concepts, and therefore, some early cases adopted the fault-related proximate cause test for the "arising out of" concept, which required that one's employment be the proximate cause of one's injury. This approach is much too narrow, and it is incompatible and in conflict with the objectives of any statutory no-fault compensation system.

b. Peculiar Risk

An early device that resulted in hardship to employees was the peculiar risk doctrine. This risk concept excluded coverage for injuries caused by risks that, admittedly, were within the course of one's employment, but were commonly shared by others, even though the employee was exposed for a longer period of time by virtue of the nature of the employee's employment. For example, an employee who suffered a sunstroke while delivering coal for his employer was viewed as not having been "peculiarly exposed" to the danger of sunstroke because he was not subjected to a materially greater risk of sunstroke than other outdoor workers. *Dougherty's Case*, 131 N.E. 167 (Mass. 1921). The peculiar risk theory is generally rejected in modern compensation cases because it is unrealistic and allows only limited coverage.

c. Increased Risk

A modern approach that provides broader coverage than the peculiar risk test is the increased risk doctrine. This approach includes within the scope of the risk those risks to which an employee has been exposed for a longer period of time than the public, even though the risk is commonly shared by all. If one's employment results in a greater exposure to a risk, there would be coverage, even though the risk is not one that is qualitatively different from that shared by others. For example, one constantly exposed to extreme heat on the job and who suffers from heatstroke should be entitled to compensation under the increased risk theory.

d. Actual Risk

A liberal approach toward the scope of the risk issue can be found in the actual risk doctrine. The sole question to be answered is whether the risk realized was in fact a risk of one's employment, regardless of whether the risk is commonly shared by the public. For example, heat prostration would be compensable if the nature of the employment exposed the employee to the risk; the fact that the risk is common to all who are exposed to the sun's rays on a hot day would be immaterial. *Hughes v. Trustees of St. Patrick's Cathedral*, 156 N.E. 665 (N.Y. 1927).

e.　*Positional Risk*

The positional risk doctrine is the most liberal of the scope of the risk theories, and it has been adopted in a minority of jurisdictions. The only inquiry under a positional risk theory is whether one's employment was responsible for one's being at the time and place where an injury occurred.

Even the most neutral of risks can be included; for example, an employee at work who was accidentally struck by an arrow fired by a small boy next door would be covered. *Gargiulo v. Gargiulo*, 93 A.2d 598 (N.J. Super. Ct. App. Div. 1952).

2.　A MISCELLANY OF RISKS AND INJURIES

a.　*Acts of God*

While acts of God, such as windstorms, tornadoes, exposure, lightning, floods, and earthquakes, would at first appear to be outside the employment risk, it is generally agreed that if one's employment has enhanced or "increased" the risk of injury from these sources, the injury would be compensable. In addition to an increased risk approach to recovery, it may be possible to recover on the basis of "actual risk" or "positional risk" theories. The "proximate cause" or "peculiar risk" approaches would disallow compensation. See generally 2 *Modern Workers Compensation* ch. 113—Weather Injuries (1998).

b. Street Risk Doctrine

Frequently, employees find themselves on the streets and highways in the course of their employment. Early decisions denied recovery to employees who were injured as a result of the realization of risks associated with the use of streets and highways because these were viewed as common risks or hazards to the general public and not risks peculiar to one's employment. The situation is somewhat different today, and an employee who is subjected to a greater exposure to the risks of the street, despite the fact that such risks are common to the public, may be covered. Coverage in these cases can be provided on the basis of the increased risk approach; also, coverage can be had on the basis of the actual risk or positional risk doctrines. See generally 2 *Modern Workers Compensation* ch. 111—Travel & Commuting (1998).

c. Imported Dangers Doctrine

It is not uncommon for employees to be exposed to a risk of harm that they or their fellow employees have imported to the worksite, such as matches, explosives, or firearms. Traditionally, risks imported by the injured employee were viewed as "personal" and outside of the scope of the risk of employment. A danger imported by one's co-employee, while it may appear to be a neutral risk, could nevertheless give rise to recovery on the basis of increased, actual, or positional risk theories. In *Ward v. Halliburton Co.*, 415 P.2d 847 (N.M. 1966), compensation was denied to an employee who was killed when his hunting gun accidentally discharged while he was getting a work uniform from his car; the court indicated that recovery would have been allowed if the gun had belonged to another employee. Additionally, an employee might be able to recover for the realization of a personal risk that the employee has imported, if it could be established that the employment had increased such a risk. See generally 2 *Modern Workers Com-*

pensation § 110:8—On–Premises Injuries—Personal Risks (1998).

d. Assault

Assaults are held to be within the scope of the risk and to arise out of one's employment when the nature of the employment (e.g., policeman or security guard) increases the likelihood of such an occurrence, or if the assault has grown out of a controversy that is work related. Ordinarily, assaults are not within the scope of the risk if they have been prompted by malice or personal motives; however, even these assaults may be included if one's work has contributed to the occurrence in some manner. Assaults in some cases, such as those made by strangers, lunatics, or children, may be viewed as neutral risks outside coverage; still, it may be possible for these to be covered through the use of the positional risk doctrine. See generally 2 *Modern Workers Compensation* ch. 114—Assaults or Firearms (1998).

Early cases recognized the aggressor defense, which denied compensation to an aggressor in work-related assaults. The aggressor defense has been discredited today because it creates a fault-based defense in a no-fault system. Despite the rejection of the aggressor defense, a substantial minority of jurisdictions by statute exclude from coverage those who have been harmed as a result of their "willful intent to injure" others. Generally, these statutes require a greater degree of fault and wrongdoing than is required for the aggressor defense.

e. Horseplay

Injuries frequently occur in the workplace as a result of horseplay. There is little difficulty in providing coverage for a non-participant who is a victim of a horseplay injury; such an injury is viewed as being within the scope of the risk of one's employment. Difficult problems are posed, however, when one instigates or actively participates in horseplay and receives an injury. These cases may be disposed of on the basis of whether they occurred "in the course of" employment; the better analysis, however, is one that focuses on the scope of the risk inquiry, with the increased, actual, or positional risk doctrines determining coverage. In any event, an instigator or willing participant may be able to recover on the basis of the longevity and customary nature of the practice. See generally *Modern Workers Compensation* § 115:3—Horseplay (1998).

f. *Heart Cases*

One of the most problematic areas in the law of workers' compensation is that of heart cases. These cases are commonly approached on the basis of whether a personal injury has occurred "by accident," and require that "unusual" strain or exertion precipitate the heart attack. This is an impractical and unsatisfactory test for coverage in heart cases; distinctions between "usual" and "unusual" strains are practically impossible to make and serve to confuse the issue. See generally J.D. Lee & B. Lindahl, 4 *Modern Tort Law: Liability and Litigation* § 43:40—Workers' Compensation—Compensable Injuries—Heart Attacks (2d ed. 2008).

The better approach is one that focuses on the scope of the risk; thus, if one's employment has contributed to the heart attack because of exertion or other work-related circumstances, the attack may be found to have arisen out of one's employment; otherwise, heart attacks occurring on the job would involve personal risks. Professor Arthur Larson advocates the utilization of both a legal test and a medical test in heart cases. The legal test would be met on the basis of work-related exertion, and the medical test would simply require proof of a causal connection between work-related exertion and the heart attack. This inquiry would be the same as that previously characterized as factual cause and would necessitate expert medical testimony.

As a result of the difficulties in this area, some jurisdictions have special provisions directed at heart and exertion cases. See generally 2 *Modern Workers Compensation* § 109:17—Heart Disease, § 109:18—Heart Disease—Public Safety Personnel, § 109:19—Stroke (1998); 3 *Modern Workers Compensation* § 307:10—Causation—Heart Conditions (1998).

g. *Pre–Existing Injury or Disease*

It is certainly not uncommon for employees to bring pre-existing medical problems to the workplace. The difficulty posed in this area stems from the fact that pre-existing medical problems constitute personal risks, which would fall outside of coverage; however, if one is able to demonstrate that one's employment exacerbated or aggravated a pre-existing medical problem, then recovery may be permitted. The obvious problem facing employees is that of factual cause and medical proof. One must establish through expert medical testimony the fact of aggravation and a causal connection between one's employment and the claimed injury. Some jurisdictions address this problem area through special provisions in their workers' compensation act. See generally 2 *Modern Workers Compensation* § 116:2—Employment Aggravation of Pre–Existing Condition (1998).

h. *Unexplained Accidents and Idiopathic Falls*

Coverage questions arise in cases of unexplained deaths, unexplained falls, and idiopathic falls. A strict application of the neutral risk or personal risk theories could result in a denial of coverage, even if a fall or death occurred in the course of employment. An application of the positional risk doctrine can result in recovery, even if the cause of a fall or death is unknown, because of the employment relation that existed at the time. The positional risk doctrine could also permit recovery in idiopathic fall situations in which the fall was the result of a purely personal condition if, for example, the fall occurred at work. See generally 2 *Modern Workers Compensation* § 116.10—Idiopathic Conditions (1998).

In an effort to resolve the problems posed by an unexplained employee death, courts will generally employ a presumption that the death was one that arose out of employment if the death occurred at the appropriate time and in the appropriate work situation. Given the objectives and policies of workers' compensation legislation, every effort should be made to resolve unexplained injury and death cases in favor of the employee or his survivors. See generally 2 *Modern Workers Compensation* § 116.5—Presumption of Accidental Injury (1998).

i. *Cumulative Stress and Trauma*

Cumulative stress or work-related traumas that cause worker disability over a long period of time or in a gradual manner are not compensable in some states, which take a strict view that accidents must occur suddenly or violently to be compensable. Gradual deteriorations or progressions of medical conditions from natural causes are excluded from coverage as not being injuries by accident. Other states recognize cumulative trauma disorders, such as carpal tunnel syndrome, when supported by proper medical diagnosis. Some states treat cumulative stress disorders as a part of occupational diseases, while others have special provisions for specifically recognized repetitive stress or trauma conditions. See generally 2 *Modern Workers Compensation* § 108:11—Cumulative Injuries, § 109:9—Repetitive Motion Diseases and Injuries (1998); 3 *Modern Workers Compensation* § 307:7.1—Causation—Pre–Existing Conditions—Gradual Onset of Injuries (1998).

j. Hearing Loss

Hearing losses can result from a sudden traumatic event, such as an explosion, or from gradual deterioration over a long period of time due to excessive noises in the workplace. Most jurisdictions have special provisions for occupational hearing loss that define the types, noise level conditions of the workplace, and decibel levels of hearing loss that are involved in a worker's proof of compensable hearing loss. Some states treat hearing loss as an occupational disease, while others treat it as both an injury by accident and as an occupational disease. Some states require that a worker be removed from excessive noise exposure for a period of six months before a claim can be filed, while other states have statutes of limitation built around the last exposure rule concept. See generally 2 *Modern Workers Compensation* § 109:25—Hearing Loss (1998); 3 *Modern Workers Compensation* § 301:5—Disease Claims—Hearing Loss, § 307:15—Disability or Impairment—Hearing Loss (1998).

k. Hernias

A number of jurisdictions have special provisions for hernia claims because they can develop gradually over a period of time and work relation is difficult to prove. Hernias that occur suddenly and with pain are typically covered in most jurisdictions. Some states restrict the recognition of gradual hernias to public safety workers who develop hernias while in service. See generally 2 *Modern Workers Compensation* § 108:13—Hernias (1998).

l. Mental or Emotional Injuries

In the majority of jurisdictions, mental or psychological injuries are compensable, but proof of work relation requires substantial and competent medical evidence. In all states, psychological injuries caused by physically traumatic compensable injuries are recognized, but in a few states, psychological injures that are not the result of physical traumas are not compensable. Special proof requirements vary from jurisdiction to jurisdiction. See generally 2 *Modern Workers Compensation* § 109:27—Mental Illness, § 109:28—Mental Illness—Trauma–Caused, § 109:29—Mental Illness—Stress–Caused, § 109:30—Mental Illness—Work Relation Requirement (1998); 3 *Modern Workers Compensation* § 307:16—Disability or Impairment—Mental Illness (1998).

m. *Explosions, Fires, and Terrorist Acts*

Compensation is usually available for injuries or deaths caused by explosions and fires if workers were engaged in the duties required by their employment at the time of injury, especially if the traumatic events occur on the employers' premises.

If a terrorist act is directed or related to the course of a worker's employment, as in the case of police, firefighters, medical responders, and the like, then any resulting injury or death should be classified as an "accident" within the act, as in assault cases. A liberal approach to the street risk doctrine and the use of the positional risk theory would allow other workers to recover. See generally 2 *Modern Workers Compensation* § 110:7—On–Premises Injuries, § 110:10—Off–Premises Injuries, § 110:11—Emergencies, § 110:12—Emergencies—Firefighters; Emergency Personnel, § 110:13—Emergencies—Police (1998).

n. *Employee False Representations*

Under workers' compensation laws, an employer takes a worker as he finds him, as far as pre-existing conditions are concerned, and therefore, most employers want to know about a worker's medical past in order to access risks and costs of employment. Some jurisdictions by statute or judicial decision specifically exclude from coverage any worker who knowingly misrepresents or makes false statements as to his physical condition on an employment application or pre-employment questionnaire. In some states, employers are required to give written notice to workers that compensation benefits can be denied for failure to provide truthful answers about their prior medical history or condition. For successful defense purposes, an employer must prove three things in order to prevail: (1) The worker misrepresented his prior injuries or medical history on an employment application; (2) the employer substantially relied on the worker's knowing misrepresentations; and (3) there is a causal connection between the worker's misrepresentation and the claimed compensable injury. As to the last requirement, the loss of a small toe in a prior job, for example, would have no relation to hearing loss due to an explosion in the plant on the worker's current job. See generally 2 *Modern Workers Compensation* § 109:34—Misrepresentation Defense, § 115:6—Employment Application Misrepresentations, § 115:7—Employment Application Misrepresentations— Knowing and Willful Misrepresentation, § 115:8—Employment Application Misrepresentations—Causal Connection, § 115:9—Employment Application Misrepresentations—Employer Reliance (1998).

It should be noted that under the Americans with Disabilities Act (ADA), 42 U.S.C.A. § 12101 *et seq.* (West 2010), employers must make a conditional offer of employment before inquiry into a potential employee's workers' compensation history. The inquiry can be pursuant to a medical examination or medical inquiry that is required for all applicants in the same worker category. The employer can refuse employment or can fire a worker who knowingly provides misrepresentations or false information in responses to lawful post-offer questionnaires about his workers' compensation history or medical history. See generally *Workers' Compensation*

Guide ch. 8—Relation to Other Laws, I. Americans with Disabilities Act § 8:3—Coverage (2008).

C. THE "IN THE COURSE OF" CONCEPT

1. AN INTRODUCTION AND PERSPECTIVE

The statutory formula for workers' compensation coverage generally requires a personal injury by accident arising out of and "in the course of" one's employment. The "in the course of" requirement refers to the necessity for a sufficiently close relationship between one's employment and injury. This inquiry focuses on considerations of time, place, and circumstances, as they relate to one's employment.

Problems in this area usually occur for two reasons. First, the "in the course of" concept may be confused with the vicarious liability requirement of the same terms used in tort cases to establish liability; for example, a master is liable for the torts of a servant committed in the course of employment. The vicarious liability "in the course of" requirement certainly may be of assistance in many workers' compensation cases in establishing the requisite employment connection or relation; however, it should not be determinative in those cases in which it conflicts with the policies and coverage objectives of workers' compensation legislation. For example, if one's employment has produced an injury that occurs or manifests itself while one is not at work and off the employer's premises, there should still be coverage. In other words, one need not be acting within the course and scope of one's employment when an employment-related harm produces injury. The only issue is causal connection between one's employment and injury. *Rogers v. Allis Chalmers Mfg. Co.*, 88 N.E.2d 234 (Ohio Ct. App. 1949); see generally A. Larson & L. Larson, 1 *Larson's Workers' Compensation Law* ch. 12—Meaning of "Course of Employment" (Rev. ed. 2000). In *Technical Tape Corp. v.*

Industrial Comm'n, 317 N.E.2d 515 (Ill. 1974), the inhalation of chemical fumes at work produced residual intoxication, causing an employee to have an automobile accident after leaving the workplace; compensation was allowed.

The second cause of difficulties in this area stems from confusing the "in the course of" requirement with the scope of the risk inquiry, which is made in conjunction with the "arising out of" requirement. In other words, the time, place, and circumstances considerations involved in the "in the course of" question may be permitted to dictate the answer to the scope of the risk issue. The scope of the risk issue should always be viewed as a question directed at the scope of workers' compensation coverage, with the necessity for a liberal and broad approach toward employment risks. The "in the course of" requirement really should do no more than establish the necessary relation to one's employment required for workers' compensation coverage. The more liberal a jurisdiction's approach is toward the selection of a risk theory, the less that will probably be required to meet the "in the course of" test. If a positional risk theory is employed, little would probably be required to establish the necessary employment relation. For example, a salesman who suffers harm some distance from the employer's place of business, and on the premises of another, could be covered. See *Wiseman v. Industrial Accident Comm'n*, 297 P.2d 649 (Cal. 1956).

2. COMMON "IN THE COURSE OF" PROBLEMS

a. *Going to and From Work*

Injuries occurring while employees are traveling to and from work have constituted a large portion of workers' compensation litigation, and there is a lack of uniformity in this area. It should be noted at the outset that the problems posed with regard to coverage stem from a failure to recognize that many of these cases should be addressed on the basis of the "arising out of" requirement with its concomitant scope of the risk inquiry.

Generally, those accidents that take place while one is on the way to or from work are viewed as outside the course of one's employment; however, if one is on the employer's premises (having not yet arrived at work or in the process of leaving work), there would ordinarily be coverage. The key issue thus becomes the boundaries of the employer's premises. Various devices have been employed to resolve coverage issues for those injured off of but near the employer's premises; included are the parking lot exception, the "so-close" rule, the "proximity" rule, and the "threshold" doctrine. Some jurisdictions have special provisions in their compensation laws to deal with "going to and from work" problems.

An employee may well be found "in the course of" in the following special circumstances, even if the injury has occurred while going to or coming from work. These special circumstances exist if the employer provides the transportation or travel expenses, the employer compensates the employee for time spent in travel, or the employee is on call and travel constitutes a significant portion of employment duties. In many situations, employees are required, as a regular part of their employment, to spend time away from home or office, and difficult questions arise here because of the myriad of circumstances in which one might receive an injury, e.g., sleeping, eating, or recreation in conjunction with work-related travel. Again, it must be emphasized that the crux of the "in the course of" problem is to be found in a failure to address many of these cases on the basis of the scope of the risk. See generally J.D. Lee & B. Lindahl, 4 *Modern Tort Law: Liability and Litigation* § 43.17—Workers' Compensation—Scope of Coverage—Injuries "Arising Out of" and "In the Course of" Employment—Going to and Coming from Place of

Employment (2d ed. 2008); 2 *Modern Workers Compensation* ch. 111—Travel & Commuting (1998).

Foreign work and travel overseas can create additional risks and problems of coverage. While foreign voluntary workers' compensation insurance is generally available, it may not always bar tort suits against employers. See e.g., Khan v. Parsons Global Services, Ltd., 428 F.3d 1079 (D.C. Cir. 2005) (employee's tort claims due to employer's mishandling of ransom demands in the Philippines were not barred by "traveling employee" exception to general "coming and going" rule of noncoverage under workers' compensation act). See generally D. Dowling Jr., Global Workplace Health and Safety Compliance: From Micro To Macro (2011), 83 *BNA Daily Labor Report* I–1, 2011.

b. *Mixed–Purpose Trips*

An area in which the rules of vicarious liability have created confusion with regard to workers' compensation coverage is that of mixed-purpose trips. On occasion, an employee may be injured while on a trip that is both for the employee's benefit and for that of the employer; these are sometimes called "dual purpose" cases. Certainly, if the trip is primarily for the benefit of the employer, there should be coverage despite the fact that the trip also involves some personal benefit or personal purpose; this is generally called the dominant purpose rule. *Marks' Dependents v. Gray*, 167 N.E. 181 (N.Y. 1929). See generally 2 *Modern Workers Compensation* § 111:18—Dual Purpose Travel (1998).

Just as in cases of vicarious liability, issues of frolic and detour arise. It should be kept in mind that in vicarious liability situations, the issue is one of possible employer liability to a third person, whereas in compensation cases, the issue is one of coverage for the injured employee. Given the question in workers' compensation cases, a more liberal approach is required and less emphasis should be placed upon the vicarious liability meaning of "in the course of." Little should be required in the way of employment connection, and the major inquiry should focus on the scope of the risk. In some jurisdictions, a liberalizing trend is evident in this area. For example, coverage was extended to an employee who, prior to going to work, was injured in an accident while driving his child to school in a company truck; this would certainly appear to have been a personal trip, but the presence of the company's name and address on the truck seemingly determined the outcome. *Thomas v. Certified Refrigeration, Inc.*, 221 N.W.2d 378 (Mich. 1974).

c. Recreation

Various approaches have been taken toward compensation coverage when accidents have occurred during recreational or social activities. There may be liability when injuries from these sources have occurred on the employer's premises. Some decisions take a scope of employment approach toward the activity that produced the injury, while others insist upon some kind of benefit to the employer, direct or indirect. Recreational cases may frequently involve "going to and from" work and personal comfort issues (see *infra*). The more liberal a jurisdiction's risk theory, the greater the likelihood of coverage in recreation cases, and the less that is required for an activity to be "in the course of" employment. See generally J.D. Lee & B. Lindahl, 4 *Modern Tort Law: Liability and Litigation* § 43.14—Workers' Compensation—Scope of Coverage—Injuries "Arising Out of" and "in the Course of" Employment—Recreational activities (2d ed. 2008); 2 *Modern Workers Compensation* § 112:24—Recreational and Social Activities, Generally (1998).

d. Personal Comfort Doctrine

Employees who are injured while engaged in activities aimed at their personal comfort, such as drinking, eating, resting, smoking, or using toilet facilities, generally enjoy compensation coverage if their activities bear the necessary relationship to their employment. An employee may, however, remove himself from the course of employment if, in efforts to satisfy personal needs, he abandons his work or employs means that move the employee outside of the employment relation, thus indicating that a purely personal or neutral risk has been realized. For example, a deliveryman injured while attempting to dislodge a rabbit from a culvert was denied compensation. *Ranger Ins. Co. v. Valerio*, 553 S.W.2d 682 (Tex. Civ. App. 1977). See generally J.D. Lee & B. Lindahl, 4 *Modern Tort Law: Liability and Litigation* § 43.13—Workers' Compensation—Scope of Coverage—Injuries "Arising Out of" and "in the Course of" Employment—Personal Comfort (2d ed. 2008); 2 *Modern Workers Compensation* § 112:5—Personal Comfort Breaks (1998).

e. Emergencies

Employees injured while attempting rescues, or otherwise in emergency situations, are viewed as having acted within the course of their employment if an interest of the employer was furthered by the effort or activity. The good will of the employer alone may constitute a sufficient interest for coverage. As a matter of policy, very little should be required for a finding of "in the course of" when employees receive injuries during rescue attempts. The positional risk theory should be employed to provide coverage when an employee, motivated by common humanity and decency, is injured while attempting to rescue a stranger who bears no relation to the employer's business. See *Food Prods. Corp. v. Industrial Comm'n*, 630

P.2d 31 (Ariz. Ct. App. 1981). See generally 2 *Modern Workers Compensation* § 110:11—Emergencies (1998).

f. Willful Misconduct and Violation of Laws, Regulations, and Safety Rules

The question of willful misconduct on the part of an employee may arise in two important contexts: (1) It may provide the basis for a statutorily created defense in a minority of jurisdictions, or (2) in the absence of such a statute, it may be relevant to the issue of whether an employee was outside of the course of employment at the time of injury. The willful misconduct defense is usually difficult to establish because employee fault should not bar recovery under workers' compensation theory. The term "willful" is strictly construed, and gross negligence will not suffice. The issue of willful misconduct may also arise in the "in the course of" context in conjunction with questions concerning personal comfort, going to and from work, recreation, etc.

Some jurisdictions provide the employer with a statutory defense when an employee has willfully violated safety rules, regulations, or statutes. The willful violation defense is in some ways comparable to the assumption of the risk defense in tort cases. The employer must establish actual knowledge of the rule or statute and an appreciation of the risk connected with non-compliance. Additionally, excuses may exist for non-compliance. The justification and wisdom of the willful violation defense is open to question in light of the no-fault nature of workers' compensation and the inevitability of employee injuries, which are in large part the result of human frailty. See generally 2 *Modern Workers Compensation* ch. 115—Employee Misconduct (1998).

g. Intoxication and Drug Abuse

Employee intoxication is addressed statutorily in a majority of jurisdictions, and it may constitute a separate defense to coverage. The key question in employee intoxication cases is one of causation. The "sole cause" approach taken by some statutes appears to be the one most compatible with the policies of workers' compensation legislation; if there has been some work-related contribution to the injury, there should be coverage. See *Hopkins v. Uninsured Employers' Fund*, 251 P.3d 118, 359 Mont. 381 (2011) (worker's marijuana use in the morning of day he was attacked and mauled by grizzlies at bear park where he worked feeding them was not the major contributing cause of his injuries, and, thus, did not preclude his receipt of benefits where there was no evidence of worker's level of impairment; it was noted that grizzly bears are "equal opportunity maulers").

The coverage question in intoxication cases may also be addressed on the basis of a scope of the risk inquiry, an "in the course of" requirement, or as an issue of whether an injury "by accident" has occurred. See generally 2 *Modern Workers Compensation* § 115:18—Alcohol or Drug Abuse (1998).

h. Suicides

Suicides have traditionally posed problems because they may be viewed as the result of a willful act on the part of an employee, which severs the causal connection between a job-related injury and one's death. The minority view, which parallels the traditional tort view, would only allow recovery in those cases in which one committed suicide in a state of delirium or as a result of an uncontrollable impulse evidencing an inability to make a conscious decision with regard to the taking of one's life. Under the minority approach, there would need to be medical testimony of a mental disorder sufficiently serious to deprive one of volition.

A more liberal approach is generally taken in many jurisdictions, and if an unbroken chain of causation can be established between a work-related injury and a mental condition that leads to a suicide, then compensation may be permitted. See *City of Tampa v. Scott*, 397 So.2d 1220 (Fla. Dist. Ct. App. 1981).

Given the difficulties involved in establishing the requisite causal relation between employment-related injuries and suicides, a better approach would be one requiring simply a demonstration of some contribution to the suicide by an employment-related physical or psychic injury. See *Lopucki v. Ford Motor Co.*, 311 N.W.2d 338 (Mich. Ct. App. 1981). A broad approach should be taken toward the scope of the risk in suicide cases, and such deaths should be viewed as in the course of one's employment when a work relation can be shown. See generally J.D. Lee & B. Lindahl, 4 *Modern Tort Law: Liability and Litigation* § 43.42—Workers' Compensation—Compensable Injuries—Suicide (2d ed. 2008); 2 *Modern Workers Compensation* § 115:5—Suicide (1998).

i. Telecommuting or Working From Home

The modern worker is frequently injured or killed while (1) traveling to and from an office in the home, (2) working at home, or (3) telecommuting from home or office. The traditional traveling to and from home cases, along with a mixed purpose or dual purpose analysis of the scope of the risk, should provide coverage guidance in these situations.

Injuries while working at home require a fact-intensive focus on any work connection for coverage, which also includes a policy analysis of the scope of the risk. *See, e.g., In re Compensation of Sandberg*;101;101, 243 Or.App. 342 (2011) (if an employer, for its own advantage, demands that a worker furnish the work premises at home, the risks of those premises encountered in connection with the performance of work are risks of the work environment, even if they are outside of the employer's control, and injuries resulting from those risks arise out of the employment). One should evaluate such factors as the specific job assignment, routine or required home *situs* as the place of harm, convenience of the employer or worker, personal comfort issues, nature of the injury or death, mixed or dual purpose analysis, quantity of work assigned to home, nature of any home office, employer-furnished equipment, and payment of expenses.

Telecommuting work-related injuries require the same factor considerations in an attempt to place the worker within the scope of the risk for coverage purposes. In many cases, this will be an *ad hoc* determination. The key factor in most situations is the specific work assignment at the time of the injury or death. See generally A. Larson & L. Larson, 1 *Larson's Workers' Compensation Law* ch. 6—The Street–Risk Doctrine, ch. 13—Going To and From Work, ch. 14—Journey Itself Part of Service, ch. 15—Employer's Conveyance, ch. 16—Dual–Purpose Trips, ch. 17—Deviations (Rev. ed. 2000); A. Larson & L. Larson, 2 *Larson's Workers' Compensation Law* ch. 21—Personal Comfort Doctrine, ch. 24—Resident Employees, ch. 25—Traveling Employees (Rev. ed. 2000); 2 *Modern Workers Compensation* § 112:20—At–Home Injuries, § 112:21—At–Home Injuries—Work–Originated Injuries, § 112:22—At–Home Injuries—Delayed–Reaction Injuries, § 112:23—At–Home Injuries—Employment Tasks Performed at Home (1998).

D.   THE NECESSITY OF "PERSONAL INJURY BY ACCIDENT"

1.   THE PROBLEMS

Traditionally, most workers' compensation acts have required as a part of their coverage formula a "personal injury by accident" or "accidental injury." Difficulties have arisen in interpreting the meanings of these terms. Historically, problems have existed in this area because of the failure to take a pragmatic and liberal approach toward these requirements as they relate to the scope of the employment risk.

Furthermore, difficulties in this area were compounded by factual causation issues, which were disposed of under the guise of "personal injury by accident," and which more appropriately should have been addressed as a part of the employment risk question, with very little required in the way of the cause in fact.

The personal injury by accident requirement has caused confusion and worked hardships in the following three major areas: occupational diseases; mental illness; and diseases, illnesses, or injuries that have developed over a gradual period of time. Additionally, controversies sometimes exist as to whether injuries to artificial limbs are excluded from coverage by the "personal injury" or "accidental injury" requirement. See *Self v. Riverside Cos., Inc.*, 382 So.2d 1037 (La. Ct. App. 1980). A growing number of jurisdictions treat artificial limb injuries by special statutory provisions.

Initially, occupational diseases were excluded from workers' compensation coverage because it was generally thought that this was an area for private health insurance. There was thus no provision for disease coverage in early compensation legislation, and the courts refused to find coverage because no "personal injury by accident" had occurred; after all, all diseases were considered to be personal or neutral risks commonly shared by everyone. In more modern times, the necessity for occupational disease coverage has been candidly recognized either by broad judicial interpretations of the formula wording or by special occupational disease provisions in the compensation acts.

Another difficulty with the "personal injury by accident" requirement is that presented by mental illnesses. Today, on the basis of medical science, mental illness is recognized as a legitimate form of injury that may be causally connected to a risk of one's employment. The basic employment-related mental illness fact patterns that commonly arise are (1) physical trauma producing a nervous disorder, (2) nervous shock producing a physical disorder, (3) nervous shock producing a nervous condition or neurosis, (4) mental distress produced by prolonged work-related stress and anxiety, and (5) compensation neurosis, i.e., an unconscious desire to prolong compensation or a fear that compensation will not be paid. Little difficulty is presented for coverage by the first two fact patterns, but the latter three may have coverage issues. There is authority for compensation recovery in all five areas, and given the current state of medical science, there should be coverage for all the patterns when a mental illness is proven and the requisite employment connection is established. Given the pace and complexity of the modern industrial state with its rapid technological changes, mental disorders may well be within the scope of the risk of one's employment. See generally *Wade v. Anchorage Sch. Dist.*, 741 P.2d 634 (Alaska 1987).

Originally, the formula coverage requirement of an "accident" was generally said to necessitate an "unusual," "unforeseen," "unexpected," or "external" event as the cause of an injury. In addition to an "unexpected event," it was also generally said that an injury had to have been sustained on a definite occasion or at a certain time. This approach created insoluble coverage problems because of the apparent necessity of distinguishing between "unexpected" or "unusual" and "expected" or "usual" risk, e.g., if the strain, exertion, or hernia was caused by an unusual or usual work-related event. Furthermore, the definite occasion requirement in "accident" cases resulted in the exclusion of occupational diseases that had gradually developed over a long period of time. See generally 2 *Modern Workers Compensation* ch. 108—Accidents & Injuries (1998).

2. THE SOLUTION

The enormous coverage problems caused by the "accident" interpretations in many jurisdictions prompted the National Commission on State Workmen's Compensation Laws to recommend the elimination of this coverage requirement. It should be pointed out that the confusion created by the language "personal injury by accident" can be avoided simply by focusing upon scope of the risk, work connection, and factual cause.

E. THE ROLE OF "PREMISES"

The mere existence of an injury on an employer's premises, without more, will not be sufficient to show work connection for compensation purposes in most jurisdictions. However, one of the most important work relation factors in the evaluation of coverage involves the employer's premises. Some jurisdictions treat as in the course of employment all injuries or deaths occurring on premises controlled by or occupied by the employer. Other jurisdictions view employer-authorized work and activities at employer-controlled or approved premises as a part of the arising out of and in the course of employment formulation. Premises defects, hazards, working conditions, idiopathic falls, adjacent premises, off-premises, and the like are related terms that workers and employers use to establish or reject coverage under the arising out of and in the course of formula. See generally 2 *Modern Workers Compensation* § 110:7—On–Premises Injuries, § 110:8—On–Premises Injuries—Personal Risks, § 110:9—On–Premises–Injuries—Neutral Risks, § 110:10—Off–Premises Injuries (1998).

F. OCCUPATIONAL DISEASE

1. COVERAGE SCHEMES

General compensation coverage for occupational diseases is currently provided in all jurisdictions, but the coverage methods vary considerably. The exclusive remedy provisions in the various acts, in recent years, have provided an increasingly important area of employer immunity. See *Buford v. American Tel. & Tel. Co.*, 881 F.2d 432 (7th Cir. 1989). At least five schemes of occupational disease coverage are identifiable: (1) use of a general definition of occupational disease in the workers' compensation act, (2) use of an expanded definition of "injury" or "personal injury" to include occupational disease, (3) use of a scheduled list of occupational diseases coupled with a general disease catch-all definition, (4) use of an unrestricted disease coverage provision, and (5) use of a separate occupational disease act. In addition to the foregoing general occupational disease coverage schemes, it is not uncommon to find specific legislative provisions dealing with loss of hearing, hernias, radiation, and various diseases of the lungs. Finally, the area of coal miner pneumoconiosis, or "black lung," has virtually been preempted by federal legislation and programs; see Chapter 1, E.5, *supra*. See generally 2 *Modern Workers Compensation* ch. 109—Diseases (1998).

2. COVERAGE PROBLEMS

a. *Occupational Disease Versus Accident*

As mentioned previously, early workers' compensation acts contained no provision for occupational disease coverage, and most courts interpreted the formula "personal injury by accident" to exclude all diseases from workers' compensation coverage. As might be expected, the gray area between the definition of personal injury and disease became a conceptually difficult one. With the passage of special occupational disease legislation, however, the distinctions between disease and injury by accident definitions became less important. It should be kept in mind that an occupational disease can in fact occur through accidental means; for example, one can contract many diseases as a result of an accidental cut or skin breakage that is work related. See *Wilson Foods Corp. v. Porter*, 612 P.2d 261 (Okla. 1980). See generally 2 *Modern Workers Compensation* ch. 109—Diseases (1998).

b. *Occupational Disease Versus Common Disease*

The major problem area today in occupational disease cases is to be found in the identification of those ordinary diseases of life that are said to be common to the public and not distinctively associated with a particular employment. Most jurisdictions attempt to give a detailed definition of the term "occupational disease," and despite the wording chosen, the ultimate issue of coverage is usually decided by the particular jurisdiction's approach to the scope of the employment risk of the disease in question. This is probably the case even though many jurisdictions fail to realize that their decisions are being made on this basis. For example, coverage problems of this nature could easily arise for a deliveryman who is regularly exposed to rain, sleet, and snow in the winter months, and who claims that his pneumonia is sufficiently work related to be compensable. Pneumonia may be an ordinary disease of life, common to the public, and certainly not peculiar to his employment; however, deliveries made in winter weather may increase the risk of pneumonia, make it an actual risk of employment, or place the deliveryman in a position to contract the disease. See generally 2 *Modern Workers Compensation* ch. 109—Diseases (1998).

c.   Occupational Disease and Medical Causation

In the foregoing example of the deliveryman who contracted pneumonia in the winter months, difficulties also arise with regard to medical causation. A medical expert might testify that the employee's exposure because of his working conditions was a minor causative factor in the contraction of the pneumonia, or the expert might testify that the employee was subjected to both employment-and non-employment-related exposure, either of which could have caused the disease. The key inquiry should be whether the employment exposure caused or substantially contributed to the pneumonia. If the employment relation, as the cause in fact of the disease, is unclear, vague, or uncertain in the medical sense, then there is a likelihood that no coverage will be found. See *Florida State Hosp. v. Potter*, 391 So.2d 322 (Fla. Dist. Ct. App. 1980).

The medical cause in fact inquiry poses real difficulties because of the frequent merger of the scope of the risk issue with the medical-factual causation question and the surrounding confusion that this produces. The entire area of occupational disease is confusing and troublesome, and as recognized by the *1972 Report of the National Commission on State Workmen's Compensation Laws*, "the determination of the etiology or 'cause' of a disease in a medical sense is often difficult or even impossible." See generally 2 *Modern Workers Compensation* ch. 109—Diseases (1998).

3.   SPECIAL COVERAGE RESTRICTIONS

It has been fairly common for various states to place unique restrictions on recovery for certain occupational diseases. Those diseases that receive restrictive treatment are generally diseases of the lungs, such as silicosis, asbestosis, and black lung. Typical restrictions preclude recovery unless death or disability has occurred within a certain number of years from the date of the last injurious exposure or from the date of the last employment in a particular area. Another example of restriction is to be found in the denial of benefits to one who has suffered less than total disability as a result of a particular occupational disease. Sometimes, one finds that employees are precluded from compensation unless they can demonstrate their exposure to the hazards of a particular disease for a specified period of time. The policies and practices of each jurisdiction should be examined. In some instances, there are even special provisions granting greater compensation than normal for certain lung diseases. See generally 2 *Modern Workers Compensation* ch. 109—Diseases (1998).

CHAPTER 6

DEATH

A. DEATH BENEFITS GENERALLY

Death benefits are provided by workers' compensation legislation to certain classes of beneficiaries. These benefits include burial expenses, with a statutory limit placed on the expenses, and compensation for the beneficiaries, which is calculated on the basis of the appropriate statutory formula of the particular jurisdiction. The right to death benefits is a right created by statute, and it is not dependent upon any rights of the deceased worker. Therefore, a worker's release, compromise, settlement, or unfavorable compensation decision would be no bar to the claims of beneficiaries. A beneficiary's claim is legally separate and distinct from the worker's claim for compensation during his lifetime, and the worker generally has no right to control or dispose of the claims of the beneficiaries. See generally 2 *Modern Workers Compensation* § 200:44—Death (1998).

B. DEPENDENCY AND PARTIAL DEPENDENCY

As a general proposition, only those beneficiaries who are viewed by the compensation act as "dependents" are entitled to death benefits. The acts vary, but generally compensation statutes require a showing of either actual dependency (complete or partial) and/or membership in a designated class or group before there can be recovery. In many instances, those bearing certain relationships to the deceased, e.g., wife or child, enjoy a presumption of dependency and need not demonstrate actual dependency.

It is always important at the outset to determine who can be classified as complete or total dependents as opposed to partial dependents, as the former group is given preference and may recover compensation to the exclusion of the latter group. Anyone claiming death benefits other than one who enjoys a statutory presumption of dependency must prove actual dependency and membership in the statutory class entitled to compensation. The statutory classes are defined differently from jurisdiction to jurisdiction. Some acts provide fixed lists of persons, such as widow or widower, child, parent, or sibling. Other acts use classes defined by the terms "next of kin," "member of the employee's family," or "member of the employee's household." While the term "next of kin" may sometimes mean blood relatives only, a liberal approach should be taken toward the classifications; for example, an unadopted dependent child living in the deceased's household should be included as a beneficiary. See generally *Ryan–Walsh Stevedoring Co., Inc. v. Trainer*, 601 F.2d 1306 (5th Cir. 1979).

In those cases in which one does not receive the benefit of a presumption of total dependency, one must prove either total or partial dependency. Generally, total dependency may be proven despite the fact that a dependent had some other minor sources of support; however, one would not be totally dependent if a substantial source of support were received from someone other than the deceased. Partial dependency is a question of fact, and can be found to exist even if one's own sources provide substantial support. A majority of jurisdictions take a liberal approach toward the definition of "dependent"; see *Tabor v. Industrial Accident Fund*, 247 P.2d 472 (Mont. 1952). See generally 1 *Modern Workers Compensation* ch. 107—Dependents (1998).

C. WIDOW

In a majority of jurisdictions, a widow is conclusively presumed to be totally dependent upon the deceased for workers' compensation purposes. Widowers should receive equal treatment. See *Wengler v. Druggists Mut. Ins. Co.*, 446 U.S. 142 (1980). When no legal presumption exists, proof of dependency would be required. A claimant's marital status at the time of the death of the worker is often a key factor because some jurisdictions fix compensation rights as of the time of death. Other jurisdictions, sometimes with inequitable results, fix relationships and dependency as of the time of the accident or injury producing death. See generally *Dunn v. Industrial Comm'n*, 866 P.2d 858 (Ariz. 1994). For example, widows have been denied death benefits when they married a worker after the date of an injury that ultimately produced death. See generally 1 *Modern Workers Compensation* § 107:7—Spouse or Cohabitant, § 107:7.1—Domestic Partner Benefits (1998).

1. LIVING WITH OR APART

In most jurisdictions, a surviving spouse enjoys a presumption of dependency only if living with the deceased worker at the time of injury or death. "Living with" does not necessarily mean residing together; for example, economic necessity or considerations of health might dictate a separation. Additionally, a separation may be the result of desertion or other wrongful conduct on the part of the deceased worker's spouse that does not affect the legal obligation to provide support. If a separation has occurred that relieves the deceased employee's spouse of the legal obligation to provide support, the "living with" requirement would not be met, and there would be no presumption of dependency.

2. COMMON–LAW MARRIAGE

The domestic relations laws of a particular jurisdiction control whether a surviving common-law spouse may recover death benefits. For example, a common-law wife may be viewed as a "widow" or "wife" for workers' compensation purposes. See *National Union Fire Ins. Co. v. Britton*, 187 F.Supp. 359 (D.D.C. 1960). Even in jurisdictions in which the relationship is considered illicit, one may be entitled to compensation benefits as an actual dependent member of the deceased's "household." Furthermore, in some jurisdictions, an illicit relationship is no bar to recovery if it was entered into in a "good faith" belief in legality by the surviving spouse. See *Dawson v. Hatfield Wire & Cable Co.*, 280 A.2d 173 (N.J. 1971). Bigamous marriage situations are often resolved on the basis of the "last marriage rule," which presumes that the last marriage was the legal one for compensation purposes. See *Gibson v. Hughes*, 192 F.Supp. 564 (S.D.N.Y. 1961).

D. CHILDREN

Death benefits are generally provided for the "child" or "children" of a deceased employee on the basis of specific statutory language that includes them within the group conclusively presumed to be dependent. Illegitimate children, stepchildren, posthumous children, and other children who were not the subject of a legal obligation for support on the part of the deceased employee have posed coverage problems. Coverage has sometimes been afforded under the dependent classifications of "member of the family" or "member of the household," and under specific statutory provisions addressing acknowledged illegitimate children. Today, the difficulties previously posed by illegitimate children have been largely eliminated by the Supreme Court decision of *Weber v. Aetna Casualty & Surety Co.*, 406 U.S. 164 (1972), in which the Louisiana Workers' Compensation Act was declared unconstitutional in so far as unacknowledged illegitimate children were denied coverage. This was held to be in violation of the Equal Protection Clause of the Fourteenth Amendment. Proof problems with regard to paternity still remain. See generally 1 *Modern Workers Compensation* § 107:8—Children (1998).

E.   FAMILY AND HOUSEHOLD MEMBERS

While the exact statutory language may vary, many workers' compensation acts permit the recovery of death benefits to one who can qualify as a "member of the family" or "member of the household." On the basis of the creation of these classifications, it may be possible for stepchildren, stepgrandchildren, stepmothers, illegitimate children, nephews, mothers-in-law, and even unrelated children who can establish some dependency upon the deceased to receive death benefits. The liberal approach taken toward these groupings is supported by the humane objectives of workers' compensation. See generally 1 *Modern Workers Compensation* ch. 107—Dependents (1998).

F.   PRIORITIES

Death benefit priorities are statutorily established in workers' compensation acts. Family relationships and/or dependency dictate priorities and benefits. For example, it is sometimes provided that a surviving spouse and minor children are to receive an entire award to the exclusion of others claiming dependency. Ordinarily, that class consisting of total dependents is entitled to receive death benefits, even if this means no recovery for partial dependents. When more than one wholly dependent claimant exists, there may be an equal division of benefits, or statutorily-fixed proportions may be allocated. It is possible, however, on the basis of some acts, for both total and partial dependents to receive compensation, but this should only occur after full compensation has been had by total dependents. As a caveat, it should be noted that compensation accrued and due a deceased employee must be paid either to the deceased's estate for distribution or to the dependents under a compensation act, depending upon the jurisdiction. See generally 1 *Modern Workers Compensation* ch. 107—Dependents (1998).

CHAPTER 7

MEDICAL EXPENSES, DISABILITIES, AND BENEFITS

A. INTRODUCTION TO RECOVERIES

The three broad categories of recovery under workers' compensation are (1) medical and related expenses, (2) disability benefits, and (3) death benefits. Under the first group, medical expenses, rehabilitation costs, nursing costs, drugs, etc., are recoverable. Disability benefits are designed to provide compensation for the loss of earnings or earning power, and they are usually determined on the basis of either medical loss or wage loss theories, or some combination thereof; these benefits are determined by statutory formulas that may result in weekly, monthly, or sometimes lump sum payments. Death benefits are paid to the dependents of a deceased worker, and such benefits are based on a statutory formula; additional amounts are specified for funeral or burial expenses. For reference and comparison purposes, the U.S. Chamber of Commerce annually compiles comprehensive charts of the state, federal, and Canadian compensation requirements and benefits. See U.S. Chamber of Commerce, *2010 Analysis of Workers' Compensation Laws*. See generally 2 *Modern Workers Compensation* pt. 9—Compensation & Benefits (1998); *Workers' Compensation Guide* ch. 7—State Laws (2008).

B. MEDICAL EXPENSES AND REHABILITATION

At one time, workers' compensation acts placed limitations on the amounts recoverable for medical expenses. Today, most jurisdictions permit the recovery of unlimited medical expenses, so long as a worker's condition necessitates continued treatment and care. A liberal approach is taken toward medical expenses, and commonly, the costs of doctors, nurses, specialists, hospitalization, medical equipment, prosthetic devices, psychiatric treatment, drugs, medicines, etc., are included. It should be noted that in those cases in which an injured worker's spouse provides home nursing services, there can be recovery for the value of such services under the heading of medical expenses. See *Kushay v. Sexton Dairy Co.*, 228 N.W.2d 205 (Mich. 1975). See generally 2 *Modern Workers Compensation* ch. 202—Medical Benefits (1998); *Workers' Compensation Guide* ch. 7—State Laws (2008).

There is a lack of uniformity among workers' compensation statutes with regard to the recovery of physical and vocational rehabilitation costs. Ordinarily, those costs reasonably necessary for medical rehabilitation are recoverable; however, very few statutes provide complete coverage for the costs of vocational rehabilitation and related expenses necessary for a worker's return to full employment. See generally 2 *Modern Workers Compensation* ch. 203—Vocational Rehabilitation (1998); *Workers' Compensation Guide* ch. 7—State Laws (2008).

It should be remembered that in those cases in which medical complications, bad results, and even greater disabilities from medical malpractice occur, these events can be viewed as a part of the employee's original "injury," and all increased medical costs and benefits should be recoverable.

See, e.g., *Mallette v. Mercury Outboard Supply Co.*, 321 S.W.2d 816 (Tenn. 1959).

It should also be noted that the avoidable consequences rule has been applied to workers' compensation cases by statutes or case law. Employees who unreasonably refuse to submit to medical aid and treatment may jeopardize their rights to benefits. See *Kentucky Dep't of Highways v. Lindon*, 380 S.W.2d 247 (Ky. 1964).

C. SELECTION OF PHYSICIAN

The right to choose freely one's physician has been the subject of a great deal of controversy under workers' compensation laws. Some acts permit an employee to select a physician, while others require that a selection be made from a panel of physicians chosen by the employer. Other acts require that treating physicians be approved by the medical profession for workers' compensation practice.

The physician selection controversy revolves around the need for physician-patient confidentiality and confidence, on the one hand, versus the need to control medical costs and to provide effective medical treatment, on the other. No matter what the physician selection rule of the particular jurisdiction may be, an injured employee cannot generally seek medical assistance without the employer's prior knowledge and consent, except for emergency situations. Of course, if after notice, an employer fails to provide the necessary medical care, an employee is free to procure medical assistance and submit a claim for reimbursement. Osteopaths and chiropractors may be selected. See *Wetzel v. Goodwin Bros., GMC Truck*, 622 P.2d 750 (Or. Ct. App. 1981). See generally 2 *Modern Workers Compensation* § 202:35—Selection of Physician (1998); *Workers' Compensation Guide* ch. 7—State Laws (2008).

D. MEDICAL LOSS AND WAGE
LOSS THEORIES

The key to understanding compensable disabilities is to be found in medical loss and wage loss theories; both theoretically compensate an injured worker for loss of earnings or earning power, but they achieve this result by different methods. The medical loss theory focuses upon the physical injury or impairment suffered by a worker. Compensation may be based on "pure" medical losses; for example, workers' compensation acts usually contain "schedules," which provide a predetermined amount of compensation for specific enumerated medical losses; i.e., a schedule might provide a specified amount of compensation for the loss of a hand, regardless of the economic impact of such a loss. In other words, certain enumerated medical losses are clearly recognized as disabilities, and a loss of earnings or earning power is conclusively presumed on the basis of the inclusion of the loss in a medical loss schedule.

The wage loss theory attempts to provide compensation for an injured employee on the basis of the employee's actual earnings that have been lost due to an injury. For example, a "pure" wage loss approach might award compensation to an injured employee on the basis of actual lost wages incurred during the period of incapacity. In many jurisdictions, wage loss determinations are made by comparing actual earnings prior to the date of injury with one's "earning capacity" after the injury. This "diminished earning capacity" concept permits an injured worker to recover compensation even if there has been no actual loss of earnings. See, e.g., *Karr v. Armstrong Tire & Rubber Co.*, 61 So.2d 789 (Miss. 1953).

No compensation system today employs pure medical loss or pure wage loss theory; rather, compensation acts utilize both in varying degrees. For example, a compensation act that contains an injury schedule may also provide compensation for an unscheduled injury resulting in a medical impairment. The severity of the impairment and the degree of one's disability (i.e., temporary total, permanent total, temporary partial, or permanent partial) commonly are used to determine the duration and amount of the employee's economic losses.

A tremendous amount of controversy exists with regard to the proper use of medical and wage loss theories in the determination of the appropriate amount of compensation for injured workers. See A. Larson, *The Wage–Loss Principle in Workers' Compensation*, 6 Wm. Mitchell L. Rev. 501 (1980). While it is desirable for compensation awards to bear a reasonable relation to one's past wages, and to be based upon a reduction in one's earning capacity, rather than on the basis of arbitrary amounts dictated by the type of medical injury sustained, it must be stressed that no wage loss or medical loss approach actually attempts to provide compensation on the basis of the injury's true economic impact on the particular worker or on the worker's earning power or earning capacity. All legislation in this area represents compromises, which has resulted in a no-fault system of reduced but fairly certain compensation for work-related injuries. See generally 2 *Modern Workers Compensation* ch. 200—Basis for Compensation (1998); *Workers' Compensation Guide* ch. 7—State Laws (2008).

E. THE AVERAGE WAGE AND FORMULAS

The cornerstone of compensation calculations is an employee's average wage, commonly specified as an "average weekly wage" or as some other average wage based upon a unit of time, such as months or days. The average weekly wage, average monthly wage, or the like represents an average earnings figure, which, when multiplied times a jurisdiction's fixed statutory percentage (typically ranging from 50% to 66 2/3%), produces the employee's basic weekly or monthly benefit. Statutory formulas vary from jurisdiction to jurisdiction, but commonly, compensation benefits are determined on the basis of weeks or months of eligibility. In addition, it is commonly provided that maximums and minimums are to be placed on the amount of the weekly or monthly benefits; further, limitations may be placed upon the number of weeks or months of eligibility.

Frequently, issues arise with regard to the composition of the average weekly wage and whether, for example, tips, fringe benefits, bonuses, meals, and transportation should be considered. Every effort should be made to make the employee's average weekly wage computation as complete as possible. See *Jess Parrish Mem'l Hosp. v. Ansell*, 390 So.2d 1201 (Fla. Dist. Ct. App. 1980); but see *Morrison–Knudsen Constr. Co. v. Director, OWCP*, 461 U.S. 624 (1983).

Difficulties may also arise because of an employee's temporary, irregular, or erratic work history. The average wage may sometimes be calculated with reference to the wages of a comparably situated employee. Most statutes permit calculations of average wages in a discretionary manner, if a just and fair result for the employee cannot be obtained by the use of the normal statutory formulas. See generally 2 *Modern Workers Compensation* ch. 200—Basis for Compensation (1998); *Workers' Compensation Guide* ch. 7—State Laws (2008).

F. DISABILITIES

1. DISABILITIES GENERALLY

Workers' compensation statutes ordinarily provide four classifications of disability, determined by the severity or extent of the disability, with the disability characterized as either partial or total. Additionally, disabilities are affected by their duration and are characterized as either permanent or temporary. The four common disability classifications are temporary partial, temporary total, permanent partial, and permanent total. These classifications, in conjunction with the employee's average wages and appropriate statutory formulas, provide the basis for disability benefit computation. See generally 2 *Modern Workers Compensation* § 200:1—Generally (1998); *Workers' Compensation Guide* ch. 7—State Laws (2008).

2.   TEMPORARY PARTIAL

A temporary partial disability is present when an employee who has been injured on the job is no longer able to perform that job, but for the period of disability is able to engage in some kind of gainful employment. Temporary partial disability compensation is designed to pay an injured worker for lost wages, and thus wage loss theory is generally employed in making awards. Additionally, this classification promotes the prompt return of an injured employee to the workforce. Examples of injuries that commonly produce temporary partial disabilities are sprains, minor fractures, contusions and lacerations. See generally 2 *Modern Workers Compensation* § 200:7—Temporary Partial Disability (1998); *Workers' Compensation Guide* ch. 7—State Laws (2008).

The critical factor in determining the temporary partial classification may be the impairment of the employee's earning capacity. For example, an employee who has received a minor injury that has resulted in no loss of time at work and who has suffered no actual wage losses may still be entitled to temporary partial compensation if some impairment to earning capacity can be proven.

3. TEMPORARY TOTAL

The condition of temporary total disability exists when an employee is unable to work at all for a temporary but undetermined amount of time. One may be totally disabled even though not completely helpless or wholly disabled. Examples of injuries that can result in temporary total disability are serious illnesses, heat exhaustion, and disabling back injuries. Temporary total disability is designed to provide compensation to an injured worker for the economic losses incurred during a recuperative period. See generally 2 *Modern Workers Compensation* § 200:8—Temporary Total Disability (1998); *Workers' Compensation Guide* ch. 7—State Laws (2008).

4. PERMANENT PARTIAL

A permanent partial disability may be found when a permanent and irreparable injury has occurred to an employee, i.e., one that probably will continue for an indefinite period with no present indication of recovery. For example, one who loses a foot on the job will experience a period of temporary total disability during hospitalization and recuperation. At the point in time when maximum medical improvement has been attained, the disability should be classified as permanent partial; a foot has been lost, but the employee is able to perform some gainful work.

The purpose of permanent partial disability is to provide compensation for the employee's reduced earning capacity, even though this is often accomplished through the use of a medical loss schedule. It should be noted that the majority view is to the effect that if a scheduled injury produces additional disability to other parts of the body, the employee will be able to recover an amount in excess of that provided in the schedule; for example, loss of a foot could produce traumatic neurosis. See *Gonzales v. Gackle Drilling Co.*, 371 P.2d 605 (N.M. 1962). See generally 2 *Modern Workers Compensation* § 200:9—Permanent Partial Disability, Generally (1998); *Workers' Compensation Guide* ch. 7—State Laws (2008).

5. PERMANENT TOTAL

The condition of permanent total disability exists when an employment-related injury renders an employee permanently and indefinitely unable to perform any gainful work. An employee need not be entirely helpless or completely incapacitated in a medical sense. The so-called "odd-lot" doctrine permits the finding of a permanent total disability for workers who are not completely incapacitated, but are handicapped to such an extent that they cannot become regularly employed in any well-known branch of the labor market; the worker is said to have been left in the position of an "odd lot" in the labor market. *Cardiff Corp. v. Hall*, [1911] 1 K.B. 1009 (Eng.).

One may receive a permanent total disability on the basis of a scheduled loss; for example, loss of sight in both eyes can be a scheduled loss that requires compensation as a permanent total disability. It is difficult to generalize about permanent total disabilities, but the following factors are generally relevant to such determinations: age, experience, skills and training, education, nature and extent of injury, employment history, and nature of employment at the time of injury. A few jurisdictions refer to permanent total as catastrophic loss. See generally 2 *Modern Workers Compensation* § 200:19—Permanent Total Disability (1998); *Workers' Compensation Guide* ch. 7—State Laws (2008).

6. DISFIGUREMENT

The great majority of jurisdictions address disfigurement by special provision. Compensation for disfigurement is generally provided in much the same way that compensation is provided for scheduled injuries. In the absence of special disfigurement provisions, it may be difficult for a worker to establish impairment to earning capacity because of disfigurement, scars, or the like. These special provisions candidly recognize the need for compensation in disfigurement cases, and thus, like medical loss schedules, conclusively presume a wage loss that dictates compensation. Occasionally, the issue may arise with regard to whether an employee may receive compensation both on the basis of a disability classification and disfigurement. It may be possible to obtain compensation on the basis of both. For example, compensation has been awarded for permanent partial disability resulting from burns with additional compensation awarded for disfigurement. *Kerr–McGee Corp. v. Washington*, 475 P.2d 815 (Okla. 1970). See generally 2 *Modern Workers Compensation* § 200:14—Disfigurement (1998); *Workers' Compensation Guide* ch. 7—State Laws (2008).

G. MULTIPLE AND SUCCESSIVE INJURIES

Difficulties sometimes arise when a worker receives multiple injuries from the same accident. This problem is often addressed statutorily in the particular workers' compensation act. In the absence of a specific provision, an approach should be taken that provides the injured employee with the greatest possible coverage and compensation for the most serious degree of disability that can be demonstrated. For example, a worker might receive concurrent injuries to two different fingers on the same hand. These injuries could result in the complete loss of use of both fingers, and the compensation paid could simply amount to twice the scheduled amount for the loss of a finger. This amount might be less than the compensation to which the worker would be entitled on the basis of a percentage disability to the hand as a whole.

In other words, an employee should not be confined to an injury schedule when multiple injuries have been sustained and the disability is greater than the sum of the scheduled losses. The reverse should also be the case, and when the sum of the scheduled losses provides greater compensation than the percentage of disability, the greater amount should be awarded. See *Emerson Elec. Co. v. Powers*, 597 S.W.2d 111 (Ark. Ct. App. 1980); *Holcombe v. Fireman's Fund Ins. Co.*, 116 S.E.2d 891 (Ga. Ct. App. 1960). See generally 2 *Modern Workers Compensation* § 200:22—Overlapping Disabilities (1998); *Workers' Compensation Guide* ch. 7—State Laws (2008).

Successive injuries may present problems because the cumulative effect of the injuries may produce a greater degree of disability and dictate greater compensation than the amount that would have been paid on the basis of separate scheduled injuries. For example, an employee who has lost one hand may lose the other hand in another work-related accident. The worker has thus suffered a much greater loss than the sum of single hand losses on a schedule. Three possible approaches are taken to the problem. First, the employer can be required to provide compensation for the entire resulting disability. Second, there may be apportionment statutes requiring the employer to provide compensation on the basis of the disability the employee would have experienced without taking into effect the previous disability. It should be noted that if a greater disability is suffered because of some pre-existing illness, disorder, weakness, or disease on the part of the employee, apportionment may not be permitted; as a general rule, an employer takes an employee as he finds him with regard to latent and pre-existing conditions that result in greater disabilities than otherwise would have been suffered. Third, "second injury funds" may exist (discussed *infra*) and therefore assure that an employee is fully compensated for an entire disability. See generally 2 *Modern Workers Compensation* § 200:25—Overlapping Disabilities—Successive Injuries (1998).

H.　SECOND INJURY FUNDS

Second injury funds (sometimes called "subsequent injury funds") offer the best solution to the problem of the worker who suffers a greater degree of disability as the result of a work-related injury because of some pre-existing disability or condition. The second injury fund is designed to encourage the employment and retention of handicapped workers. There is little incentive for their employment if the last employer faces entire liability for a disability in part due to pre-existing causes. The second injury fund provides an equitable solution to the problem of the handicapped employee by allowing the employer to pay only that amount he would have been required to pay in the absence of the pre-existing difficulty. An issue exists in second injury situations with regard to what will qualify as an "injury" or "disability" for purposes of the utilization of the second injury fund.

Traditionally, employers take their employees as they find them; however, it is questionable whether the last employer of an injured employee should bear the complete burden of an employee's disability that is in part the result of a previous work-related injury or disability. It is also questionable whether the last employer should bear the complete burden of an employee's disability that is in part the result of a previous non-work-related injury. See *Lawson v. Suwannee Fruit & S.S. Co.*, 336 U.S. 198 (1949). It should be noted that second injury fund liability cannot be established when the sequence of injuries is reversed; subsequent non-work-related accidents make no difference in compensation awards.

A liberal approach should be taken toward the utilization of second injury funds because handicapped workers are often the subject of job discrimination. Furthermore, workers' compensation legislation should strive to provide compensation for the entire extent of a disability suffered as a result of a work-related injury, regardless of whether that disability has been contributed to by some purely personal condition or previous work-related injury. It should be noted that the Americans with Disabilities Act (ADA), 42 U.S.C.A § 12101 *et seq.* (West 2010), promotes employment of physically disabled workers by providing remedies for employment disability discrimination. Because of this special protection, some have argued that second injury funds are no longer needed. See C. Doud, Comment, *Oklahoma's Special Indemnity Fund: A Fund Without a Function?*, 30 Tulsa L. Rev. 745 (1995). This is one of the reasons that Alabama, Colorado, Georgia, and Kansas have repealed their second injury fund laws. See generally 2 *Modern Workers Compensation* § 204:4—Second Injury Fund Claims (1998); *Workers' Compensation Guide* ch. 7—State Laws (2008).

I. DEATH AFTER DISABILITY

When death follows disability, several issues may arise. In analyzing the problems in this area, it should always be remembered that an employee's right to compensation benefits is separate and distinct from the right of an employee's dependents to death benefits. See Chapter 6, A, *supra*. For that reason, death benefits should not be reduced by compensation paid to an injured worker prior to the worker's death unless there is a statutory provision to the contrary; for example, some jurisdictions statutorily reduce the dependency period by the period of disability compensation payments. An additional problem area is that of accrued compensation benefits that have not been paid prior to a worker's death. Generally, these accrued amounts are paid to the employee's estate or the employee's dependents, depending on the jurisdiction. Reference should be had to particular statutes that address this issue. See generally 2 *Modern Workers Compensation* § 200:44—Death (1998).

J. DEATH COMPENSATION BENEFITS

In the case of complete or total dependents, death compensation benefits are generally computed on the basis of statutorily fixed percentages of a workers' average wage, just as in the case of computing a worker's disability compensation benefits. The majority of compensation acts place maximum limits on death benefits. Statutes vary considerably with regard to the computation of death benefits for those classified as partial dependents. A popular method of computing benefits for partial dependents is to provide compensation on the basis of the amounts of the deceased worker's contributions. It must be stressed that the formulas and methods employed in computing death benefits for all dependents vary considerably, and generalizations are inappropriate regarding exact computations. Usually, the most important legal issues involved in this area are those mentioned in Chapter 6, *supra*. See generally 2 *Modern Workers Compensation* § 200:44—Death (1998); *Workers' Compensation Guide* ch. 7—State Laws (2008).

CHAPTER 8

ADMINISTRATION

A. INTRODUCTION

A statutory scheme of no-fault compensation can be no better than its administration. Efficient and effective administration is especially necessary in the workers' compensation context because a majority of claims are uncontested, and the prompt delivery of compensation benefits is of critical importance to a worker and his family.

According to the *1972 Report of the National Commission on State Workmen's Compensation Laws*, there are six primary obligations of administration:

(1) To take initiatives in administering the act,

(2) To provide for continuing review and seek periodic revision of both the workmen's compensation statute and supporting regulations and procedures, based on research findings, changing needs, and the evidence of experience,

(3) To advise employees of their rights and obligations and to assure workers of their benefits under the law,

(4) To apprise employers, carriers, and others involved of their rights, obligations, and privileges,

(5) To assist voluntary resolutions of disputes, consistent with the law, and

(6) To adjudicate disputes that do not yield to voluntary negotiation.

The National Commission clearly pointed out that the adjudication of disputes should be the least burdensome of the six obligations when the other five obligations are properly executed. See generally 3 *Modern Workers Compensation* pt. 12—Administrative Proceedings (1998).

B. COMMISSIONS VERSUS COURTS

Only a few jurisdictions permit the initial judicial adjudication of disputed compensation claims. The great majority of the states have administrative agencies that supervise, administer, and adjudicate workers' compensation matters, subject to subsequent judicial appellate review.

It is generally accepted that the judiciary is ill equipped to administer adequately and effectively compensation matters and accomplish the six primary obligations of administration identified by the National Commission on State Workmen's Compensation Laws, Chapter 8, A, *supra*. Furthermore, the adversary nature of judicial proceedings ensures unhealthy conflict between employers and employees and is incompatible with the goals and objectives of workers' compensation. State systems of administration vary, but the best approach appears to be the one recommended by the National Commission. Under its recommendation, there would be an executive officer and staff who devote their time solely to administration, with a separate and independent board of compensation appeals. The appellate board would review the decisions of hearing officers in contested compensation cases. An informal procedures unit would handle all claims initially, and those claims that are incapable of voluntary resolution would be forwarded to a hearing officer for a formal determination. Only questions of law from the appellate board would receive judicial review. See generally 3–4 *Modern Workers Compensation* pt. 13—Judicial Proceedings (1998); U.S. Chamber of

Commerce, *2010 Analysis of Workers' Compensation Laws*; *Workers' Compensation Guide* ch. 7—State Laws (2008).

C. NOTICES

Almost all workers' compensation acts contain provisions requiring that an employee promptly inform the employer of an injury. Some statutes may require that notice of injury be given within a specified period of time. The purpose of the notice requirement is to facilitate prompt medical treatment and care, and to minimize the extent of an employee's injury. Additionally, notice provides the employer with a timely opportunity to investigate the causes and conditions of injury.

A rigid approach should not be taken, and generally it is not taken toward notice requirements. The employee's failure to comply with the notice requirement should be excused if there is actual knowledge on the part of the employer or one whose knowledge can be imputed to the employer. Certainly, knowledge can be found on the basis of compensation or medical payments to an employee. Additionally, an employee's lack of compliance should be excused if it has not resulted in prejudice to the employer. Many reasonable excuses can exist for non-compliance with formal notice requirements. See generally 3 *Modern Workers Compensation* ch. 303—Notice & Claim; Pleadings (1998); *Workers' Compensation Guide* ch. 7—State Laws (2008).

D. STATUTES OF LIMITATION

There are generally two types of limitation statutes that govern the timely filing of workers' compensation claims for disability. In one type of statute, the limitation period runs from the date of injury, and in the other type of statute, the period commences on the date of the employee's accident. In jurisdictions using date of injury, a liberal approach is usually taken, and the appropriate date may be the time when the injury became apparent or reasonably should have become apparent to the employee. In date of accident jurisdictions, an inflexible and literal approach is sometimes taken toward the time of the accident; this may result in the loss of a worker's claim because of a personal failure to discover the injury or its work connection prior to the running of the statute. This type of statute of limitations has been the subject of a great deal of criticism. See A. Larson & L. Larson, 7 *Larson's Workers' Compensation Law* ch. 126—Notice and Claim Periods (Rev. ed. 2000).

Generally, in death cases, statutes of limitation begin to run at the date of an employee's death; however, some statutes of limitation commence at the time of the accident or injury producing death. A literal approach should not be taken to date of accident or injury statutes in recognition of the fact that dependents' rights do not arise until the date of an employee's death.

The possibility always exists for a finding of a waiver of the limitations period on the part of the employer. The recognition of liability, the payment of compensation or medical benefits, or the failure to raise the defense of the statute of limitations in a timely manner can result in waiver. See generally 3 *Modern Workers Compensation* ch. 301—Time Limitations (1998).

E. WAITING PERIODS

Waiting periods may be found in workers' compensation statutes. These provisions authorize compensation only after the passage of a specific amount of time from the date of an employee's injury. Waiting periods are generally inapplicable to medical benefits and to death benefits. In an effort to discourage malingering and to promote a prompt return to the workforce, many waiting period provisions are directed specifically at temporary total disability claims.

By way of illustration, the Council of State Governments' Model Act, Part III, Section 15, proposes a waiting period of three days, with retroactive payment if the total period of disability exceeds fourteen days. This follows the recommendation of the *1972 Report of the National Commission on State Workmen's Compensation Laws*. As a general proposition, it should be noted that the longer the waiting or qualifying periods, then the less the costs of workers' compensation programs; however, this results in reduced benefits for workers. See generally 2 *Modern Workers Compensation* § 200:45— Waiting Period (1998); U.S. Chamber of Commerce, *2010 Analysis of Workers' Compensation Laws*; *Workers' Compensation Guide* ch. 7—State Laws (2008).

F. HEARINGS, EVIDENCE, AND REVIEW

In practically all jurisdictions, disputed workers' compensation cases are handled by an administrative process rather than by the courts. A less formal, more expeditious, and more flexible approach is taken than in a normal judicial civil trial. It is always desirable for some part of the administrative machinery to be available for the resolution of contested claims through the use of an informal procedure; however, a formal administrative adjudicative process must be available for those contested claims that cannot otherwise be resolved informally. See generally 3 *Modern Workers Compensation* pt. 12—Administrative Proceedings (1998).

The workers' compensation administrative process may vary somewhat from jurisdiction to jurisdiction, and despite occasional commentary to the contrary, the proceedings in contested cases are all marked by a degree of practical formality consistent with the adjudication of substantive rights. One should exercise some caution when one encounters the often repeated phrase that compensation proceedings are to be informal with the ordinary rules of evidence relaxed.

In every jurisdiction, administrative compensation decisions can ultimately be the subject of judicial review. In most jurisdictions, judicial review is limited to questions of law, and administrative findings of fact will not generally be disturbed.

The common-law rules of evidence generally do not apply to compensation proceedings; however, they can serve as a guide. Appellate review sometimes occurs because of the admission of hearsay evidence. Wide discretion is permitted in compensation hearings, and the admission of evidence that would be inadmissible in a court of law is allowed. While the admission of hearsay evidence may not constitute error, if an undue amount of weight has been given to such evidence in the administrative decision, then error may have been committed. A jurisdiction's approach to the treatment of hearsay is particularly important to claimants who are prone to present a great deal of hearsay evidence; indeed, in many cases, only hearsay evidence may be available on key issues.

In reviewing compensation decisions, four different approaches have been taken toward the use of hearsay evidence. First, hearsay is admissible and may provide the basis for the decision. Second is the residuum and majority rule, which permits administrative decisions to be based upon hearsay evidence, but some of the evidence supporting the decision must have been admissible. Third, the admission of the hearsay is not reversible error; however, if the decision would not have been rendered but for the hearsay evidence, the decision must be reversed. Finally, there is some authority declaring hearsay evidence inadmissible and its admission to be reversible error. See generally 3 *Modern Workers Compensation* ch. 306—Admissibility of Evidence (1998).

Generally, the standard of review in appeals of administratively-decided compensation cases is whether there is substantial evidence to support the decision. For variations on the above standard of review, see generally A. Larson & L. Larson, 8 *Larson's Workers' Compensation Law* ch. 130—Review of Awards (Rev. ed. 2000); 3 *Modern Workers Compensation* ch. 315—Scope of Review (1998).

G.   COMPROMISE, SETTLEMENT, AND LUMP SUM COMMUTATION

The policy considerations in workers' compensation cases differ from those found in the adversary and uncertain environment of the tort system with regard to compromises, agreements, and settlements. As a result of these differences, most jurisdictions by statute or by judicial decision deny the claimants the right to settle, adjust, or compromise a claim for less than the statutory amount, regardless of whether the claim is disputed or undisputed. See *Southern v. Department of Labor and Indus.*, 236 P.2d 548 (Wash. 1951). The minority view would permit compromises and settlements for less than the statutory amounts when disputed questions of liability exist; even so, approval of the compromise, agreement, or settlement would ordinarily be required by the appropriate workers' compensation authority.

It may be possible for a claimant to receive compensation benefits in a "lump sum" rather than by way of periodic payments, depending upon the jurisdiction. This method of payment is subject to criticism, given the objectives of compensation benefits to replace lost wages and to provide economic benefits over a period of time. Lump summing generally takes the form of a reduction of periodic benefits to present value with the use of a percentage discount. There may be some situations in which the best interests of a claimant can dictate a lump sum approval, as for example, in the cases of a worker who needs the entire amount for legitimate educational, retraining, or rehabilitation costs. Tremendous potential for harm exists, however, when lump summing is indiscriminately permitted because of the likelihood that the entire award will be quickly and unwisely spent. See *Malmedal v. Industrial Accident Bd.*, 342 P.2d 745 (Mont. 1959). The use of lump sums and the difficulties that surround their use have been exacerbated by the desire of some claimants' attorneys to obtain their entire fees at once rather than over a period of time. See generally 2 *Modern Workers Compensation* ch. 204— Compensation Agreements (1998).

H.   REOPENING, MODIFICATION, TERMINATION, AND REDISTRIBUTION

Statutes vary from jurisdiction to jurisdiction with regard to the details of reopening and modification of compensation awards; however, reopening and modification is usually permitted on the basis of a disabled worker's changed condition. Modification may take the form of increased or decreased benefits, or a cessation of benefits. Time limits for reopening can be found in a majority of jurisdictions. Fraud, mutual mistake of fact, and sometimes "any good cause" can provide grounds for reopening. A minority of jurisdictions permit reopening at any time for changed conditions.

In death benefit cases, the possibility exists for termination or redistribution of benefits based upon certain dependents' changes in status. For example, the remarriage of a widow may result in the termination of benefits; a redistribution could also occur as a result of the death of a minor dependent.

See generally 3 *Modern Workers Compensation* ch. 309—Award (1998).

I. INSURANCE

There are three methods of insuring workers' compensation benefits. First, there is the private insurance system, which provides a majority of the benefits paid in the United States, and which may be utilized in the vast majority of states. Secondly, there is self-insurance, which is also available in a vast majority of states, but which provides a small overall percentage of the benefits paid in the United States. Third, there are state insurance fund systems, which provide almost a fourth of the benefits paid in the United States; six states mandate participation in the state fund, while twelve states permit private insurance competition with their state insurance funds. It is difficult to determine whether any one insurance method is superior to another, and as long as proper controls exist for the adequate protection of compensation claimants, any of the methods accomplish their purposes. Lower insurance costs can perhaps be achieved through the use of state insurance funds.

It must be stressed that the object of insurance in workers' compensation systems is to provide security for the payment of benefits. If for some reason the insurance carrier or employer is unable to provide insurance or to guarantee benefits, then machinery and resources should be in existence to provide workers and their dependents the benefits to which they are entitled. For example, Michigan has a self-insurer's security fund. See *McQueen v. Great Markwestern Packing Co.*, 214 N.W.2d 882 (Mich. Ct. App. 1974). Most states do not have direct security systems, but rely upon indirect or administrative supervision of insurance carriers and self-insurers. The Council of State Governments' Model Workmen's Compensation and Rehabilitation Law contains special fund provisions that would provide payments in the case of insolvent employers or insurers. See Model Workmen's Compensation and Rehabilitation Law pt. IV—Insurance, § 55—Special Fund (1974).

Workers' compensation insurance is designed for the benefit and protection of both the employee and the employer. In an effort to maximize the security of the employee and dependent claimants, the defenses that could be used by an insurer against an employer should not be available against claimants. For example, the employer's failure to pay a premium should not provide an effective bar to an otherwise eligible compensation claimant. See *Home Life & Accident Co. v. Orchard*, 227 S.W. 705 (Tex. Civ. App. 1920).

Each state has a workers' compensation insurance regulatory authority that establishes rates based upon experience ratings and loss experiences. Rate-making service organizations have a direct impact on this process. While a few states have independent data-gathering organizations, the majority of states use the National Council on Compensation Insurance (NCCI) to collect data for rate-making purposes. Its website is http://www.ncci.com.

J. REMOVAL FROM STATE TO FEDERAL COURT

Under 28 U.S.C.A. § 1445 (West 2010), actions brought under the FELA and Jones Act in state court generally cannot be removed to federal court. The same code section also prohibits removal of actions under workers' compensation laws of the state in which the federal district court is sitting. This would include suits for retaliatory discharge for filing a worker's compensation claim. See *Sherrod v. American Airlines, Inc.*, 132 F.3d 1112 (5th Cir. 1998) (applying Texas law);

Wallace v. Ryan–Walsh Stevedoring Co., 708 F.Supp. 144 (E.D. Tex. 1989). The federal statute reflects a congressional policy of allowing states local control over their workers' compensation systems without federal court interference in the local administrative process. It should be noted that 28 U.S.C.A. § 1332(c) (West 2010), the direct action provision, does not apply to actions initiated in federal court by a workers' compensation insurer; actions against such an insurer initiated in federal court are not allowed. *Northbrook Nat'l Ins. Co. v. Brewer*, 493 U.S. 6 (1989).

However, removal has been permitted in a suit to set aside, for fraud or misrepresentation, a compromise settlement agreement between a claimant and the workers' compensation insurer because the action arose under state common law and not under the state workers' compensation statute. *Ehler v. St. Paul Fire and Marine Ins.*, 66 F.3d 771 (5th Cir. 1995). See generally 77 C.J.S. *Removal of Cases* § 19 (2010).

K. ARBITRATION

Some jurisdictions provide for the arbitration of workers' compensation claims. While some states permit an agreement by the parties to submit the entire compensation claim for arbitration, others provide that only certain issues be submitted. See generally 3 *Modern Workers Compensation* § 300:11—Arbitration (1998).

It should be noted that the Federal Arbitration Act (FAA), 9 U.S.C.A. § 1 *et seq.* (West 2010), might preempt state workers' compensation laws and cause parties with a valid arbitration agreement to enter into binding arbitration rather than seek judicial remedies available in the courts. See, e.g., *Ryan's Family Steakhouse, Inc. v. Kilpatric*, 966 So.2d 273 (Ala. Civ. App. 2006).

In addition, under the FAA, a federal district court cannot decide a claim by a worker that an arbitration agreement, signed as a condition of employment, is unconscionable when the parties to the contract have clearly and unmistakably assigned this "gateway" issue to the arbitrator for decision. See *Rent–A–Center, West, Inc. v. Jackson*, ___ U.S. ___, 130 S.Ct. 2772 (2010).

L. DRUG AND ALCOHOL TESTING

Many jurisdictions enacted special provisions permitting the drug and alcohol testing of workers as a part of managed drug-free workplace programs to promote worker safety. Typically, workers are notified that being subject to testing is a condition of employment and that positive tests and/or refusal to submit to testing could result in a loss of employment or workers' compensation benefits. See generally 2 *Modern Workers Compensation* § 115:20—Alcohol or Drug Abuse—Drug and Alcohol Testing (1998).

It should be noted that most federal contractors are required to establish drug-free workplace programs pursuant to the Drug Free Workplace Act of 1988, 41 U.S.C.A. § 701 *et seq.* (West 2010).

M. HIPAA EXCEPTION FOR WORKERS' COMPENSATION

The Federal Health Insurance Portability and Accountability Act of 1996 (HIPAA), Pub. L. No. 104–191, 110 Stat. 19356, and federal regulations thereunder include provisions that mandate the adoption of federal privacy protections for individually identifiable health information. According to 45 C.F.R. § 160.103 (2006), this information includes information that (1) is created or received by a health care provider, (2) relates to the past, present, or future physical or mental health or condition of an individual, and (3) with respect to which, there is a reasonable basis to believe the information can be used to identify the individual. The relevant rules relating to privacy are found at 45 C.F.R. §§ 160, 162, and 164 (2006).

An exception exists for workers' compensation cases, as indicated in 45 C.F.R. § 164.512(*l*) (2006), which states:

Standard: Disclosures for workers' compensation. A covered entity may disclose protected health information as authorized by and to the extent necessary to comply with laws relating to workers' compensation or other similar programs, established by law, that provide benefits for work-related injuries or illness without regard to fault.

Despite the exception, litigants routinely obtain a HIPAA order out of caution and because many healthcare providers insist on one or on an acceptable HIPAA release for full disclosure of records.

One should also be aware of the changes to HIPAA that were enacted in 2009, which significantly increased civil monetary penalties for HIPAA violations. See D. Gue and S. Fox, *Guide to Medical Privacy and HIPAA* ¶ 830—Enforcement Penalties (2002).

N. WORKERS' COMPENSATION AND SOCIAL SECURITY

For occupational accidents in which there is an impairment that can be expected to result in death or that has lasted or can be expected to last for a 12–month continuous period, there is a potential Social Security disability claim. See 42 U.S.C.A §§ 423–425 (West 2010). Non-occupational accidents and illnesses can also give rise to Social Security disability claims. However, in many injury situations, there will be both a workers' compensation claim and a potential Social Security disability claim. See generally C. Hall, *Social Security Disability Practice* (2010).

In 1965, Social Security amendments started an offset program for workers eligible for both Social Security disability benefits and workers' compensation benefits. The law provided for a reduction or offset in federal Social Security disability benefits for workers receiving workers' compensation payments. The combined limit of both was not to exceed 80% of the worker's prior earnings, but states were allowed to enact their own offset laws so that workers' compensation payments would be reduced rather than the worker's Social Security disability payments. The following states took advantage of this provision and enacted "reverse offset" laws: California, Colorado, Florida, Hawaii, Illinois, Louisiana, Minnesota, Montana, Nevada, New Jersey, New York, North Dakota, Ohio, Oregon, Washington, and Wisconsin. In 1981, federal laws were enacted to prevent states from adopting reverse offset laws, but the states with offsets in place were allowed to retain them.

The Social Security Act, 42 U.S.C.A. § 424a (West 2010), presently provides that there is an offset or reduction in Social Security benefits for workers' compensation. See 20 C.F.R. § 404.408 (2006). Careful planning may offer some savings for particular workers. See generally 2 *Modern Workers Compensation* § 207:1—Social Security Offset—Generally, § 207:2—Social Security Offset—Request for Average Current Earnings Information, § 207:3—Social Security Offset—Computation Sheet for Social Security Offset, § 207:4—Motion for Recognition of Right to Social Security Offset, § 207:5—Order Recognizing Right to Social Security Offset, § 207:6—Statutes Governing Workers' Compensation Offsets (1998).

In situations involving Medicare beneficiaries, the Centers for Medicare and Medicaid Services (formerly the Health Care Financing Administration), pursuant to the Medicare secondary payor statute, 42 U.S.C.A. § 1395y (West 2010), may undertake actions to collect moneys in situations in which workers' compensation settlements have been reached without the agency's knowledge or consent. Both insurance carriers and workers' attorneys may be at risk for failure to obtain Medicare approval of settlements and for failure to set aside the proper funding amounts to cover workers' future medical expenses. Medicare generally resists all attempts by insurance carriers to shift liability for lifetime medicals to Medicare in workers' compensation cases. 42 C.F.R. § 411.46(d)(2) (2006).

A Medicare Set Aside Trust or Custodial Agreement is frequently used to avoid problems with Medicare, with savings to the workers. Only the medicals that Medicare would normally cover are placed in a trust or under a custodial agreement, leaving out allocations for nursing homes, prescriptions, custodial care, and any other medicals not covered by Medicare. See generally 2 *Modern Workers Compensation* § 206:1— Liens Against Workers' Compensation Benefits—Generally, § 206:4—Medicare Lien, § 206:5—Medicaid Lien (1998).

As of July 1, 2009, liability insurers are required to report information on settled claims for all claimants that are Medicare beneficiaries. Congress tasked the Centers for Medicare and Medicaid Services (CMS) with enforcement, and a civil penalty of $1,000–day for non-compliance can be imposed. This greatly broadens the ability of CMS to reach beyond workers' compensation to tort and no-fault recoveries. The operative provisions were enacted as a part of the Medicare, Medicaid, and SCHIP Extension Act of 2007. In November 2010, the Department of Health and Human Services announced that enforcement of the Medicare Secondary Payer reporting requirements, which require plaintiffs, attorneys, and insurers to report personal injury settlements, judgments, or other awards to the Centers for Medicare and Medicaid Services, had been delayed until January 1, 2012.

CHAPTER 9

EXTRATERRITORIAL PROBLEMS AND OVERLAPPING COVERAGES

A. CONFLICT OF LAWS

Conflict of laws and full faith and credit problems often arise in workers' compensation cases because of the inevitable multi-state contacts encountered by today's employees. For example, an employee may reside in Texas, sign a contract of employment in Oklahoma, work for a company whose home office is in Arkansas, on a job based in Wyoming, and receive a compensable injury while on company business in Louisiana. Conflicts questions ordinarily are concerned with which state's workers' compensation statute is applicable. As a general rule, the rights provided by the workers' compensation act of one state cannot be enforced in other states. See A. Larson & L. Larson, 9 *Larson's Workers' Compensation Law* ch. 140—Nature of Compensation Conflicts Problem (Rev. ed. 2000).

The following fact patterns usually give rise to most conflicts problems: (1) The accident is local and the employment contract is foreign, (2) the employment contract is local and the accident is foreign, (3) both the accident and the employment contract are foreign, and (4) the accident is foreign to the state of the employer's principal place of business or legal residence. Most states have specific statutory provisions that address conflict of laws issues. Normally, if a compensable injury has taken place within a state, that fact alone may provide a basis for the utilization of local law.

State statutes addressing out-of-state injuries commonly provide for the application of the law of the forum on the basis of the contract of employment being entered into within the forum state, or on the basis of employment connections, relations, or contacts with the forum state. Where both the employment contract and state of injury are foreign, a proceeding under the law of an unrelated forum is generally inappropriate. Finally, the domicile or residence of the claimant and/or the location of the employer's home office or legal residence can affect the application of a particular state's workers' compensation act.

In order to avoid the conflicts difficulties in workers' compensation cases, the *1972 Report of the National Commission on State Workmen's Compensation Laws* recommended that a worker or dependents have the choice of claiming compensation in the state where the injury or death occurred, where the employment was principally localized, or where the employee was hired. This recommendation would probably eliminate the problem of the employee who could be without compensation coverage in any state because of multi-state contacts. The Restatement (Second) of Conflict of Laws § 181 (1971) takes a liberal and expansive approach toward the circumstances that may bring the workers' compensation law of the forum into play. It is suggested that resort should be had to this Restatement section when statutes of a forum state fail to address a workers' compensation conflict problem, as this section is compatible with the objectives and policies of workers' compensation legislation. See generally 1 *Modern Workers Compensation* pt. 4—Governing Law (1998).

B. FULL FAITH AND CREDIT

The Full Faith and Credit Clause of the U.S. Constitution has posed two major problems for workers' compensation: (1)

the extent to which the workers' compensation laws of one state should be recognized and given weight in the decisions of another state, and (2) the extent that successive compensation awards should be permitted from state to state for the same injury or death.

The primary difficulties created in the first situation were the result of *Bradford Elec. Light Co. v. Clapper*, 286 U.S. 145 (1932), in which the Supreme Court held that New Hampshire was forced to recognize the Vermont workers' compensation statute under the Full Faith and Credit Clause. A subsequent series of Supreme Court decisions have virtually abolished the *Clapper* doctrine, and the Full Faith and Credit Clause's requirement of the recognition of foreign law now presents few problems when the forum state wishes to apply its own workers' compensation act. See *Carroll v. Lanza*, 349 U.S. 408 (1955); *Kelly v. Guyon Gen. Piping, Inc.*, 882 F.2d 108 (4th Cir. 1989) (Virginia would apply North Carolina exclusive remedy provision to bar tort claim arising out of accident in South Carolina).

The Full Faith and Credit Clause has also been the source of a great deal of controversy because of the difficulties posed when more than one state awards compensation to a claimant for the same injury or death. The Supreme Court resolved a major area of controversy in *Thomas v. Washington Gas Light Co.*, 448 U.S. 261 (1980), in which it held that one jurisdiction has no legitimate interest in preventing another jurisdiction from awarding supplemental compensation when that second jurisdiction had the power in the first instance to apply its compensation law and to make an award. The Full Faith and Credit Clause is not to be construed in such a way as to bar another state's successive award of workers' compensation, so long as credit is given for the prior state's award. In other words, a worker is entitled to receive the largest single amount of compensation to which he would be entitled under the applicable compensation acts. See generally A. Larson & L. Larson, 9 *Larson's Workers' Compensation Law* ch. 141—Successive Awards in Different States (Rev. ed. 2000); 1 *Modern Workers Compensation* § 104.6—Full Faith and Credit Requirements (1998).

C. THE PROBLEM OF OVERLAPPING COVERAGE

The coverage boundaries between state workers' compensation acts and certain federal remedies and programs are unclear. These vague boundaries create difficulties for claimants because of the possibility of federal preemption and an improper election of remedies, which could result in a denial of compensation or in a lesser award than that to which a claimant could be entitled. The federal remedies that pose potential problems in this area are the Longshore and Harbor Workers' Compensation Act (LHWCA); personal injury and death actions by seamen or their survivors based upon Jones Act negligence, general maritime law unseaworthiness, and maintenance and cure; and personal injury and death actions based upon the Federal Employers' Liability Act (FELA).

The Supreme Court has recognized the "twilight zone" doctrine in LHWCA situations. *Davis v. Department of Labor & Indus.*, 317 U.S. 249 (1942). This doctrine eliminates the risk of an initial mistake on the part of a claimant by allowing a presumption of coverage under the first act providing a basis for the claim. Additionally, the Supreme Court has indicated that concurrent jurisdiction may exist in borderline cases, particularly in regard to injuries or deaths occurring on land. *Sun Ship, Inc. v. Pennsylvania*, 447 U.S. 715 (1980). The possibility of successive and supplementary awards exists in the LHWCA area by analogy to the policies contained in *Thomas v. Washington Gas Light Co.*, *supra*, even though the constitutional bases would be different. Certainly, no double recovery should be permitted. It should be noted that the LHWCA generally provides more generous benefits than the various state compensation acts.

The coverage problems of seamen involving either the LHWCA or state workers' compensation acts usually depend upon a factual determination of one's status as a seaman. The LHWCA specifically excludes from coverage a master or member of the crew of a vessel. Borderline cases involving state compensation acts may also receive "twilight zone" doctrine treatment. See *Maryland Cas. Co. v. Toups*, 172 F.2d 542 (5th Cir. 1949). But see *Anderson v. Alaska Packers Ass'n*, 635 P.2d 1182 (Alaska 1981). Successive awards are sometimes allowed on the basis of concurrent jurisdiction theories when federal seamen's remedies are pursued after an acceptance of state workers' compensation benefits. See *Manuel Caceres v. San Juan Barge Co.*, 520 F.2d 305 (1st Cir. 1975).

The FELA provides a negligence remedy for all interstate railway workers whose jobs affect interstate commerce, including employees engaged in auxiliary activities related to interstate railroads. Motor carrier, airline, and other interstate transportation workers are not covered by the FELA. If an employee is covered by the FELA, then it is said to be the exclusive remedy because of federal preemption in the field of interstate commerce, and thus state compensation acts have no application. The LHWCA provides the exclusive remedy for covered workers and bars actions under the FELA. See *Chesapeake & Ohio Ry. Co. v. Schwalb*, 493 U.S. 40 (1989).

As an additional note on overlapping coverage, it should be remembered that the payment of workers' compensation benefits may have a direct impact upon one's Social Security benefits because the Social Security Act provides for the reduction of benefits to the extent that they are duplicated by state or federal workers' compensation payments. See 42 U.S.C.A. § 424a (West 2010); *Sciarotta v. Bowen*, 837 F.2d 135 (3d Cir. 1988); 20 C.F.R. § 404.408 (2006). In 14 states, however, statutory provisions reduce workers' compensation benefits when a worker is entitled to Social Security. The FELA is not considered a workers' compensation law or plan for the purposes of 42 U.S.C.A. § 424a.

In addition, approximately half of the states treat workers' compensation payments as disqualifying income for unemployment compensation purposes. There is a lack of uniformity on this issue. See *Page v. General Elec. Co.*, 391 A.2d 303 (Me. 1978).

It should also be noted that tensions can arise in the context of the Americans with Disabilities Act (ADA) and workers' compensation. For example, settlement of permanent partial disability claims usually involves carefully crafted releases. Other issues include the effects of ADA violations on state claims for compensation. See *Caldwell v. Aarlin/Holcombe Armature*, 481 S.E.2d 196 (Ga. 1997). In 1996, the EEOC published a guide entitled *Workers' Compensation and the ADA* (Pub. No. 915.002, 1996).

Finally, an issue of claim preclusion can arise when a workers' compensation or Social Security disability claimant alleges total disability but seeks to maintain an ADA action. See *Dush v. Appleton Elec. Co.*, 124 F.3d 957 (8th Cir. 1997); *Swanks v. Washington Metro. Area Transit Auth.*, 116 F.3d 582 (D.C. Cir. 1997). See generally 1 *Modern Workers Compensation* pt. 4—Governing Law (1998).

CHAPTER 10

THIRD-PARTY ACTIONS

A. EXCLUSIVE NATURE OF COMPENSATION ACT

Workers' compensation legislation provides employees and their dependents with their exclusive remedy against the employer and insurance carrier for all injuries and deaths that arise out of and in the course of employment. The exclusivity provisions of workers' compensation acts have generally withstood constitutional attacks in recent times, and their continued vitality remains the keystone of compensation legislation. Constitutional questions concerning exclusivity may, however, be of importance in certain areas. See Chapter 3, B., *supra*; see also *Fleischman v. Flowers*, 267 N.E.2d 318 (Ohio 1971). Generally, the immunities provided to the employer and others are difficult to avoid. *Kimball v. Millet*, 762 P.2d 10 (Wash. Ct. App. 1988).

The exclusive nature of the workers' compensation remedy can sometimes result in a denial of compensation in cases in which damage has clearly occurred. For example, injuries to sexual organs, the senses, the psyche, non-disabling pain and suffering, and sometimes disfigurement may go uncompensated if the injuries producing these results fall within the workers' compensation formula, because most workers' compensation acts fail to provide compensation for these results.

It should always be remembered that an employer may be sued in tort despite the exclusivity provision, on the basis of intentional tort theories and in situations giving rise to nonphysical torts. *Lopez v. S.B. Thomas, Inc.*, 831 F.2d 1184 (2d Cir. 1987) (emotional distress under 42 U.S.C.A. § 1981). See Chapter 3, B., *supra*. See generally 1 *Modern Workers Compensation* pt. 3—Exclusivity (1998).

B.   WHO ARE THIRD PARTIES?

The exclusivity provision of workers' compensation legislation applies only to employers and others who may be so treated, such as insurance carriers and co-employees. Generally, the rights of employees and survivors to pursue common law and statutory remedies against a "third party" whose conduct has caused or contributed to an injury or a death remain intact. Issues frequently arise with regard to who "third parties" are, subject to separate actions for damages. One of the most troublesome groups is that of co-employees. A majority of jurisdictions, either on the basis of statute or judicial decision, have extended the employer's immunity to co-employees, while a minority of jurisdictions view co-employees as "third persons" outside of the immunity enjoyed by the employer.

It is difficult to generalize about who third parties are; however, third parties have from time to time been found among the following: physicians, product manufacturers, co-employees (including possibly corporate officers, directors, or stockholders), supervisory employees, compensation carriers and their safety inspectors, unions and their safety inspectors, governmental entities, and owners and occupiers of land. See Chapter 3, *supra*. See generally 1 *Modern Workers Compensation* ch. 103—Remedies Against Third Persons (1998).

C. THIRD–PARTY ACTIONS AGAINST
THE EMPLOYER

Questions of contribution and indemnity may arise when third parties attempt to recover over against the employers of injured or killed employees. Most jurisdictions deny a third party the right to contribution from an employer whose negligence has played a part in an employee's harm, due to the general common-law rule that there can only be contribution from one who is liable to the plaintiff. The exclusivity provision of workers' compensation legislation relieves the employer of tort liability for injuries or deaths falling within the coverage formula; thus, generally employers cannot be the subjects of contribution actions. Third party indemnity actions present a problem for all workers' compensation jurisdictions.

Prof. Larson describes this issue as an evenly-balanced controversy in workers' compensation law. A. Larson, *Third–Party Action Over Against Workers' Compensation Employer*, 1982 Duke L.J. 483, 484 (1982). Despite the exclusivity provisions in workers' compensation acts, and despite the necessity of inquiries directed at fault in non-contractual indemnity situations, the possibility of employer liability certainly exists under substantive indemnity law. See *Lockheed Aircraft Corp. v. United States*, 460 U.S. 190 (1983). Additionally, in appropriate cases, indemnity may be obtained from an employer on the basis of an express or implied agreement, or on the basis of a separate and independent duty owed by the employer to the third person. See *Carneiro v. Alfred B. King Co.*, 347 A.2d 120 (Conn. Super. Ct. 1975).

D. DEFENSES OF THIRD PARTIES

Normally, third parties who are defendants in actions brought by employees, employers, or insurance carriers may employ any defenses that could be utilized against the employee. Thus, regardless of whether the action is one for damages on the part of the employee, or a subrogation action brought by an employer or insurer, the employee's negligence or the statute of limitations may be used as defenses. Since the action, even in subrogation cases, is that of the employee, the contributory fault of an employer may not generally be raised as a defense. *Mermigis v. Servicemaster Indus., Inc.*, 437 N.W.2d 242 (Iowa 1989) (jury not allowed to consider employer negligence in order to reduce award); see *Baker v. Traders & Gen. Ins. Co.*, 199 F.2d 289 (10th Cir. 1952). See generally 1 *Modern Workers Compensation* § 103:55—Third–Party Defenses—Employee Negligence (1998).

E. SUBROGATION

It is difficult to generalize about subrogation rights and procedures, but almost all jurisdictions have subrogation statutes that affect workers' compensation cases. The common-law background of subrogation arose out of duties that are no longer popular. See W. Seavey, *Liability to Master for Negligent Harm to Servant*, 1956 Wash. U. L.Q. 309 (1956). There appears to be a common-law basis for subrogation in some compensation cases. See *Federal Marine Terminals, Inc. v. Burnside Shipping Co.*, 394 U.S. 404 (1969). A variety of statutory approaches may be found. Some statutes grant employees priority in actions against third parties, and if the employee fails to take advantage of the priority, then the subrogee may maintain the action. Other statutes provide the employer or carrier with priority to proceed against third parties. Still other statutes grant no priority and allow both to proceed against third parties independently or jointly. A few jurisdictions deny subrogation rights altogether, while others bestow all rights upon the subrogee.

The central policy issue to be found in the subrogation area centers on the conflict between the desire for full and adequate compensation and the potential problem of double recovery if subrogation is not allowed. Additional policy issues involve the following: the possibility of workers' compensation payments inuring to the benefit of a wrongdoer, the desire to impose liability on a third party at fault, and the need for a third party to indemnify those who have been required to pay workers' compensation benefits. See generally 1 *Modern Workers Compensation* § 103:55—Assessment and Subrogation of Claim to Compensation Payor (1998).

F.   UNINSURED MOTORIST INSURANCE AND NO–FAULT INSURANCE

The off-set provisions contained in uninsured motorist and no-fault insurance policies have created special problems when claims also involve workers' compensation benefits. No uniform solution to these problems has been found, and each state's insurance statutes and public policy must be examined.

Where there is uninsured motorist insurance, some courts have held the off-set provisions invalid or void as being contrary to public policy because the insurance provision reduces effective coverage below that required by statute. Often legislation is enacted to alter this result. See also *National Union Fire Ins. Co. v. Figaratto*, 667 N.E.2d 877 (Mass. 1996). See generally *Mountain States Mut. Cas. Co. v. Vigil*, 918 P.2d 728 (N.M. Ct. App. 1996). Other courts have held that insurance contracts are valid that allow insurers to reduce uninsured motorist liability by the amount of workers' compensation paid. *Ullman v. Wolverine Ins. Co.*, 269 N.E.2d 295 (Ill. 1970). In those states that allow the off-set for workers' compensation, there are divided authorities on the issue of whether reduction should be made from an insured's total damages or from the amount of insurer liability under the insurance policy; see, e.g., *Waggaman v. Northwestern Sec. Ins. Co.*, 94 Cal.Rptr. 170 (App. 1971); *American Ins. Co. v. Tutt*, 314 A.2d 481 (D.C. 1974); *Michigan Mut. Liab. Co. v. Mesner*, 139 N.W.2d 913 (Mich. Ct. App. 1966). See generally 1 *Modern Workers Compensation* § 103:45—No–Fault Insurance, § 103:46—Uninsured Motorist Claims (1998).

No-fault insurance creates a similar off-set problem when a workers' compensation claim is involved. See, e.g., *Neel v. Utah*, 889 P.2d 922 (Utah 1995). It can be argued that the exclusive remedy provision in the workers' compensation act precludes any recovery of no-fault benefits, regardless of statutes that would require workers' compensation benefits to be off-set. On the other hand, the exclusive remedy provision does not bar receipt of no-fault benefits, and due process and equal protection are not violated. *Mathis v. Interstate Motor Freight Sys.*, 289 N.W.2d 708 (Mich. 1980). In jurisdictions where reduction or off-set is allowed, no-fault coverage should be recoverable only to the extent that damages exceed workers' compensation benefits received by an injured worker.

CHAPTER 11

FUTURE OF WORKERS' COMPENSATION

A. THE NATIONAL COMMISSION ON STATE WORKMEN'S COMPENSATION LAWS

Section 27 of the Occupational Safety and Health Act of 1970 (OSHA), 29 U.S.C.A. § 651 *et seq.* (West 2010), established a National Commission on State Workmen's Compensation Laws and authorized "an effective study and objective evaluation of state workmen's compensation laws in order to determine if such laws provide an adequate, prompt, and equitable system of compensation for injury or death arising out of or in the course of employment." OSHA, Pub. L. No. 91–596, § 27(a)(2), 84 Stat. 1590, 1616 (1970). The National Commission submitted its report to the President and Congress on July 31, 1972, in which it made 84 recommendations for minimum state standards. The report indicated that 19 of its proposed state standards were "essential," and that the states should comply with these by July 1, 1975, or else congressional action should be taken in the form of a national minimum standards law. The National Commission found five major objectives for modern workers' compensation programs:

(1) Broad coverage of employees and work-related injuries and diseases,

(2) Substantial protection against interruption of income,

(3) Provision of sufficient medical care and rehabilitation services,

(4) Encouragement of safety, and

(5) An effective system for delivery of benefits and services.

Some of the National Commission's recommended "essential" elements of workers' compensation laws were:

(1) Compulsory coverage,

(2) No Occupational or Numerical Exemptions to coverage,

(3) Full coverage of work-related diseases,

(4) Full medical and physical rehabilitation services without arbitrary limits,

(5) Employee's choice of jurisdiction for filing interstate claims,

(6) Adequate weekly cash benefits for temporary total, permanent total, and death cases, and

(7) No arbitrary limits on duration or sum of benefits.

To date, the 19 "essential" recommendations of the National Commission have not been adopted by any state, but many states have used the recommendations as a basis for the improvement of their particular workers' compensation acts. In 1976, an Inter–Agency Workers' Compensation Task Force reported in its findings that there was a need to reform state workers' compensation programs. The recommendations of both the National Commission and the Task Force have been used as a basis for a proposed National Workers' Compensation Standards Act.

The Council of State Governments took the 84 recommendations and incorporated them into a Model Act (as revised). This effort brought about some modifications in state workers' compensation laws.

The International Association of Industrial Accident Boards and Commissions (IAIABC) studies workers' compensation issues and makes recommendations for legislative changes. Its website is http://www.iaiabc.org.

B. NATIONAL WORKERS' COMPENSATION STANDARDS ACT PROPOSALS

Neither the National Commission nor the Inter–Agency Task Force (later merged with the Division of State Workers' Compensation Standards within the Department of Labor's Office of Workers' Compensation Programs) recommended the replacement of state workers' compensation laws with an overall federal program, but both emphasized the overall need to reform state programs. As a result of these studies, several bills have been introduced in Congress to set federal "minimum standards" for all state workers' compensation systems with one overall federal program. For example, Senate Bill 420 was introduced in the 96th Congress in an effort to create the "National Workers' Compensation Standards Act of 1979." There has never been sufficient political support for these proposals in Congress.

As recently as 2009, House Bill 635 was introduced in Congress. This bill would have established a National Commission on State Workers' Compensation Laws Act, calling for a review of the findings and recommendations of the previous National Commission on State Workmen's Compensation Laws and a study and evaluation of state workers' compensation laws to determine their adequacy and whether additional remedies should be available to ensure the payment of benefits and medical care. The proposal made little in the way of legislative progress.

C. ALLOCATION OF FUTURE ECONOMIC AND SOCIAL BURDENS FOR INDUSTRIAL ACCIDENTS AND DISEASES

Despite the many justifiable criticisms of state workers' compensation laws, these acts will probably continue to serve as the chief vehicles for compensating workers for employment-related injuries and deaths. The *1972 Report of the National Commission on State Workmen's Compensation Laws* indicates that workers' compensation is preferable to tort actions because of the fact that (1) in many cases, both employee and employer fault and causation produce industrial accidents, (2) the tort process is expensive, lengthy, and uncertain in nature, with an assurance of no compensation to some victims, and (3) the tort system contains an inherent deterrence to rehabilitation.

The National Commission also indicated that presently it would be impracticable and unbeneficial to attempt to disassemble the present workers' compensation system and place its various branches under other social programs. The report further noted that it is unlikely that acceptable medical program alternatives to workers' compensation with regard to medical care will be established in the foreseeable future. Furthermore, the report observed that no other delivery system is more effective than workers' compensation. In summary, the conclusion of the National Commission was to the effect that workers' compensation systems, with recommended changes, should continue. See *1972 Report of the National Commission on State Workmen's Compensation Laws*, pp. 119–21 (1972).

It is certainly likely that in the future, there will be federal and state social programs that, to some extent, may overlap with workers' compensation. Every effort should be made to avoid a duplication of benefits and to insure the coordination of complementary systems. See A. Larson & L. Larson, 9 *Larson's Workers' Compensation Law* ch. 156—Compensation as Part of General Wage–Loss System (Rev. ed. 2000).

The national healthcare debate, which began in earnest in the early 1990s and culminated in the Healthcare Reform Law of 2010 (Patient Protection and Affordable Care Act of 2010 ("PPACA") (Pub. L. No. 111–148, 124 Stat. 119)), as amended by the Health Care and Education Reconciliation Act of 2010 ("HCERA"), Pub. L. No. 111–152, 124 Stat 1029 (together, the Healthcare Reform Law), saw some discussions about the possible merger of the workers' compensation system into a national healthcare system. For example, a fully integrated national system would allocate responsibilities to the state workers' compensation systems for the definition and oversight of wage replacement disability benefits, while the national healthcare program would provide and oversee medical and rehabilitation benefits. In 2009, House Bill 635 was introduced to establish a National Commission on State Workers' Compensation Laws, which would study state workers' compensation laws and programs. See *supra*. Some have argued that this is the forerunner of an attempt to merge or federalize all workers' compensation programs under U.S. jurisdiction. Thus far, the political and economic interests have not shown a willingness to adopt an integrated or even partially integrated national system. For further background arguments about a possible national merger, see D. Ballen, *The Sleeper Issue in Health Care Reform: The Threat To Workers' Compensation*, 79 Cornell L. Rev. 1291 (1994).

On the horizon are federal and state proposals to prevent employers from misclassifying workers as independent contractors rather than employees. Some employers have used this method to avoid tax, wage and hour, safety, health insurance, and workers' compensation obligations. For example, see the proposed federal legislation contained in House

Bill 3408/Senate Resolution 2882, entitled the Taxpayer Responsibility, Accountability, and Consistency Act of 2009, and House Bill 5107/Senate Resolution 3254, entitled the Misclassification Prevention Act.

It is also possible that tort reform in the future will look to the workers' compensation model for guidance, particularly in the areas of medical malpractice and catastrophic injuries.

There is definitely a trend toward managed health care in workers' compensation programs throughout the states. See D. Hashimoto, *The Future Role of Managed Care and Capitation in Workers' Compensation*, 22 Am. J.L. & Med. 233 (1996).

The insurance industry has debated genetic testing as a part of various insurance plans, including workers' compensation, but to date the political environment has not been receptive to these ideas. In 2008, Congress enacted the Genetic Information Nondiscrimination Act (GINA), 42 U.S.C.A. § 2000ff *et seq.* (West 2010), which was designed to protect individuals against discrimination based on their genetic information when it comes to health insurance and employment.

For comparisons of state law changes, see generally 4 *Modern Workers Compensation* ch. 321—Statutory Comparison Table (1998).

PART 3

EMPLOYEE PROTECTION LAWS

CHAPTER 12

OCCUPATIONAL SAFETY AND HEALTH ACT (OSHA)

A. BACKGROUND AND SCOPE

In 1970, Congress enacted the Occupational Safety and Health Act, 29 U.S.C.A. § 651 *et seq.* (West 2010), for the purpose of assuring as far as possible that safe and healthful working conditions exist for all workers in the United States. The basic act has withstood constitutional challenge, *Atlas Roofing Co. v. OSHRC*, 430 U.S. 442 (1977), but some procedural difficulties have been encountered. See *Marshall v. Barlow's, Inc.*, 436 U.S. 307 (1978). The act extends geographically to all areas under U.S. jurisdiction, including territories, possessions, and the outer continental shelves. It provides coverage and applies to all employers engaged in a business that affects interstate commerce, and its jurisdictional scope has been broadly construed. See *Usery v. Lacy*, 628 F.2d 1226 (9th Cir. 1980). State and local governments are excluded from coverage. Federal employees are not covered, but special safety and health programs are required by Executive Order 12196. See 29 C.F.R. pt. 1960 (2006).

Since its enactment in 1970, no substantive changes have been made to OSHA except for the extension of coverage to the U.S. Postal Service and penalty increases. The latest range of monetary penalties was included in the Omnibus Budget and Reconciliation Act of 1990 and included the following potential assessments: de minimis notice $0; non-serious violation $0—$7,000; serious violation $1—$7,000; repeated violation $0—$70,000; willful violation $5,000—$70,000; failure to abate $0—$7,000; and failure to post $0—$7,000.

Essentially, the act imposes a twofold obligation upon all employers: (1) There is a "general duty" clause requiring employers to furnish a workplace free from recognized hazards that are likely to cause serious injury or death to workers, and (2) there are safety and health standards that employers must meet. The act also requires employers to keep records of accidents, illnesses, deaths, and particular hazards; to post OSHA information and citations for violations; and to make reports to OSHA.

Of importance to both employers and employees is OSHA's Hazard Communication Program. 29 C.F.R. § 1926.59 (2006). The purpose of this program is to give employers and employees vital information about chemical hazards through product container labeling and dissemination of "material safety data sheets." Some states have enacted "right to know" legislation that may be preempted by OSHA unless the particular state is operating under an approved plan.

Several federal agencies administer and enforce the act. Safety and health standards are usually recommended on the basis of research by the National Institute for Occupational Safety and Health, and they fall under the responsibility of the Secretary of Health and Human Services. The Occupational Safety and Health Administration of the U.S. Department of Labor promulgates and enforces standards. An independent agency, the Occupational Safety and Health Review Commission, adjudicates contested cases through the use of administrative law judges. Judicial review of commission decisions rests with the U.S. Circuit Courts of Appeals.

The act provides that the states may assume responsibility for workplace safety and health by adopting a plan of standards and enforcement that is at least as effective as the federal one. See generally *Gade v. National Solid Wastes Mgmt. Ass'n.*, 505 U.S. 88 (1992). All state plans must receive approval from the Occupational Safety and Health Administration, and upon approval, the states are entitled to enforce their own laws. A minority of states have adopted these plans.

It should be kept in mind that no private rights of action are created against employers for violation of standards under the act. See *Russell v. Bartley*, 494 F.2d 334 (6th Cir. 1974). Citations and standards, however, can have a significant impact on private damage actions. The safety and health standards can be evidence of an employer's standard of care in tort actions. See *Donovan v. General Motors*, 762 F.2d 701 (8th Cir. 1985) (standard of care issue); *Schroeder v. C.F. Braun & Co.*, 502 F.2d 235 (7th Cir. 1974); see also *Hines v. Brandon Steel Decks, Inc.*, 886 F.2d 299 (11th Cir. 1989) (use of OSHA reports as evidence in civil trial).

B. STANDARDS AND VARIANCES

There are three types of safety and health standards, and two types of variances that come into play under the act. First, there are interim or "start-up" standards based upon existing federal and national consensus standards. The federal standards originate from the Service Contract Act, the Longshore and Harbor Workers' Compensation Act, the Construction Safety Act, and the Walsh–Healey Act. The consensus standards originate from national standards organizations such as the American National Standards Institute, the National Fire Protection Association, and the American Society for Testing and Materials. Consensus standards also originate from federal procedures permitting consideration of opposing views or from designated standards of the Secretary of Labor after consultation with particular federal agencies.

A second type of standard is called a permanent standard. Permanent standards are designed to replace or supplement the interim standards, and they generally come into being after advisory committee recommendation, publication in the Federal Register, receipt of comment by interested parties, and public hearing. The Secretary of Labor then makes a permanent standard determination.

The third type of safety and health standard is called a temporary emergency standard, which the Secretary of Labor establishes when the Secretary determines that new safety and health findings demonstrate that employees are exposed to grave dangers.

All of the three foregoing types of safety and health standards are subject to judicial review by the U.S. Circuit Courts of Appeals upon petition by any person affected by the standard, within 60 days of a standard being set. The development and promulgation of safety and health standards can be the subject of serious judicial scrutiny. See *Industrial Union Dep't, AFL–CIO v. American Petroleum Inst.*, 448 U.S. 607 (1980).

An employer may obtain either a permanent or a temporary variance from the safety and health standards in certain circumstances. A permanent variance is obtained after application and a showing that an employer's working conditions, practices, methods, etc., are as safe and healthful as those provided by the standards. Applications are filed with the Assistant Secretary of Labor for Occupational Safety and Health. Temporary variances may be obtained from the Secretary of Labor if an employer can demonstrate either that necessary equipment or personnel are not immediately available, or that the construction or alteration of required facilities or controls cannot be completed by a standard's effective date. Economic hardship is not a consideration in these determinations, and temporary variances are only good for a limited time period.

C. ENFORCEMENT AND PROCEDURES

The enforcement of the act usually involves OSHA inspections and citations of employers for (1) breach of the general duty obligation, (2) breach of specific safety and health standards, or (3) failure to keep records, make reports, or post notices required by the act.

Upon the presentation of appropriate credentials, OSHA inspectors are authorized to enter an employer's premises without delay. These investigations are to occur at reasonable times and within reasonable limits, and to be conducted in a reasonable manner. OSHA inspectors are entitled to private interviews with employers, owners, agents, employees, and operators. If an OSHA inspector is denied entry, a search warrant may be obtained from a U.S. District Court by the Solicitor of Labor. The probable cause requirements are less stringent than those in criminal cases. See *Marshall v. Barlow's, Inc., supra.* Ex parte warrants are obtainable under OSHA regulations. It should be noted that it is unlawful to discriminate against employees or to discharge them for OSHA inspection requests, testimony in OSHA inspection requests, testimony in OSHA proceedings, or for the exercise of any rights under the act.

When a violation is discovered, a written citation, proposed penalty, and correction date are furnished to the employer. Citations may be contested, and in such cases, administrative law judges are assigned by the Occupational Safety and Health

Review Commission to conduct hearings. The commission may grant review of an administrative law judge's decision; commission review is not a matter of right. If commission review is not undertaken, then the judge's decision becomes the final order of the commission 30 days after receipt. In any event, once a decision is final, it may be appealed by any aggrieved party to the appropriate U.S. Circuit Court of Appeals within 60 days.

Civil and criminal penalties exist for various violations. Penalties are usually assessed on a monetary, per-day, per-violation basis, and criminal fines, along with imprisonment, are allowed. In cases involving civil penalties, it is important, as a matter of practice, to distinguish between serious and non-serious violations. Serious violations require that a penalty be proposed, but non-serious violation cases seldom have penalties proposed. It should be noted that employers can be cited by OSHA and still be subject to prosecution without violating the ban on double jeopardy. See *Herman v. S.A. Healy Co.*, 522 U.S. 1025 (1997); *Hudson v. United States*, 522 U.S. 93 (1997).

The Secretary of Labor is further empowered by the act to obtain temporary restraining orders shutting down business operations that create imminent dangers of death or serious injury. This procedure is available when imminent dangers cannot be eliminated through regular OSHA enforcement procedures. See generally M. Rothstein, *Occupational Safety and Health Law* (2010 ed.).

The U.S. Department of Labor maintains a useful website at http://www.dol.gov/compliance/guide/osha.htm.

CHAPTER 13

AMERICANS WITH DISABILITIES ACT OF 1990 (ADA) AND THE REHABILITATION ACT OF 1973

A. BACKGROUND

Title I of the Americans with Disabilities Act of 1990 ("ADA"), 42 U.S.C.A. §§ 12101–12213 (West 2010), represents the first comprehensive national legislation banning employment discrimination on the basis of physical or mental disability. In 2008, Congress enacted the ADA Amendments Act of 2008 ("ADAAA"), Pub. L. No. 110–324, 122 Stat. 3553, which was a legislative rejection of the Supreme Court's holdings in *Sutton v. United Air Lines, Inc.*, 527 U.S. 471 (1999) and *Toyota Motor Mfg., Ky., Inc. v. Williams*, 534 U.S. 184 (2002), with an affirmation of the rationale in *School Bd. of Nassau Cnty. v. Arline*, 480 U.S. 273 (1987). It should be noted that in *Board of Trs. of the Univ. of Ala. v. Garrett*, 531 U.S. 356 (2001), the Court held that the Eleventh Amendment to the Constitution barred a private individual action for money damages against a state under the ADA.

Like employment discrimination under Title VII, the ADA prohibits not only intentional or "disparate treatment" discrimination on the part of covered employers—those with 15 or more employees—but also generally applied, facially "neutral" employment tests, practices, or standards that have a disproportionately adverse impact on the disabled. The latter may be justified only if the employer shows them to be "job-related and consistent with business necessity." One set of neutral practices—medical inquiries or examinations (other than those testing for the use of illegal drugs)—is specifically outlawed until an offer of employment is made; thereafter, actual employment may be conditioned on the results of medical history questions and examinations, but those must meet the job-relatedness/business necessity requirement, and their results must be held confidential. But while pre-offer inquiries to applicants concerning the existence or severity of a disability are prohibited, employers may ask whether the employee can perform essential job-related functions.

In 1978, Congress amended Section 504 of the Rehabilitation Act of 1973 ("RHA"), Pub. L. No. 93–112, 87 Stat. 355 (codified at 29 U.S.C.A. § 701 *et seq.* (West 2010)), to cover federal agency programs and activities. Also amended was Section 501, under which regulations were required to enforce the non-discrimination policies. 29 U.S.C.A. § 791 (West 2010). Most importantly, Section 505(a) gave federal job applicants and employees the same rights, remedies, and procedures for disability claims that were given to federal employees under the Title VII discrimination laws. 29 U.S.C.A. § 794a (West 2010). This includes the right to a jury trial but no right to punitive damages. 42 U.S.C.A. § 1981a (West 2010).

It should be noted that the Act does not extend to uniformed military personnel or to the reserves or National Guard. Discrimination protections are afforded federal executive branch employees by the Government Employee Rights Act of 1991 (2 U.S.C.A. §§ 1202, 1219(b) (West 2010)), which prohibits discrimination to the same extent as in other federal employments under the ADA, the Rehabilitation Act, Title VII, and the ADEA. Congressional employees are protected from discrimination in a similar fashion pursuant to the Congressional Accountability Act of 1995, Pub. L. No. 104–1,

§ 201(a), 109 Stat. 3, 7 (codified at 2 U.S.C.A. § 1311 (West 2010)).

The ADA is distinct from standard employment discrimination laws in its affirmative additional requirement that employers provide "qualified" disabled individuals "reasonable accommodation." An individual is "qualified" if, with or without such accommodation, she can perform the "essential" (not all) functions of the job in question. The employer bears the burden of showing the infeasibility, excessive cost, or other undue hardship involved in providing the accommodation proposed by the disabled employee. See generally R. Colker & A. Milani, *Federal Disability Law in a Nutshell* (4th ed. 2010).

In this respect and others, the ADA is an outgrowth of Section 504 of the RHA, which prohibits federal funds recipients from excluding or discriminating against any "otherwise qualified handicapped individual" in "any program or activity receiving federal financial assistance." 29 U.S.C.A. § 794 (West 2010). See generally U.S. Department of Labor website, http://www.dol.gov/dol/topic/disability/ada.htm.

The Civil Rights Restoration Act of 1987 effectively banned discrimination in all recipient institutions' operations, not merely in programs or activities for which federal assistance is granted. RHA Section 504 is enforced by the administrative procedures of Title VI, which may lead to termination of funding or refusal to extend future assistance.

In 1974, Congress amended the definition of "handicapped individual" for Section 504 purposes to include not just those with actual physical impairments, "but also those who are regarded as impaired and who, as a result, are substantially limited in a major life activity...." *Sch. Bd. of Nassau Cnty. v. Arline, supra.* Moreover, a person suffering impairment of major life activities from tuberculosis is considered handicapped even though his disease is contagious. *Id.* But to be eligible for relief, a plaintiff must generally also be "otherwise qualified" or able to perform the "essential functions" of the particular job. And while inability to function may not be inferred simply from the fact of a handicap, a tuberculosis sufferer may not be "otherwise qualified" if his contagion poses "a serious health threat to others."

The ADA and decisions construing it adhere for the most part to the RHA model, expanding it to private employment. The ADA excludes from coverage as employers wholly-owned United States corporations and tax-exempt private membership clubs. An employer may require that every employee be qualified to perform the "essential functions" of a job (the phrase is part of the definition of a "qualified person" with a disability), but the judgment of whether a disabled employee can so perform must take into account feasible "reasonable accommodations." Thus, employers can continue to require that all applicants and employees, including those with disabilities, be able, or with reasonable accommodation be enabled, to perform the essential, non-marginal functions of the job in question.

The Supreme Court has held that the application for or receipt of Social Security disability benefits will not by itself defeat an ADA claim through the doctrine of judicial estoppel. *Cleveland v. Policy Mgmt. Sys. Corp.*, 526 U.S. 795 (1999). While a Social Security Disability claim can comfortably exist side by side with an ADA claim, an ADA plaintiff cannot evade the apparent contradiction that arises out of an earlier Social Security total disability claim; rather, the plaintiff must proffer a sufficient explanation. The Court noted in this regard that it is frequently appropriate for an employer to be granted summary judgment unless an ADA plaintiff's explanation would warrant a reasonable juror's concluding that, assuming the truth of, or the plaintiff's good faith belief in, the earlier statement, the plaintiff could nonetheless perform the essential functions of the plaintiff's job, with or without reasonable accommodation. *Id.* See generally *Americans with Disabilities: Practice and Compliance Manual* ch. 7—Employment Provisions Under the Americans with Disabilities Act, I. Overview, B. Relationship to Other Laws; Conflicts (1992).

B. PROHIBITIONS AND REMEDIES

The determination of whether a person is qualified should be made at the time of an employment action, for example, hiring or promotion. The "qualification" of an applicant should not be based on the possibility that the employee or applicant will become incapacitated and unqualified in the future. And the ADA frowns on paternalistic concerns about what would be best for the person with the disability, since these serve to foreclose employment opportunities.

Under the ADA, an employer remains free to select the most qualified applicant available and to make decisions based on reasons unrelated to the existence or consequence of a disability. Employment decisions must not have the purpose or effect of subjecting a qualified individual with a disability to discrimination based on that disability. The non-discrimination concept does not prohibit an employer from devising physical or other job criteria or tests for a job, so long as the criteria and tests are job-related and consistent with job necessity. Even a nondiscriminating employer, however, must on an applicant or employee's request determine whether a reasonable accommodation would enable the disabled person to perform the essential functions of the job without imposing an undue hardship on the business.

Title I prohibits discrimination by employers, unions, employment agencies, and union management committees against "any qualified individual with a disability" regarding any term, condition, or privilege of employment. This includes within employment protections all matters related to employment applications, hiring, tests, evaluations, medical exams, training, assignments, promotions, compensation, leave, fringe benefits, discipline, layoffs, recalls, terminations, and employer activities, including recreation and social events.

Section 3(2) of the ADA defines "disability" as:

(1) a physical or mental impairment that substantially limits one or more of an individual's "major life activities" (e.g., walking, standing, lifting, bending, seeing, speaking, hearing, caring for oneself, performing manual tasks, eating, sleeping, breathing, learning, reading, concentrating, thinking, communicating, or working);

(2) a record of having such an impairment; or

(3) being regarded as having such an impairment.

42 U.S.C.A. § 12102 (West 2010). See generally 29 C.F.R. § 1630.2(g) (2006); L. Rothstein and J. Rothstein, *Disabilities and the Law* § 4:8 (4th ed. 2009)

Section 101(8) of the ADA, 42 U.S.C.A. § 12111 (West 2010), explains that a "qualified" disabled person is "an individual who, with or without reasonable accommodation, can perform the essential functions of the employment position that such individual holds or desires." This prohibition extends to job applications, hiring, advancement, discharge, compensation, training, or other terms of employment. ADA § 102(a), 42 U.S.C.A. § 12112 (West 2010). Job descriptions are considered primary evidence in establishing the scope of essential functions. ADA § 101(8), 42 U.S.C.A. § 12111 (West 2010).

Title I's broad anti-discrimination policy blends the concepts of equal treatment and affirmative support. Thus, an employer may not (1) classify a disabled applicant or employee in a way that adversely affects the opportunities or status of the person; (2) participate in an arrangement with another organization that has the effect of discriminating against the disabled individual; (3) utilize standards, criteria, or methods of administration that have the effect of discriminating on the basis of the disability or perpetuating discrimination by others subject to common administrative control; (4) exclude or deny equal jobs or benefits to an individual because she has a relationship with a disabled individual; (5) use standards or tests that screen out or tend to screen out an individual with disabilities (unless the standard is job-related and consistent with business necessity); (6) use tests whose results reflect the impairment of the individual rather than the skills or aptitude of the test-taker; or (7) fail to make reasonable accommodations to the known physical or mental limitations of an otherwise qualified individual (unless the accommodation would impose undue hardship). ADA § 102(b), 42 U.S.C.A. § 12112 (West 2010).

The ADA does not exclude infected or contagious applicants or employees from its definition of the "qualified individual with a disability" who is entitled to reasonable accommodation. See *Bragdon v. Abbott*, 524 U.S. 624 (1998). Claims of disability must be evaluated on a case-by-case basis. *Albertson's, Inc. v. Kirkingburg*, 527 U.S. 555 (1999).

Section 103 of the ADA does allow employers the defense of showing that a person poses a "direct threat to the health or safety of other individuals in the workplace" and that his safe performance "cannot be accomplished by reasonable accommodation. . . ." 42 U.S.C.A. § 12113 (West 2010). See *Chevron U.S.A. Inc. v. Echazabal*, 536 U.S. 73 (2002); see also *Allmond v. Akal Sec., Inc.*, 558 F.3d 1312 (11th Cir. 2009) (the business-necessity defense applied to plaintiff's challenge to a hearing aid ban).

The Act neither prohibits nor authorizes testing for illegal drugs, although such tests are not considered medical examinations and, accordingly, may be conducted even prior to a job offer. Employers may ban the use of illegal drugs and alcohol at the workplace and may hold alcoholics and drug users to the same qualifications and job performance standards as other employees, even if unsatisfactory performance is related to alcoholism.

Section 501(c) provides that ADA may not be construed to restrict a health care provider from classifying or administering risks unless it does so as a "subterfuge" to evade the purposes of the Act. 42 U.S.C.A. § 12201 (West 2010).

CHAPTER 14

SOCIAL SECURITY

A. INTRODUCTION

The federal Social Security system began in 1935 in an effort to provide limited retirement or death benefits for workers in commerce and industry. Since 1935, the system has greatly expanded, and benefits have increased dramatically. See Social Security Act, 42 U.S.C.A. § 401 *et seq.* (West 2010).

Generally, the constitutionality of the Act has been upheld. See *Helvering v. Davis*, 301 U.S. 619 (1937); *Charles C. Steward Mach. Co. v. Davis*, 301 U.S. 548 (1937). One should note that individuals can challenge portions of the Act as violations of equal protection under the Due Process Clause of the Fifth Amendment if they have colorable constitutional arguments, however. *Califano v. Sanders*, 430 U.S. 99 (1977); *Flemming v. Nestor*, 363 U.S. 603 (1960).

Historically significant changes occurred as follows: In 1954, coverage became almost universal; in 1956, disability insurance benefits were added; in 1958, disability eligibility was liberalized and benefits were added for dependents of disability insurance recipients; in 1961, early but reduced retirement was permitted for men at age 62; in 1965, Medicare benefits were added; in 1972, automatic cost-of-living-adjustments (COLA) were added to the benefit system; in 1977, substantial increases in tax rates were enacted to cover projected long term deficits; and in 1981, short-term deficits were financed by inter-fund borrowing.

Amendments in 1983 resulted in the taxation of certain Social Security benefits for the first time, called for the normal retirement age to be gradually changed from 65 to 67, established mandatory coverage for employees of nonprofit organizations, resulted in some federal workers being covered by Social Security rather than by civil service, established deferred compensation plan taxation for Social Security purposes, prohibited states from terminating coverage of state and local government employees, altered cost-of-living-adjustment computation methods, and eliminated several gender-based distinctions previously made by the Social Security laws.

The Social Security Disability Benefits Reform Act of 1984 changed the standard of review for terminating disability benefits and, among other changes, provided for the evaluation of pain. Technical amendments were passed in 1986 and 1987. Catastrophic health care coverage and financing was enacted under the Medicare Catastrophic Coverage Act of 1988, but Congress voted to repeal this Act in 1989.

The Omnibus Budget Reconciliation Act of 1990, Omnibus Budget Reconciliation Act of 1993, and Social Security Domestic Employment Reform Act of 1994 brought other policy changes, while the Social Security Independence and Program Improvements Act of 1994 caused the Social Security Administration to be taken out from under the control of the Department of Health and Human Services.

The Contract with America Advancement Act of 1996; Personal Responsibility and Work Opportunity Reconciliation Act of 1996; Omnibus Consolidated Rescissions and Appropriations Act of 1996; Department of Defense Appropriations Act,1997; Balanced Budget Act of 1997; Omnibus Consolidated and Emergency Supplemental Appropriations Act, 1999; Foster Care Independence Act of 1999; Ticket to Work and Work Incentives Improvement Act of 1999; Senior Citizens' Freedom to Work Act of 2000; Medicare Prescription Drug, Improvement, and Modernization Act of 2003; Social Security Protection Act of 2004; American Recovery and Reinvestment Act of 2009; and No Social Security Benefits for Prisoners Act of 2009 have added other changes in policies.

The Healthcare Reform Law of 2010 (Patient Protection and Affordable Care Act of 2010 ("PPACA") (Pub. L. No. 111–148, 124 Stat. 119)), as amended by the Health Care and Education Reconciliation Act of 2010 ("HCERA"), Pub. L. No. 111–152, 124 Stat 1029 (together, the Healthcare Reform Law) is supposed to extend the life of the Medicare Trust Fund as a result of waste reduction, new fraud and abuse provisions, and a slowing of the costs of Medicare growth. There is much debate about the impact of the Healthcare Reform Law, and the courts are in the process of deciding constitutional issues about the legislation. See *Virginia ex rel. Cuccinelli v. Sebelius*, 728 F. Supp. 2d 768 (E.D. Va. 2010) (minimum-coverage mandate for individuals unconstitutional); *Thomas More Law Ctr. v. Obama*, 720 F. Supp. 2d 882 (E.D. Mich. 2010) (mandate constitutional).

Today, the Social Security system contains the following benefit programs:

(1) Retirement and survivors benefits (Old–Age and Survivors Insurance—OASI);

(2) Disability benefits (Disability Insurance—DI);

(3) Medicare benefits in four parts:

(a) Hospitalization Insurance—HI (Part A), which provides inpatient hospital care, skilled nursing care after a hospital stay, and, to some extent, home health care and hospice care;

(b) A separate Medicare Medical Insurance (MI) program (Part B), which pays for physicians, medical services, medical supplies, and costs not covered by HI;

(c) Medicare Advantage (MA), another insurance program (Part C), which allows provider organizations to offer healthcare services for persons eligible for Part A and Part B benefits; and

(d) Prescription drug (PD) coverage (Part D), which provides Medicare beneficiaries with prescription drug payment assistance; and

(4) Supplemental Security Income benefits (SSI).

Coverage is generally mandatory, with the exception of state and local governments and certain nonprofit organizations, which may elect to have coverage. See 20 C.F.R. §§ 404.1200–.1299 (2006) (employees of state and local governments).

For the most part, Social Security benefits are financed by taxes or "contributions" collected from employers, employees, and self-employed persons who work in employments covered by Social Security. The Federal Insurance Contributions Act (FICA), which falls within the Internal Revenue Code, governs taxation and collection.

For 2011, the Social Security tax rate (combined OASDI and HI 2004 FICA withholding) on wages was reduced for employees from 7.65% (6.2% plus 1.45% for Medicare (Part A—Hospital Insurance)) to 5.65% (4.2% plus 1.45% for Medicare (Part A—Hospital Insurance)). Employers pay an equal rate, and this established a total rate of 11.3%. The self-employment rate was 15.3% for OASDI and 2.9% for Medicare (15.3% total). The maximum OASDI wage base for 2011 was $106,800. There was no limit on the Medicare wage tax portion.

These collected taxes pay for retirement, survivors, disability, and hospital insurance benefits. In the case of certain persons, however, hospital insurance benefits are paid from the general revenues of the United States, and supplementary medical insurance benefits are generally financed through the collection of monthly premiums. The general revenues of the United States pay for supplemental security income benefits (SSI).

Three basic trust funds hold Social Security contributions: (1) the Old–Age and Survivors Insurance Trust Fund, (2) the Disability Insurance Trust Fund, and (3) the Hospital Insurance Trust Fund (which also receives general revenues in order to pay benefits to uninsured persons age 65 and older). The Supplementary Medical Insurance Trust Fund receives premium collections and general revenues that have been appropriated for the fund. A Board of Trustees, consisting of the Secretaries of Health and Human Services, Treasury, and Labor, hold these funds, and amounts not currently needed are invested in federal securities that bear interest.

The Social Security Administration basically administers the retirement, survivors, disability, and supplemental security income programs. While the Centers for Medicare and Medicaid Services are responsible for the four Medicare benefit programs, the Social Security Administration processes applications for the benefits.

Other public assistance and welfare services programs are financed separately, and they are generally administered by the states in cooperation with the federal government's supervision through the Department of Health and Human Services. Since 1997, these include (1) the Temporary Assistance for Needy Families (TANF) program, which succeeded the Aid to Families with Dependent Children legislation and provides cash assistance to indigent families with dependent children, and (2) the State Children's Health Insurance Program (SCHIP), which provides matching funds with the states in order to provide health insurance to families with children.

It should be noted that Medicare and Medicaid are separate programs. Persons with low income and few resources are entitled to Medicaid, which is a program administered by the various states with federal supervision. While some persons can qualify for both Medicare and Medicaid, eligibility rules and benefits are determined by the states. Local social services and welfare offices are the intake offices for claimants under the Medicaid program.

The Department of Health and Human Services and the Social Security Administration maintain websites at http://www.hhs.gov and http://www.ssa.gov.

B.   RETIREMENT AND SURVIVORS INSURANCE (OASI)

1.   ELIGIBILITY FOR OASI

Eligibility for retirement and survivors benefits depends upon the "insured status" of an employee. Generally, an employee's insured status is established by the number of "quarters of coverage" or work credits that have been earned in work covered by Social Security. A worker and family can become "fully insured" with as little as 31 quarters (eight years) of work. The requisite age and quarters of coverage can vary. 20 C.F.R. § 404.115 (2006) (table of ages and quarters). If a worker is "currently insured," benefits can be paid to survivors upon the worker's death; six quarters of coverage in the 13 quarters preceding death gives rise to this "currently insured status." See 20 C.F.R. pt. 404 (2006).

OASI benefits, which are in the form of monthly benefit payments, are conditioned upon the attainment of retirement age or death. The retirement age at which full retirement benefits may be received is 65 years of age for a claimant who attains early retirement age, that is, age 62, before January 1,

2000. For claimants who attain early retirement age after December 31, 1999 but before January 1, 2005, the retirement age is scheduled to gradually rise to 66 years of age by increasing the age for full benefits by two months per year for six years so that the normal age of retirement in the year 2005 will be 66 years of age. For workers who reach early retirement age of 62 after December 31, 2004 but before January 1, 2017, the full retirement age is set at age 66. In 2017, the retirement age is scheduled to increase by upping the age for full benefits by two months per year for six years for workers who reach early retirement age after December 31, 2016 but before January 1, 2022; thus, for the years 2022 and beyond, the full retirement age will be 67. Some other adjustments due to age increase factors are allowed under the Act. See 42 U.S.C.A. § 416(*l*) (West 2010). Reduced benefits are available beginning at age 62. Other OASI benefits have age eligibility variations.

2. OASI BENEFIT CALCULATIONS

The past earnings of covered workers generally determine the benefit levels that are to be paid to retired employees, disabled workers, dependents, and survivors. Four basic concepts govern benefit calculations: (1) computation years, (2) index earnings, (3) average indexed monthly earnings (AIME), and (4) primary insurance amount (PIA). The "computation years" are essentially the number of years worked in employment covered by Social Security. The "index earnings" represents the earnings of each year, converted to reflect increases in wage levels over the years; this indexing creates an earnings record. The AIME is the result of having divided the total indexed earnings by the number of months in the computation years. Finally, a PIA or basic benefit level is obtained by applying a percentage formula to the AIME; this includes using certain "bend points" or dollar amounts in the formula. All benefit levels are subject to periodic cost-of-living-adjustments. See 42 U.S.C.A. § 415 (West 2010); 20 C.F.R. §§ 404.201–.290 (2006).

3.   OASI BENEFITS

The figure that provides the basis for almost all benefit amounts is the primary insurance amount (PIA). Lump-sum death benefits are fixed, and special benefits are sometimes paid without reference to the PIA. The OASI types of benefits payable and the percentage of the PIA receivable for retirees, disabled workers, dependents, and survivors are generally as follows (eligible ages subject to change):

(1) *Full retirement*—100% of PIA (eligible at age 65); reduced benefits available at 62.

(2) *Widowed spouses*—100% of PIA (eligible at age 65); reduced benefits available at 60.

(3) *Spouses*—50% of the PIA (eligible at age 65 or younger if caring for a disabled child or child under 16); reduced benefits available at 62.

(4) *Divorced spouses*—50% of PIA (eligible on the same basis as spouses, *supra*, but ten years of marriage also required).

(5) *Children*—50% of PIA (eligible until age 18 if a child of a retired or deceased insured employee; eligible while attending full-time elementary or secondary school).

(6) *Surviving children*—75% of PIA (eligible on the same basis as children, *supra*).

(7) *Parents*—82 1/2% of PIA if one parent entitled; 75% of PIA if more than one parent entitled.

(8) *Maximum family benefits*—175% of PIA.

(9) *Lump-sum death benefit*—$255 payment to survivors (not a percentage of PIA).

(10) *Transitionally insured benefits*—Not a percentage of PIA (eligible if over 65 with insufficient quarters of coverage).

(11) *Special age 72*—Not a percentage of PIA (eligible if over 72 with insufficient quarters of coverage to permit retiree benefits; must not receive public assistance).

(12) *Special minimum*—Not a percentage of PIA (eligible are workers with low average earnings).

(13) *Currently insured*—OASDI benefits (eligible if survivor of worker not fully insured so long as deceased employee worked at least 6 of the 13 quarters in covered employment preceding death).

See 42 U.S.C.A. § 402 (West 2010); 20 C.F.R. §§ 404.301–.392 (2006).

It should be noted that there can be reduction in all benefits based upon a beneficiary's annual earnings. See 20 C.F.R. §§ 404.401–.480 (2006). This reduction can vary, but generally, all benefits are charged on the basis of $1 of excess earnings for each $1 of monthly benefits. In 1996, Congress enacted changes that gradually increased the annual exempt amount for beneficiaries ages 65 to 69. Self-employment at age 70 and thereafter is exempt.

C. DISABILITY INSURANCE (DI)

1. ELIGIBILITY

In general, the test for disability benefit eligibility employs the same "insured status" concept used by OASI, *supra*. Disability eligibility requires that an employee be both (1) "fully insured" under OASI and (2) "disability insured." The disability insured requirement is met if a worker has 20 quarters of coverage in the 40 quarters immediately preceding disability. A waiting period of five months exists before these benefits can be paid. At age 65, disability benefits cease, and regular full retirement benefits are paid. In making eligibility determinations, "disability" is generally defined as the inability to engage in gainful activity by reason of any medically determinable physical or mental impairment that can be expected to last at least 12 continuous months or to result in death. Social Security disability benefits are generally offset by any other disability benefits. See 20 C.F.R. § 404.317 (2006). See generally A. Sacks, *CCH Social Security Explained* (2010 ed.).

2. DI BENEFITS

Generally, there are five fundamental types of disability insurance benefits:

(1) *Disabled worker*—100% of PIA (eligible five months after disability if fully insured under OASI and disability insured).

(2) *Disabled surviving spouse*—100% of PIA (eligible at age 60; benefits available at 50 if disabled).

(3) *Disabled surviving divorced spouse*—50% of PIA (eligible at age 60; benefits available at 50 if disabled).

(4) *Disabled child*—50% of PIA (eligible at 18).

(5) *Disabled surviving child*—75% of PIA (eligible at 18).

See 20 C.F.R. §§ 404.301–.392 (2006).

It must be pointed out that the Disability Insurance Trust Fund only pays benefits to disabled workers and their dependents. The benefits payable to "disabled surviving spouses" and "disabled surviving children" are paid from the Old–Age and Survivors Insurance Trust Fund. The 1980 amendments provided for the review and assessment of eligibility every three years with the exception of cases of permanent disability. This policy generated a great deal of controversy and litigation, and resulted in the Disability Reform Act of 1984.

3. DI EVALUATION

There is a stepped sequential approach to disability insurance (DI) and supplemental security income disability (SSI) determinations. See 20 C.F.R. §§ 404.1520, 416.920 (2006). Initially, the claimant must demonstrate physical and/or mental impairments that are severe and meet the duration requirements. There is then a five-step evaluation that asks and answers certain key questions, and favorable disability determinations for claimants can be made at steps three and five:

(1) Is the claimant working in a substantial gainful activity? If so, then no disability will be found regardless of medical condition or age, education, and work experience.

(2) Does the claimant have a severe impairment? If there is no impairment or combination of impairments that significantly limit physical or mental ability, then no disability will be found. If a severe impairment does exist, then the following question is necessary.

(3) Does the claimant's impairment or impairments meet or equal the "listings" in 20 C.F.R. pt. 404, subpt. P, app. 1 (2006), which contain specific medical criteria? if so, then a finding of disability will be made without considering age, education, and work experience.

(4) If a claimant does not meet the "listings," then inquiry is made whether the claimant's impairment(s) prevents the claimant from performing past relevant work. A review of residual functional capacity and the physical and mental

demands of past work are evaluated at this point. If the claimant is found able to perform past relevant work, then a finding of no disability will be made.

(5) If the claimant cannot perform past relevant work because of severe impairment(s), then the burden shifts to the agency to prove the claimant capable of performing other gainful employment. The question of residual functional capacity to perform other work is therefore evaluated, considering the age, education, and past work experience of the claimant. At this point, vocational expert testimony or the Medical–Vocational Guidelines contained in 20 C.F.R. pt. 404, subpt. P, app. 2 (2006) (commonly known as the "Grids") may be used to aid in the ultimate determination of disability. See *Bowen v. Yuckert*, 482 U.S. 137 (1987) ("severity regulation" upheld); *Heckler v. Campbell*, 461 U.S. 458 (1983) (medical-vocational guidelines are valid).

See generally C. Hall, *Social Security Disability Practice* (2010 ed.).

It should be noted that a constitutional tort challenge to the continuing disability review program was made in *Schweiker v. Chilicky*, 487 U.S. 412 (1988), but the Supreme Court rejected the cause of action by a narrow margin.

It should also be noted that claims under the Americans with Disabilities Act (ADA) are not automatically barred by the receipt of Social Security disability benefits, but credibility issues for the plaintiff are generally raised by these circumstances. See *Cleveland v. Policy Mgmt. Sys. Corp.*, 526 U.S. 795 (1999).

D. MEDICARE—HOSPITAL INSURANCE (HI) (PART A) AND MEDICARE—MEDICAL INSURANCE (MI) (PART B)

Certain disabled and aged persons are entitled to the benefits of a national health insurance program called Medicare. Most persons over 65 are eligible automatically; if not eligible, coverage can be purchased for an annual premium. There are two fundamental Medicare programs: (1) Part A, Hospital Insurance (HI), which is basically financed through special payroll taxes similar to FICA taxes that are held in the Hospital Insurance Trust Fund, and (2) Part B, Medicare Medical Insurance (MI), which is fundamentally financed through individual medical premiums and general revenues of the United States, which are held in the Supplementary Medical Insurance Trust Fund. Both Part A and Part B benefit programs contain cost-sharing measures, usually in the form of coinsurance and deductibles.

The Centers for Medicare & Medicaid Services (CMS) supervises both programs. Part A (HI) payments are generally tied to "benefit periods." If a patient has not been hospitalized for 60 consecutive days, a benefit period is available; there are no limits on the number of benefit periods that patients can have during their lifetime, except for inpatient psychiatric hospital services. Each benefit period under Part A pays for (1) inpatient hospital care (subject to 90 days of coverage and other limitations), (2) extended care services up to 100 days during each benefit period, (3) home health services, and (4) in lieu of certain other benefits, hospice care, subject to limitation periods.

Part B (MI) was designed as a voluntary program that essentially paid 80% of reasonable charges for doctors, osteopaths, chiropractors, psychiatrists, independent therapists, and most medical, outpatient, and laboratory services that

Part A does not cover. The elderly and disabled pay only portions of program premiums and the difference is paid by the federal government from general revenues.

E. MEDICARE ADVANTAGE (MA) (PART C) AND PRESCRIPTION DRUG (PD) (PART D)

Persons with Medicare Parts A and B are entitled to enroll in a Medicare Advantage plan (Part C). By doing so, enrollees can avoid the purchase of Medigap insurance policies, which would otherwise cover the extra costs of hospitalizations not covered by Medicare under Parts A and B. Many enrollees in Medicare Advantage plans pay monthly premiums for extra benefits that are offered. Most Medicare Advantage plans include Medicare-managed care plans, preferred provider organization plans, private fee-for-service plans, and specialty plans.

Persons with Medicare Parts A and B or Part C are entitled to enroll for prescription drug (PD) coverage (Part D). The drug plan is voluntary and an additional monthly premium is required, with some higher income enrollees having to pay increased monthly premiums. Waiting to join the part D plan can cause an enrollee to pay a penalty if the enrollee otherwise has prescription drug coverage inferior to Medicare prescription drug coverage.

F. SUPPLEMENTAL SECURITY INCOME (SSI)

The Supplemental Security Income (SSI) program provides financial assistance to U.S. citizens and lawfully admitted aliens who meet income and resource criteria. The SSI program provides a "floor of income" for these persons, and it is financed by general tax revenues. SSI benefits are paid monthly to persons who are age 65 or older, blind, or disabled. See generally C. Hall, *Social Security Disability Practice* (2010 ed.). Typically, these persons must be U.S. citizens or lawful residents of the 50 states, the District of Columbia, or the Northern Mariana Islands. "Federal Benefit Rates" (FBR) help determine the eligibility of individuals and couples; these rates are increased periodically, and the FBR is employed on a per-month basis in order to compare the income and resource criteria in an effort to determine eligibility. The periodic redetermination of eligibility is required for all recipients.

The receipt of Social Security insurance benefits does not necessarily disqualify persons from receiving SSI benefits, but Social Security insurance benefits are included in the income determinations that must be made before SSI benefits can be paid.

G. PROCEDURE

The claims procedure for most Social Security benefits under retirement, survivors, disability, and Medicare insurance programs, and under the SSI program, is initiated on special forms provided by the Social Security Administration. These claim forms are usually filed with a local Social Security office, which makes an initial determination of eligibility. If there is a dispute, the claimant or the claimant's representative must request a reconsideration of the initial decision.

A claimant who is dissatisfied with a reconsideration decision is entitled to a hearing before an administrative law judge. The judge's decision becomes final unless Appeals Council review is requested within 60 days of receipt by the claimant, or unless the Appeals Council decides to review the decision on its own motion. An expedited appeals process may be requested in certain instances. Denials of review or decisions of the Appeals Council can be appealed within 60 days to the U.S. District Courts. Attorney's fees are permitted for the representation of claimants.

Furthermore, in some cases, the claimant may be entitled to an additional award of attorney's fees under the Equal Access to Justice Act ("EAJA"), 28 U.S.C.A. § 2412(b) (West 2010).

CHAPTER 15

UNEMPLOYMENT COMPENSATION

A. BACKGROUND

In 1935, an unemployment insurance system was established in order to provide economic security for workers during periods of temporary unemployment. The original system was created by Title IX of the Social Security Act of 1935. In 1939, the tax provisions of Title IX became the Federal Unemployment Tax Act under the Internal Revenue Code. Today, the Social Security Act, the Federal Unemployment Tax Act, and numerous amendments to these acts provide the statutory basis for federal unemployment compensation programs in the United States. Constitutional challenges to the system have met with little success. See *Charles C. Steward Mach. Co. v. Davis*, 301 U.S. 548 (1937); *Carmichael v. Southern Coal & Coke Co.*, 301 U.S. 495 (1937); *W.H.H. Chamberlin v. Andrews*, 299 U.S. 515 (1936). Recent constitutional challenges have generally been unsuccessful. See *McKay v. Horn*, 529 F.Supp. 847 (D.N.J. 1981). This is not to say that the unemployment insurance system is free from all constitutional problems. For example, payment or nonpayment of compensation during labor disputes creates a federal preemption question under the Supremacy Clause; see *Nash v. Florida Indus. Comm'n*, 389 U.S. 235 (1967). First Amendment rights can also pose problems. See *Frazee v. Illinois Dept. of Emp't Sec.*, 489 U.S. 829 (1989).

The principal federal statutes comprising the basis of the unemployment insurance system today are the Federal Unemployment Tax Act (I.R.C. §§ 3301–3311); the Social Security Act, Titles III, IX, and XII; 5 U.S.C.A. §§ 8501–8508, 8521–8525; the Wagner–Peyser Act; the Social Security Amendments of 1960; the Manpower Development and Training Act of 1962; the Federal–State Extended Unemployment Compensation Act of 1970; the Employment Security Amendments of 1970; the Disaster Relief Act of 1970; the Emergency Unemployment Compensation Act of 1971; the Disaster Relief Act of 1974; the Trade Act of 1974; the Emergency Unemployment Compensation Act of 1974; the Emergency Jobs and Unemployment Assistance Act of 1974, as amended; the Emergency Compensation and Special Unemployment Assistance Extension Act of 1975; the Unemployment Compensation Act Amendments of 1976; the Emergency Unemployment Compensation Act of 1977; the Omnibus Reconciliation Act of 1980; the Omnibus Budget Reconciliation Act of 1981; the Tax Equity and Fiscal Responsibility Act of 1982; the Social Security Amendments of 1983; the Omnibus Budget Reconciliation Acts of 1987 and 1990; the Emergency Unemployment Compensation Act of 1991; the Unemployment Compensation Amendments of 1993; the Personal Responsibility and Work Opportunity Reconciliation Act of 1996; the Balanced Budget Act of 1997; the Taxpayer Relief Act of 1997; the Workforce Investment Act of 1998; the Noncitizen Benefit Clarification and Other Technical Amendments Act of 1998; the Ticket to Work and Work Incentives Improvement Act of 1999; the Victims of Trafficking and Violence Protection Act of 2000; the Consolidated Appropriations Act, 2001; the Economic Growth and Tax Relief Reconciliation Act of 2001; the No Child Left Behind Act of 2001; September 11th Victim Compensation Fund of 2001; the Job Creation and Worker Assistance Act of 2002; The Trade Act of 2002; the Emergency Wartime Supplemental Appropriations Act, 2003; the Unemployment Compensation Amendments of 2003; the Consolidated Appropriations Act, 2004; the SUTA Dumping Prevention Act of 2004; the QI, TMA, and Abstinence Programs Extension and Hurricane Katrina Unemployment Relief Act of 2005; the Department of Defense Appropriations Act, 2006; the Katrina Emergency Assistance Act of 2006; the Pension Protection Act of 2006; the Energy Independence and Security Act of 2007; the Consolidated Appropriations Act, 2008; the Supplemental Appropriations Act, 2008; the Energy Improvement and Extension Act of 2008; the Unemployment Compensation Extension Act of 2008; the Worker, Retiree, and Employer Recovery Act of 2008; the SSI Extension for Elderly and Disabled Refugees Act; the Consolidated Security, Disaster Assistance, and Continuing Appropriations Act, 2009; the American Recovery and Reinvestment Act of 2009; the Omnibus Appropriation Act, 2009; the Worker, Homeownership, and Business Assistance Act of 2009; the Trade and Globalization Adjustment Assistance Act of 2009; the Department of Defense Appropriations Act, 2010; the Temporary Extension Act of 2010; the Continuing Extension Act of 2010; the Unemployment Compensation Extension Act of 2010; Omnibus Trade Act of 2010; and the Tax Relief, Unemployment Insurance Reauthorization, and Job Creation Act of 2010. See generally CCH Unemployment Insurance Reporter—Federal Only, available at http://hr.cch.com.

In addition to the foregoing, each state, the District of Columbia, Puerto Rico, and the Virgin Islands have separate unemployment compensation laws. See generally CCH Unemployment Insurance Reporter—All States, available at http://hr.cch.com. The U.S. Department of Labor maintains a state law comparison and information website at http://workforce security.doleta.gov/unemploy/statelaws.asp.

The unemployment insurance system relies on cooperative federal-state programs. Federal laws provide general guidelines, standards, and requirements, with administration left to the states under their particular unemployment legislation. The unemployment compensation system is generally funded by unemployment insurance taxes or "contributions" imposed upon employers. The federal taxes are generally applied to the costs of administration, while the state taxes provide trust funds for the payment of benefits. Federal taxes are paid into a Federal Unemployment Trust Fund from which administrative costs and the federal share of extended benefits are paid. The Fund is also used to establish a Federal Unemployment Account from which the states can borrow if their state trust funds become depleted. Unemployment taxes should not be confused with the separate Social Security taxes imposed by the federal government or with the separate disability benefits taxes imposed by some states. It should be noted that unemployment benefits are taxable as ordinary income.

The U.S. Department of Labor maintains a useful website at http://www.dol.gov/dol/topic/unemployment-insurance/index.htm.

B.   FEDERAL UNEMPLOYMENT INSURANCE PROGRAMS

1.   REGULAR STATE PROGRAMS

a.   Overview

The principal vehicle for providing weekly unemployment benefits is referred to as the regular state program. Subject to federal guidelines, the states determine (1) qualifying requirements, (2) amounts of benefits, (3) duration, and (4) grounds for disqualification.

While state unemployment compensation laws can vary, ordinarily, qualification requires a demonstration of employment by an employer subject to the unemployment tax of a particular jurisdiction, and employment during a "base period" (a recent 12–month period). Generally, one must have been employed in more than one quarter.

Payments usually take the form of weekly benefits, and the weekly amount is calculated on the basis of a particular jurisdiction's formula. Commonly, an employee's average weekly wage provides the basis for the weekly benefit amount. This average amount is determined by dividing one's high quarter wages by the 13 weeks in a quarter; one-half of the result is the weekly benefit amount paid to the worker. There may be a waiting period prior to the initial payment of benefits, which may be referred to as the "waiting week." However, not all jurisdictions impose such an unemployment period prior to the payment of compensation. Normally, claimants have a "benefit year" of a designated 52 weeks within which to receive or "draw out" all compensation entitlements.

The duration of unemployment compensation benefits varies with the particular jurisdiction, but the vast majority of jurisdictions determine duration on the basis of the length of employment or the amount earned (variable duration approach). The longer the length or the greater the amount, the more weeks of benefits one can receive. A minority of jurisdictions considers an employee's work history to be irrelevant, and all claimants who qualify for benefits are treated in the same manner; i.e., each uniformly receives the same number of weeks of benefits on the theory that benefits should be tied to that period of time necessary to secure new employment (uniform duration approach).

Workers are denied compensation benefits if certain grounds for disqualification exist. Unemployment compensation policy dictates payment only to those employees who have lost their jobs through no fault on their part. In all jurisdictions, an employee is disqualified from benefits if the employee (1) voluntarily quits employment without good cause or (2) is discharged for employment-related misconduct. Additionally, disqualification can occur at any time if a claimant or benefit recipient refuses to accept suitable employment without good cause. Finally, in order for benefits to continue, a claimant must (1) register for employment with the jurisdiction's Employment Service, (2) be able to work, (3) be available for work, and (4) seek work on his own.

b. *Procedures and Appeals*

Representatives of the state employment agencies, who may be called deputies or claims examiners, make initial findings of fact (usually on the basis of interviews), which lead to a grant or denial of unemployment compensation benefits. The appellate rights of a dissatisfied claimant are generally guaranteed by Title III of the Social Security Act, Section 303(a), which requires administration by the states in a manner "reasonably calculated to insure full payment of unemployment when due," and which requires an "opportunity for a fair hearing, before an impartial tribunal, for all individuals whose claims for unemployment compensation are denied." 42 U.S.C.A. § 503(a) (West 2010). See *Graves v. Meystrik*, 425 F.Supp. 40 (E.D. Mo. 1977).

It should be noted that employers have appellate rights as well, and they frequently exercise these rights because an employer's unemployment experience rating affects the amounts that an employer is required to contribute. Appellate procedures vary from state to state, but all jurisdictions allow access to the state judicial system for appellate review, once administrative remedies have been exhausted (usually after a hearing before an appeals tribunal, whose decision may or may not be then reviewed by a board or some other state administrative body). A state administrative practice of permitting the automatic suspension of benefit payments upon the filing of an appeal by an employer was enjoined by the

Supreme Court. *California Dep't of Human Res. Dev. v. Java*, 402 U.S. 121 (1971). See *Jenkins v. Bowling*, 691 F.2d 1225 (7th Cir. 1982).

c. *Extended and Supplemental Benefits*

In recent times, certain amendments have provided extended, supplemental, or special unemployment benefits, thus increasing unemployment compensation for many unemployed persons in the United States. The Federal–State Extended Benefits Program pays "exhaustees" (individuals who have exhausted their regular program entitlements) further unemployment compensation, with the costs shared equally by the federal and state governments. The Federal Supplemental Compensation Act of 1982 made additional unemployment benefits available in states experiencing periods of "higher unemployment"; these benefits are funded out of general federal revenues. The Social Security Amendments of 1983 extended the Federal Supplemental Compensation program. On almost an annual basis since 2001, federal legislative acts have made similar adjustments in extending or supplementing benefits. See generally U.S. Department of Labor website, http://workforcesecurity.doleta.gov/unemploy/extenben.asp.

2. FEDERAL EMPLOYEES AND EX–SERVICEMEN

In 1956, unemployment compensation coverage was extended to federal employees. The state law of the jurisdiction in which a claimant worked as a federal employee usually determines an employee's eligibility. This eligibility may also be determined by the law of the state in which a claimant subsequently worked in privately covered employment, or by the law of the state in which a claimant resides at the time of the filing of the claim. The amount of benefits is determined by state law. The conditions and eligibility requirements for compensation are also governed by state law, but findings of fact provided by the employing federal agency with regard to federal employment, wages, and the reasons for separation (which have been made under U.S. Department of Labor procedures) are binding upon the states. See generally U.S. Department of Labor website, http://workforcesecurity.doleta. gov/unemploy/unemcomp.asp.

In 1958, unemployment compensation coverage was extended to ex-servicemen. The program also currently covers members of the National Oceanographic and Atmospheric Administration (NOAA) and U.S. Public Health Service (USPHS) Commissioned Corps. The state law of the jurisdiction in which a claimant first files an unemployment compensation claim, which establishes a benefit year after the claimant's most recent separation from active duty, determines eligibility. A U.S. Department of Labor schedule prescribes applicable wages for benefit purposes. These are based upon a claimant's pay grade at the time of his latest discharge or release from federal service. If a claimant is eligible for certain Veterans Administration benefits (subsistence or educational), the claimant is not entitled to unemployment compensation during these periods of eligibility. See generally U.S. Department of Labor website, http://workforcesecurity.doleta.gov/ unemploy/ucx.asp.

3. DISASTER UNEMPLOYMENT ASSISTANCE

Those employees who suffer unemployment as a result of major disasters are entitled to unemployment benefit assistance. This program is now generally known as the Disaster Relief and Emergency Assistance (DREA) Program. The President makes disaster area declarations. The states generally administer the payment of benefits, and these are strictly derived from federal revenues. Individual benefits are payable for the period of unemployment caused by the disaster, or until suitable reemployment is obtained, but in no event longer than the prescribed disaster assistance period. See generally U.S. Department of Labor website, http://workforce security.doleta.gov/unemploy/disaster.asp.

On April 20, 2010, the Deepwater Horizon semi-submersible mobile offshore oil drilling rig exploded and created an oil spill in the Gulf of Mexico, which generated extensive environmental and economic damage in the nearby coastal areas. Pursuant to the Oil Pollution Act of 1990 (OPA), Pub. L. 101–380, 104 Stat. 484, British Petroleum Exploration & Production, Inc., as a "responsible party," created a Gulf Coast Claims Facility as a vehicle for businesses and individuals to settle claims for damages as a result of the oil spill disaster. In general, claimants apply to an Administrator for funds to compensate for losses and in turn give up their rights to seek judicial redress against the company. Many of the claims have been for loss of employment by individuals impacted by the oil spill. There is an off-set for collateral source compensation which includes insurance payments, health insurance payments, unemployment benefits, and payments by federal, state, or local governments. Claims payments are considered income by the Internal Revenue Service, and they are taxable just like unemployment compensation. A website was created to facilitate the claims process at http://www.gulfcoastclaims facility.com

4.   TRADE READJUSTMENT ALLOWANCES (TRA)

Direct assistance is provided to employees who find themselves unemployed because of foreign competition. These benefits are provided only to those employees whose terminations are the result of foreign imports, and these imports must be a substantial cause of actual or threatened termination. Allowances are paid out of federal revenues and are generally administered by the states. This assistance takes the form of weekly benefits, training allowances, relocation allowances, and job search allowances. See generally U.S. Department of Labor website, http://workforcesecurity.doleta.gov/unemploy/tra.asp.

C. STATE–FINANCED PROGRAMS

1. EXTENDED AND ADDITIONAL BENEFITS

A few states have enacted supplemental unemployment programs. These programs are financed completely by the particular jurisdiction, and they are usually aimed at providing extended benefits during high unemployment periods. California, Connecticut, and Puerto Rico have state extended-benefit programs. Hawaii has enacted an Additional Unemployment Compensation Benefits Law that provides benefits for unemployment resulting from disasters. See generally U.S. Department of Labor website, http://workforcesecurity.doleta.gov/unemploy/pdf/uilawcompar/2010/special.pdf.

2. UNEMPLOYMENT COMPENSATION DISABILITY BENEFITS

Six jurisdictions in the United States have enacted special disability benefit programs to assist workers who are ineligible for either unemployment compensation or workers' compensation. Workers' compensation generally excludes disabilities arising out of non-work-related diseases or injuries; benefits are not payable through unemployment insurance programs to disabled workers because the ability to work is a condition of eligibility. California, Hawaii, New Jersey, New York, Rhode Island, and Puerto Rico have special unemployment disability benefit programs that fill the gap between workers' compensation and unemployment compensation laws. A branch of the particular jurisdiction's labor agency administers the program. Contributions by employers to state funds, private insurance, or self-insurance finance the programs. Some states make distinctions between the employed and the unemployed in their benefit formulas, while other jurisdictions do not. See generally U.S. Department of Labor website, http://workforce security.doleta.gov/unemploy/pdf/uilawcompar/2010/disability. pdf.

3. SELF–EMPLOYMENT ASSISTANCE

Seven jurisdictions in the United States (Delaware, Maine, Maryland, New Jersey, New York, Oregon, and Pennsylvania) participate in a voluntary program that seeks to return the unemployed to active work through the promotion of small businesses. Weekly benefits are paid to workers who are employed full-time in start-up businesses. See generally U.S. Department of Labor website, http://workforcesecurity.doleta. gov/unemploy/self.asp.

CHAPTER 16

FAIR LABOR STANDARDS ACT (FLSA)

A. INTRODUCTION

The federal attempt to regulate the wages and hours of employees began in 1892 with the passage of the Eight–Hour Law. Later, in *Hammer v. Dagenhart*, 247 U.S. 251 (1918), the Supreme Court held that Congress could not properly exercise its power under the Commerce Clause to prohibit the shipment of goods produced by child labor in interstate commerce. The Fair Labor Standards Act of 1938, 29 U.S.C.A. § 201 *et seq.* (West 2010) (hereinafter referred to as "FLSA") was enacted to regulate wages and hours (set minimum wage and overtime requirements) and child labor. The FLSA was upheld as constitutional in *United States v. Darby*, 312 U.S. 100 (1941), in which *Hammer v. Dagenhart*, *supra*, was overruled.

Over the years, Congress has amended the FLSA and added major and minor acts to the federal wage-hour laws as follows: the Fair Labor Standards Amendments of 1949; the Fair Labor Standards Amendments of 1955; the American Samoa Labor Standards Amendments of 1956; the Fair Labor Standards Amendments of 1961; the Equal Pay Act of 1963; the Fair Labor Standards Amendments of 1966; the Fair Labor Standards Amendments of 1974; the Fair Labor Standards Amendments of 1977; the Fair Labor Standards Amendments of 1985; the Fair Labor Standards Amendments of 1989; the Court Reporter Fair Labor Amendments of 1995; the Minimum Wage Increase Act of 1996; the Amy Somers Volunteers at Food Banks Act; the Drive for Teen Employment Act; the

Worker Economic Opportunity Act; the Fair Minimum Wage Act of 2007; and the Genetic Information Nondiscrimination Act of 2008.

The Equal Pay Act of 1963 was an important amendment to the FLSA; it generally prohibits sex-based wage discrimination by requiring equal pay for equal work regardless of sex. The Congressional extension of wage and hour coverage to public schools and hospitals was upheld as constitutional in *Maryland v. Wirtz*, 392 U.S. 183 (1968), but this decision was overruled in *National League of Cities v. Usery*, 426 U.S. 833 (1976). In this latter case, the Supreme Court held that the attempted Congressional regulation of wages and hours of employees of state and local governments constituted an unconstitutional infringement on state sovereignty. Constitutional issues again reached the Supreme Court in *Garcia v. San Antonio Metropolitan Transit Authority*, 469 U.S. 528 (1985), in which a divided Court upheld the application of the FLSA to state and local governments and overruled *National League of Cities v. Usery*. Congress passed the Fair Labor Standards Amendments of 1985 in order to lessen the impact of *Garcia* by authorizing the use of compensatory time in the place of overtime for state and local government employees.

The FLSA may be applied to a nonprofit religious organization that derives income largely from commercial business, despite constitutional challenges based upon the First Amendment. *Tony & Susan Alamo Found. v. Secretary of Labor*, 471 U.S. 290 (1985).

The Fair Labor Standards Amendments of 1989 created a "training wage" for eligible employees under 19 years of age at rates less than the minimum wage. The Small Business Job Protection Act of 1996 increased the minimum wage and replaced the "training wage" with an "opportunity wage." The Fair Minimum Wage Act of 2007 set the current minimum wage, and the Genetic Information Nondiscrimination Act of 2008 increased the child labor, minimum wage, and overtime penalties.

In *Kasten v. Saint–Gobain Performance Plastics Corp.*, ___ U.S. ___, 131 S.Ct. 1325 (2011), the Supreme Court held that a worker's oral complaints concerning workplace conditions made to a employer's supervisor are covered by the anti-retaliation provisions of the Fair Labor Standards Act, contained in 29 U.S.C.A. § 215(a)(3).

The FLSA is given liberal construction by the courts, and, with certain exceptions, it applies generally to interstate commerce and industry. *Mitchell v. Lublin, McGaughy & Associates*, 358 U.S. 207 (1959) (FLSA is to be construed liberally to apply to the furthest reaches consistent with congressional direction).

Today the FLSA, as amended, provides compensation standards and regulation in four basic areas: (1) minimum wages, (2) overtime compensation, (3) sex-based wage discrimination (equal pay for equal work), and (4) child labor. Other important federal acts apply compensation standards to federally financed public works contracts (Davis–Bacon Act), government service contracts (Service Contract Act), and government supply contracts (Walsh–Healey Public Contracts Act). The Copeland (Anti–Kickback) Act prevents circumvention of these mandates by contractors requiring workers to "kick-back" a part of their wages. See generally L. Schneider & J. Stine, *Wage and Hour Law: Compliance and Practice* (1995); CCH, *U.S. Master Wage–Hour Guide* (2009 ed.).

Some states have enacted higher compensation standards than those existing under federal law. These higher state standards are not superseded or preempted, and the federal standards cannot be used to excuse noncompliance with the higher state ones. If employees are covered by both federal and state compensation standards, then the stricter federal or state standards are applicable.

The following U.S. Department of Labor website is useful: http://www.dol.gov/WHD/.

B. STANDARDS AND REQUIREMENTS

1. MINIMUM WAGE

Congress changes the minimum wage rate from time to time, and as of July 24, 2009, the FLSA established the minimum hourly rate for all covered employees at $7.25. 29 U.S.C.A. § 206 (West 2010). Thus, for example, an employee working a 40–hour week and paid weekly is entitled to $290.00 per week under the current minimum wage requirement. It must always be remembered that the workweek is the longest unit of time over which wages can be averaged in order to determine whether the minimum wage has been paid. This does not mean that all employees must be paid solely on an hourly rate basis; they can be paid on a salary, commission, or piecework basis that is monthly, semi-monthly, or weekly, but they must receive the minimum hourly rate.

The FLSA requires that an employee's regular rate of pay be not less than the minimum wage. If wages or salary payments are made on other than a weekly basis, then the weekly pay must be established so that the regular rate of pay and overtime can be properly computed. For example, a monthly salary must be multiplied by 12 and the result divided by 52; an employee paid on a monthly basis who is working 40–hour weeks, under the current minimum wage, must be paid $1,256.66 per month. As a further example, a semi-monthly salary must be multiplied by 24 and the result divided by 52; an employee paid on a semi-monthly basis who is working 40–hour weeks, under the current minimum wage, must be paid $628.33 twice per month. The foregoing are monthly, semi-monthly, and weekly average standards which must be met (based upon eight-hour workdays, 40–hour workweeks, and 2,080 work hours in a year).

Under the FLSA, the workweek is established as a period of 168 hours during seven consecutive 24–hour periods. An employer can set a workweek for wage purposes to begin on any day of the week and at any hour of the day, but for purposes of minimum wage and overtime payments, each workweek stands alone. The averaging of two or more workweeks is prohibited. Generally, the workweek is the basis for determination of coverage of employees, compliance with wage payment mandates, and most of the exemption applications.

It should be noted that if an employee is at least 16 years of age, the FLSA does not limit the number of hours in a day or days in a week an employee may be required or scheduled to work, including overtime hours. Also, tipped employees have a minimum wage that is currently set at $2.13 per hour. Employers are permitted to pay youthful employees that are under 20 years of age a minimum wage of not less than $4.25 per hour for the first 90 consecutive calendar days (Youth Minimum Wage). Employees can be paid on a piece-rate or incentive plan basis, but employers must pay them at least the mandated minimum wage and overtime rates for all hours in excess of 40 per workweek. Subminimum wage provisions, with certificates from the U.S. Department of Labor, allow the payment of less than the minimum wage to student-learners (vocational education students); full-time students in retail or service establishments, agriculture, or institutions of higher education; and individuals whose earning capacity is impaired by physical or mental disabilities, including those related to age or injury. Special wage provisions apply to workers in American Samoa and the Commonwealth of the Northern Mariana Islands. There are also certain employees that are exempt from the overtime requirements or both the minimum wage and overtime requirements for various policy reasons.

Problems can further arise because certain deductions may be legally made from an employee's wages. Wages must be paid in cash or "facilities furnished," and thus the reasonable costs of board, lodging, or other facilities can be used in meeting minimum wage requirements. Payment in scrip, tokens, coupons, etc., is prohibited. Gifts, talent fees, discretionary bonuses, and certain other payments are excluded from wage calculations.

The application of the minimum wage to particular employees requires detailed research because of the complexity and exceptions contained in the FLSA and related wage and hour laws. See generally U.S. Department of Labor website, http://www.dol.gov/whd/regs/compliance/hrg.htm.

2. OVERTIME COMPENSATION

The federal wage and hour laws do not limit the number of hours that an employee can work in a workweek, but the employee must be paid time and one-half the employee's regular rate of pay for each hour worked over 40 in a workweek. It should be noted that an employee's regular rate of pay can be higher than the minimum hourly rate set by law for these purposes. The workweek is the longest period over which earnings may be averaged in arriving at an employee's regular hourly rate of pay. For example, if an employee works 45 hours in one week and 35 in the next week, the employee must be paid overtime for five hours in the first week, despite the fact that the employee's hourly average over two weeks is 40 hours per week. Time lost on the job must be made up in the same workweek, or else overtime must be paid for all hours subsequently worked over 40 in any other workweek.

Overtime exceptions and exemptions exist that must be researched in particular cases.

Many disputes arise because employers and employees fail to agree on what activities are to be considered "working time." For example, time spent on call may or may not be considered working time. The Portal-to-Portal Act of 1947 excludes preliminary and postliminary activities from working time not otherwise compensable by contract, custom, or practice. Overtime calculation difficulties also arise from premium pay, which is pay received in excess of basic straight-time wages; it can take the form of holiday pay, contracted overtime, gifts, bonuses, sick pay, etc. If premium pay is considered to be part of an employee's regular earnings, then FLSA overtime is increased; otherwise, premium pay may be offset against the statutory overtime pay.

It should be noted that effective August 23, 2004, overtime regulations promulgated by the U.S. Department of Labor changed the overtime rules for white-collar workers. See 29 C.F.R. pt. 541—Defining and Delimiting the Exemptions for Executive, Administrative, Professional, Computer and Outside Sales Employees (2006). Those workers who earn more than $100,000 per year are automatically exempt from overtime pay requirements under the changes. Further, a white-collar employee must be paid overtime unless the worker meets three tests: (1) The worker is paid a set salary and not hourly; (2) the salary is at least $455 per week, or $23,600 per year; and (3) the worker's job qualifies as administrative, professional, or executive. These changes were the first in over 50 years in this area, and they are controversial. Labor unions opposed the changes, while employers generally supported them. One of the reasons for the changes has been the marked increase in overtime lawsuits brought by employees in the past ten years. Employers were hopeful that the changes would reduce overtime litigation. See generally L. Schneider &

J. Stine, 1 *Wage and Hour Law: Compliance and Practice* ch. 10—Overtime (1995).

3. SEX–BASED WAGE DISCRIMINATION

The Equal Pay Act of 1963 amended the minimum wage provisions of the FLSA and prohibited wage discrimination based upon sex. 29 U.S.C.A. § 206(d) (West 2010).The provisions require equal pay for equal work for men and women doing equal work on jobs requiring equal skill, effort, and responsibility, and that are performed under similar working conditions. Minimum, overtime, and premium wages for men and women must be equal if the work is equal, and the wages of one sex cannot be lowered in order to comply with the law. Exceptions are allowed for (1) seniority systems, (2) merit systems, (3) systems measuring earnings by quantity or quality of production, and (4) factors other than sex. The act prohibits sex-based wage discrimination only in "any establishment" operated by an employer. The act does not cover discriminatory rates as between an employer's two or more legitimate "establishments."

It should be noted that wage differences authorized by the Equal Pay Act are valid pay practices for the purposes of the Civil Rights Act of 1964, Title VII; however, it is possible for sex-based discrimination involving pay practices, beyond the reach of the Equal Pay Act, to be remedied under Title VII. In order for equal pay coverage to exist, an employee generally must be covered by the FLSA minimum wage provisions. It should also be pointed out that amendments in 1972 placed executive, administrative, and professional employees within equal pay coverage. See generally L. Schneider & J. Stine, 2 *Wage and Hour Law: Compliance and Practice* ch. 16—Equal Pay (1995).

4.　CHILD LABOR

The FLSA prohibits "oppressive child labor" in commerce or in the production of goods for commerce. There is a "hot goods" ban that prohibits the interstate shipment of goods from establishments that have employed oppressive child labor. Enterprise coverage is used to prohibit the use of oppressive child labor, regardless of whether the work of children has an interstate impact or is purely local in nature. The FLSA defines "oppressive child labor" through the use of age restrictions. Essentially, minors under the age of 14 cannot be employed except in agriculture, minors 14 to 16 can work limited hours outside of their school hours in a limited class of jobs, and minors 16 to 18 cannot be employed in certain hazardous occupations. Employers generally obtain age or permit certificates for each minor in accordance with Department of Labor regulations and state guidelines.

Effective July 19, 2010, a Final Rule was implemented by the U.S. Department of Labor's Wage and Hour Division that was intended to protect working children from hazards in the workplace while also recognizing the value of safe work to children and their families. The Final Rule contained ambitious and far-reaching revisions to the child labor regulations. See generally L. Schneider & J. Stine, 2 *Wage and Hour Law: Compliance and Practice* ch. 14—Child Labor (1995).

The U.S. Department of Labor maintains a useful website at http://www.dol.gov/whd/childlabor.htm.

C.　COVERAGES

Congress has imposed compensation standards through the exercise of its powers to regulate interstate commerce and through its powers to control federal government contracts and federally financed projects. All geographical areas under the jurisdiction of the United States, including possessions and leased bases in foreign countries, are subject to the FLSA. Two forms of coverage are provided by the FLSA: (1) "enterprise" coverage and (2) "individual employee" coverage. Enterprise coverage generally exists if an employer has two or more workers engaged in interstate commerce, or in the production of goods for interstate commerce, while meeting a requirement of business volume. If enterprise coverage exists, then all employees of the enterprise are covered. Individual employee coverage can exist even if an employer's business does not qualify for enterprise coverage. An individual employee can be covered if the employee is engaged in commerce or in the production of goods for commerce, or is employed in a closely related process or occupation directly essential to the production of goods. The FLSA contains a number of exemptions based upon the type of industry or the type of employee. Once FLSA coverage is found to exist, the minimum wage, overtime, equal pay, and child labor provisions are applicable, unless a specific exemption governs. See generally L. Schneider & J. Stine, 1 *Wage and Hour Law: Compliance and Practice* ch. 3—Employment, ch. 4—Coverage, ch. 5—Exemptions (1995).

In those situations in which government contract laws impose compensation standards, the particular transaction and the appropriate federal act must be considered. For example, the Walsh–Healey Act imposes employee compensation standards through the terms and conditions of federal government supply contracts.

D. ENFORCEMENT AND REMEDIES

The administration and enforcement of federal compensation standards primarily rests with the U.S. Department of Labor, Employment Standards Administration. The Wage and

Hour Division performs inspections and investigations, makes compliance determinations, and issues rules and regulations. The Equal Employment Opportunity Commission is now charged with the enforcement of the equal pay provisions.

The Secretary of Labor is authorized to file suit on behalf of employees to collect wages and overtime, plus liquidated damages in an equal amount. The Secretary is empowered to file suits enjoining or restraining employer violations, and can also seek civil contempt citations against employers for continued violations of decrees. It should be noted that a "clearly erroneous" standard of review is to be used by courts of appeals in reviewing the application of an exemption to the FLSA; the employer has the burden of proof and strict construction is applied against any claimed exemption. See *Icicle Seafoods, Inc. v. Worthington*, 475 U.S. 709 (1986).

The U.S. Department of Justice can prosecute willful violators in criminal proceedings. 18 U.S.C.A. § 3571; 29 U.S.C.A. § 216(a) (West 2010).

Employees are authorized to file suit for reinstatement, back wages, liquidated damages in an equal amount, reasonable attorney's fees, and costs. A three-year statute of limitations exists for willful violations, while a two-year statute exists for other violations. *McLaughlin v. Richland Shoe Co.*, 486 U.S. 128 (1988) (definition of "willful" in connection with three-year statute of limitations). It should be noted also that employees generally do not have the right to release employers for less than the full amounts owing or to waive their rights to compensation. See *D.A. Schulte, Inc. v. Gangi*, 328 U.S. 108 (1946); *Brooklyn Sav. Bank v. O'Neil*, 324 U.S. 697 (1945). See generally L. Schneider & J. Stine, 2 *Wage and Hour Law: Compliance and Practice* ch. 21—Damages and Remedies (1995).

CHAPTER 17

FAMILY AND MEDICAL LEAVE
ACT OF 1993 (FMLA)

The Family and Medical Leave Act of 1993 ("FMLA"), as amended, 29 U.S.C.A. § 2601 *et seq.* (West 2010), see 29 C.F.R. pt. 825 (2006), mandates that covered employers who have 50 or more workers employed within a 75–mile radius must give up to 12 weeks of unpaid job-protected leave to eligible employees for certain family and medical reasons. The reasons include (1) birth and care of the newborn child of a worker, (2) placement with the worker of a child for adoption or foster, (3) care for an immediate family member (spouse, child, or parent) with a serious health condition, and (4) medical leave when the employee is unable to work because of a serious health condition. Leave for pregnancy complications can be counted against the 12 weeks. See generally G. Phelan & J. Arterton, 1 *Disability Discrimination in the Workplace* § 17:2 (2009).

To be eligible, a worker must have worked for an employer at least 12 months and been employed at least 1,250 hours at a location where the employer has 50 or more workers within a 75–mile radius. In addition to private employers, all public agencies and public and private elementary and secondary schools are covered by the FMLA; there are special rules for local education agency workers. New military family leave provisions were enacted pursuant to the National Defense Authorization Acts for Fiscal Years 2008 and 2010. In 2009, the FMLA was amended to establish special minimum eligibility requirements for airline flight attendants and flight crew members.

The Supreme Court upheld the application of the FMLA to the states over claims of state sovereign immunity, *Nevada Dept. of Human Res. v. Hibbs*, 538 U.S. 721 (2003), but U.S. Department of Labor regulations granting more than 12 months of leave have been stricken. *Ragsdale v. Wolverine World Wide, Inc.*, 535 U.S. 81 (2002).

For FMLA purposes, a "serious health condition" entitling an employee to FMLA leave means "an illness, injury, impairment or physical or mental condition that involves inpatient care as defined in § 825.114 or continuing treatment by a health care provider as defined in § 825.115." 29 C.F.R. § 825.113. A worker can take FMLA leave all at one time, or intermittent leave can be taken with a showing of medical necessity. A reduced FMLA leave schedule is also possible.

A worker requesting leave for the worker's own health reasons can be required by the employer to provide a certification from a health care provider that contains the following: (1) the name, address, telephone number, and fax number of the health care provider and type of medical practice/specialization; (2) the date the serious health condition began and the condition's probable duration; (3) a description of appropriate medical facts regarding the patient's health condition for which FMLA leave is requested (the medical facts must be sufficient to support the need for leave, and such medical facts may include information on symptoms, diagnosis, hospitalization, doctor visits, whether medication has been prescribed, any referrals for evaluation or treatment (physical therapy, for example), or any other regimen of continuing treatment); and (4) if the worker is the patient, information sufficient to establish that the worker cannot perform the essential functions of the worker's job as well as the nature of any other work restrictions, and the likely duration of such inability. 29 C.F.R. § 825.306(a) (2006).

The certification is required to indicate whether a worker's medical leave is necessary for absence from work because of the worker's own condition (including absences due to pregnancy or a chronic condition), and further, whether the worker (1) is unable to perform work of any kind; (2) is unable to perform any one or more of the essential functions of the worker's position, including a statement of the essential functions that the worker is unable to perform, based on either information provided by a statement from the employer about the essential functions of the position or, if not provided, discussion with the worker about his job functions; or (3) must be absent from work for treatment. 29 C.F.R. 825.306(b) (2006). See generally *Workers' Compensation Guide* ch. 8— Relationship to Other Laws, II. Federal Family and Medical Leave Act (2008).

The FMLA provides that nothing it contains shall be construed to modify or affect any federal or state law prohibiting discrimination on the basis of disability. 29 U.S.C.A. § 2651(a) (West 2010). FMLA regulations indicate that an employer must provide leave under whichever statutory provision provides the greater rights to workers. 29 C.F.R. § 825.702 (2006). If an employer violates both the FMLA and the Americans with Disabilities Act of 1990 ("ADA"), then an employee can have recovery under either or both.

A worker who is a qualified individual with a disability under the ADA is entitled to a reasonable accommodation by the employer unless undue hardship can be shown. The employer is also required to provide FMLA rights. The FMLA's serious health condition concept and the ADA's disability concept are different, and they must be analyzed separately. Under the FMLA, a worker is entitled to 12 weeks of leave in any 12–month period, whereas the ADA, as a reasonable accommodation, requires an indeterminate amount of leave unless undue hardship is demonstrated. The FMLA requires the maintenance of a worker's group health plan coverage, but the ADA does not unless other workers receive coverage during leave under the same circumstances.

The FMLA allows an employer to transfer a worker on a temporary basis if intermittent leave is taken or if the worker is on a reduced leave schedule to an alternate position. The ADA permits an accommodation of reassignment to an equivalent, vacant position only if the worker cannot perform the essential functions of the worker's present position and an accommodation is not possible in the worker's present position, or an accommodation in the worker's present position would cause undue hardship. 29 U.S.C.A. § 2601 *et seq.* (West 2010).

An example of the interaction of the FMLA and the ADA can be shown by the example of a qualified worker with a disability under the ADA who is also entitled to FMLA leave. If the worker requests 10 weeks of medical leave as a reasonable accommodation, the employer should grant the leave because there is no undue hardship. The employer should then advise that the 10 weeks of leave is being designated as FMLA leave to count against the worker's FMLA leave entitlement. The designation allows the parties to also treat the leave as a reasonable accommodation and reinstate the worker into the same job, as required by the ADA, rather than into an equivalent position under the FMLA, if that is in fact the greater right available to the worker. The worker would also be entitled to have the employer maintain group health coverage during leave because that requirement provides a greater right to the worker.

At the end of FMLA leave entitlement, the FMLA requires the employer to reinstate a worker in the same or an equivalent position, with equivalent pay and benefits, to that which the worker held when leave commenced. FMLA requirements would be satisfied if the employer offered the worker an equivalent full-time position. For a worker who was unable to perform the essential functions of that equivalent position, even with reasonable accommodation, because of a disability, the ADA may require the employer to make a reasonable accommodation at that time by allowing the worker to be employed part-time or by reassigning the worker to a vacant position, unless undue hardship can be demonstrated.

When the FMLA grants a worker leave, an employer may not, in lieu of FMLA leave entitlement, require a worker to take a job with a reasonable accommodation. But, the ADA may require an employer to offer a worker the opportunity to take such a position, and the employer may not change the essential functions of the job in order to deny FMLA leave.

An employee on a workers' compensation absence may also qualify as having a serious health condition under FMLA. A workers' compensation absence and FMLA leave may run concurrently. At some point, the workers' compensation health care provider may certify the worker is able to return to work in a light-duty position. If the employer offers such a position, a worker is permitted but not required to accept the position. As a result, the worker may no longer qualify for payments from workers' compensation, but the worker is entitled to continue on unpaid FMLA leave either (1) until the worker is able to return to the same or equivalent job the worker left, or (2) until the 12–week FMLA leave entitlement has expired. If a worker returning from the workers' compensation injury or illness is a qualified individual with a disability, he will have rights under the ADA.

If an employer requires certifications of a worker's fitness for duty in order to return to work, as permitted by FMLA, the employer must comply with the ADA requirement that a fitness for duty physical be job-related and consistent with business necessity.

The FMLA explicitly allows an employer to obtain a certification of medical information when a worker makes a FMLA request, while the ADA prohibits an employer from requiring medical exams of a current worker or inquiry into a worker's disability, unless an exam or inquiry is job-related and consistent with business necessity. No regulations or policy guidance has been provided despite the apparent conflicts in these laws.

Pursuant to Title VII of the Civil Rights Act of 1964 (as amended by the Pregnancy Discrimination Act), employers should provide the same benefits for women who are pregnant as the employers furnish to other workers with short-term disabilities. This means that a worker employed for less than 12 months, who is not eligible for FMLA leave, may not be denied maternity leave if the employer normally provides short-term disability benefits to employees with the same tenure who are experiencing other short-term disabilities. 29 U.S.C.A. § 2601 *et seq.* (West 2010).

A worker on leave for the worker's own serious health condition may be entitled to benefits under the FMLA and the ADA, but an employer's recommendation or granting of FMLA leave to a worker does not automatically mean that the worker is "regarded as" disabled under the ADA. See *Berry v. T–Mobile USA, Inc.*, 490 F.3d 1211 (10th Cir. 2007).

Pursuant to 29 U.S.C.A. § 2614(a) (West 2010), a worker must be restored by his employer to the position of employment held by the worker when his leave commenced or be restored to an equivalent position with equivalent employment benefits, pay, and other terms and conditions of employment.

There is an exception for certain highly compensated workers. 29 U.S.C.A. § 2614(b) (West 2010).

FMLA violations can result in suits for up to double the amount of wages, salary, employment benefits, or other compensation lost, as well as attorneys' fees and costs. 29 U.S.C.A. § 2617 (West 2010). Emotional distress and punitive damages are not permitted. *Nevada Dept. of Human Res. v. Hibbs*, 538 U.S. 721, 739–40 (2003).

A worker's FMLA interference claim must show that (1) the worker is an eligible "employee" under the FMLA, (2) the defendant is an "employer" under the FMLA, (3) the worker was entitled to leave under the FMLA, (4) the worker gave the employer notice of his intention to take leave, and (5) the employer denied the worker FMLA benefits to which he was entitled. See *Wysong v. Dow Chem. Co.*, 503 F.3d 441 (6th Cir. 2007).

A worker's FMLA retaliation claim must show that (1) the worker engaged in a statutorily protected activity, (2) the worker suffered an adverse employment action, and (3) there was a causal connection between the adverse employment action and the protected activity. 29 U.S.C.A. § 2615(a)(2) (West 2010).

FMLA claims must be made not later than two years after the date of the last event constituting the alleged violation for which the action is brought, but for alleged willful violations, claims must be made within three years of the date of the last event constituting the alleged violation for which the action is brought. 29 U.S.C.A. § 2617(c) (West 2010).

At present, there is a legal controversy and split in the federal circuits over the issue of whether public agency supervisors can be held individually liable, similar to private sector supervisors. Compare *Darby v. Bratch*, 287 F.3d 673 (8th Cir. 2002) (allowed) with *Mitchell v. Chapman*, 343 F.3d 811 (6th

Cir. 2003) (not allowed); *Wascura v. Carver*, 169 F.3d 683 (11th Cir. 1999) (not allowed).

FLMA complaints are processed, investigated, and resolved by the U.S. Department of Labor, Wage and Hour Division. The Secretary of Labor can also file suit in the district courts of the United States to (1) restrain violations, including any improper withholding of payment of wages, salary, employment benefits, or other compensation, plus interest, found by the court to be due to eligible employees; or (2) award such other equitable relief as may be appropriate, including employment, reinstatement, and promotion. The Solicitor of Labor can appear for and represent the Secretary on any litigation brought under 29 U.S.C.A. § 2617. Although the FMLA is administered by the U.S. Department of Labor, Wage and Hour Division, the Office of Personnel Management administers the FMLA for federal employees. See generally U.S. Department of Labor website, http://www.dol.gov/whd/fmla.

CHAPTER 18

EMPLOYEE RETIREMENT INCOME SECURITY ACT OF 1974 (ERISA)

In 1974, Congress enacted the Employee Retirement Income Security Act, 29 U.S.C.A. § 1001 *et seq.* (West 2010), for the purpose of safeguarding employee retirement and pension benefits. The following significant legislative changes have been made since that time: the Multiemployer Pension Plan Amendments Act of 1980; the Retirement Equity Act of 1984; the Single–Employer Pension Plan Amendments Act of 1986; the Rural Telephone Cooperative Associations ERISA Amendments Act of 1991; the Pension Annuitants Protection Act of 1994; the Savings Are Vital to Everyone's Retirement Act of 1997; the Pension Funding Equity Act of 2004; the Pension Protection Act of 2006; the Worker, Retiree, and Employer Recovery Act of 2008; and the Preservation of Access to Care for Medicare Beneficiaries and Pension Relief Act of 2010.

ERISA established minimum standards for employee participation, vesting standards that create non-forfeitable rights and funding guidelines. Generally speaking, federal laws preempt all state laws and causes of action relating to ERISA pension or welfare plans, directly or indirectly. *Ellenburg v. Brockway, Inc.*, 763 F.2d 1091 (9th Cir. 1985). For example, ERISA preempts state tort and contract actions involving ERISA-covered plans. See, e.g., *Jackson v. Martin Marietta Corp.*, 805 F.2d 1498 (11th Cir. 1986) (contract); *Dependahl v. Falstaff Brewing Corp.*, 653 F.2d 1208 (8th Cir. 1981) (tort).

As a result of preemption, damages in an ERISA proceeding are limited, but attorney's fees are recoverable. Punitive damages are not allowed. *Massachusetts Mut. Life Ins. Co. v. Russell*, 473 U.S. 134 (1985). ERISA preemption is an area of heavy litigation. See Cigna v. Amara, ___ U.S. ___, 131 S.Ct. 1866 (2011) (under ERISA's equitable remedies provision, monetary relief in the form of a surcharge is available to claimants; in other words, an ERISA fiduciary can be surcharged or ordered to pay money damages under the ERISA provision allowing a participant or beneficiary of ERISA plan to obtain "other appropriate equitable relief" upon a showing of actual harm proved by a preponderance of the evidence; however, ERISA's required summary plan descriptions cannot be enforced as terms of pension plan itself). See generally R. Cooke, *ERISA Practice and Procedure* (2d ed. 1996). ERISA's broad preemption of state laws that would otherwise regulate employee health plans has been the subject of criticism because gaps in insurance regulatory coverage, traditionally left to the states, have been created. See B. Cohen, *Saving the Savings Clause: Advocating a Broader Reading of the* Miller *Test to Enable States to Protect ERISA Health Plan Members By Regulating Insurance*, 18 Geo. Mason L. Rev. 125 (2010).

Since 1974, Congress has enacted many other laws that have had a significant impact on the ERISA provisions. Some of these are: the Health Insurance Portability and Accountability Act of 1996 ("HIPAA"); the Small Business Job Protection Act of 1996; the Defense of Marriage Act; the Newborns' and Mothers' Health Protection Act of 1996; the Mental Health Parity Act of 1996; the Savings Are Vital to Everyone's Retirement Act of 1997; the Women's Health and Cancer Rights Act of 1998; the Medicare Prescription Drug, Improvement, and Modernization Act of 2003; the Working Families Tax Relief Act of 2004; and the Genetic Information Nondiscrimination Act of 2008.

Of course, many changes have been brought about in ERISA by the Healthcare Reform Law of 2010 (Patient Protection and Affordable Care Act of 2010 ("PPACA") (Pub. L. No. 111–148, 124 Stat. 119)), as amended by the Health Care and Education Reconciliation Act of 2010 ("HCERA"), Pub. L. No. 111–152, 124 Stat 1029 (together, the Healthcare Reform Law). Some of the topics and issues for ERISA created by the Healthcare Reform Law include treatment of grandfathered plans; new adult dependent coverage; prohibition of preexisting condition limitations; prohibition of annual or lifetime limits; rescission restrictions; new patient protections; internal appeals and external review procedures; new rules for flexible spending arrangements ("FSAs"), health savings accounts ("HASs"), health reimbursement accounts ("HRAs") and Archer medical savings accounts ("MSAs"); W–2 reporting of the aggregate value of health benefits for each worker; waiting periods for coverage limited to 90 days; and new employer requirements.

Under ERISA, investments are regulated and minimum standards of fiduciary conduct for trustees and administrators are established, with civil and criminal enforcement measures provided.

The U.S. Department of Labor maintains a health plan website at http://www.dol.gov/dol/topic/health-plans/erisa.htm.

ERISA plan administrators have a special fiduciary relationship toward plan participants and beneficiaries. Most federal courts of appeal had applied an arbitrary and capricious standard of review to decisions of plan administration denying benefits. However, the Supreme Court in *Firestone Tire & Rubber Co. v. Bruch*, 489 U.S. 101 (1989), placed limits on the utilization of this standard of review, and provided for de novo review unless a plan expressly grants the necessary discretion to an administrator to construe terms and determine benefits.

It should be pointed out that if an employer is found to have acted as a fiduciary toward its employees in misleading them about their benefits, recovery becomes much easier. *Varity Corp. v. Howe*, 516 U.S. 489 (1996). Payment of pensions has been assured through the Pension Benefit Guaranty Corporation, which administers the termination insurance provisions. The Retiree Benefits Bankruptcy Protection Act of 1988 also affords workers health, disability, and life insurance protection from insolvent businesses. See J. Conison, *Employee Benefit Plans in a Nutshell* (3d ed. 2003).

The U.S. Department of Labor maintains a pension website at http://www.dol.gov/ebsa/pensionreform.html.

Offset or reduction provisions in retirement or benefit plans that are equal to state workers' compensation benefits are permitted, and state laws prohibiting reductions or offsets are preempted by ERISA. *Alessi v. Raybestos–Manhattan, Inc.*, 451 U.S. 504 (1981); *PPG Indus. Pension Plan A (CIO) v. Crews*, 902 F.2d 1148 (4th Cir. 1990).

CHAPTER 19

CONSOLIDATED OMNIBUS BUDGET RECONCILIATION ACT OF 1985 (COBRA)

From a historical standpoint, the states have been predominately the legal and policy regulators of the insurance industry, but Congress entered the picture in a significant and fundamental manner with its passage of the Consolidated Omnibus Budget Reconciliation Act of 1985 ("COBRA"), Pub. L. No. 99–272, 100 Stat. 222. The purpose of COBRA was to add some uniformity to the nation's healthcare system, and the method chosen was the amendment of three laws: (1) the Employee Retirement Income Security Act of 1974 (ERISA), (2) the Internal Revenue Code, and (3) the Public Health Service Act (PHSA). The goal was to provide continuation of health insurance coverage for workers and their dependents or "qualified beneficiaries" when a worker's coverage is lost under a group plan. Loss of coverage is tied to a "qualifying event" that triggers COBRA rights. Generally, workers and/or beneficiaries are allowed to continue health insurance at their own expense. ERISA and IRS penalties are imposed on employers and plan administrators who failed to give workers and their beneficiaries required notices about their COBRA rights. The continuation of coverage under COBRA is allowed for an initial period of 18 months and then for a maximum of 36 months, depending on the type and number of "qualifying events."

The "qualifying events" causing COBRA coverage eligibility are: (1) a reduction in the number of hours of employment below what is required to maintain health care coverage under the terms of the employer's plan, (2) any voluntary or involuntary termination of an employee other than for gross misconduct, (3) death, (4) Medicare entitlement, (5) a divorce or legal separation, (6) the changing of a dependent child's status, and (7) an employer's bankruptcy. Since 2009, provisions were added to create COBRA premium subsidies (65%) for "assistance-eligible individuals" who meet certain income categories and job loss time frames. See generally P. Hamburger, *Mandated Health Benefits—The COBRA Guide* (2010).

The law, as amended, and its regulations are complex. Four different federal agencies have COBRA regulatory responsibilities and authority: (1) Internal Revenue Service (IRS), (2) U.S. Department of Labor (DOL), (3) U.S. Department of Health and Human Services (HHS), and (4) Office of Personnel Management (OPM).

Since 1985, there have been numerous amendments affecting COBRA rights and obligations: the Omnibus Budget Reconciliation Act of 1986; the Tax Reform Act of 1986 ("TRA"); the Technical and Miscellaneous Revenue Act of 1988 ("TAMRA"); the Federal Health Benefits Amendments Act of 1988; the Omnibus Budget Reconciliation Act of 1989; the Federal Deposit Insurance Corporation Improvement Act of 1991; the Omnibus Budget Reconciliation Act of 1993; the National Defense Authorization Act for Fiscal Year 1993; the Uniformed Services Employment and Reemployment Rights Act of 1994 ("USERRA"); the Health Insurance Portability and Accountability Act of 1996 ("HIPAA"); the Small Business Job Protection Act of 1996; The Trade Act of 2002; the American Recovery and Reinvestment Act of 2009 ("Stimulus Bill"); the Department of Defense Appropriations Act, 2010; the Temporary Extension Act of 2010; and the Continuing Extension Act of 2010. It is noteworthy that the Healthcare Reform Law of 2010 did not significantly alter obligations mandated by COBRA. The law did alter health plan obligations with required dependent coverage for dependents through age 26, elimination of preexisting condition exclusions, and the requirement for employers to report the value of group health plan coverage on workers' W–2 forms. By 2014, even with mandated health care coverage for everyone, there will still be a need for COBRA because employer-sponsored group health care plans will still exist. See generally P. Hamburger, *Mandated Health Benefits—The COBRA Guide* (2010).

Workers' compensation is not deemed or considered to be a group health plan under ERISA, and therefore, worker's compensation does not come under COBRA. However, leave caused by worker's compensation can be considered in certain circumstances a "qualifying event" that triggers COBRA coverage. Three "qualifying events" for COBRA purposes that may be related to workers' compensation disability leave are: (1) a reductions in hours, (2) termination, and (3) Medicare eligibility. See generally *Workers' Compensation Guide* ch. 8—Relationship to Other Laws, V. Consolidated Omnibus Budget Reconciliation Act of 1985 (2008). Many employers avoid COBRA issues in these circumstances by providing "alternative coverage" for those on workers' compensation or disability leave by treating these workers as active employees under the group benefit plans.

CHAPTER 20

FEDERAL AND STATE ANTI-DISCRIM-INATION, FAIR EMPLOYMENT, AND OTHER LAWS

A. FEDERAL LAWS IN GENERAL

Federal and state laws provide workers with significant safeguards against discrimination in the workplace. The First, Fifth, Thirteenth, and Fourteenth Amendments to the U.S. Constitution, together with the Commerce Clause, form the foundation for most federal anti-discrimination measures affecting employment. Three of the Reconstruction Civil Rights Acts passed in the aftermath of the Civil War—42 U.S.C. §§ 1981, 1983, and 1985(3)—are still useful, to differing degrees, in challenging particular kinds of discrimination by state, local, or private employers.

Title VII of the Civil Rights Act of 1964, Pub. L. No. 88–352, 78 Stat. 241, 42 U.S.C.A. § 2000e (West 2010), is the most broadly-based and influential federal statute prohibiting discrimination in employment. Its prohibitions on discrimination based on race, color, sex, religion, or national origin extend to all "terms, conditions or privileges" of employment. Title VII § 703(a)(1), 42 U.S.C.A. § 2000e–2(a)(1). The federal courts have construed this language quite broadly to embrace any benefit actually conferred or burden actually imposed in the workplace, whether or not provided for by contract. See, e.g., *Hishon v. King & Spalding*, 467 U.S. 69 (1984) (right to be considered for law firm partnership). The concept embraces such intangible aspects of employment as workplace assignments, environment, and even mentoring opportunities, as well as more tangible problems like refusals to hire or promote, unequal pay, or discriminatory discharge.

Interestingly, although the Supreme Court has described an actionable level of harm for claims of retaliation under section 704 of Title VII, see *Burlington N. & Santa Fe Ry. Co. v. White*, 548 U.S. 53 (2006), there is no national consensus on the comparable level of harm sufficient to state a discrimination claim under section 703 of Title VII. See A. George, Comment, *"Adverse Employment Action"—How Much Harm Must be Shown to Sustain a Claim of Discrimination Under Title VII?*, 60 Mercer L. Rev. 1075 (2009) (collecting cases). Unfavorable employee evaluations that do not translate immediately into economic harm, and lateral transfers without reduced responsibility or pay, have proved particularly vexing. A typical circuit court formulation requires that the plaintiff must demonstrate "a serious and material change in the terms, conditions, or privileges of employment," *Butler v. Alabama Dep't of Transp.*, 536 F.3d 1209 (11th Cir. 2008), although an occasional opinion still requires that the discrimination affect an "ultimate" term like a job or promotion.

Decisions interpreting Title VII have frequently served as interpretive models for the Age Discrimination in Employment Act of 1967, 29 U.S.C.A. §§ 621 *et seq.* (West 2010) ("ADEA"), and other statutes, including the Reconstruction Civil Rights Acts. See *Western Air Lines, Inc. v. Criswell*, 472 U.S. 400 (1985) (ADEA). But when Title VII was amended by the Civil Rights Act of 1991, Pub. L. No. 102–166, § 3(1), (3), and (4), 105 Stat. 1071, to "provide appropriate remedies for intentional discrimination and unlawful harassment in the workplace," to "confirm statutory authority and provide statutory guidelines for the adjudication of disparate impact suits under Title VII," and to "respond to recent decisions of the Supreme Court by expanding the scope of relevant civil rights statutes," Congress did not amend certain critical counterpart provisions in ADEA or the Civil Rights Act of 1866, 42 U.S.C.A. § 1981 (West 2010). In addition to Title VII and the Reconstruction Civil Rights Acts, the federal laws, rules, regulations, and remedies affecting employment discrimination include ADEA; the Age Discrimination Act of 1975; the Civil Rights Act of 1964; the Civil Rights Act of 1968, Title I; the Civil Rights Attorney's Fees Awards Act of 1976; the Education Amendments of 1972, Title IX (banning sex discrimination in federally funded education programs); the Equal Pay Act of 1963 ("EPA"); Executive Order 11141 (Age Discrimination); Executive Order 11246 (Government Contractors and Subcontractors); the Foreign Boycott Laws (Export Administration Act of 1969, as amended); the Immigration Reform and Control Act of 1986 ("IRCA"); the Intergovernmental Personnel Act of 1970; the Labor Management Relations Act; the Rehabilitation Act of 1973 ("RHA") and Americans with Disabilities Act of 1990 ("ADA") (prohibiting disability discrimination); and the Vietnam Era Veterans Readjustment Act of 1974. For a fuller treatment of these protections, see Lewis and Norman, Civil Rights Law and Practice (Thomson/West 2004), and Lewis and Norman, Employment Discrimination Law and Practice (2d ed. Thomson/West 2004). Some of these laws and others are also summarized in Chapters 21 and 22.

Title VII's broad sweep distinguishes it from statutes like the EPA that prohibit employment discrimination solely with respect to one term or condition of employment, such as compensation. Further, the Title VII prohibitions on race, color, sex, religious, and national origin discrimination set it apart from single-focus employment-related statutes that ban only sex discrimination (EPA and Title IX); age discrimination (ADEA); race, ancestry, and possibly national origin discrimination (42 U.S.C.A. § 1981); or disability discrimination (RHA or ADA).

1. U.S. CONSTITUTION

In limited circumstances the Constitution provides direct protection against certain forms of employment discrimination. The Fifth Amendment prohibits federal government deprivations of life, liberty, or property without due process, while the Fourteenth Amendment prohibits the same deprivations by state and local governments. The Fourteenth Amendment also prohibits states from denying the equal protection of the laws; this prohibition has been judicially extended to federal action as part of the Fifth Amendment right of due process. See *Bolling v. Sharpe*, 347 U.S. 497 (1954).

The Supreme Court has recognized an implied private right of action against individual federal agents for Constitutional violations. *Bivens v. Six Unknown Named Agents of Fed. Bureau of Narcotics*, 403 U.S. 388 (1971), It has also upheld a "*Bivens*" claim for employment discrimination against a member of Congress under the equal protection component of the Fifth Amendment's Due Process Clause. *Davis v. Passman*, 442 U.S. 228 (1979) Individual federal officers sued under *Bivens* receive the same immunities available to individual state and local officers sued under § 1983. See, e.g., *Harlow v. Fitzgerald*, 457 U.S. 800, 818 n.30 (1982); *Butz v. Economou*, 438 U.S. 478, 496–504 (1978). The Court has declined to recognized a similar implied constitutional claim against federal agencies.

Additionally, the Court has crafted an exception to *Bivens*-based suits that radically reduces their utility as a remedy for employment discrimination. It has refused to imply a *Bivens* claim against a federal officer where the government action in question is subject to an elaborate statutory remedial scheme, even when the alternative does not afford as generous a remedy, or perhaps any remedy, against the offending agent. *Schweiker v. Chilicky*, 487 U.S. 412 (1988); *United States v.*

Stanley, 483 U.S. 669 (1987). Most federal employees work for an agency that is a covered "employer" within § 717 of Title VII, 42 U.S.C.A. § 2000e–16 (West 2010), and therefore enjoy the protection against discrimination afforded by that statute. See *Brown v. General Servs. Admin.*, 425 U.S. 820 (1976). Moreover, those employees may not maintain a *Bivens* claim alleging unconstitutional employment discrimination remediable by Title VII.

Even for employment claims other than discrimination, the Supreme Court has held that Congress's complete occupation of the federal personnel field is a "special factor" counseling against the *Bivens* damages remedy in matters related to "federal personnel policy." *Bush v. Lucas*, 462 U.S. 367, 380–81 (1983). After enactment of the Civil Service Reform Act of 1978, Pub. L. No. 95–454, 92 Stat. 111 ("CSRA"), the Court rejected a claim under the Back Pay Act that would have indirectly provided for review of adverse federal personnel action by a court that was not an "appropriate authority" to review that action under the CSRA. The Court concluded that Congress intended to withhold such review by failing to provide for it in the CSRA, which it deemed a comprehensive and exhaustive charter of protections and remedies for federal employees. *United States v. Fausto*, 484 U.S. 439 (1988). *Schweiker v. Chilicky*, 487 U.S. 412 (1988), extended this trend, declining to recognize a claim that federal officials violated the plaintiff's due process rights in denying Social Security disability benefits even while recognizing that the Social Security Act, although affording an elaborate administrative and judicial framework for review of benefits denials, offered no remedy for the claim of the plaintiff there. Following the Court's lead, the circuits have routinely denied federal employees review of adverse agency action under *Bivens*, the Back Pay Act, or the Administrative Procedure Act, except to the extent authorized by the CSRA. See, e.g., *Ayrault v. Pena*,

60 F.3d 346, 348 (7th Cir. 1995). And the Supreme Court has refused to extend *Bivens* to reach any claim against the United States or its agencies, *FDIC v. Meyer*, 510 U.S. 471 (1994), or private companies conducting federal functions under contract. *Correctional Services Corp. v. Malesko*, 534 U.S. 61 (2001).

2. CIVIL RIGHTS ACTS OF 1866, 1870, AND 1871

a. *In General*

The Civil Rights Acts of 1866, 1870, and 1871 are generally referred to as the Reconstruction Civil Rights Acts, and they were originally intended to enforce the Thirteenth and Fourteenth Amendments in the post-Civil War era. The most frequently invoked provisions are codified at 42 U.S.C. §§ 1981, 1983, and 1985(3). These acts remained dormant for many years but were resurrected in the 1960s.

What is now § 1981 was first enacted in 1866 under the authority of the Thirteenth Amendment, and re-enacted in 1870, two years after ratification of the Fourteenth Amendment. This history has spawned doctrinal schisms and jurisprudential inconsistencies. On one hand, the Supreme Court has relied on the Thirteenth Amendment origins of § 1981 (and § 1982, its legislative companion that bars discrimination in the acquiring, holding, and disposing of property) to apply these statutes to purely private defendants, at least with respect to transactions held open to the public. On the other, the court has relied on the Fourteenth Amendment origins of § 1981 to limit its reach to violations that reflect race discrimination that is intentional in character. And while the Court has insisted that it is the intent of the enacting Congress that controls the breadth of the §§ 1981 and 1982 definitions of "race," its reliance on the Thirteenth Amendment origins of these statutes seemingly caused it to depart from the norms of that Congress by holding the statutes to bar purely private discrimination, subject only to possible First Amendment limitations related to freedom of association.

b. Section 1981

Section 1981 secures equal contracting rights without regard to race. It affords "all persons" in the United States "the same right ... to make and enforce contracts ... and to the full and equal benefit of all laws ... as is enjoyed by white citizens." 42 U.S.C.A. § 1981(a) (West 2010). By its terms, § 1981 reaches not just employment but a host of contracting relationships—with private schools, to name just one—not reached by Title VII of the Civil Rights Act of 1964, as amended. And § 1981, unlike Title VII, has no minimum-employee numerical threshold for employer liability; § 1981 also provides for individual liability in several circuits. Section 1981 has been interpreted to provide a civil damages remedy for racial discrimination arising from contracts of employment, even though Congress comprehensively addressed employment discrimination much more recently in Title VII. Moreover, the Supreme Court has held, *Runyon v. McCrary*, 427 U.S. 160 (1976), and reaffirmed, *Patterson v. McLean Credit Union*, 491 U.S. 164 (1989), that § 1981, long assumed to reach only state action, also reaches purely private conduct. 42 U.S.C. § 1981(c), added by the 1991 Amendments to § 1981, codifies that decision. A contract for § 1981 purposes is not necessarily written or for a particular term. Also, in *Patterson*, the Court impliedly acknowledged that an at-will employee may bring an action under § 1981.

The Supreme Court has construed the language that secures to all the same contracting rights as "white citizens" to refer only to the racial (not gender-or religious-based) character of the prohibited discrimination, rather than to limit the class of appropriate plaintiffs to non-whites. Whites as well as blacks may assert contract denial claims under § 1981 on the basis of race. *McDonald v. Santa Fe Trail Transp. Co.*, 427 U.S. 273 (1976).

The Supreme Court has construed § 1981's ban on "race" discrimination to also include discrimination on the basis of ancestry. The Court has understood ancestry, in turn, to mean membership in an "ethnically and physiognomically distinctive sub-grouping." This somewhat vague formulation has generated predictable confusion among the lower federal courts. Thus, the § 1981 "ancestry" that equates to "race" has sometimes but not always been held to include national origin and alienage discrimination, but not discrimination based on religion as such.

A sharply limited protection from employment discrimination on the basis of non-citizenship, i.e., alienage status, is now provided by the Immigration Reform and Control Act of 1986, Pub. L. No. 99–603, 100 Stat. 3359. Aliens, like other "persons within the jurisdiction of the United States," may complain of race or ancestry (including possibly alienage) discrimination under § 1981, as well as of discrimination due to race, gender, religion, or national origin, but not ancestry or citizenship, under Title VII. None of the Reconstruction Civil Rights Acts reaches gender or religious discrimination as such, although discrimination on those grounds might violate equal protection and accordingly would be redressable under § 1983.

A showing of disparate impact does not suffice to prove a § 1981 employment violation, which requires instead a direct or inferential demonstration of discriminatory intent. *General Bldg. Contractors Ass'n v. Pennsylvania*, 458 U.S. 375 (1982). The Court, in *Patterson v. McLean Credit Union*, 491 U.S. 164 (1989), approved for use in § 1981 actions the Title VII intentional yet inferential disparate treatment mode of proof first outlined in *McDonnell Douglas Corp. v. Green*, 411 U.S. 792 (1973). Those requirements continue to be routinely applied to actions under § 1981.

For more than two decades after Title VII became effective in 1965, circuit courts consistently recognized § 1981 claims of unlawful harassment and retaliation, despite statutory silence on the subject. But in *Patterson*, 491 U.S. 164 (1989), the Supreme Court held that most discriminatory conduct directed against an employee after her initial hiring—including, presumably, claims of harassment and retaliation—falls outside the right granted by § 1981 to "make" a "contract" free from racial discrimination. The Court stated that the plaintiff might have a cause of action against her employer for certain refusals to promote, depending on "whether the nature of the change in position was such that it involved the opportunity to enter into a new contract with the employer." *Id.* at 185. The 1991 Amendments overturned this aspect of *Patterson* and thereby restored § 1981 as a wide-ranging supplementary vehicle for redressing intentional race or ancestry discrimination in contracting. The legislation provides that the right to "make" a contract extends beyond initial formation to include "performance, modification and termination" and thus reaches not only dismissal but also ongoing terms and conditions of employment, including not only all promotions and demotions but also compensation and discipline decisions and harassment. § 1981(b) (West 2010). The Supreme Court has since held that the 1991 legislation restored § 1981 post-hiring retaliation claims. *CBOCS West v. Humphries*, 553 U.S. 442 (2008). The retaliatory conduct, to be actionable, must respond to an employee's opposition to the denial of rights protected by § 1981; thus, the claim would fail if the underlying opposition were to discrimination based on sex or religion, grounds that are not reached by § 1981.

But what if, after the plaintiff proves intentional "race" discrimination, the § 1981 defendant is able to prove a defense the Supreme Court afforded in *Mt. Healthy City School District Board of Education v. Doyle*, 429 U.S. 274 (1977): that the challenged employment decision would have been made for lawful reasons independent of the racial component of the employer's overall motivation? The effect of this showing under § 1983 appears to be (except with respect to procedural due process and certain express or facial equal protection violations) that no federal law violation is established and the defendant may not be mulcted in damages. Under Title VII, as amended in 1991, the defendant who makes this "same-decision" showing is relieved only of retroactive, monetary relief; she is still considered to have violated the law and is therefore subject to prospective relief and attorneys' fees. The 1991 amendments did not, however, make the same amendment to the ADEA, although they amended those statutes in other respects. For this reason, the Supreme Court has held that an ADEA defendant never carries a burden of persuasion to show that it would have reached the same decision for lawful reasons. *Gross v. FBL Fin. Servs.*, ___ U.S. ___, 129 S.Ct. 2343 (2009). Because the 1991 Act's amendments to causation were likewise not made to § 1981, the *Mt. Healthy*, pre–1991 regime governing § 1981 defendants who carry the "same decision" showing—a complete defense to liability—is therefore still likely to prevail if that rule were challenged in the Supreme Court, as it prevails in most circuits. Accordingly, the § 1981 defendant, by making a "same decision" showing, may escape without liability, whereas the Title VII discrimination plaintiff (although perhaps not the Title VII retaliation plaintiff) will establish a violation and thereby have an opportunity to receive declaratory and injunctive relief and, in turn, attorney's fees as a "prevailing party."

Lower courts have permitted the assertion of § 1981 claims where intimate or associational rights of the plaintiff are allegedly invaded by a defendant whose conduct was aimed at third parties; these decisions are likely to stand in light of a recent Supreme Court Title VII ruling that Title VII prohibits an employer from retaliating against a plaintiff who opposed unlawful discrimination by firing the plaintiff's fiancée. *Thompson v. North Am. Stainless, LP,* ___ U.S. ___, 131 S.Ct. 863 (2011). A related question is whether the defendant must be the party with whom the plaintiff contracts or seeks to contract. Courts have answered this question in the negative, holding § 1981 is violated by a racially motivated interference with a plaintiff's right to enter into contracts with non-whites and by third parties' attempts to punish the plaintiff for making such contracts.

28 U.S.C. § 1658(a) is a four-year "catchall" statute of limitations governing claims "arising under an Act of Congress enacted after [December 1, 1990]." One such post-December 1, 1990 statute is the Civil Rights Act of 1991, Pub. L. No. 102–166, 105 Stat. 1071, which amended § 1981 by overruling the Supreme Court's decision in *Patterson* and thus restored the reach of § 1981 to the full spectrum of terms and conditions of employment arising after initial contract formation. The question that then divided the circuit courts of appeals was whether a § 1981 claim asserting racial discrimination respecting a post-hire term of employment—that is, a claim made possible only by the Civil Rights Act of 1991's overruling of *Patterson*—was eligible for § 1658's four-year statute of limitations even though the underlying statute that the 1991 Act amended, § 1981, predated December 1, 1990 by 124 years.

In *Jones v. R.R. Donnelley & Sons Co.,* 541 U.S. 369 (2004), the Court concluded that a cause of action "aris[es] under an Act of Congress enacted after" December 1, 1990—and there-

fore gets the benefit of § 1658's four-year limitations period—
if the plaintiff's claims were made possible by a post–1990
enactment. Because the *Jones* petitioners' hostile work environment, wrongful termination, and failure-to-transfer claims
alleged § 1981 violations that, under *Patterson*, would not
have stated a claim before December 1, 1990, but were actionable by virtue of the Civil Rights Act of 1991 amendments,
they "ar[ose] under" the 1991 amendments to § 1981 and
accordingly fit within the terms of § 1658. Because the vast
majority of claims under § 1981—indeed, virtually all such
claims other than alleged racially discriminatory refusals to
hire or major promotions—depend on the 1991 amendments
to § 1981 that overruled *Patterson*, almost all § 1981 claims
will now be eligible for § 1658's generous four-year limitations
period, regardless of shorter limitations periods of the forum
state. Under the other Reconstruction Civil Rights Acts, notably § 1983, the Supreme Court has held that federal courts
must use the forum state's general or residual personal injury
limitations period rather than, for example, a statute geared
specifically to intentional torts. *Owens v. Okure*, 488 U.S. 235
(1989). That approach should persist because the rights created by those statutes, unlike most rights under § 1981 that
were revived by the Civil Rights Act of 1991, have not been
substantively amended since § 1658's December 1, 1990 cutoff
date. The liberal approach to claim accrual embraced by the
Supreme Court in *National Railroad Passenger Corp. v. Morgan*, 536 U.S. 101 (2002), for "hostile environment" claims of
harassment under Title VII, discussed below, likely also extends to § 1981 harassment claims.

42 U.S.C. § 1977A(a)(1), added by § 102 of the Civil Rights
Act of 1991, bars double recovery under Title VII or 1981 for
the same injury, but does not bar parallel proceedings under
the two statutes. Putative plaintiffs with intentional race
discrimination claims against employers large enough to be

covered by and not exempt from Title VII can choose whether to proceed under Title VII or § 1981 or both, provided they meet the particular deadlines and procedures applicable to each such claim. See *Johnson v. Railway Exp. Agency, Inc.*, 421 U.S. 454 (1975).

The choice of statutory vehicle will be heavily influenced by the availability of unlimited compensatory and punitive damages under § 1981, free of Title VII's variable caps, and by the immediate access to court under § 1981, free of the Title VII state and federal administrative prerequisite requirements with their rather early filing deadlines. In practice, § 1981 will usually look more attractive. The national four-year limitations period that now governs most § 1981 claims, and even the usually shorter personal injury limitation periods still borrowed from state law to govern the rest, are normally longer than the 180–day or 240/300–day Title VII deadline for filing administrative charges with federal or state agencies. Although jury trials are now available under either statute with respect to claims of intentional discrimination, the nineteenth-century statutes offer compensatory and punitive damages unlimited in amount; even after the Civil Rights Act of 1991, Title VII plaintiffs who prove intentional discrimination are subject to caps on those damages that vary with the number of employees working for the defendant employer. In one respect, Title VII lines up precisely with § 1983 and § 1981: Punitive damages are not available against a defendant government entity.

A potential plaintiff with an intentional race discrimination claim actionable under both statutes may prefer Title VII if she cannot afford counsel and believes that state or federal agency administrative processing of her charge will induce her employer to settle. In addition, it remains possible for a plaintiff who cannot prove intentional discrimination, and would therefore fail under § 1981, to succeed under Title VII by establishing that an employer's neutral practice had a disproportionate adverse impact on her group and that the employer cannot justify the practice as a matter of job relatedness and business necessity.

In *Jett v. Dallas Independent School District*, 491 U.S. 701 (1989) the Supreme Court held that municipalities are liable under § 1981 only if they would be liable under the more stringent standards of § 1983. In an apparent attempt to overrule *Jett*, Congress in § 101 of the Civil Rights Act of 1991 appended to § 1981 the following paragraph:

> (c) The rights protected by this section are protected against impairment by nongovernmental discrimination and impairment under color of State law.

The protection against impairment by nongovernmental discrimination simply codifies the *Runyon* holding, reaffirmed by *Patterson*, that § 1981 extends to purely private, as well as governmental, discrimination. Indeed, the Sponsors' Interpretive Memorandum identifies only this purpose for the entirely new paragraph (c). Does the paragraph's last clause, then, asserting that the rights protected by § 1981 are protected from "impairment under color of State law," overrule *Jett*? Circuit decisions hold that *Jett* survives, because that decision never denied that the § 1981 right to be free of race discrimination in contracting was enforceable to some degree against state and local government. It held only that in actions against those entities, the § 1981 plaintiff must establish the "policy" element of the § 1983 prima facie case, and that § 1981 is not available on its own terms and instead the plaintiff must surmount the additional proof requirements and defenses available under § 1983. Title VII therefore remains a far more attractive option than § 1981 for asserting intentional race discrimination claims against state or local government employers. Title VII is also the only remedy for race discrimination in federal employment, which has been held outside the reach of § 1981.

And suppose the finder of fact determines that the employer acted with mixed lawful and unlawful motives and would have made the same decision against the plaintiff (not hired, not promoted, disciplined, or fired) based on the lawful ground alone. Authority under § 1981, drawing on the Supreme Court's *Mt. Healthy* ruling under § 1983, treats this "same-decision" affirmative defense as a complete defense to § 1981 liability, not merely a limitation on remedy. By contrast, the mixed-motive Title VII plaintiff alleging intentional discrimination remains eligible for prospective (mainly injunctive) relief and, in turn, attorney's fees, even if that defense succeeds.

Often, however, § 1981 will be the only game in town: It contains no threshold numerical requirement for employer coverage, and it is therefore the only protection against race or ancestry discrimination for those millions of applicants or employees whose employers are too small to be covered by Title VII. The 1991 amendments to Title VII make no attempt to protect those applicants or employees against the forms of discrimination prohibited only by Title VII, such as sex, religion, or possibly national origin discrimination, or against non-intentional race discrimination resulting solely from the effects of a neutral practice.

In § 1981 disparate treatment discrimination cases, courts commonly permit the showing of intent requisite under the Reconstruction Acts to be made inferentially, that is, through the *McDonnell Douglas* formula of shifting evidentiary burdens that is paradigmatic under Title VII. Similarly, once a plaintiff has established a prima facie case of retaliation under § 1981, most circuits will consider *McDonnell Douglas* inferential evidence to discredit any neutral employer reason for the adverse action at issue.

Nevertheless, there are at least five situations in which the advocate contemplating a race-based employment discrimination claim should endure Title VII's procedural prerequisites and limitations on damages rather than proceed under § 1981 alone. First, § 1981 is unavailable because the plaintiff alleges unintentional discrimination—that is, the plaintiff's sole complaint is that the employer utilized one or more neutral employment practices (tests, height-weight requirements, nospouse rule) that had a disproportionate adverse impact on a group defined by race. That claim is actionable only under Title VII. Second, the plaintiff has an intentional race-based employment discrimination claim actionable under § 1981 but fears that defendant could succeed with the "same decision" complete affirmative defense; in that situation, only Title VII affords any relief, namely a declaratory judgment and an injunction, and an injunction may also support an award of attorneys' fees. Third, under the Supreme Court's *Jett* decision, the plaintiff who sues state or local governments for intentional, race-based employment discrimination either has no claim at all under § 1981 or must satisfy its requirements by proving the exceptionally exacting elements of a claim under § 1983. Fourth, the unrepresented or impecunious plaintiff may choose to pursue a Title VII claim, at least initially, to capitalize on any free assistance in investigation or settlement that may be provided by the regional office of the Equal Employment Opportunity Commission. Fifth, in some cases where the claim is brought by someone other than the injured employee, so that the plaintiff is asserting the right of a third party, broader standing has been recognized under Title VII than under § 1981.

c. *Section 1983*

Section 1983 authorizes actions at law or suits in equity against any "person" for the deprivation of rights, privileges, or immunities secured by the federal Constitution or laws, so long as the defendant acted "under color of" state law, custom, or usage. For most employment discrimination claimants, § 1983 is of less utility than § 1981. First, it vindicates only rights, notably equal protection, protected by the U.S. Constitution or other federal statutes. Second, deprivations of those rights are actionable only if imposed "under color of" state law—i.e., during state or local government employment. Third, while the Supreme Court has held that municipalities and other local governments are "persons," and hence appropriate defendants, for purposes of § 1983, it simultaneously concluded that municipalities are not subject to liability vicariously, i.e., through respondeat superior, but only for conduct composing a well-established entity "custom"; for official policies or actions taken or approved by employees with "final policymaking authority," a question to be decided by the court before trial by reference to local law; or for omissions so likely to result in unconstitutional harm as to amount to "deliberate indifference." *Monell v. Department of Soc. Servs. of City of N.Y.*, 436 U.S. 658 (1978); see *Jett v. Dallas Indep. Sch. Dist.*, 491 U.S. 701 (1989) (five-member majority opinion); *St. Louis v. Praprotnik*, 485 U.S. 112 (1988) (plurality opinion); *Pembaur v. Cincinnati*, 475 U.S. 469 (1986) (plurality opinion).

The § 1983 liability of individual government employees, state or local, has been sharply circumscribed by a series of Supreme Court rulings expanding the range of absolute immunity for government officials respecting conduct constituting a legislative, judicial, or prosecutorial function, and by an increasingly generous brand of qualified immunity for discretionary executive or administrative acts. See generally *Burns v. Reed*, 500 U.S. 478 (1991) (prosecutorial immunity); *Forrester v. White*, 484 U.S. 219 (1988) (judicial immunity); *Anderson v. Creighton*, 483 U.S. 635 (1987), and *Harlow v. Fitzgerald*, 457 U.S. 800 (1982) (qualified immunity).

Still, while Title VII does not support claims against individual employer agents like supervisors, § 1983 does, and it subjects them not only to uncapped compensatory damages but, in appropriate cases, to punitive awards as well. The Supreme Court has yet to decide whether Title VII provides the exclusive remedy for employment discrimination against state actors, thus impliedly preempting § 1983, but the federal circuit courts are largely in accord that the mere availability of a Title VII claim does not altogether preempt a § 1983 claim arising from the same facts. But see *Hughes v. Bedsole*, 48 F.3d 1376, 1383 n.6 (4th Cir. 1995). Most, however, also hold that the § 1983 employment discrimination plaintiff cannot rest simply on the "and laws" branch of that statute, which provides a remedy for action under color of state law that violates a federal statutory right. See, e.g., *Pontarelli v. Stone*, 930 F.2d 104 (1st Cir. 1991). This means that in general, § 1983 can be used by state or local government employees only to challenge discrimination that violates the Equal Protection or Due Process Clauses of the Constitution, not Title VII. Employer conduct that violates only the Title VII "neutral practice/disparate impact" theory fails to show the intentional discrimination requisite for a violation of the Equal Protection Clause. See *Washington v. Davis*, 426 U.S. 229 (1976).

3. TITLE VII OF THE 1964 CIVIL RIGHTS ACT, AS AMENDED

a. Scope and Coverage

(1) PROTECTION FOR INDIVIDUALS

Title VII's principal provisions defining unlawful employment practices, contained in section 703, extend protection to any "individual," whether or not an employee. Relying on section 703's broad protection of "any individual," courts have had no difficulty according plaintiff status and standing on former employees as well as applicants. Further, they have sometimes even recognized claims on behalf of persons who fall outside any common-law understanding of the employee-employer relationship, provided the circumstances satisfy an "economic realities" test that protects those in a position to suffer the kind of discrimination Title VII was designed to prevent. The key factor in the inquiry is the employer's right to control the means and manner of the plaintiff's performance of his work. Occasionally, however, a court will rely on the "employee" definition to deny protection to persons, mainly independent contractors, who do not satisfy the common law's test for employee status, the "totality of the working relationship." For example, employees working for independent contractors are not generally considered employees of the other contracting party.

Relying on the statutory language "any individual," courts have permitted plaintiffs to sue for harm respecting employment with third parties. These courts reason that while the Title VII defendant must be a defined "employer," the plaintiff need not be an "employee," but instead is referred to in the statute as a "person aggrieved." (For the same reason, the statute applies to defendant labor unions and employment agencies, which may have no direct employment relationship with a plaintiff.)

By contrast, the section 704 protection against retaliation for opposing unlawful employment practices or participating in proceedings to protest them extends to "employees or applicants for employment." The Supreme Court has agreed with the overwhelming view of the circuit courts that, despite the possible implication that "employees" refers only to those currently working, former employees also enjoy protection from retaliation. *Robinson v. Shell Oil Co.*, 519 U.S. 337 (1997).

(2) EMPLOYERS GOVERNED BY TITLE VII/ADEA

Title VII applies to employers, employment agencies, apprenticeship programs, and labor organizations whose activities affect interstate commerce. There are very few categorical exclusions from the definition of "employer" in either Title VII or ADEA. Title VII expressly exempts private membership clubs exempt from taxation under the Internal Revenue Code and Indian tribes. 42 U.S.C.A. § 2000e(b) (West 2010). ADEA contains neither such exemption in express terms, but Indian tribes have been exempted by judicial construction. By far the most significant exclusion is numerical: An employer is covered by Title VII only if it has 15 or more employees, and by ADEA only if it has 20 or more employees for each working day in 20 or more calendar weeks in the current or prior calendar year. Persons holding an employment relationship with the employer during a calendar week (usually manifested by presence on the payroll) are counted regardless of how many of them actually worked or received compensation on any particular working day in that week.

Courts have wrestled with whether to aggregate for coverage purposes the number of employees employed by affiliated enterprises, for example by subjecting a parent corporation to potential liability for the conduct of a subsidiary; whether to consider all of an employer's employees when the alleged unlawful employment practice is confined to a discrete operating location; whether to impose liability on a successor employer after a sale of the business or bankruptcy; whether a government-appointed receiver is a Title VII "employer" of employees of a failed financial institution; whether a contractor is liable for a subcontractor's unlawful employment practice; whether a nonprofit organization qualifies as an "employer"; and whether an employment agency or union meets the statutory "employer" definition even when it has fewer than 15 employees. These and other coverage questions are capably discussed in detail in several standard works.

Unions may be liable as labor organizations representing employees in collective bargaining without regard to the number of employees represented, but are liable in their capacity as "employer" only if they satisfy the employer definition, including the requirement of at least fifteen employees under Title VII. States, their political subdivisions, and agencies of each are also employers under Title VII. The constitutionality of applying Title VII to state defendants, and their amenability to suit in federal court is settled.

The federal government and its agencies are not defined "employers," but special provisions in each statute mandate that personnel actions affecting most federal employees be made free from discrimination based on any of the grounds those statutes address. Title VII generally does not apply to uniformed members of the armed services because of the *Feres* non-justiciability doctrine.

Both Title VII and ADEA define a covered "employer" to include any "agent" of an employer. See 29 U.S.C.A. § 630(b) (West 2010); 42 U.S.C.A. § 2000e(b) (West 2010). With the conspicuous exception of liability for hostile work environment harassment by supervisors or co-workers of the plaintiff, this definition makes the employer liable for the acts of subordinates by means of respondeat superior or "scope of employment" liability. The circuits that have confronted the issue have uniformly concluded, however, that neither a supervisor nor other individual can be subjected to personal liability.

(3) AMERICAN CORPORATIONS' EMPLOYEES WORKING ABROAD; "FOR-
EIGN" EMPLOYERS' PERSONNEL IN THE U.S. AND OVERSEAS; AND
NATIONAL ORIGIN, ALIENAGE, AND ANCESTRY DISCRIMINATION
UNDER TITLE VII, IRCA, AND 42 U.S.C.A. § 1981

Discrimination on any ground against an alien (for this
purpose, someone who has not yet attained full American
citizenship) working outside the United States for either a
U.S. or non-U.S. company is not prohibited by either Title VII
or ADEA. This results from an exemption to Title VII and a
restriction in the ADEA's definition of "employee." Somewhat
more difficult questions concern the statutory protection available to citizen employees of American companies stationed
overseas and to the U.S.-and overseas-based employees of
foreign enterprises.

Unlike the ADEA, which was amended in 1984 to apply to
the overseas work of American corporations and American-
controlled foreign corporations, Title VII initially had no language specifically extending its application to work performed
abroad. The Civil Rights Act of 1991 amendments to Title VII
now define covered employees to include U.S. citizens employed by U.S. corporations or their subsidiaries "with respect
to employment in a foreign country." 42 U.S.C.A. § 2000e(f)
(West 2010).

This protection for U.S. citizens is now coextensive with
that earlier provided by the ADEA. The 1991 Act subjects to
Title VII jurisdiction not only U.S. corporations but also those
foreign corporations "controlled" by American employers, and
it appears to provide dual defendants in this situation by
presuming that unlawful employment practices of the controlled foreign affiliate are engaged in by the controlling
(American) employer as well. But it exempts conduct that
would cause any employer to violate the national law of the
foreign workplace. This exemption is not triggered simply
because the type of discrimination in question (e.g., gender or

religious) is permitted by foreign law; rather, that law must affirmatively prohibit the particular employer conduct (e.g., hiring a woman as a driver in Saudi Arabia) that compliance with Title VII would otherwise require the employer to permit. The foreign "law" that would be violated if ADEA were respected may also include a collective bargaining agreement with a foreign labor union.

Truly foreign corporations—those not "controlled" by a U.S. business—are not subject to Title VII with respect to work outside the United States. U.S. citizens working abroad meet the amended section 701 definition of "employee," and firms chartered in other nations are not excluded from the definition of "employer." To relieve foreign corporations of liability with respect to foreign work, therefore, Congress in 1991 had to specifically provide that the basic prohibitions of the Title do not apply "with respect to the foreign operations of an employer that is a foreign person."

If the employer is not shielded by a treaty authorizing discrimination in the selection of executives on the basis of citizenship, the more than half a million U.S.-based employees of foreign corporations may rely on Title VII and ADEA. But those statutes may not afford them protection against some of the more common forms of discrimination they may encounter. In the first place, although Title VII prohibits national origin discrimination, it does not reach discrimination based on alienage status (i.e., non-citizenship) or undocumented status, which are dealt with by the Immigration Reform and Control Act of 1986, Pub. L. No. 99–603, 100 Stat. 3359 ("IRCA"), and also likely by § 1981, or based ancestry (e.g., discrimination against Arabs or Jews), covered by § 1981. Title VII, therefore, will not avail a plaintiff whose employer, whether American or foreign, excludes applicants solely because they lack U.S. citizenship or belong to a distinct cultural subgroup. Further, although both Title VII and IRCA prohibit discrimination on the basis of national origin, evidence that the plaintiff's compatriots are as well as or better represented in such an employer's workforce than others can defeat a claim that a U.S. citizenship requirement is in fact a smokescreen for intentional discrimination based on national origin. But a neutral practice may have the effect of discriminating on the basis of national origin, and if that is the case, a plaintiff excluded as a result of that practice may be able to state a prima facie national origin claim notwithstanding the fair or favorable treatment of her group as a whole.

Since 1988, limited protection against discrimination in hiring because of alienage (i.e., citizenship status) is separately provided to lawfully admitted aliens, and a few others, by IRCA. But unlike the IRCA protection against national origin, which extends to "any individual," the protection against alienage discrimination applies only to a rather narrowly defined "protected individual" who is well on the way to achieving full U.S. citizenship or has been granted refugee or asylum status. 8 U.S.C.A. § 1324b(a)(1) (West 2010). Indeed, IRCA imposes fines and imprisonment on employers who knowingly hire or employ undocumented persons or fail to check their authorization to work—in other words, it requires employers to discriminate against those aliens. *Id.* § 1324a(f)(1).

A charge of discrimination under IRCA may be filed within 180 days after the occurrence of a violation before a U.S. Justice Department Office of Special Counsel for Immigration–Related Unfair Employment Practices. If an administrative law judge finds a violation after hearing, the employer may be ordered to hire the charging party with or without back pay, to pay attorney fees, and to pay civil penalties of amounts that vary with the number of persons discriminated against and the number of prior offenses.

The fact that an alien is neither lawfully admitted for permanent U.S. residence within the meaning of IRCA nor authorized by law to work does not deprive him of the capacity to sue and receive at least some remedies under Title VII for the kinds of discrimination that are prohibited by that statute. *Espinoza v. Farah Mfg Co.*, 414 U.S. 86 (1973). This follows not only from the fact that Title VII defines "employees" broadly as "individuals" employed by an employer, but also from a negative implication of its alien exemption clause, which precludes application of the statute to the employment of aliens outside the United States. The problem is that alien victims of the kinds of discrimination Title VII bans will often as a practical matter be ineligible for important Title VII remedies. If hire or reinstatement would require the employer to violate IRCA, Title VII's mixed-motive or after-acquired-evidence doctrines would probably preclude a reinstatement order. Although the issue is unsettled, see *Rivera v. NIBCO, Inc.*, 364 F.3d 1057 (9th Cir. 2004), a worker's undocumented status may also affect her eligibility for, or the appropriate amount of, back or front pay, since she may be "unavailable" for work after termination—either literally (e.g., out of the country) or legally, because of IRCA. A Fourth Circuit decision appears to go further, denying an undocumented alien working in violation of IRCA any claim under Title VII. *Egbuna v. Time–Life Libraries, Inc.*, 153 F.3d 184 (4th Cir. 1998) (en banc). The Equal Employment Opportunity Commission ("EEOC") takes the position that the plaintiff's undocumented status has no effect on the availability of injunctive relief or other more appropriate damages; precludes the ordinary presumption favoring reinstatement or instatement only if the worker is unable to satisfy IRCA's verification requirements within a reasonable period of time; and limits back pay only where the worker is unavailable in the sense of being out of the country. The Commission does recognize that the worker's unauthorized status may form the basis for limited remedies in a mixed motives or after-acquired evidence case. A claim alleging private employer alienage discrimination under 42 U.S.C.A. § 1981 did not offend IRCA, even though the plaintiff was an unauthorized alien, because the court did not deem his complaint to be on the ground of his unauthorized status. *Anderson v. Conboy*, 156 F.3d 167 (2d Cir. 1998).

Discrimination against aliens in general is not, absent adverse impact, treated as discrimination on the basis of any particular national origin, and is therefore not condemned by Title VII. But discrimination against U.S. citizens in favor of citizens of a particular nation does amount to prohibited national origin discrimination under Title VII as well as IRCA. Title VII protection from this "anti-American" discrimination based on national origin is limited, however, by treaty exemptions designed to give foreign companies operating in the United States a free hand in selecting their own citizens for executive positions. The U.S.–Japanese Treaty of Friendship, Commerce and Navigation, art. VIII, Apr. 2, 1953, 4 U.S.T. 2063, for example, authorizes "companies of either party," such as a Japanese-chartered employer, "to engage, within the territories of the other Party … executive personnel … of their choice." Companies of signatory countries are, despite these treaties, subject to liability, in their executive hiring and firing, for intentional discrimination based on national origin (but not citizenship), but they cannot be liable for a citizenship-preference practice that merely has a disproportionate adverse impact on a particular national origin.

(4) Purely or Partly Religious Employers: Coverage, Exemptions, Defenses

Religious organizations are also viewed as Title VII "employers," and as such may be subject to a specially defined duty not to discriminate on that ground. But they are specifically permitted to make certain employment decisions on the basis of religion. A welter of related and somewhat overlapping statutory and constitutional provisions afford different kinds of covered employers exemptions from or exceptions to liability for religious discrimination. In addition, the special prohibition on religious discrimination—subsuming the ordinary imperative not to discriminate and a duty to make "reasonable accommodation" to an employee's religious beliefs and practices—is subject to the general affirmative defense that permits an employer to discriminate under circumstances where the exclusion is a "bona fide occupational qualification." Title VII § 703 (West 2010).

i.   Overview: Discrimination Because of Religion

The section 702 exemption, strictly limited to pervasively religious institutions like churches, missions, and seminaries, declares Title VII inapplicable with respect to the employment "of individuals of a particular religion" in any of its activities, for any position. It does not exempt them from regulation for sex, race, national origin, or age discrimination. Section 702 has been upheld against the objection that it unconstitutionally "establishes" the institutions it protects, at least with respect to their nonprofitmaking activities. *Corporation of the Presiding Bishop v. Amos*, 483 U.S. 327 (1987).

Section 703(e)(2) excludes from the definition of "unlawful employment practice" the hiring of employees of a particular religion by educational institutions insufficiently religious to qualify for the section 702 exemption but that are (a) substantially owned, supported, controlled, or managed by a particular religion or (b) direct their curriculum "toward the propagation of" a particular religion.

If the ground alleged is sex, race, national origin, or age—where, that is, neither of the foregoing exemptions aids the employer—it may invoke the "ministerial exception," a Free

Exercise or Establishment Clause (excessive government entanglement) override of Title VII or ADEA regulation. This may succeed where the position (e.g., minister) or duties (e.g., teacher of theology, church music director) in question lie close to the religious core of the institution, or perhaps where the reason for discharge relates to malperformance of subsidiary religious duties. See *Werft v. Desert Sw. Annual Conference*, 377 F.3d 1099 (9th Cir. 2004); *Combs v. Central Tex. Annual Conference*, 173 F.3d 343 (5th Cir. 1999).

ii.   Prima Facie Prohibitions

If no statutory or constitutional exemption applies, one turns to the prima facie case. Section 703(a)(1), amplified by the section 701(j) definition of "religion," raises two questions:

(1) Has the employer drawn a distinction because of "religion"? And has it disparately treated the plaintiff "because of" religion, or rather imposed a neutral practice, not specifically targeted to religion, that has adverse impact on the plaintiff's particular religion? If the latter, the practice may be defended as justified by job relatedness and business necessity.

(2) Even if an employer has made no hostile discrimination, has it breached the separate section 701(j) duty to accommodate?

(a) "Reasonable accommodation" need not fully meet the needs of an employee's religious belief or practice, or be costless to the employee, and the employer need not accept the particular accommodation proposed by employee; and

(b) A reasonable accommodation works "undue hardship" and is thus not legally mandated if it requires an employer to incur more than de minimis cost.

So diluted, section 701(j) does not violate the Establishment Clause.

iii.   BFOQ Defense

In a refusal to hire case, if statutory exemptions and constitutional overrides fail, and the plaintiff establishes a prima facie case of disparate treatment because of religion, an employer still has the 'BFOQ'—"bona fide occupational qualification"—defense of section 703(e)(1). As restrictively construed by *International Union, UAW v. Johnson Controls, Inc.*, 499 U.S. 187 (1991), an employer must show that its religious exclusion relates to the "essence" of its business and that all or substantially all persons of the excluded faiths could not fulfill the requirements of the job in question.

(5) "PURELY" RELIGIOUS ORGANIZATION

Any pervasively "religious" employer—paradigmatically a church, mission, seminary, or one of their branches or subunits—is exempt by virtue of section 702(a) from liability for religious discrimination. This section exempts a "religious corporation, association, educational institution, or society" from Title VII "with respect to the employment of individuals of a particular religion to perform work connected with the carrying on" of any of the institution's "activities." But except for ministerial or quasi-ministerial positions, as discussed above, the exemption does not ban discrimination based on race, gender, or national origin.

For the most part, only churches or institutions owned or partly owned by them have qualified for the section 702 exemption. The determination whether an organization, including an educational institution, is eligible for its sweeping protection hinges on whether "the corporation's purpose and character are primarily religious." That question, in turn, is answered on a case-by-case basis, with the court weighing "[a]ll significant religious and secular characteristics." The section 702 exemption extends to any of the religious employer's activities, secular or sectarian, and applies regardless of the particular term and condition of employment involved. The exemption nevertheless survived a challenge as an unconstitutional establishment of religion in *Corporation of the Presiding Bishop v. Amos*, 483 U.S. 327 (1987).

(6) RELIGIOUSLY AFFILIATED EDUCATIONAL INSTITUTIONS

Because relatively few organizations are sufficiently religious to qualify for the broad exemption from Title VII afforded by section 702, Congress added a seemingly more limited exception from liability designed to benefit religiously affiliated schools.

Under section 703(e)(2) of Title VII, an educational institution not qualifying as sufficiently religious to be exempt under section 702(a), but which is substantially supported or directed by a particular religion, or has a religiously oriented curriculum, may "hire and employ" persons of the particular religion with which it is affiliated. Textually, therefore, it insulates schools that are sufficiently religious only from charges of religious discrimination related to hiring. In contrast, section 702(a), it will be remembered, provides that Title VII "shall not apply" to the more pervasively religious institutions it protects. Determining what schools qualify for even this limited protection is vexing. Section 703(e)(2) states that it is not an "unlawful employment practice" for an "educational institution or institution of learning to hire and employ employees of a particular religion" if that employer is "in whole or in substantial part, owned, supported, controlled, or managed by a particular religion" (hereinafter the "structure clause") or maintains a curriculum "directed toward the propagation of a particular religion" (the "curriculum clause"). Different circuits use different factors to determine whether an educational institution is dominantly religious under this definition. See *Killinger v. Samford Univ.*, 113 F.3d 196 (11th Cir. 1997).

The courts have consistently held that the section 703(e)(2) exception to the definition of an unlawful employment practice by a religiously affiliated school, like the section 702 exemption from Title VII for pervasively religious organizations, does not shield the defendant from Title VII liability when the institution discriminates against an employee or applicant (say, one who seeks a secular job like science teacher or custodian of a seminary or university) on some basis other than religion—sex, race, national origin, or retaliation. In such cases, the defendant may still occasionally succeed, however, if the position or duties involved are "ministerial."

ADEA has no express exemption for religious or religiously affiliated institutions, but because ADEA's substantive prohibitions are derived *in haec verba* from Title VII, courts have crafted an immunity from age discrimination liability of the same scope, and with the same limitations, for religious organizations that meet the section 702 (or, apparently, section 703(e)(2)) requirements.

(7) ALL EMPLOYERS, RELIGIOUS OR NOT: THE "BFOQ" AFFIRMATIVE DEFENSE

Under section 703(e)(1), any employer, even one wholly sectarian, may "hire and employ" (a labor organization may "admit or employ" in apprenticeship or retraining programs) on the basis of religion where religion is a "bona fide occupational qualification reasonably necessary to the normal operation" of the enterprise. The principal discussion of the 'BFOQ' defense, as it applies to express gender and national origin discrimination, is set forth immediately following. The discussion here will be confined to its role in defending against express discrimination based on religion.

Section 703(e)(1) has the same textual limitation to hiring as does Section 703(e)(2). Accordingly, the BFOQ affirmative defense protects employers from liability only for certain religiously discriminatory hiring decisions; it does not excuse discrimination concerning subsequent terms and conditions of employment like compensation, promotion, discipline, harassment, or discharge.

Moreover, the Supreme Court's decision in *International Union, UAW v. Johnson Controls*, 499 U.S. 187 (1991) confirms the narrowness of the BFOQ exception—in any context, i.e., gender or national origin as well as religion. The bare language of section 703(e)(1) would appear satisfied if an employer can show that a refusal to hire based on religion, sex, or national origin is reasonably necessary to the normal operation of the defendant's overall "enterprise." As a textual matter, that is, the employer need not show that the exclusion on those grounds is conducive to the sound performance of the particular plaintiff's job, only that it will further general business goals. Nor does the text of the BFOQ defense suggest that the discriminatory job qualification must relate to the heart of employer's business, only to its "normal operation." Yet the Court has concluded that to prevent the exception from virtually eliminating an applicant's protection against these forms of express discrimination, the employer must show that its discriminatory rule bears a "high correlation" to the plaintiff's ability to perform the job in question and relates to the "essence" or "central mission" of the employer's business. *Id.* at 201. Relying on *Johnson Controls*, an appellate court has denied the BFOQ defense to schools that insisted on hiring Protestant teachers to maintain a Protestant "presence" assertedly important to their general educational operations. *EEOC v. Kamehameha Sch./Bishop Estate*, 990 F.2d 458 (9th Cir. 1993).

b. *Title VII: The Basic Substantive Prohibitions*

Section 703(a)(1) declares it an "unlawful employment practice" for a covered employer "to fail or refuse to hire or to discharge any individual, or otherwise to discriminate against any individual with respect to his compensation, terms, conditions or privileges of employment, because of such individual's race, color, religion, sex, or national origin."

Section 703(a)(2) forbids limiting the employment "opportunities" of an applicant or incumbent employee on any of the same grounds. The controversies addressed by the case law have centered on two intertwined issues. First, what employer conduct or classifications correspond to the forbidden kinds of discrimination—what, in other words, constitutes discrimination on the grounds of "race, color, religion, sex or national origin"? The answers to these questions are not always self-evident. Discrimination based on alienage status, for example, is not tantamount to the prohibited discrimination based on national origin, even though a non-U.S. citizen would not have that status unless she or an ancestor recently arrived here from another nation. Whites may sue for race discrimination, as may blacks, based on the racial animus directed against them by other blacks.

The second pervasive issue concerns the nature and degree of the nexus that must exist between prohibited employer conduct and harm to a plaintiff's employment status. When, in other words, is adverse action taken by the employer "because of" prohibited discrimination? For example, the Supreme Court has treated as prohibited gender discrimination certain forms of employer speech and action characterized by sex stereotyping, but it has simultaneously demanded evidence that the employer actually relied on the stereotype as a factor in the challenged employment decision before that decision could constitute an unlawful employment practice under Title VII. *Price Waterhouse v. Hopkins*, 490 U.S. 228 (1989).

The courts have answered the statute's definitional silence on this causation or nexus question by developing different evidentiary allocations and burdens that are deemed equivalent to proof that adverse action was imposed "because of" an employer's reliance on a prohibited characteristic. These proof modes are discussed below.

(1) The Meaning of Discrimination Because of "Race," "Color," "National Origin," "Religion," and "Sex"

i. Race

For the most part, the Supreme Court has defined the concept of "race" in connection with actions under 42 U.S.C.A. § 1981 (West 2010), the 1866 statute that secures to all persons the same right to make and enforce contracts, including contracts of employment, as is enjoyed by white citizens. In one of those decisions, however, *McDonald v. Santa Fe Trail Transportation Co.*, 427 U.S. 273 (1976), the Court held that the Title VII prohibition on race discrimination is enforceable by whites as well as blacks. Whites have been granted standing to assert discrimination based on their association with or marriage to blacks, where the court is persuaded that a black plaintiff with those associations would not have endured similar treatment. But some circuits have required in cases alleging discrimination against whites evidence of "background circumstances" tending to prove that the defendant is the "unusual employer who discriminates against the majority." In a failure to promote situation, the white or male plaintiff can meet this burden by proving that the plaintiff's qualifications were superior to those of the successful minority applicant—a showing the Supreme Court has specifically ruled is not required in the ordinary Title VII case.

The EEOC and the courts apply the same "subjective" and "objective" prima facie elements and defenses developed in sexual harassment cases to assess claims of unlawful harassment based on race, religion, or national origin. The majority's recognition in *Faragher v. City of Boca Raton*, 524 U.S. 775 (1998), that the elements of actionable sexual harassment derive from earlier race and national origin decisions has also resulted in the use of the *Faragher* and *Burlington* standards to determine employer liability for racial or national origin harassment.

The race concept has been viewed even more broadly under § 1981. In *St. Francis College v. Al–Khazraji*, 481 U.S. 604 (1987), and *Shaare Tefila Congregation v. Cobb*, 481 U.S. 615 (1987), the Court held that the § 1981 ban on race discrimination could be enforced by Arabs and Jews, respectively, if they could prove adverse treatment on the basis of their ancestry. Observing that these holdings in effect mean that whites can maintain a viable § 1981 claim against other whites, a court has concluded that a black plaintiff may maintain a Title VII claim based on alleged race discrimination by a black supervisor. Subsequent lower court decisions extend § 1981 to provide a claim against discrimination on the ground of alienage or non-citizenship, and a few such decisions even reach national origin. Title VII has a distinct prohibition on discrimination because of "color" that has supported claims by lighter-or darker-skinned blacks based on discrimination by a black employer agent with skin of a different hue. There is authority permitting proof of discrimination on dual grounds, e.g., gender and race.

ii. National Origin, Including Accent Discrimination and Language Rules

Discrimination because of national origin presents special difficulties because it is relatively seldom that defendants refer explicitly to the particular country of origin of the plaintiff or his ancestors. An employer rule requiring citizenship as a precondition to hire is an example. Because citizenship as such is not a forbidden ground of discrimination, the rule might violate Title VII if but only if in operation it has disproportionate adverse impact on persons of an identifiable national origin. Similarly, ethnic slurs more commonly stain an individual's ancestry (e.g., slurs pertaining to Arabs, Jews, or persons hailing from Asia, Africa, Central or South America, Mexico, or Puerto Rico), another basis of discrimination not forbidden by Title VII. In addition, employer practices or rules based on language characteristics will usually also be neutral on their face. They therefore could violate Title VII only if applied in ways that are designed to injure or that have disproportionate adverse impact on persons of a particular national origin.

Two language problems of this kind have surfaced in the cases: discrimination based on foreign accent, and "speak-English-only" rules. Several circuit courts have considered discrimination because of accent, where the adverse employer action is typically meted out ad hoc, rather than pursuant to an across-the-board rule. Consequently, the decisions evaluate the evidence in these cases under the theory of individual disparate treatment, rather than disproportionate adverse impact. The leading case, *Fragante v. City & County of Honolulu*, 888 F.2d 591 (9th Cir. 1989), relied on an EEOC Guideline in assuming without deciding that proof of discrimination based on foreign accent establishes a prima facie case of discrimination based on national origin. But it upheld the employer's bona fide occupational qualification defense, writing that an adverse employment decision taken because of accent is lawful only when the accent "interferes materially with job performance." *Id.* at 596. Nevertheless, because accent and national origin "are obviously inextricably intertwined in many cases," the court cautioned that a "searching look" is demanded to ensure that employer assertions about a candidate's poor communications skills are not used as a cover or pretext for national origin discrimination. *Id.*

The Ninth Circuit rejected the EEOC Guideline in *Garcia v. Spun Steak Co.*, 998 F.2d 1480 (9th Cir. 1993). In *Spun Steak*, the court insisted that adverse impact must be proved and not merely presumed. But the scope of *Spun Steak* as applied to varying employer rules is uncertain. For example, there, the court found that the employer's English-only rule had no disproportionate adverse impact because the plaintiff, being bilingual, could readily comply without jeopardizing his employment. Further, the company's policy was justified as a business necessity because it facilitated worker safety on a production line. That defense might not be available where a similar rule is applied to office personnel or to off-duty inter-employee conversations.

iii.   Discrimination Based on Gender

Whereas the problem with national origin discrimination is that it is often not relied on expressly, the definitional problem with many permutations of sex discrimination frequently is that sex, while an explicit part of an employer's decision or rule, is not the sole factor. For example, the employer's rule in *Phillips v. Martin Marietta Corp.*, 400 U.S. 542 (1971), disqualified from employment women, though not men, with preschool-aged children. The rule, then, excluded only women, but not all women. The question was whether this was the kind of express discrimination on the basis of sex that would require the greatest level of employer justification. The Supreme Court found express discrimination, holding that the rule impermissibly created "one hiring policy for women and another for men." *Id.* at 544. It was no defense that the policy discriminated not because of sex alone but because of "sex-plus"—with the plus factor here being the early stages of motherhood.

Although Title VII does not expressly prohibit employers from using marital status to make employment distinctions, the logic of *Martin Marietta* and decisions of other federal courts and the EEOC demonstrate that such distinctions may constitute unlawful discrimination if sex is one of the factors the employer took into account when making such distinctions. For example, it is unlawful sex discrimination to reject applicants or fail to promote employees who are married women, but not married men. Similar reasoning underpins the Pregnancy Discrimination Act, Pub. L. No. 95–555, 92 Stat. 2076 (1978), which prohibits discrimination because of pregnancy or related medical conditions even though employer rules adversely affecting pregnant women do not affect other women.

Federal appellate courts have long held, with substantial unanimity, that discrimination solely based on the plaintiff's sexual orientation does not amount to gender discrimination prohibited by Title VII. These courts have relied heavily on the repeated failure in Congress of bills that would have prohibited sexual orientation discrimination. For these courts, unless an anti-homosexual policy is disparately enforced in favor of or against members of a particular gender, the employer rule is simply not on the basis of gender. Efforts to circumvent this barrier, either by proceeding on a disparate impact theory or by asserting that a campaign of anti-homosexual hostility amounted to unlawful environmental harassment based on gender, have also generally failed. For example, an anti-homosexual practice, gender-neutral on its face and neutrally applied, may nevertheless result in disproportionately greater exclusion of male homosexuals (as will be the case, if, for example, they are more readily identifiable) and might therefore be said to discriminate because of gender. But since the impetus for the discrimination is anti-homosexual rather than anti-male animus, the circuit opinions accordingly conclude that recognizing the impact theory would amount to an end-run around the Congressional purpose not to forbid discrimination based on sexual orientation. By contrast, disparate enforcement of an anti-homosexual policy in favor of or against members of a particular gender would presumably violate the statute. Despite the absence of national protection, numerous state and local laws provide protection from this type of employment discrimination.

Relying on *Price Waterhouse v. Hopkins*, 490 U.S. 228 (1989), however, several circuits have permitted plaintiffs to proceed where they alleged they were discriminated against because they failed to meet certain gender stereotypes. In *Price Waterhouse*, the Supreme Court held that a woman who was denied partnership in an accounting firm because she did not match a sex stereotype—her appearance and behavior were considered too masculine—had an actionable claim under Title VII. In *Nichols v. Azteca Restaurant Enterprises*, 256 F.3d 864 (9th Cir. 2001), the Ninth Circuit applied the same principle in holding that a male employee was entitled to redress under Title VII because his employer (through its employees) discriminated against him for not comporting with the employer's stereotypical notion of how a man should behave. Transsexuals sometimes, see *Smith v. City of Salem*, 378 F.3d 566 (6th Cir. 2004), but not always, see *Vickers v. Fairfield Med. Ctr.*, 453 F.3d 757 (6th Cir. 2006), can prove that they were adversely treated because of an appearance or mannerisms atypical of other members of their gender, which is actionable, rather than because of practices attributed to them that are characteristic of a same-sex sexual orientation, which is not.

Rules prohibiting the employment of spouses in the same office, department, or plant of one company have been viewed as neutral on their face, actionable only if they are disparately enforced against members of a particular gender or if they have the statistical effect of disproportionately adversely impacting wives or husbands. A no-dating rule is likewise neutral on its face and could violate Title VII only if disparately enforced or disproportionately impacting.

Grooming and dress code regulations that on their face pertain only to one gender—men must have short hair, for example—have nevertheless been judicially assessed as neutral rather than as a form of express disparate treatment. See *Willingham v. Macon Tel. Publ'g Co.*, 507 F.2d 1084 (5th Cir. 1975) (en banc).

The same approach has disadvantaged women with respect to regulations governing attire and grooming. Even when the employer's rule specifically imposes more demanding clothing and coiffure requirements on one gender than the other, the tendency has been for the courts to assert that the employer has one omnibus grooming regime that naturally has distinctive variations to account for gender differences. In a variation on this theme, courts will observe that the employer has some grooming standard for each gender and will treat that standard as the common, neutral employer practice. The fact that the employer imposes different, or more stringent, or differentially applied dress or grooming requirements on its employees of different genders is usually just ignored or treated as de minimis unless the plaintiff can prove that the policy imposed an "unequal burden" of compliance on his or her gender. *Jespersen v. Harrah's Operating Co.*, 444 F.3d 1104 (9th Cir. 2006) (en banc). Plaintiffs have also been compelled to litigate no-beard rules within the framework of disproportionate adverse impact rather than disparate treatment. The consequence of these decisions is that employers are far more easily able to justify such rules as a matter of business necessity or job relatedness than they would be if the rules were classified as discriminating facially on the basis of gender.

The general judicial rejection of women's gender discrimination complaints about harsher grooming or clothing requirements represents an exception to the Supreme Court's general recognition that employer practices driven by sex stereotyping unlawfully discriminate because of gender.

There are a number of other frequently litigated issues that wrestle with the question when grounds of discrimination that correlate differentially or exclusively with one gender amount to the prohibited discrimination "because of sex." Most of these are specially treated by Title VII or related statutes and are considered below.

iv. Sexual Harassment

a. Scope and Requirements

Early decisions doubted whether a supervisor's imposition of adverse terms and conditions of employment on a subordinate employee for resisting the superior's sexual advances constituted discrimination "because of sex" even where the superior and subordinate were of different genders. After all, these cases reasoned, the selection of a "target" would usually not be based on the factor of gender alone, except perhaps if the superior targeted all subordinate employees of the opposite gender. That is, there would usually be a "plus" factor in the superior employee's calculus, usually the target's relative attractiveness or vulnerability to the superior. Subsequently, however, the Supreme Court has appeared to assume that, as in *Martin Marietta*, the target's gender need not be the sole motivating factor in the superior's advance in order for the subsequent reprisal to be actionable. The court held in *Meritor Savings Bank, FSB v. Vinson*, 477 U.S. 57 (1986), that it is sufficient if gender is a "but-for" cause of the advance. This of course would be the case in the most commonly charged sexual harassment scenario, an advance by a heterosexual directed toward a person of the opposite gender.

Nevertheless, the requirement that the discrimination be based on and directed against a particular gender, and not merely against sexual behavior attributable to persons of either gender, has some continuing significance in the law governing harassment. It undercuts claims based on anti-homosexual harassment unless the discrimination is limited to homosexuals of one gender (e.g., lesbians), or there is evidence that homosexuality by an employee of a different gender would be tolerated. It apparently also exempts from Title VII scrutiny sexual advances or reprisals made by a bisexual supervisor, who by hypothesis would not usually be selecting a target because of the target's particular gender. Yet claims have been upheld based on non-sexually-oriented "equal opportunity harassment" of both men and women where the evidence supports the conclusion that the harasser would not have sought to demean either victim except for their respective genders. By the same token, where a male supervisor's nonsexual but gender-based harassing conduct is in fact directed only against women, it is no defense to conjecture that men might find the supervisor's conduct equally offensive.

Same-sex harassment is actionable when the evidence shows that a male harasses another male (or a female harasses another female) not because of the harassee's sexual orientation, but because of the harassee's gender. As the EEOC's Compliance Manual, § 615.2(b)(3) (2006), asserts, "the crucial inquiry is whether the harasser treats ... members of one sex differently from members of the other sex." A unanimous Supreme Court endorsed this reasoning in *Oncale v. Sundowner Offshore Services, Inc.*, 523 U.S. 75 (1998). The victim's gender must be a "but-for" factor in the harassment. Thus, workplace harassment does not automatically constitute sex discrimination "merely because the words used have sexual content or connotations." *Id.* 80. at This evidentiary minimum is exactly, and only, what the Court in *Meritor* required in the classic case of opposite gender heterosexual harassment. Thus, conduct motivated by the harasser's homosexual interest in the harassee (rather than by the plaintiff-harassee's own sexual orientation) falls on the actionable side of the line because such conduct would not occur unless the victim were of a particular gender. By contrast, same-sex harassment inspired by the particular victim's prudishness, shyness, or apparent relative vulnerability to sexually-tinged teasing or taunting would generally not be actionable if the particular harasser would for the same reasons harass members of the other gender, too.

The Court in *Oncale* identified several ways that a same-sex harassee can prove that he was targeted "because of" his gender. The most direct way, of course, is to prove that men and women were treated differently. In single-gender workplaces, like the offshore drilling platform in *Oncale*, this type of evidence is impossible to produce. Alternatively, a plaintiff can proffer credible evidence that the harasser is gay or lesbian; courts can reasonably assume that such a harasser would not sexually harass members of the other sex. A third approach, useful in cases factually similar to *Oncale*, is to prove that the harassee was harassed "in such sex-specific and derogatory terms" as to make it clear that the harasser is motivated by a general animus toward persons of plaintiff's gender. *Id.* at 80. Sometimes, a combination of two or more approaches is necessary to survive a summary judgment motion. It should be noted that the third approach requires the plaintiff to adduce evidence of the specific nature of the allegedly derogatory comments and to carefully avoid any admission that the harassment was on the basis of sexual orientation. *Rene v. MGM Grand Hotel, Inc.*, 305 F.3d 1061 (9th Cir. 2002). Same-race racial harassment has also been found to be actionable after *Oncale*. *Ross v. Douglas Cnty.*, 234 F.3d 391 (8th Cir. 2000).

The "because of sex" requirement will also usually defeat the typical claim of sexual favoritism, in which a plaintiff denied a job or benefit alleges that another employee was hired or promoted because he or she participated in a consensual romantic relationship with a supervisory or managerial agent of the employer. In that situation, both women and men are disadvantaged for a reason other than, or in addition to, their gender, viz., they were not the object of the agent's sexual interest. Thus, in these settings, the "gender-plus" liability avoidance persists, despite the Supreme Court's repudiation of it in *Phillips* and *Meritor*. If, however, an employee is coerced into sexual participation as a condition of receiving a job benefit, other employees of the same gender could prevail if they could prove that sexual favors were demanded generally as the "quid pro quo" for advancement.

Ultimately, the judicial rationale for relieving employers of liability based on sexual orientation and sexual favoritism discrimination is extra-textual. It rests instead on a judicial perception about the underlying or motivating purposes of Title VII: to free applicants and employees from the imposition of adverse (thus excluding sexual favoritism discrimination) working conditions on the basis of the very few characteristics protected by Title VII (thus excluding sexual orientation discrimination).

Courts have also been cautious before deciding that sexual harassment constitutes unlawful gender discrimination because in some cases, the alleged harasser's proposition or advance may have been invited or received as welcome. Any sexual harassment plaintiff must therefore show that she or he subjectively perceived a proposition or advance as "unwelcome." This requires first a showing that there was in fact a sexual advance. An amendment to the Federal Rules of Evidence, applicable to trials commencing on or after December 1, 1994, eases the plaintiff's proof on this issue in those harassment cases that are "predicated on a party's [i.e., an alleged employer agent's] alleged commission of conduct constituting an offense of sexual assault." In such cases, Rule 415 provides that "evidence of that party's commission of another offense or offenses of sexual assault . . . is admissible and may be considered. . . ." Textually, Rule 415 overrides other rules that ordinarily might result in the exclusion of such evidence—for example, where the prejudicial effect of the evidence outweighs its probative value, or where the evidence is introduced in the form of hearsay (not eligible for one of the usual hearsay exceptions), or where it is admissible only in the form of reputation or opinion testimony.

If there was an advance, its welcomeness *vel non* is determined by a subjective test. Until recently, sufficient evidence of the plaintiff's off-hours conduct and attitudes has sufficed to refute her assertion that workplace harassment was unwelcome. An employer may attempt to overcome a showing that an actionable level of interference was unwelcome with evidence about the plaintiff's past sexual conduct, "fantasies," or failure to object to sexual advances. But recent decisions caution against equating participation in off-duty sex-related activities with acquiescence to sexual advances on the job. For example, evidence that the plaintiff had posed nude for a magazine did not negate her evidence that she did not welcome the employer's sexual advances in the workplace. Indeed even a plaintiff's "vulgar and unladylike" language and behavior on the job did not negate her showing that she did not welcome the crude sexual epithets, sexually insulting messages, and offensive demonstrative conduct (including urination and self-exposure) directed at her by her male co-workers. On this issue it was important to the court that the plaintiff plainly resented their conduct and complained of it repeatedly to her supervisor.

Rule 412(b)(2), applicable to trials commencing after December 1, 1994, may rule out all but the most probative evidence of the plaintiff's prior sexual behavior. Rule 412 provides that in a civil action, "evidence offered to prove the sexual behavior or sexual predisposition of any alleged victim is admissible if ... its probative value substantially outweighs the danger of harm to any victim and of unfair prejudice to any party." The Rule 412 amendment tilts the scales against admissibility in three respects, as compared to standard probative value-prejudicial impact balancing under Rule 403. First, it reverses the presumptive weighting, by requiring the proponent to justify admissibility rather than requiring the opponent to justify exclusion. Second, the prerequisites for admissibility are more stringent, because the value of the proffered evidence must "substantially" outweigh the specified dangers. Third, harm to the victim must be explicitly placed on the exclusion side of the balance, in addition to party prejudice.

Accordingly, evidence of consensual sexual conduct in a plaintiff's prior or contemporaneous private life will seldom be admissible. The amendment even casts doubt on the likely admissibility of evidence of the plaintiff's response to or initiation of sexual jokes, sexually-tinged language, or erotic pictorial displays in the workplace, which the Rule treats as tangential to her receptivity to an unconsented touching or sexual proposition. Indeed, it may lead even to the exclusion of evidence of the plaintiff's actual consensual sexual relationships with co-employees, including even the alleged harasser.

   b. "Quid Pro Quo" or "Tangible Terms" Harassment

Title VII is violated when submission to an employer's sexual demands is expressly made the "quid pro quo" of gaining a job, promotion, continued employment, pay increase, work assignment, or other economic job benefit, or of avoiding demotion, diminished compensation, a disadvantageous transfer, or formal discipline or discharge. The Court, in *Burlington Industries v. Ellerth*, 524 U.S. 742, 753–54 (1998), re-labeling "quid pro quo" as "tangible terms" harassment, stated that a tangible employment action "constitutes a significant change in employment status, such as hiring, firing, failing to promote, reassignment with significantly different responsibilities, or a decision causing a significant change in benefits." The EEOC's Guidelines assert that quid pro quo harassment also occurs when submission to unwelcome sexual advances or conduct is "implicitly" made a term of condition of the target's employment and made the basis for an employment decision. 29 C.F.R. § 1604.11(a) (2010). Relying on the Guidelines, a circuit opinion has held that "quid pro quo sexual harassment occurs whenever an individual explicitly or implicitly conditions a job, a job benefit, or the absence of a job detriment, upon an employee's acceptance of sexual conduct." *Nichols v. Frank*, 42 F.3d 503, 511 (9th Cir. 1994). However, a victim need not provide evidence of a direct and express sexual demand to make a claim under the "tangible employment action" analysis. "[A] supervisor may simply intimate that a subordinate's career prospects will suffer if she does not submit to his advances, with the hope of concealing his harassment if his statements are repeated to a third party." *Frederick v. Sprint/United Mgmt.*, 246 F.3d 1305, 1312 (11th Cir. 2001).

Where a harassing superior officer of the employer did not carry out threats to adversely alter the plaintiff's tangible terms of employment because of her refusal to submit to a sexual proposition or demand, the Supreme Court and the circuit courts have treated the discrimination as an instance of hostile work environment rather than "tangible terms" harassment, limiting the latter classification to situations in which the threat is consummated. This suggests that the Court might analyze scenarios where the target submits to such a proposition or demand as hostile environment harassment, unless perhaps the employer agent does adversely alter the target's terms of employment despite her submission.

In sum, the "quid pro quo" or "tangible terms" sexual harassment plaintiff must prove that (1) he or she encountered verbal, visual, or physical propositions or advances of a sexual nature; (2) the harassment was based on her or his gender, and not, for example, sexual orientation; (3) he or she experienced the propositions or advances as subjectively unwelcome; and (4) the harassment was perpetrated by a supervisor, manager, or other high-ranking agent of the employer who had the authority to and did in fact give the plaintiff a tangible employment benefit for submitting, or imposed a tangible detriment for resisting, the proposition or advance.

Since *Burlington*, one appellate decision has held that merely assigning extra work to the plaintiff was not sufficiently "tangible" to impute automatic, vicarious liability to an employer. *Reinhold v. Virginia*, 151 F.3d 172 (4th Cir. 1998). But another has held that forcing the plaintiff to give up her office and her secretary was a tangible adverse action. *Durham Life Ins. Co. v. Evans*, 166 F.3d 139 (3d Cir. 1999). In most cases, but not always, "a tangible employment action ... inflicts direct economic harm." *Burlington*, 524 U.S. at 762.

Where harassment is treated as tangible, the available remedies include back pay representing the economic value of a lost job or promotion; injunctive relief directing the award of any lost position; emotional distress and other compensatory damages; for a willful or reckless violation, punitive damages (with the combined total of any compensatory and punitive damages capped at $50,000 to $300,000 depending on the number of persons employed by the defendant); and attorney's fees and costs.

c. Employer Liability for Quid Pro Quo (Tangible Terms) Discrimination

Because only supervisors or managers can alter such tangible terms of employment, and because they are clothed by the employer with at least apparent authority to do so, a finding of quid pro quo harassment results, as with most other violations of Title VII, in automatic or "strict" liability of the employer. Dictum in companion cases decided by the Supreme Court in June 1998 confirms that the employer is not only vicariously but strictly or "automatically" liable without more for tangible terms harassment by a supervisor or other employer agent who has the means to and does in fact alter the plaintiff's tangible terms and conditions of employment. Strict liability means that if the plaintiff demonstrates that her obtaining a tangible job benefit or avoiding a tangible job detriment turned on her compliance or noncompliance with an unwelcome sexual advance, and the employer agent carried out such a promise or threat, the employer, even if it was unaware of the harassment, will have no affirmative defense. In a "tangible terms" case, the Court reasons, "there is assurance the injury could not have been inflicted absent the agency relation" between the supervisor and a defendant employer. *Burlington*, 524 U.S. at 761–62.

But evidence of an adequate anti-harassment policy and prompt and effective remedial action may be admissible even in tangible benefit cases on the issue of punitive damages. Under 42 U.S.C.A. § 1981a(b)(1) (West 2010) and the Supreme Court's decision in *Kolstad v. American Dental Ass'n*, 527 U.S. 526 (1999), a party may recover punitive damages if his employer engaged in intentional discrimination "with malice or with reckless indifference to the federally protected rights of an aggrieved individual." The terms "malice" and "reckless indifference" refer to the employer's knowledge that it may be violating federal law, not its awareness that it is engaging in discrimination. Thus, the employer must perceive some risk that its actions violate federal law in order to be liable for punitive damages. In a case involving vicarious liability, the plaintiff must also establish a basis for imputing liability to the employer by showing that the employee who discriminated against him was a manager acting within the scope of his employment. An employer may escape punitive damages liability for its manager's acts, however, if it can demonstrate a good faith attempt to establish and enforce an antidiscrimination policy. According to *Kolstad*, "an employer may not be vicariously liable [for punitive damages] for the discriminatory employment decisions of managerial agents where these decisions are contrary to the employer's 'good-faith efforts to comply with Title VII.'" 527 U.S. at 545. Such good-faith efforts, if proven, demonstrate that the employer itself did not act in reckless disregard of federally protected rights, thus making it inappropriate to punish the employer for its manager's contravention of its established policies.

d.   "Hostile Environment" Discrimination

Suppose the victim is subjected to worsened working conditions or other "environmental" harassment that affects only intangible aspects of the job. Until Title VII was amended by the Civil Rights Act of 1991, a plaintiff who could prove only an abusive or hostile work environment, without tangible detriment to her employment status, could recover no monetary relief. There was thus little incentive to sue under Title VII for environmental sexual harassment, unaccompanied by termination, demotion, or other adverse action resulting in a reduction or loss of pay or benefits. But Section 102 of the Civil Rights Act of 1991 authorized compensatory and, if appropriate, punitive damages for all intentional forms of unlawful discrimination, including harassment. (Punitive damages are not available against government employers.) These damages are capped in amounts that vary with the number of employees employed by the defendant.

In *Meritor* and *Oncale*, the Supreme Court reaffirmed its traditional broad interpretation of covered "terms and conditions of employment," holding that harassment is actionable, even if it does not affect a tangible term of employment, provided it is sufficiently severe or pervasive to create a hostile or abusive working environment. The "hostile environment" label defines all actionable sexual harassment claims other than "tangible terms." Thus, it includes situations in which the harasser is (a) a coworker, customer, or subordinate without authority to reward or punish with tangible job benefits or detriments; (b) a supervisor whose conduct consists of unwanted verbal or physical sexually-oriented advances (or of speech or conduct demeaning to the abilities or status of women), unaccompanied by a tangible job detriment, as in *Faragher*; or (c) a supervisor who threatens but does not fulfill a threat respecting the target's tangible terms of employment, as in *Burlington*. The Court explains that labeling a harasser's conduct as "hostile environment" rather than "tangible terms" means that the plaintiff will have to show more aggravated or persistent conduct to prove sex discrimination violating Title VII, but does not by itself control whether the employer is liable for that conduct.

The "hostile environment" sexual harassment plaintiff must prove that (1) she or he encountered verbal, visual, or physical propositions, advances, insults, or invasions of person; (2) those propositions or insults were based on her or his gender, as distinct from, for example, her or his sexual orientation; (3) he or she experienced the alleged harasser's conduct as subjectively unwelcome; (4) the harassment was of sufficient nature and magnitude (e.g., on one hand, a one-time flagrant physical assault or intimate touching, or, on the other, ongoing, relatively frequent or continual physical or verbal propositions, advances, or insults) to have created an objectively intimidating, hostile, offensive, or abusive work environment of a kind that would have unreasonably interfered with the work performance, working conditions, or general well-being of a reasonable person in her position; and (5) the harassment was perpetrated either by a supervisor, manager, or high-ranking agent of the employer, or by a coworker, subordinate, customer, or other business invitee in circumstances that fasten liability on the employer under modified principles of agency law.

The plaintiff's most formidable obstacle here is usually establishing the objectively hostile or abusive work environment, element (4). Whether conduct reaches a level of unreasonable interference with the employee's ability to work, or creates a sufficiently intimidating work environment, "should be evaluated from the objective standpoint of a 'reasonable person.'" Thus a "normal" level of workplace obscenity, isolated sexual suggestiveness or propositions, or even some single instances of unwelcome touching may not amount to unreasonable interference. And although the terminology "sexual harassment" implies that the harassment must be sexual in nature, the Court in *Oncale* explained that the "harassing conduct need not be motivated by sexual desire to support an inference of discrimination on the basis of sex." 523 U.S. at 80.

The circuit courts are still sorting out whether the "person" from whose standpoint reasonableness should be assessed is the genderless prototype of torts litigation (the "reasonable man") or a reasonable victim—usually, in this context, a woman. The EEOC blurs this division in its Policy Guidance, advocating a "reasonable person" standard but adding that in applying that standard the factfinder "should consider the victim's perspective and not stereotyped notions of acceptable behavior." The Supreme Court in *Harris v. Forklift Systems*, 510 U.S. 17, 21 (1993) described the required environment as one "that a reasonable person would find hostile or abusive...." Subsequently, in *Oncale*, the Court characterized that requirement as meaning "that the objective severity of harassment should be judged from the perspective of a reasonable person in the plaintiff's position, considering 'all the circumstances.'" 523 U.S. at 81. Neither of these statements unequivocally indicates that the "position" or "circumstances" of the plaintiff that may permissibly be considered include his or her race or gender, although one circuit so concludes.

The Supreme Court has upheld a "hostile environment" claim when workplace intimidation, ridicule, and insult are "sufficiently severe or pervasive to alter the conditions of the victim's environment and create an abusive working environment." *Harris*, 510 U.S. at 21. The plaintiff suffered a series of gender-related insults and unwanted sexual innuendos. Because in totality this conduct may have been sufficient to create an abusive work environment from the standpoint of a hypothetical reasonable person, the Court held that the plaintiff was not required to show that it seriously affected her psychological well-being. The Court located the required level of injury somewhere "between making actionable any conduct that is merely offensive and requiring the conduct to cause a tangible psychological injury." *Id.* Psychological harm is just another, nonessential factor relevant to the issue of abusiveness. A plaintiff can meet the *Harris* threshold without showing that the harassment affected her psychologically, diminished her work performance, or caused her to quit or even want to quit her job.

Justice O'Connor's opinion for the *Harris* majority emphasizes that when the defendant's conduct consists entirely of epithets or sexual innuendo, those must be sufficiently severe or pervasive "to create an objectively hostile or abusive work environment," one that a "reasonable person would find hostile or abusive." *Id.* (In addition, the victim must "subjectively perceive the environment to be abusive." *Id.*) The opinion does little more than identify a number of unweighted, non-exhaustive factors relevant to the objective question of an "abusive" or "hostile" work environment: the nature of the discriminatory conduct, i.e., whether it is merely offensive or also physically threatening or humiliating; the conduct's frequency and severity; and whether it unreasonably interfered with the plaintiff's work performance. None of these is identified as indispensable or even preeminent, and this leads the EEOC to conclude that none is.

Justice Ginsburg, concurring, opined that the inquiry should "center, dominantly, on whether the discriminatory conduct has interfered with the plaintiff's work performance." *Id.* at 25 (Ginsburg, J., concurring). For her, this would mean that the plaintiff need show only that the defendant's conduct made it more difficult for her to do her job, and not that the plaintiff's productivity actually declined. Several court of appeals decisions appear to hold just that: A supervisor's sexual innuendo and banter was actionable because it was unwelcome and made it more difficult for plaintiff to do her job, even though it was not of sufficient severity to prevent her from timely meeting her work obligations. But the *Harris* majority did not hold that a showing that the plaintiff's job has been made more difficult suffices. On the other hand, interference with the plaintiff's work performance is not essential to the required demonstration of hostility or abusiveness. It is enough if the offensive conduct is shown, through the totality of the circumstances, to create, cumulatively or in the aggregate, an abusive work environment, or even just that it adversely affected plaintiff's daily working conditions.

Because no bright line separates merely vulgar banter (usually lawful) from a consistently hostile or severely abusive environment (usually unlawful), some circuits confide the pervasiveness and severity questions to a jury, so long as the district judge is satisfied that the harasser's comments or conducts were "because of sex." Others, however, consider actionable harassment a question of law and accordingly reserve decision on the sufficiency of severity and pervasiveness for the district courts or for themselves. The standards for ruling on the employer's motion for summary judgment are key. In *Reeves v. C.H. Robinson Worldwide, Inc.*, 594 F.3d 798 (11th Cir. 2010) (en banc), the Eleventh Circuit repeated and applied the Supreme Court's directive that determining whether the *Harris* "sufficiently pervasive" line has been crossed (in cases where the harassment is not "severe") must be judged cumulatively, from all the evidence, and take into account the totality of the circumstances. The court also ruled that it is no defense that the work environment may have been hostile to members of plaintiff's group before her arrival, and that discriminatory conduct can be actionable even though it is not aimed directly at the plaintiff herself, but rather at other members of her group.

Where environmental harassment is severe and obvious, as with intensive physical sexual abuse, assault, or rape, the limitations period begins to run immediately. But where such conduct is so severe as to disable a plaintiff from taking the steps necessary to prosecute a claim, equitable tolling may extend the duration of the period.

e. Employer Liability for Prohibited Hostile Environment Harassment by Supervisors and Coworkers

The plaintiff will ordinarily receive no remedy for sexually harassing conduct of the "hostile environment type" unless the employer as an entity is liable for that conduct. This is because the federal appellate circuits addressing the question have held that supervisors, managers, and most high officials of a covered "employer" cannot be held individually liable, even though the statute defines a covered "employer" to include "any agent of" that employer. So the requirements of employer liability for environmental harassment are critical.

While recognizing that a supervisor's sexually harassing conduct is probably a "frolic and detour" outside the scope of his authority, the Supreme Court has nevertheless held that an employer "is subject to vicarious liability to a victimized employee for an actionable hostile environment created by a supervisor with immediate (or successively higher) authority over the employee." *Faragher*, 524 U.S. at 807. As observed above, where the supervisor's harassment culminates in a tangible employment detriment to the victim, employer liability is not only vicarious but strict. Thus, there is no employer defense where actionable harassment of the tangible type results directly in an actual or even constructive discharge. *Pennsylvania State Police v. Suders*, 542 U.S. 129 (2004). But where the supervisor does not impose a tangible employment detriment for non-submission to a sexual demand—that is, in an "intangible" or "hostile environment" case—the employer may avoid liability if by a preponderance of the evidence it carries both elements of the following affirmative defense: "(a) that the employer exercised reasonable care to prevent and correct promptly any sexually harassing behavior, and (b) that the plaintiff employee unreasonably failed to take advantage of any corrective opportunities provided by the employer or to avoid harm otherwise." *Faragher*, 524 U.S. at 807; see *Burlington*, 524 U.S. at 762–63.

This test expands employer liability for unlawful hostile environment harassment by supervisors or other high officials. Applied literally, an employer avoids liability for otherwise actionable supervisory harassment only when it exercised reasonable care to "prevent" and "correct" unlawful environmental harassment and when the plaintiff unreasonably failed to use available employer-provided channels of complaint or other remedies. To show that it took "reasonable care to prevent" under prong (a) and to meet prong (b)—that the plaintiff "unreasonably" failed to utilize corrective opportunities—the employer must typically prove that it had in place a policy that specifically condemned sexual harassment and that it maintained an internal effective complaints procedure with reasonable reporting procedures, including a mechanism that assured victims a means of bypassing the alleged harasser to register a complaint, and that was widely disseminated among employees, and adequately enforced (with appropriate training of managers) in a climate that did not discourage complaints. But because alleged victims will usually take advantage of such policies and procedures, the defense would frequently founder on this second prong.

Unreasonable failure to invoke the employer's procedures has been widely found where plaintiffs waited to report the harassment or failed to report ongoing harassment altogether because they fear retaliation or were uncertain allegations would be held confidential, especially where employers' anti-harassment policies contain express anti-retaliation provisions. Indeed, employers may be at risk in honoring complainants' requests for strict confidentiality, since doing so impedes full investigation, which in turn may prevent them from taking the prompt and appropriate corrective action required by *Burlington* and *Faragher* to satisfy the affirmative defense. *Gallagher v. Delaney*, 139 F.3d 338 (2d Cir. 1998). It has even been held that an employee cannot maintain a work environment claim if she coupled an internal complaint with a request for confidentiality, at least absent evidence of the kind of egregious harassment that would predictably lead to serious physical or psychological harm if the employer does not act.

Torres v. Pisano, 116 F.3d 625 (2d Cir. 1997). And the employer will be able to show plaintiff's noncompliance under prong (b) if her complaint, although timely, does not provide notice that the agent's offensive conduct was of a sexual or gender-based nature.

But there may be considerably more flexibility as to when the employee must complain where harassment has been extreme. In the statute of limitations context, equitable tolling may extend the time in which plaintiff may comply with prerequisites to suit where the harassment is so severe as to be disabling. This concept might easily be transplanted to enable a plaintiff to resist the employer's evidence that she unreasonably failed timely to invoke an available internal complaints procedure.

While a literal application of the two-pronged defense often prevents even explicit, fair, and fairly enforced internal grievance procedures from avoiding liability altogether, employers still have an incentive to adopt them. Such procedures will encourage internal complaints, thereby enhancing the employer's ability to take prompt corrective action that will limit its exposure for emotional distress, punitive damages, and attorney fees. And a complete avoidance of liability for supervisory environmental harassment is still possible, even when the plaintiff invokes a complaints procedure and a court applies the literal reading of the compound affirmative defense, for the plaintiff must still carry her prima facie burden of showing a sufficiently severe or hostile environment. The Court hinted in *Faragher* itself that it intended to continue to insist on palpable harm to the plaintiff's work environment, observing that the *Harris* standards for judging actionable interference "are sufficiently demanding to ensure that Title VII does not become a 'general civility code.'" 524 U.S. at 788.

In dictum in *Faragher*, the Court confirmed the "negligence" standard widely used by most circuit courts and EEOC to determine employer liability for actionable environmental harassment by a plaintiff's co-worker (or subordinate or customer). This negligence standard has been carried forward in post-*Burlington/Faragher* circuit decisions. Because a coworker, subordinate, or customer cannot independently adversely alter the plaintiff's tangible terms of employment, the underlying violation here is of the "hostile environment" rather than "tangible terms" variety. It is even clearer with coworker, as with supervisory environmental harassment, that the harasser is not acting on behalf of the employer or carrying out its business. In those cases, therefore, the circuit courts, with the Supreme Court's apparent approval, are unanimous that the employer will be liable only if it actually knew or should have known of the coworker's (or subordinate's, customer's, or supplier's) unlawful harassment and failed to take prompt and effective corrective action. In coworker or subordinate cases, then, the employer can assure its non-liability by its own unilateral action.

The liability of the defendant employer, then, in hostile work environment cases, will often turn on whether the harasser is a supervisor or a coworker. If the harasser is a coworker, the plaintiff bears the burden of proving that the employer was negligent, i.e., that the employer knew or should have known of the harassment and despite that knowledge failed to take prompt and appropriate corrective action. But if the harasser is a supervisor, the burden is on the defendant to establish the two-pronged *Burlington/Faragher* affirmative defense. Of course, summary judgment or judgment as a matter of law is uncommon when the moving party has the burden at trial on the targeted issue, as would the defendant-employer, in a case where the harasser is a supervisor, on the *Burlington/Faragher* affirmative defense.

Although the circuits have articulated various formulations for identifying supervisory status, a central question is whether the harasser had the authority to affect the terms and conditions of the harassee's work environment. The Tenth Circuit has limited the term "supervisor" to those persons having actual and immediate authority over the plaintiff. In *Harrison v. Eddy Potash, Inc.*, 158 F.3d 1371 (10th Cir. 1998), the court rejected both an "alter ego" and apparent authority jury instruction requested by the plaintiff. Relying on *Burlington*, the court stated that employer liability cannot be grounded on a theory that a supervisor was an alter ego of the employer. The court further stated that to be a supervisor, the person must have actual authority; the false impression of authority is not sufficient. Only the misuse of actual authority can create employer liability.

Resolving a circuit split, the Supreme Court has held that an employer may ordinarily assert the *Burlington/Faragher* affirmative defense when a supervisor's hostile and abusive environmental harassment causes a constructive discharge of the plaintiff. The defense would be precluded only if, as a part of or following that harassment, the constructive discharge were precipitated by an official company act that imposed a tangible detriment on the plaintiff, such as a severe demotion, extreme pay decrease, or humiliating transfer. The Court stressed, however, that as with other uses of the defense, the employer must establish by a preponderance of the evidence both that it exercised reasonable care to prevent and promptly correct the harassing behavior and that the plaintiff unreasonably failed to take advantage of employer-provided preventive or corrective opportunities or failed to mitigate harm. *Suders*, 542 U.S. 129, 142–52.

Employers have asserted rights to indemnity or contribution for supervisory harassment that has resulted in employer liability. But the Supreme Court has held that no such right is provided by Title VII itself or at common law. Claims by supervisors disciplined for violating their employer's anti-sexual harassment policy have generally not fared well, most courts reasoning that the employer must enjoy reasonable latitude to conduct a vigorous internal examination without risking additional charges of sexual harassment. Thus, even a hostile, unprofessional, and abusive employer investigation of sexual harassment charges ultimately determined to be unfounded could not support a separate sexual harassment claim by the exonerated suspect.

Unsuccessful sexual harassment charges have also spawned defamation suits by alleged harassers, both against accusers and employers who placed stock in the charges and took unilateral corrective action. These have been defeated by employers' assertions of a conditional privilege that arises where the recipient of an alleged defamatory statement has an important interest that is advanced by frank communication or for want of sufficient evidence of the "actual malice" state law may require to recover for defamation.

f.　First Amendment Implications of Imposing Liability for Environmentally Harassing Speech

It seems clear after *Harris* that gender-based speech alone, when sufficiently repeated or hostile, may violate Title VII. Therefore, mandated federal procedures and sanctions will sometimes implicate First Amendment concerns. These concerns are heightened because, as the *Harris* language underscores, the contours of the violation are somewhat vague. The only guidance given employers is that "verbal . . . conduct of a sexual nature [that] has the purpose or effect of unreasonably interfering with an individual's work performance or creating an intimidating, hostile, or offensive work environment" is harassment. 29 C.F.R. § 1604.11(a) (2010). Moreover, the existence of a hostile environment is determined by a totality of the circumstances test; the employer may therefore be uncertain as to whether a hostile environment exists until a court makes that determination.

An effective policy and procedure against sexual harassment may avoid employer liability for harassment by subordinate employees and for environmental harassment by supervisors. Accordingly, when, as will frequently be the case, the employer is in doubt, it has the incentive, in order to avoid the vagaries of liability for uncertain workplace speech and pictorial displays, to overregulate and over-punish. Nevertheless, fired managers have generally had difficulty persuading courts that their discipline or discharge as the result of an internal investigation violates their rights to free speech. Still, while an employer may discipline supervisors for engaging in sexual harassment, supervisors enjoy protection against retaliation for their participation in an investigation of that harassment.

v.   The Special Statutory Concept of "Religion"

Employers not qualifying for immunity from liability for religious discrimination under sections 702 or 703(e)(2), or for the BFOQ defense with respect to religiously-based hiring decisions, are subject to a special affirmative obligation somewhat distinct from the normal duty not to discriminate. Section 703(a)(1) forbids an employer from discriminating because of "religion," and section 701(j), added in 1972, in turn defines "religion" to include "all aspects of religious observance and practice as well as belief, unless an employer demonstrates that he is unable to reasonably accommodate to an employee's . . . religious observance or practice without undue hardship."

Employees may assert various theories of religious discrimination, including disparate treatment, religious harassment, and failure to accommodate. To prove a claim under the disparate treatment theory, the prima facie case and evidentiary burdens of an employee alleging religious discrimination mirror those of an employee alleging race or sex discrimination. Accordingly, the courts apply the familiar burden-shifting framework of *McDonnell Douglas*. The plaintiff must demonstrate that she (1) is a member of a protected class, (2) was qualified and rejected for the position she sought, and (3) nonmembers of the protected class were treated more favorably. Harassment on the basis of religion similarly tracks the now-familiar sexual or racial harassment cases.

More typically, the religious discrimination plaintiff complains of a particular employer practice that burdens the practice of his religion. The prima facie case consists of evidence that an employer practice conflicts with the employee's exercise of a sincerely held religious belief, that the employee has put the employer on notice of the conflict, and the employer has nevertheless imposed an employment detriment. The employer then defends by showing either that it fulfilled its obligation to reasonably accommodate or that any accommodation of the plaintiff's religious needs would work an undue hardship. But two Supreme Court decisions have greatly eased the resulting employer obligation to reasonably accommodate the religious practice.

In *Ansonia Board of Education v. Philbrook*, 479 U.S. 60 (1986), the Court suggested that if an employer's schedule conflicts with the plaintiff's religious need to refrain from secular employment on holy days, the employer could ordinarily satisfy its accommodation obligation by offering the employee additional unpaid leave rather than affording additional paid leave. In particular, the employer was not required to accept the plaintiff's proffered fuller accommodation if the employer's own accommodation is "reasonable."

Second, *Trans World Airlines, Inc. v. Hardison*, 432 U.S. 63, 74–84 (1977), held that an employer's reasonable accommodation, even as alleviated by *Ansonia*, works "undue hardship" whenever it results "in more than a de minimis cost." An accommodation that requires the employer to hire an additional worker in order to permit the plaintiff to observe his religion every Saturday works undue hardship. So do accommodations that permit a religious observer to skip assignments that would have to be picked up by others, or that allow the observer to work less than others, even if he reimburses the employer for the resulting additional costs. Largely because the duty to accommodate has thus been substantially diluted by judicial construction, section 701(j) has survived challenge under the First Amendment's Establishment Clause.

vi. Wage Discrimination and the Equal Pay Act

The Equal Pay Act of 1963, 29 U.S.C.A. § 206(d) (West 2010) ("EPA"), prohibits only sex-based pay differentials for "equal work," defined to mean jobs involving substantially the same skill, effort, and responsibility. The EPA also contains four listed affirmative defenses to a claim of unequal pay for equal work.

The "Bennett Amendment" to Title VII, the last sentence of section 703(h), attempts to harmonize the two statutes' treatment of sex-based wage discrimination. It provides that a successful affirmative defense to an EPA claim does double duty as a defense to liability under Title VII. Lower courts are divided, however, on the converse question, whether EPA liability automatically means Title VII liability as well.

On the other hand, intentional sex-based wage discrimination may violate Title VII even if no member of the opposite sex performs "equal work" within the meaning of EPA. But the related "comparable worth" theory has generally been rejected. An employer does not violate Title VII merely by observing market norms that result in its paying more for male-dominated jobs than for female-dominated jobs that have similar value to the employer but would not be considered "equal" under the EPA. Nor can the EPA be used to assert a claim for equal benefits based on the alleged "comparable worth" of male-and female-dominated jobs when those jobs do not entail the substantially equal skill, effort, and responsibility that EPA claims require.

Even without explicit authorizing text in the EPA, the circuit courts have held unlawful employer retaliation against employees for asserting an EPA claim or protesting an EPA violation.

(2) PARTICULAR PRACTICES GIVEN SPECIAL STATUTORY TREATMENT

i. Restrictions Relative to Pregnancy and Abortion

The Pregnancy Discrimination Act, Pub. L. 95–555, 92 Stat. 2076 (1978) ("PDA"), added to Title VII a new section, 701(k). This amendment defines the sex discrimination prohibited by section 703 to include distinctions "on the basis of pregnancy, childbirth, or related medical conditions." The PDA, in other words, effectively equates pregnancy discrimination with discrimination "because of sex" within the meaning of section 703. Refusing to hire or firing someone because she is pregnant therefore violates section 703, and such a violation is a form of facial or express gender discrimination, defensible only if the employer establishes a BFOQ.

The PDA does not require an employer to provide leave or benefits for pregnancy that it does not provide to male employees for "comparable" conditions; as the Court wrote in *California Federal Savings & Loan Ass'n v. Guerra*, 479 U.S. 272, 286–87 (1987), the amendment's dominant principle, drawn from its second, "equality of treatment" clause, is nondiscrimination, rather than preference. The PDA does not require an employer to provide any leave or benefits for pregnancy, let alone greater leave or benefits, if it treats similar disabilities the same. For the same reason, the PDA does not require more indulgence for absence or tardiness occasioned by pregnancy than for absences or tardiness attributable to any other ailment or medical condition.

Yet, permission for employers to accord pregnancy some degree of preferential treatment is inferable from the first clause of the Amendment. Thus, an employer is not forbidden from offering greater health insurance benefits for pregnancy than for other medical conditions as a matter of contract. But this degree of preference is limited: An employer may not give mothers childcare leave, keyed to the fact of childbirth rather than the duration of pregnancy disability, if fathers are denied leave under similar circumstances. See *Johnson v. University of Iowa*, 431 F.3d 325 (8th Cir. 2005). Further, as the Court held in *Guerra*, 429 U.S. at 288–92, the PDA does not preempt state legislation that preferentially treats pregnant employees by affirmatively requiring employers to offer leave benefits to pregnancy-disabled employees that the employer does not offer to others. The state statute in question was not preempted because it "is not inconsistent with the purposes of the ... [PDA], nor does it require the doing of an act which is unlawful under Title VII." *Id.* at 292.

Where the plaintiff produces evidence that the adverse action was based on pregnancy, and the employer fails to offer comparative evidence involving the disabilities of other employees, the first clause of the PDA has supported the per se equation of distinctions based on pregnancy with discrimination "because of sex." In effect, this was the path the Supreme Court followed in *International Union, UAW v. Johnson Controls*, 499 U.S. 187 (1991), where an employer rule denying women jobs in positions where they would encounter significant levels of lead was applied only to fertile women, not all women.

Although the legislative history of the PDA focused on the health and medical requirements of female employees, a majority of the Court has held that the amendment also prohibits employer-sponsored health insurance provisions that exclude spousal pregnancies and thereby offer male employees inferior total coverage than their female co-workers. The PDA also proscribes discriminating against an employee for undergoing an abortion, either by terminating her employment or, apparently, denying her sick leave available for other medical disabilities. But the PDA explicitly relieves employers from subsidizing abortions through health insurance benefits, except in cases of "medical complications" or "where the life of the mother would be endangered if the fetus were carried to term."

Courts are still exploring the full reaches of the medical conditions related to pregnancy with respect to which the PDA applies. In *Johnson Controls*, 499 U.S. at 210–11, the Supreme Court held an employer policy that applied to all women who were fertile, whether or not pregnant, violative of the PDA.

While the PDA does not compel employers covered by Title VII to afford maternity leaves or benefits not provided for other disabilities, the Family & Medical Leave Act of 1993, Pub. L. 103–3, 107 Stat. 6, requires employers with 50 or more employees to permit eligible employees, female and male alike, to take up to 12 weeks of unpaid leave per year after the birth or adoption of a child, as well as for serious health emergencies affecting the employee or his close relatives.

ii.   Fetal Vulnerability Rules

Because the fetal vulnerability rules are prima facie subject to the PDA, they must be treated as a form of express gender discrimination that can survive scrutiny only if they pass muster under the BFOQ defense. For example, the Supreme Court in *Johnson Controls*, 499 U.S. 187, definitively ruled that fetal protection policies exclude fertile women from employment opportunities expressly on the basis of gender and are accordingly defensible, if at all, only as bona fide occupational qualifications, or BFOQs. Further, the Court stringently applied the BFOQ defense. In attempting to prove that fertile employees lacked essential job qualifications, employers had sought to justify their exclusion by invoking protection of the fetus. The Court held that the safety of an employee's fetus, as distinct from the safety of plant visitors or customers, is not essential to the operation of the employer's business in the sense meant by the BFOQ defense. Perhaps the broadest significance of *Johnson Controls* is its explication of dual requirements for any BFOQ. Not only must the employer's gender-, religion-, or national-origin-based exclusion substantially relate to the plaintiff's ability to perform her particular job, it must also go to the "essence" or "central mission" of the employer's business. *Id.* at 203.

    iii.   Seniority Systems

Two neutral practices are singled out for special treatment by the text of Title VII. Section 703(h) provides that "notwithstanding any other provision" of Title VII, an employer does not commit an unlawful employment practice by imposing different terms or conditions of employment pursuant to a bona fide seniority or merit system. The employer is immune from liability even if the effect or impact of these systems falls more heavily on the plaintiff's protected group. Judicial construction of these provisions, however, has afforded far greater protection for seniority and merit systems than for professionally developed ability tests.

Unless the plaintiff is able to prove that a seniority system was initially adopted or maintained with a specific discriminatory purpose, and is thus not "bona fide," a seniority system cannot be the basis of employer liability. And such a system is lawful even though it was first adopted after the enactment of Title VII. Absent proof of discriminatory purpose by the employer and union in adopting or maintaining such a system, section 703(h) insulates a bona fide seniority system from being declared an unlawful employment practice notwithstanding that it perpetuates underlying hiring, assignment or promotion discrimination that took place before or even after the effective date of Title VII. *International Bhd. of Teamsters v. United States*, 431 U.S. 324 (1977). Thus, a bona fide system may not be dismantled wholesale by declaratory judgment or injunction. But where other, primary unlawful employment practices are proved—hiring, assignment, or promotion discrimination, for example—courts have the remedial authority in effect to adjust the system's seniority ladder incrementally by awarding retroactive seniority for bidding or other competitive purposes to proven victims of discrimination.

A system will not forfeit its status as bona fide merely because it has the effect of disproportionately "locking in" minority employees to lower-paying or less skilled positions— for example, by discouraging them from transferring to better jobs in separate bargaining units where they might forfeit accumulated seniority with the company. The mere impact of the system does not, standing alone, demonstrate the requisite discriminatory purpose. Factors in assessing a system's bona fides include whether it discourages different protected groups equally from transferring between units; whether, if the seniority units are in separate bargaining units, the bargaining unit structure is rational and conforms to industry practice; whether the system has its "genesis" in prohibited discrimination; and whether subsequent negotiations that have maintained the system were tainted by unlawful motivation.

The Court has broadly interpreted the kinds of collectively bargained arrangements that qualify as "seniority systems" entitled to the special protection of section 703(h). For example, a requirement that an employee work for a specified time before entering the permanent employees' seniority ladder has itself was held to constitute part of a protected seniority system. On occasion, however, a plaintiff has succeeded in sidestepping section 703(h) by framing a challenge to an employer decision that is related to but distinct from the functioning of a seniority system.

iv. Professionally Developed Ability Tests

Section 703(h) permits employers to act upon the results of a "professionally developed ability test." But in sharp contrast to the great deference shown seniority systems, the judicial protection accorded these tests has been inconsistent. In many cases, it has proven even more difficult for an employer to defend the adverse impact of a paper-and-pencil test than to avoid liability for other neutral practices. This is because, soon after Title VII became effective, the EEOC issued guidelines on employee selection procedures that require employers to conduct highly technical and demanding "validation" studies of ability tests to demonstrate that they reliably pinpoint desired employee traits essential to a particular job. The Supreme Court's deferral to those guidelines in *Albemarle Paper Co. v. Moody*, 422 U.S. 405, 430 (1975), required employers to incur considerable expense in validation efforts before they could safely hinge employment decisions on the results of tests having significant differential adverse impact.

Lower courts have since somewhat eased validation requirements, holding that employers need not slavishly adhere to the difficult and complex EEOC guidelines. Instead, employers may defend more generally with evidence that tests are "predictive of or significantly correlated with important elements of work behavior ... relevant to the job ... for which candidates are being evaluated." *Contreras v. City of Los Angeles,*

656 F.2d 1267, 1276 (9th Cir. 1981). Nevertheless, even this version of the validation defense places a considerably greater burden on an employer than merely producing evidence that "a challenged practice serves, in a significant way," one of many possible "legitimate employment goals." *Wards Cove Packing Co., Inc. v. Atonio*, 490 U.S. 642, 659 (1989).

By its terms, the Civil Rights Act of 1991, in an effort to restore the rigor of the defense, requires employers to justify the adverse impact of a particularly identified neutral practice by demonstrating the practice to be "job related for the position in question and consistent with business necessity." The 1991 amendments do not address validation standards in particular, but add a prohibition against the practice known as "race norming." The Act makes it unlawful in selecting, referring, or promoting employees to adjust or use different cutoff scores or otherwise alter test results because of race, color, religion, sex, or national origin.

(3) RETALIATION

To protect employees who seek to vindicate their rights under section 703, a separate provision, section 704(a), broadly prohibits retaliation. Two basic species of conduct are protected: (1) participation in any administrative or judicial investigation, proceeding, or hearing to enforce Title VII rights; and (2) less formal, reasonably conducted opposition to practices that an employee reasonably believes to be prohibited by the Act.

The participation protection is much broader than opposition protection. But once either type of activity is characterized as protected, the prima facie case is straightforward. The plaintiff must produce evidence of (1) her voluntary or involuntary participation in proceedings authorized by Title VII, or her opposition to what she reasonably believes is one or more apparently prohibited practices (the practice opposed must be one "made an unlawful employment practice by" Title VII, although the plaintiff may prevail even if the employer was not in fact violating the statute); (2) her employer's awareness of her protected participation or opposition; (3) an adverse employment action thereafter; and (4) a causal connection between the adverse employment action and the protected opposition or participation. Evidence that the adverse action was taken shortly after the protected participation or opposition fortifies or, if it is very short, even suffices to show the required causal link; the passage of several years between the protected conduct and the act of alleged retaliation will defeat the inference of retaliatory motive; but the passage of a shorter yet still substantial period of time does not conclusively refute the required causation, provided there is other causation evidence. A plaintiff creates a jury question on causation with evidence, including circumstantial evidence, that the employer was aware of the protected activity or expression at the time it took the adverse action, and temporal proximity between the protected activity and the adverse action may permit the jury to find the required causal link.

In *Clark County School District v. Breeden*, 532 U.S. 268 (2001), the Court carefully re-reviewed the timing of the protected conduct and the adverse job action and found that although the plaintiff was transferred one month after the decision-maker learned of the filing of the lawsuit, the plaintiff failed to satisfy the temporal nexus because the decision-maker had discussed the possibility of transfer before she had knowledge of the suit. The plaintiff rebutted this evidence in her appellate reply brief with evidence that the decision-maker knew of the filing of the EEOC charge, but the Court stressed the 20-month lapse of time between the charge and the transfer. "The cases that accept mere temporal proximity between an employer's knowledge of protected activity and an adverse employment action as sufficient evidence of causality to establish a prima facie case uniformly hold that the temporal proximity must be 'very close'.... Action taken (as here) 20 months later suggests, by itself, no causality at all." *Id.* at 273–74. Circuit courts have found that a three-month gap will also not suffice, standing alone, to show the required link between employer awareness of protected activity and imposition of the adverse term and condition of employment. See, e.g., *Meiners v. University of Kan.*, 359 F.3d 1222 (10th Cir. 2004).

Once the employee satisfies her prima facie burden, the resulting presumption of retaliation must be rebutted by the employer by producing evidence of a legitimate nondiscriminatory reason for the adverse employment action. If the employer meets this burden, the presumption of retaliation disappears, and the plaintiff must present evidence sufficient to prove to the fact-finder that the reason proffered by the employer was a pretext for unlawful retaliation. Section 703(m), the "mixed motives" provision that relieves an employer of retroactive relief when it demonstrates that it would have taken the same action apart from an unlawful ground, includes among such grounds only "race, color, religion, sex, or national origin," with no mention of retaliation.

The "opposition" right has been subject to two important fact-dependent qualifications, developed case by case, concerning (a) the reasonableness of the plaintiff's belief that the employer practice he opposed was unlawfully discriminatory under section 703, and (b) the reasonableness of the manner and means of the plaintiff's opposition to that practice.

One circuit specifically demands two separate components to the "reasonable belief" requirement: The "plaintiff must not only show that he subjectively (that is, in good faith) believed that his employer was engaged in unlawful employment practices, but also that his belief was objectively reasonable in light of the facts and record presented." *Butler v. Alabama Dep't of Transp.*, 536 F.3d 1209 (11th Cir. 2008). And in *Breeden*, 532 U.S. 268, the Supreme Court resolved the objectively reasonable belief question against the plaintiff as a matter of law. The Court concluded that no reasonable person could have believed that the sexually tinged comments to which supervisors exposed the plaintiff on one occasion satisfied the *Harris* "sufficiently serious or pervasive" standard for hostile work environment harassment.

The reasonableness of the manner and means of opposition is judged case by case on the facts. Certainly, employers are not required to "absolve" employees who engage in "unlawful activity against it." *McDonnell Douglas Corp. v. Green*, 411 U.S. 792, 803 (1973). Employee protests that constitute both opposition to practices made unlawful by Title VII as well as violations of established, legitimate work rules have posed especially difficult problems. The linchpin is the objective "reasonableness" of the opposition; the law protects employees in making informal protests of discrimination, including making complaints to management, writing critical letters to customers, protesting against discrimination by industry or society in general, and expressing support of co-workers who have filed formal charges. But not all forms of protest are protected by Title VII's prohibition on retaliation. For instance, Title VII "does not constitute a license for employees to engage in physical violence in order to protest discrimination." *Cruz v. Coach Stores, Inc.*, 202 F.3d 560, 566 (2d Cir. 2000). When a court adjudges an employee's manner of opposition to have gone beyond what is necessary for effective protest—when, for example, she gratuitously embarrasses a superior, see *Jennings v. Tinley Park Cmty. Consol. Sch. Dist. No. 146*, 864 F.2d 1368 (7th Cir. 1988)—employee discipline will likely be upheld. Some circuits locate this principle in the prima facie case, the first step in the burden-shifting under

McDonnell Douglas. For example, in *Laughlin v. Metropolitan Washington Airports Authority*, 149 F.3d 253 (4th Cir. 1998), the Fourth Circuit held "as a matter of law," that the plaintiff "did not engage in protected oppositional activity and, therefore, did not establish a prima facie case of retaliatory discharge." Other courts have treated unreasonable opposition activities as the employer's legitimate nondiscriminatory reason for the adverse employment action.

By contrast, the "participation" protection, designed to assure free access to the administrative and judicial bodies empowered to investigate and adjudicate Title VII violations, is virtually unlimited in scope. Just as an "opposing" plaintiff's underlying informal complaint need not have been in fact well founded under section 703 to support a claim of unlawful retaliation under section 704, so a "participating" plaintiff need not have prevailed in the proceeding initiated by her formal charge or lawsuit. Indeed it has been held that an employer's unilateral view that an employee lied in the EEOC charge documents cannot justify retaliatory action against him.

The dual limitations on the scope of the "opposition" protection make characterization of protected activity as "participation" or mere "opposition" critical. In *Clover v. Total System Services, Inc.*, 176 F.3d 1346 (11th Cir. 1999), the Eleventh Circuit held that participation in an employer's internal investigation that is prompted only by internal complaints and not an EEOC charge is not protected activity. See also *EEOC v. Total System Services, Inc.*, 221 F.3d 1171 (11th Cir. 2000). This approach appears to have been followed by the Supreme Court in *Crawford v. Metropolitan Government of Nashville*, 555 U.S. 271 (2009). The plaintiff was terminated after disclosing information during an informal employer internal investigation of sexual harassment. While acknowledging that plaintiff's response to employer questions could qualify as opposition, the Court did not even consider whether it might also be deemed eligible for the more robust "participation" protection, even though employer internal investigations of sexual harassment charges are strongly encouraged by the Supreme Court's _Faragher_ and _Burlington_ decisions, discussed above.

A plaintiff who has filed a section 703 discrimination charge with EEOC and then also asserts in court that he was retaliated against for having filed the charge generally need not have filed a distinct section 704 retaliation charge with EEOC or otherwise exhaust administrative remedies before suing. Such retaliation is actionable even if it occurs after dismissal of the plaintiff's EEOC charge.

Section 704 in terms protects only "employees or applicants," narrower than section 703's embrace of "any individual." But the Supreme Court held it to protect former employees as well, for example, from retaliation taking the form of adverse references. _Robinson v. Shell Oil Co._, 519 U.S. 337 (1997). Consistently, the Court has since held that the scope of section 704 extends beyond workplace-or employment-related retaliation to condemn any employer act that is "materially adverse" in the sense that it might dissuade a reasonable employee from opposing or participating in proceedings to challenge apparently discriminatory employer conduct. _Burlington_, 548 U.S. 53.

Most circuits treat the "mixed motive" provisions of section 107 of the Civil Rights Act of 1991 as inapplicable to retaliation; accordingly, if the employer can demonstrate that it would have taken the same action against the plaintiff apart from its retaliatory motive, the retaliation claim fails altogether. See, e.g., _Pennington v. City of Huntsville_, 261 F.3d 1262 (11th Cir. 2001); _Speedy v. Rexnord Corp._, 243 F.3d 397 (7th Cir. 2001); _Matima v. Celli_, 228 F.3d 68 (2d Cir. 2000). These opinions note that on its face, section 107 amends only section

703, the main Title VII discrimination prohibition, and not section 704. This approach is fortified by similar reasoning in *Gross v. FBL Financial Services*, ___ U.S. ___, 129 S.Ct. 2343 (2009), which reverted to pre–1991 causation standards for ADEA cases because the 1991 amendments did not amend ADEA in this respect. Even if employers facing retaliation claims cannot show they would have made the "same decision" for lawful reasons, they may rely on the section 703 doctrine of "after-acquired evidence" doctrine that relieves them of reinstatement or hiring orders and cuts off back pay when they discover after-the-fact information that would have led them to terminate the plaintiff on lawful grounds. See *McKennon v. Nashville Banner Publ'g Co.*, 513 U.S. 352 (1995), discussed below.

The plaintiff who is retaliated against because someone with whom he has a close relationship participated in a formal Title VII proceeding or reasonably opposed an apparently discriminatory practice has standing and a claim under section 704. The Supreme Court recently so held in a case where the plaintiff's fiancée filed an EEOC charge and the plaintiff was subsequently fired by their common employer. *Thompson v. North Am. Stainless, LP*, ___ U.S. ___, 131 S.Ct. 863 (2011). The Court declined to specify the characteristics of the required "closeness" between the protester and the plaintiff suffering the retaliation, but concluded it was obvious, in the terms of the *Burlington* "materially adverse" test, that a reasonable employee might be dissuaded from engaging in protected activity if she thought the consequence would be the firing of her fiancé.

(4) CONSTRUCTIVE DISCHARGE

Closely related to but distinguishable from environmental harassment and retaliation is the doctrine of constructive discharge. In essence, the claim avails an employee whose departure is in form voluntary but who in fact was virtually compelled to quit as the result of discriminatory job terms or harassment extreme in significance, duration, or offensiveness. The consequence of establishing the claim is a broader remedy: The plaintiff who succeeds will be eligible for an order directing reinstatement as well as available monetary relief.

At a minimum, the claim requires the standard showing that the plaintiff's involuntary resignation was caused by differential, unwelcome, and intolerable treatment unlawful because it was based on her race, sex, religion, national origin, or age. Evidence that the plaintiff would have resigned for independent personal reasons or work-related reasons unconnected with substantial, aggravated discrimination breaks the causal connection and therefore defeats the constructive discharge claim. This is akin to the same-decision showing which, under *Price Waterhouse*, sufficed to avoid employer liability altogether and today, under the Civil Rights Act of 1991, still limits available relief. The date of the forced resignation triggers the running of the applicable 180–or 300–day administrative charge filing period.

The element that has generated the most litigation centers on the reasonableness of the employee's decision to quit in relation to particular unlawful employer conduct. The decisions are uniform that an employee has been constructively discharged when the termination results from intolerable working conditions that the employer created with the specific intent of forcing the employee to resign. Some circuits have considered evidence of subjective intent, or of "aggravating circumstances," indispensable to constructive discharge. The Supreme Court, however, in formally approving the doctrine for the first time, has recently articulated a purely "objective" formulation previously endorsed by other circuits: The plaintiff must prove "working conditions so intolerable that a reasonable person would have felt compelled to resign." *Suders*, 542 U.S. at 147. The Court specifically observed that this standard for constructive discharge is more stringent than what is required to prove a case of hostile racial or sexual environmental harassment: a showing of offending behavior "sufficiently severe or pervasive to alter the conditions of the victim's employment and create an abusive working environment." *Id.* at 146–47. The plaintiff who alleges that constructive discharge resulted from the creation of a hostile environment must therefore make both those showings. Because the employer conduct that gives rise to colorable claims of constructive discharge is usually extreme or persistent, those claims are often joined with companion claims under state law for such torts as outrage or intentional infliction of emotional distress.

Most acts of discrimination are such that a "reasonable" employee should stay on the job, oppose the employer practice informally or by filing a charge, and trust in the efficacy of the separate section 704 protection against retaliation. Classic instances include wage discrimination, non-promotion, or assignment to less attractive or lucrative (but not intolerably demeaning) positions. At the other end of the spectrum, where the prospects of proving constructive discharge are much improved, lie the "aggravating circumstances" sometimes required to meet the objective test of "intolerable" working conditions. These include subjecting the plaintiff to repeated slurs, assigning him especially demeaning work for unlawful discriminatory reasons, or subjecting him to egregious, unrelenting, and unremedied harassment. Sexual harassment in particular has served as a predicate for constructive discharge but is not necessarily sufficiently severe to meet a particular circuit's test.

The employee must therefore make a critical decision, usually without benefit of counsel, concerning how to respond to varied employer actions. If racial slurs are so offensive or repeated that an employee who quit over them would later be deemed by a court to have acted reasonably, the employee could safely quit or take the lesser measure of remaining on the job and demanding an apology. If he keeps working but his demand leads to his discharge, he might well have a claim for retaliation in violation of section 704. But if he overestimates the seriousness or offensiveness of the employer's discrimination and quits, he may find that his only remedy is back pay from the time of the underlying discrimination until the date of his "voluntary" termination.

Employers in constructive discharge cases not precipitated by the employer's imposition of a tangible employment detriment but growing out of supervisory hostile work environment sexual harassment may invoke the *Burlington/Faragher* two-pronged defense discussed above. *Id.* at. 149.

(5) UNION LIABILITY

Labor unions are not excluded from the general definition of "employer," and consequently may be liable for violations of section 703(a) on the same terms as any other employer. In addition, section 703(c) declares distinct unlawful practices applicable to labor organizations alone. One, found in section 703(c)(3), is to "cause or attempt to cause an employer" to discriminate in violation of section 703. Another, declared by section 703(c)(2), is to rely on prohibited grounds in segregating or classifying union members or applicants, or in failing to refer individuals for employment, so as to deprive them of employment opportunities. Finally, wholly apart from any effect on employment opportunities, labor organizations are prohibited by section 703(c)(1) from excluding applicants from membership or otherwise discriminating against them. Construing this last prohibition quite broadly, the Supreme Court has held that a union commits an unlawful employment practice by refusing to file race-bias grievances presented by black members, even when it does so in order to avoid antagonizing the employer and in turn to improve its chances of success on other collective bargaining issues, and even though the percentage of all types of grievances filed on behalf of black members is proportional to their representation in the union. Courts typically find that a union violates Title VII when it breaches it duty to provide fair representation on the basis of race, color, religion, sex, or national origin.

Unions may also be liable for retaliation under section 704. For example, a union that refused to process race discrimination grievances under a collective bargaining contract whenever the would-be grievant had a charge pending against the union with a state or federal antidiscrimination agency was found to have violated Title VII. Liability attached even though the union processed other grievances as fairly for black as for white members and claimed that its policy was compelled by the employer. *Johnson v. Palma*, 931 F.2d 203 (2nd Cir. 1991).

Whether an international can be held liable for the acts of a local depends on whether the local was acting as an agent for the international. Common law agency principles determine whether such a relationship exists. If the local engages in illegal conduct in furtherance of its role as an agent of the international, the international will be liable for the local's actions. However, if the local exercises considerable autonomy in conducting its affairs, it cannot be regarded as an agent of the international, and the international accordingly cannot be held liable under an agency theory for the local's actions.

c. *Title VII Modes of Proof, Administrative Procedures, and Remedies*

The most critical and frequently litigated questions under Title VII concern the theories on which liability may be predicated and the corresponding modes of proof. In general, there are two generic forms of employer conduct actionable under Title VII. First, there are a variety of forms of intentional discrimination or "disparate treatment"; a broad legislative and social consensus supports imposing liability on employers when such conduct can be proved. More controversial is employer liability for "neutral," that is facially nondiscriminatory, work practices that have greater adverse statistical impact on members of the plaintiff's protected group than on others. Liability imposed in such circumstances is denoted by the terms "disproportionate adverse impact" or "disparate impact." Distinct proof modes have been developed to provide guidance to judges and juries in determining liability under each of these theories. Each mode presents its own conceptual and practical difficulties, and these in turn have generated a burgeoning body of judicial decisions. It should be noted that particular employer practices may implicate two or more modes of proof.

(1) INDIVIDUAL DISPARATE TREATMENT—"DIRECT" EVIDENCE

i. In General

The most obvious way of showing an unlawful employment practice is to offer "evidence that can be interpreted as an acknowledgment of discriminatory intent by the defendant or its agents." *Troupe v. May Dep't Stores Co.*, 20 F.3d 734 (7th Cir. 1994). Examples include epithets or slurs uttered by an authorized agent of the employer, a decision-maker's admission that he would or did act against the plaintiff because of his protected characteristic, or, even more clearly, an employer policy framed squarely in terms of race, sex, religion, or national origin. When produced, such "direct" evidence will without more ordinarily suffice to show that an adverse employment condition, or limitation on an employment opportunity, was imposed "because of" the plaintiff's protected group characteristic—that is, discrimination is presumed from the admission of evidence deemed "direct." Circuit opinions sometimes define direct evidence as evidence that, if believed, would prove the existence of the fact without inferences or presumption. Others subscribe to an "animus" position that deems any kind of evidence "direct" if it is tied to—that is, directly reflects—the alleged discriminatory animus. This approach is hospitable to circumstantial evidence, but excludes evidence of "stray" remarks not sufficiently tied to the challenged decision as to shed light on the employer agent's intention in making it. Still other circuits, the "animus-plus" courts, have insisted not just on evidence of animus but also that the statements reflecting the animus bear squarely on the contested employment decision. Under any of these formulations, it appears that statements weakly proved or inherently ambiguous cannot be considered "direct" for the purpose of relieving a plaintiff from proving the elements of inferential, *McDonnell Douglas* proof.

Even if courts refuse to characterize particular evidence as direct, the same evidence may sometimes fortify the inferential *McDonnell Douglas* prima facie case. Moreover, the Supreme Court's decision, discussed below, in *Desert Palace, Inc. v. Costa*, 539 U.S. 90 (2003), reduces the significance of the "direct"/"indirect" classification by allowing a plaintiff to cast the burden of the "mixed-motive" showing on a defendant regardless of the nature of a plaintiff's prima facie case.

Unsurprisingly, outside the realm of policies that discriminate by their clear terms on the basis of a protected characteristic, cases presenting smoking-gun exemplars of "direct," "express," or "facial" evidence are relative rarities. Nearly five decades after the effective date of Title VII, employers are familiar with the requirements and penalties of the statute, and consequently are more apt to comply or better skilled in disguising noncompliance. In *Price Waterhouse v.*

Hopkins, 490 U.S. 228 (1989) (plurality opinion and opinion of O'Connor, J.), the Supreme Court treated employers' agents' statements reflecting stereotypical views of women as direct evidence of gender discrimination, even when the views expressed bear somewhat tangentially on the plaintiff's capacity to perform the core elements of the position.

Justice O'Connor's concurring opinion sets out three prerequisites for employer speech to constitute "direct" evidence: The remarks must be by the applicable decision-maker, be related to the decision process, and not "stray." *Price Waterhouse*, 490 U.S. at 277 (O'Connor, J., concurring). In practice, however, this standard gives rise to multiple, interrelated issues. At a minimum, for a plaintiff's evidence to be deemed "direct"—thus enabling her to avoid the difficult evidentiary requirements of the inferential *McDonnell Douglas/St. Mary's* mode of proof—the statements she relies on must have been made by the person who made the adverse employment decision of which she complains, by someone with power to make effective recommendations to that decision-maker, or by someone in the control group to which that decision-maker belongs. Second, the content of the statement or statements, together with the context in which they were made, must suggest to the trier of fact that the decision-maker in fact relied on the bias those statements reflect in making the decision in question. For this reason, statements made by or to the decision-maker in connection with the making of the decision at issue are treated as far more probative of prohibited discrimination than those made by the decision-maker or others at times remote or on matters unrelated to the employment decision plaintiff is challenging. And evidence of the bias of a subordinate is relevant where the ultimate decision-maker is not insulated from the subordinate's influence.

There remains considerable uncertainty about how to differentiate those gender- or age-related comments or conduct that amount to "direct" evidence of discrimination—and therefore, standing alone, create a prima facie case—from merely "isolated" incidents or "stray" remarks. Even though slurs and stereotypes are sometimes treated as "direct" evidence of discriminatory intent, their real meaning or purpose may be equivocal. The frequent ambiguity of language and intent lends support to Judge Posner's observation that perhaps the "only truly direct evidence of intent that will ever be available" consists of outright litigation admissions or policies that discriminate by their own terms on grounds prohibited by the statute. *Troupe*, 20 F.3d at 736.

Even if such comments are accepted as "direct" evidence of discrimination, the plaintiff may also have to prove that the attitudes they reflect played at least a motivating part in the employment decision under challenge. Discrimination "in the air" must be brought to ground, lest Title VII be used as a mechanism for controlling pure thought or speech. To do so, the plaintiff must show first that a discriminatory attitude was to some degree actually relied on by the relevant decisionmaker.

The consequences of appellate court reluctance to label evidence "direct" were first moderated by a Supreme Court decision that aids plaintiffs in surviving motions for summary judgment or judgment as a matter of law in cases presenting evidence of slurs or other derogatory references to the abilities or characteristics of the members of plaintiff's protected group. In *Reeves v. Sanderson Plumbing Products, Inc.*, 530 U.S. 133 (2000), the Court, reversing an appellate court's grant of judgment as a matter of law pursuant to Federal Rule of Civil Procedure 50, wrote that the lower courts impermissibly supplanted the jury's judgment about the weight of the evidence. In particular, it criticized the appellate court for failing to draw all reasonable inferences in the plaintiff's favor on the question of whether the slur utterer was the actual decision-maker and for discounting the decision-maker's age-related comments on the ground that they were not made directly in the context of the plaintiff's termination.

Indeed, the Supreme Court's subsequent decision in *Desert Palace v. Costa*, 539 U.S. 90 (2003), more directly reduces the significance of the "direct"/"indirect" taxonomy. The Court held that regardless of whether a plaintiff used "direct" or "indirect" evidence to demonstrate prima facie that the employer relied in part on an unlawful reason, a Title VII plaintiff may obtain an instruction requiring the defendant to persuade that it would have made the same employment decision for an independent lawful reason. *Desert Palace* thus treats as immaterial the purported direct-indirect distinction in deciding the very issue for which the distinction was principally devised and used. Accordingly, whatever the pre-*Desert Palace* definitions of "direct" evidence, plaintiffs can now impose the same-decision limited defense on defendants in mixed-motive cases either by establishing the *McDonnell Douglas* prima facie case and persuading the fact-finder that the defendant's legitimate nondiscriminatory reasons are unworthy of credence, or by demonstrating through other evidence that a discriminatory reason more likely than not motivated the defendant in imposing the adverse term or condition of employment. On the one hand, therefore, a plaintiff may not be compelled to invoke the *McDonnell Douglas* proof mode and presumption; but on the other, if she does, she suffers no legal disadvantage relative to the plaintiff who has proceeded with evidence heretofore labeled as "direct."

Further, rejecting the dominant view of academic commentary, a consensus of lower federal courts treats *Desert Palace* as leaving intact the highly indirect *McDonnell Douglas* mode of proving individual disparate treatment for the many plaintiffs who cannot adduce "more direct" like slurs, stereotypes uttered by decision-makers in connection with the challenged decision, evidence of non-protected group "comparators" treated more favorably or less harshly under similar circumstances, statistical evidence of adverse treatment of the plaintiff's group, or anecdotal evidence of discriminatory treatment of, or suspicious or ambiguous statements made about, other members of that group. See, e.g., *Suits v. Heil Co.*, 192 F. App'x 399 (6th Cir. 2006); cf. *Sallis v. University of Minn.*, 408 F.3d 470 (8th Cir. 2005). Still, there is evidence that Title VII plaintiffs are most likely to prevail when they are able to present evidence that a comparator of a different gender, race, religion, or national origin was treated more favorably or less harshly under similar circumstances. C. Sullivan, *The Phoenix from the Ash: Proving Discrimination by Comparators*, 60 Ala. L. Rev. 191 (2009) (citing cases and elaborating circuit requirements for acceptable comparators).

Plaintiffs should take care that their "comparator" is in fact similarly situated from the standpoint of status or conduct. In one appellate decision, the court in effect viewed the Hispanic plaintiff laid off in a force reduction as a member of a (white) racial group, rather than as representing a particular national origin. Accordingly, it compared him not to non-Hispanics, who fared well in the force reduction, but to African–American employees, none of whom were terminated. *Jackson v. E.J. Brach Corp.*, 176 F.3d 971 (7th Cir. 1999). A pair of contemporaneous circuit decisions illustrate through comparator evidence the unlawfulness of differential race-based job assignments—in one case driven by actual customer preference, in the other by stereotypical assumptions about managerial effectiveness. *Ferrill v. Parker Group, Inc.*, 168 F.3d 468 (11th Cir. 1999); *Johnson v. Zema Sys. Corp.*, 170 F.3d 734 (7th Cir. 1999).

ii.   The "BFOQ" Affirmative Defense

Section 703(e)(1) affords an employer its only defense to policies or work rules that expressly or facially discriminate in hiring, and the defense is available only to discrimination on the basis of gender, religion, or national origin. It authorizes the employer to "hire and employ," and a labor organization or joint labor management committee to "admit or employ" to membership or apprenticeship or retraining programs, on the basis of gender, religion, or national origin, when that group status is a "bona fide occupational qualification ['BFOQ'] reasonably necessary to the normal operation" of the enterprise. It does not excuse discrimination in post-hire terms and conditions of employment—compensation, promotion, discipline, harassment, or discharge. See *EEOC v. Fremont Christian Sch.*, 781 F.2d 1362, 1367 (9th Cir. 1986). Nor does it defend against any discrimination on the basis of race. ADEA contains a similarly-worded BFOQ defense, and the Court has construed the corresponding provisions of the two statutes virtually identically. See, e.g., *Western Air Lines, Inc. v. Criswell*, 472 U.S. 400 (1985).

As its text would suggest, BFOQ is a true affirmative defense that the employer therefore has the burden of pleading and proving by a preponderance of the evidence. Still, the language of section 703(e)(1) would appear satisfied if an employer could show that a refusal to hire based on religion, sex, or national origin is reasonably necessary to the normal operation of the defendant's overall business. Yet, in order to prevent the exception from virtually eliminating an applicant's protection against these forms of express discrimination, the Supreme Court has required the employer to show that its discriminatory rule relates to a trait that goes to the "essence" of the enterprise, and that the rule bears a "high correlation" to the plaintiff's ability to perform her particular job. *Johnson Controls*, 499 U.S. at 202.

An early Supreme Court decision, still good law on its extreme facts, upheld the exclusion of women from contact positions as guards in unusually dangerous maximum security prisons in Alabama, even though the state failed to offer evidence that substantially all of the women who would seek those jobs would be incapable of maintaining order and safety. The Court merely hypothesized that women guards would be attacked because they were women—skipping over the fact that all guards in the Alabama maximum security system were targets simply because they were despised authority symbols. *Dothard v. Rawlinson*, 433 U.S. 321 (1977).

But the Court's decision in *Johnson Controls* confirmed the narrowness of the BFOQ defense. The employer's rule barred all still-fertile women of any age, marital status, or child-bearing inclination from holding a job in which they would likely be exposed to levels of lead that endangered the health of a fetus they might be carrying. Relying on the "occupational" limitation in section 703(e)(1), the Court concluded that the defense fails unless the employer demonstrates objectively that the exclusion is not only "reasonably necessary" to the "normal operation" of the "particular" business but also relates to "job-related skills and aptitudes." 499 U.S. at 201. The Court rejected the defense because, so far as the record revealed, "Fertile women ... participate in the manufacture of batteries as efficiently as anyone else." *Id*. at 206. Distinguishing *Dothard*, the Court wrote that third-party safety concerns had figured in the BFOQ analysis there only because inmate safety "went to the core of the employee's job performance"—something demonstrably not the case with battery making. *Id*. at 203.

Johnson Controls also restricted the employer's option to show only that some, rather than "substantially all" members of the excluded group, lack traits essential to the job and business when it is "impracticable" to ascertain the other members of the group who do. When the two BFOQ requirements, refined by *Johnson Controls*, are combined, the defendant faces a formidable task: "[A]n employer must direct its concerns about a woman's ability to perform her job safely and efficiently to those aspects of the woman's job-related activities that fall within the 'essence' of the particular business." *Id.* at 206.

Given the stringency of the BFOQ defense, its principal remaining utility may lie in resisting claims of age discrimination, especially where an employee's deteriorating physical capabilities correlate strongly with aging and would impair safe hands-on performance. See *Usery v. Tamiami Trail Tours, Inc.*, 531 F.2d 224 (5th Cir. 1976). It is unlikely that the BFOQ defense could justify a slur, as opposed to an employer policy. Lower courts have, however, upheld relaxed applications of the defense to accommodate a legitimate business need to assure customer privacy. *Healey v. Southwood Psychiatric Hosp.*, 78 F.3d 128 (3d Cir. 1996). Moreover, EEOC guidelines relax the rules where employers have an interest in the gender authenticity of such employees as actresses, actors, strippers, and food and drink servers at restaurants or bars where a primary job and business function is the projection of a sexually provocative display. See 29 C.F.R. § 1604.2 (2010) (actors and actresses). Finally, in actions under Title VII, the Supreme Court has dispensed altogether with the necessity of a BFOQ showing to justify otherwise permissible "benign," "voluntary" employer affirmative action programs favoring women. *Johnson v. Transportation Agency*, 480 U.S. 616 (1987).

(2) INDIVIDUAL DISPARATE TREATMENT—INDIRECT OR INFERENTIAL EVIDENCE OF DISCRIMINATION

i. The *McDonnell Douglas* Proof Mode

Because direct evidence of intent has been so rarely accepted or even classified as "direct," courts have recognized alternative ways of establishing unlawful discrimination through circumstantial evidence.

The indirect method of proving "individual disparate treatment" owes its origin to *McDonnell Douglas Corp. v. Green*, 411 U.S. 792 (1973), as later elaborated in several other Supreme Court decisions. The plaintiff makes a *McDonnell Douglas* prima facie showing in a failure to hire case—and thereby survives a Federal Rule of Civil Procedure 41(b) involuntary dismissal motion, or, in the jury trials authorized by the Civil Rights Act of 1991, a Rule 50(a)(1) motion for judgment as a matter of law at the close of her case in chief—by offering evidence that she (1) belongs to a protected group, (2) applied for or continued to desire the position in question, (3) met minimum uniform qualifications to receive or retain the position at the time of the adverse action, and (4) was rejected, and thereafter the employer continued to receive applications from persons having the complainant's qualifications. This evidence, the Court has explained, eliminates several of the most common nondiscriminatory reasons for the plaintiff's failure to be hired (or other rejection, non-promotion, discipline, or discharge) and thus makes it more likely that the employer's real reason, or one of them, was a status protected by Title VII. In brief, when a qualified employee who is a member of a racial minority traditionally victimized by workplace discrimination is not hired for a vacant job, the failure to hire alone suffices to raise an inference of discrimination, which the employer must then rebut by producing evidence of a legitimate, nondiscriminatory reason.

The elements, as the Court in *McDonnell Douglas* noted, are flexibly adapted to the facts of a given case. For example, the first of the numbered prima facie elements is pro forma—anyone, even a white male, can claim protected group status by contrasting himself in racial, religious, national origin, or gender terms to the group he claims was preferred. Further, an employee complaining of promotion denial need not show element (2), that she applied for the higher position, if it was the employer's routine practice to offer promotions to persons with her seniority and position. *Loyd v. Phillips Bros., Inc.*, 25 F.3d 518 (7th Cir. 1994). In general, however, courts read *McDonnell Douglas* to require a plaintiff to allege that she applied for a specific position for which she was rejected, rather than merely asserting that from time to time she requested promotion at large. *Dotson v. Delta Consol. Indus., Inc.*, 251 F.3d 780 (8th Cir. 2001). But a number of circuits have relieved plaintiffs of submitting a formal application for a particular position where the position was not posted, there was no formal application mechanism, and the employee had no knowledge of the position or applied informally for a specific position in a manner endorsed by the employer. The third element, qualifications for the position sought, has the greatest practical importance, as it eliminates the most common nondiscriminatory reason for rejection where an application for hire or promotion has been made. The Court has now declared relatively clearly that this showing refers, at the prima facie case stage, simply to minimal or absolute rather than relative or comparative qualifications. *Patterson v. Mc-Lean Credit Union*, 491 U.S. 164 (1989). The final element, sometimes relaxed or waived by lower courts, is evidence that the employer, after rejecting the plaintiff, continued to seek applicants with her general qualifications or selected a person from outside her protected group. In rehiring cases, the plaintiff need not show that he was identically situated with others of a different race who were initially terminated or who resigned at the same time; it suffices that the plaintiff's former position was filled by a member of a different race or simply that he was qualified for the new job for which he was rejected. *Richardson v. Leeds Police Dep't*, 71 F.3d 801 (11th Cir. 1995). A minority of the circuits treating the question also streamline the prima facie promotion denial case, requiring evidence only that the plaintiff be a protected group member and an unsuccessful applicant for a position for which he was qualified, and that thereafter the employer continued to seek applicants. *Mauro v. Southern New Eng. Telecomm., Inc.*, 208 F.3d 384, 386 (2d Cir. 2000) (citing *Brown v. Coach Stores, Inc.*, 163 F.3d 706, 709 (2d Cir. 1998)).

But if the employer responds to the prima facie showing of failure to promote by offering evidence of a legitimate non-discriminatory reason, the plaintiff will have a much more difficult job of proving the ultimate fact of unlawful discrimination. Rejecting an even more demanding circuit court standard—the qualifications difference between the plaintiff and the selected candidate must "jump off the page and slap you in the face"—the Supreme Court substituted the still daunting test that the disparity "must be of such weight and significance that no reasonable person, in the exercise of impartial judgment, could have chosen the candidate selected over the plaintiff." *Ash v. Tyson Foods*, 546 U.S. 454, 456–57 (2006). But some lower court opinions recognize that an inference of discrimination is also supported if the employer promoted someone unqualified under the employer's own criteria, and that when evidence of a qualifications disparity is not the sole evidence that the employer's proffered legitimate reason is pretextual, the disparity need not be so dramatic.

Accepting the Supreme Court's invitation to modify the basic template for differing circumstances, the circuit courts have adapted the *McDonnell Douglas* failure-to-hire elements to meet the realities of claims alleging unlawful discharge, promotion, discipline, and unequal pay. In an age discrimination case, the Court itself held unanimously that a terminated plaintiff need not invariably show that he was replaced by someone outside the protected class—there, someone younger than 40—so long as he was replaced by someone sufficiently younger as to generate a plausible inference that age was a determinative factor. *O'Connor v. Consol. Coin Caterers Corp.*,

517 U.S. 308, 312 (1996). This is consistent with the approach *McDonnell Douglas* took in failure-to-hire situations, where the Court never described element (4)—the employer continued to seek applications from qualified persons after plaintiff's rejection—as requiring evidence that the employer hired, or by implication replaced plaintiff with, someone outside plaintiff's protected class. Such a requirement would preclude otherwise meritorious claims by a woman or minority member deemed too feminist or assertive, provided their replacement was another woman or minority member; it would also doom claims against employers who replace the plaintiff with another member of her group solely in order to avoid the consequences of threatened or actual litigation.

Circuit courts have followed suit, generally listing the required prima facie elements in a termination case as follows: (1) plaintiff belongs to a protected class (a requirement that can be met under the right circumstances by anyone, even a white male); (2) plaintiff possessed the absolute, or minimum uniformly required, qualifications for the job she held; (3) despite those qualifications, she was discharged; and (4) the job was not eliminated after the discharge. Significantly, element (4) does not require the plaintiff, except perhaps a non-white plaintiff alleging race discrimination, to show that her job was filled by a person outside her protected group. Thus, the termination plaintiff usually satisfies element (4) simply by producing evidence that the employer had a continuing need for someone to perform the plaintiff's work, or, even more clearly, that the employer in fact filled plaintiff's former position, but not necessarily with someone from another protected class.

On the other hand, in cases where an employer alleges and the court agrees that plaintiff's termination was part of a classic, true reduction in force ("RIF"), i.e., where the plaintiff was not replaced, "it would make no sense to require a plaintiff to show the position from which she had been terminated 'remained open.' " *Bellaver v. Quanex Corp.*, 200 F.3d 485, 494 (7th Cir. 2000). One circuit modifies the plaintiff's burden in that situation by substituting for the "remain open" requirement a showing that similarly situated employees not members of plaintiff's protected class were treated more favorably. *Id.* at 494–95 (part of alternative holding). A plaintiff might carry that burden, in turn, with evidence that a non-protected class member was given plaintiff's work or that a purportedly "riffed" non-protected class member was moved to another job with the employer. *Thorn v. Sundstrand Aerospace Corp.*, 207 F.3d 383 (7th Cir. 2000). But a replacement employee's work performance following a RIF is irrelevant to the critical question whether management had an economic or unlawful discriminatory motive at the time of terminating the plaintiff. *Cullen v. Olin Corp.*, 195 F.3d 317 (7th Cir. 1999).

The Title VII prima facie case of sex-based wage or salary discrimination is in most circuits more exacting than the required counterpart demonstration under the Equal Pay Act. Like the EPA plaintiff, the Title VII plaintiff must show that she is paid less for performing substantially comparable work to that performed by one or more members of the opposite gender. That showing suffices for a form of strict prima facie liability under EPA. In a Title VII action, however, the plaintiff must also offer at least inferential evidence, per *McDonnell Douglas*, that the salary shortfall is a product of the employer's intentional discrimination against her because of her or his gender. Thus, she must first show, as under EPA, that (1) she is a member of a protected class and (2) that she was paid less than non-members of that class for work requiring substantially the same skill, effort, and responsibility. Then she must also show, to establish a claim under Title VII, that the underpayment occurred under circumstances raising an inference of discrimination.

Claims of disparate treatment in discipline present fewer complications. The plaintiff must show prima facie that (1) he belongs to a class protected by Title VII, (2) he was qualified for the job he holds or held, and (3) a similarly situated employee engaged in identical or similar misconduct but received lesser or no discipline. There are alternative formulations for a prima facie case of discriminatory demotion: that the misconduct resulting in the demotion was substantially the same as that engaged in by a similarly situated comparator outside plaintiff's protected class, yet the discipline plaintiff received was more severe; or that plaintiff, a member of a protected class, was qualified for the job he held, but was demoted and replaced by someone outside his class. See *Rioux v. City of Atlanta*, 520 F.3d 1269 (11th Cir. 2008) (dictum).

If the plaintiff establishes the prima facie case, a judicially created presumption declares the resulting inference of discrimination conclusive unless the defendant offers evidence that it had one or more "legitimate, nondiscriminatory reasons" for an employment decision. *McDonnell Douglas*, 411 U.S. at 802. The defendant must set forth this reason "clearly" and through "admissible evidence." *Burdine*, 450 U.S. at 255. Moreover, the reason must relate to what the defendant knew and relied on at the time of the challenged decision.

The preliminary question of whether the plaintiff established a prima facie case loses all significance once the defendant presents its proof. Put otherwise, the definition of the prima facie case merely aids the court in determining whether to grant a defendant's motion for judgment as a matter of law under Federal Rule of Civil Procedure 50(a) at the close of the plaintiff's case (or "directed verdict," as it is still known in most state courts). Once both sides rest, the trier of fact must evaluate all admitted evidence, including but not limited to the plaintiff's prima facie evidence, to decide if the plaintiff has carried the ultimate burden of demonstrating intentional discrimination. Thus, jury instructions in an age discrimination case that in effect permitted the jurors to find that age was a determining factor in the plaintiff's termination if they believed his prima facie evidence that younger employees were treated more favorably during a reduction in force have been held harmfully prejudicial to the employer. *Seman v. Coplay Cement Co.*, 26 F.3d 428 (3d Cir. 1994). A trial judge's ultimate determination about discriminatory intent—whether shown through direct or indirect evidence—is one of fact and may therefore be overturned on appeal only if "clearly erroneous." *Anderson v. City of Bessemer*, 470 U.S. 564, 573 (1985); Federal Rule of Civil Procedure 52(a).

Traditionally, most courts have viewed as "legitimate" virtually any reason the employer shows it relied on that can be distinguished from the five group characteristics protected by statute and from the few "proxy" factors that perfectly correspond to one of those groups. Thus, personality conflicts between the plaintiff and a supervisor, or management's genuine perception, accurate or not, that a plaintiff is adversarial, are classic "legitimate, nondiscriminatory reasons" that will absolve the employer of liability unless the plaintiff proves them to have been offered as a pretext for unlawful discrimination. This view is evidently driven by deference to the employer's superior knowledge of its own productivity, safety, and efficiency requirements. See *Hazen Paper Co. v. Biggins*, 507 U.S. 604 (1993).

Although the opinion in *McDonnell Douglas* suggested that the employer need only "articulate" a legitimate, nondiscriminatory reason, perhaps simply in an argument or brief, the Court definitively determined in *Burdine* that the employer's burden, while not onerous, may be discharged only through evidence that clearly explains its proffered reason or reasons. The reason may be anything other than race, sex, religion, or national origin—or a factor that correlates perfectly with one of those grounds—and suffices to respond to the prima facie case provided it is reasonably specific and an employer witness testifies that he relied on that reason at the time of the challenged decision. *Walker v. Mortham*, 158 F.3d 1177 (11th Cir. 1998). The reason need only be honestly held, not correct. See *Dvorak v. Mostardi Platt Assocs., Inc.*, 289 F.3d 479 (7th Cir. 2002). The Supreme Court has insisted that the defendant's burden is one of production only and that the burden of persuading about intentional discrimination resides with the plaintiff throughout. *Texas Department of Community Affairs v. Burdine*, 450 U.S. 248 (1981). Accordingly, like the presumptions described in Federal Rule of Evidence 301, the *McDonnell Douglas* presumption of unlawful discriminatory motive that arises from a successful prima facie case disappears and has no further force in the litigation if the employer discharges its relatively modest burden of producing evidence of a legitimate, nondiscriminatory reason for the challenged employment action—in other words, the bubble bursts.

A plaintiff can nevertheless prevail on rebuttal. To do so, the plaintiff must persuade the court that the defendant's purported legitimate reason is a smokescreen or "pretext" for intentional discrimination. It bears emphasis, however, that the plaintiff does not encounter this burden until after the defendant has produced evidence of one or more specific legitimate, nondiscriminatory reasons.

The Court had written that the plaintiff could make the pretext showing, by the standard preponderance of the evidence quantum, in either of two generic ways: by demonstrating through the plaintiff's own affirmative evidence, including that previously adduced prima facie, that the employer, in reaching its decision, explicitly relied on the plaintiff's protected group status, rather than on its proffered legitimate reason; or, less directly, simply by convincing the judge or jury that the proffered reason is an implausible explanation for the challenged decision. *Aikens*, 460 U.S. at 716; *Burdine*, 450 U.S. at 256. The Supreme Court held, in *St. Mary's Honor Center v. Hicks*, 509 U.S. 502 (1993), that the latter showing merely permits but does not mandate a judgment for the plaintiff.

In *Reeves v. Sanderson Plumbing Products, Inc.*, 530 U.S. 133 (2000), a case under the ADEA, the Court, taking note of differing passages in *St. Mary's* that the circuits had found to be in tension, wrote that the jury may, but need not, conclude that the defendant intentionally discriminated on a prohibited ground simply from two kinds of evidence: (1) evidence establishing the modest *McDonnell Douglas* prima facie case, coupled with (2) "sufficient" evidence that the employer's asserted legitimate nondiscriminatory explanation is false. The Court considered this approach consistent with general evidence law: "the factfinder is entitled to consider a party's dishonesty about a material fact as 'affirmative evidence of guilt' "; and once the employer's asserted reason is rejected, unlawful discrimination "may well be the most likely alternative explanation." *Id.* at 147. But the Court qualified this holding by requiring as well that the jury may properly find liability on such evidence only if, after proper instructions, it makes dual findings: (1) that the reason the employer offered for taking adverse action against the plaintiff was not its real reason and (2) the unlawful ground was in fact the employer's real reason. See *id.* at 153.

As long as the plaintiff's counsel substantially impeaches or contradicts defendant-favorable evidence, a court should not consider that evidence in determining whether to uphold a plaintiff's verdict. In effect, *Reeves* affirms the approach that a defendant is not entitled to judgment as a matter of law either when its uncorroborated evidence is contradicted by evidence favoring the plaintiff or even when the plaintiff's evidence merely impeaches the decision-maker's testimony of legitimate, nondiscriminatory reasons.

In theory, then, judgment as a matter of law should accordingly after *Reeves* be granted only in the presumably rare case that a court—considering all of the plaintiff's evidence, but only the uncontradicted, unimpeached evidence favoring the defendant—determines that a jury could not rationally find (or, after verdict, could not have rationally found) by a preponderance of that evidence the ultimate fact of unlawful race, sex, religious, national origin, or age discrimination. In such a case, judgment for the defendant is warranted even if the jury reasonably believes the plaintiff's prima facie case and the falsity of the employer's stated legitimate, nondiscriminatory reason. It is evident from the *Reeves* opinion that the Supreme Court intends these rules to apply to cases under Title VII, where a plaintiff, after the 1991 amendments, need only prove that race, sex, religion, or national origin was a "motivating" factor in the employer's decision, not just to cases under the ADEA, where the plaintiff, since *Hazen Paper Co. v. Biggins*, 507 U.S. 604 (1993), discussed below, has been required to show that age was a "determinative" or "but for" factor. However, in the wake of *Reeves*, while the lower federal courts cite and purport to apply *Reeves*, few apply it literally to permit a plaintiff to survive summary or trial judgment merely because a defense witness testifying to a legitimate, nondiscriminatory reason is impeached by minimal or doubtful evidence or by equivocal cross-examination. Instead, when plaintiffs proceed with *McDonnell Douglas* inferential evidence alone, "substantial" plaintiff's impeachment evidence or "affirmative" (that is, more direct) evidence of unlawful discrimination is generally required to prevent the defendant from receiving summary judgment or judgment as a matter of law, before or after the verdict. See, e.g., *Schnabel v. Abramson*, 232 F.3d 83 (2d Cir. 2000); *Chapman v. AI Transport*, 229 F.3d 1012 (11th Cir. 2000) (en banc).

After *Reeves*, one may imagine a fairly complex, sequential series of decisions to be made by the judge, or instructions to be followed by the jury, in post–1991 Act intentional discrimination actions. In rare cases, the trial judge at the close of defendant's case should grant the plaintiff judgment as a matter of law under Federal Rule of Civil Procedure 50(a)(1). This would happen only if any rational jury would have to find by a preponderance the existence of the facts constituting the plaintiff's prima facie case, and the defendant failed even to produce evidence recognized as a nondiscriminatory reason for the challenged action.

Far more commonly, the judge at the close of all the evidence may, at the employer's request, charge the members of the jury that if the plaintiff has persuaded them not to believe the evidence the employer produced about a purported legitimate nondiscriminatory reason, they nevertheless need not conclude that the employer relied on that reason as a pretext for unlawful discrimination.

But the judge may also have to charge, at the plaintiff's request, that the jury members may find unlawful pretext, and hence the ultimate fact of intentional discrimination, based solely on their disbelief of the defendant's proffered legitimate reason, together with the prima facie evidence earlier presented by the plaintiff during her case in chief, even absent other, more "direct" or "affirmative," evidence of unlawful pretext. *Reeves* supports this position:

> In appropriate circumstances, the trier of fact can reasonably infer from the falsity of the explanation that the employer is dissembling to cover up a discriminatory purpose. Such an inference is consistent with the general prin-

ciple of evidence law that the factfinder is entitled to consider a party's dishonesty about a material fact as "affirmative evidence of guilt." Moreover, once the employer's justification has been eliminated, discrimination may well be the most likely alternative explanation, especially since the employer is in the best position to put forth the actual reason for its decision."

530 U.S. at 147 (internal citations omitted). Some circuits have held, however, that it is not reversible error, and indeed is preferable, for trial courts not to give pretext instructions at all. See, e.g., *Moore v. Robertson Fire Prot. Dist.*, 249 F.3d 786 (8th Cir. 2001).

It should be remembered that even after *Reeves*, a plaintiff is well advised to buttress its case about the falsity of the employer's stated reason with more direct or affirmative evidence that the employer relied on a group characteristic prohibited by statute. Alternatively, such "more direct" evidence may suffice by itself to show intentional discrimination—e.g., cases involving slurs or stereotypes by employer agents, cases presenting persuasive evidence that a "comparator" outside the plaintiff's protected group received more favorable or less disadvantageous treatment than the plaintiff, or evidence of discrimination against others members of plaintiff's group.

A plaintiff's demonstration that he was in fact the most qualified applicant is neither required nor is it sufficient. It is not necessarily tantamount to a showing that the employer understood or agreed with that assessment and promoted another as a pretext for discrimination. The employer's explanation, in other words, may be erroneous in fact but sincerely believed by the decision-maker and therefore non-pretextual in the sense intended by *St. Mary's*. An employer's decision may be subjective, mistaken, unwise, erroneous, or reflect a misjudging of relevant credentials, without necessarily being motivated by a consideration prohibited by Title VII or ADEA.

A standard legitimate, nondiscriminatory reason is that plaintiff violated a customary work rule of the employer. The decisions outline a number of specific ways in which a plaintiff may show such a reason pretextual. First, a plaintiff may persuade a jury that she did not violate the rule in question if the testimony about many of her alleged deficiencies does not accurately reflect the work situation. Of course, evidence that the plaintiff did not in fact violate the rule does not preclude the possibility that the employer honestly believed she did, but nevertheless it has been held to preclude summary judgment; on the other hand, summary judgment for the employer is improper if a plaintiff who concededly did violate a work rule offers evidence that other employees outside her protected class were not similarly disciplined for committing a similar infraction. Evidence that the decision-maker herself engaged in the same policy violation as the plaintiff is "especially compelling" evidence of pretext. *Ross v. Rhodes Furniture, Inc.*, 146 F.3d 1286, 1291 (11th Cir. 1998).

McDonnell Douglas, in describing the variety of evidence the plaintiff may use to rebut a proffered legitimate, nondiscriminatory reason, makes clear that the individual disparate treatment plaintiff who sues alone may fortify the inference of discrimination with anecdotal evidence that one or more similarly situated members of his protected group experienced discriminatory treatment at the hands of the same employer. Statistical evidence of the adverse differential treatment of the plaintiff's group may also fortify the case of the solo disparate treatment plaintiff. Testimony of prior discriminatory acts against members of the plaintiff's protected group by the particular employer agent alleged to have discriminated against the plaintiff is particularly probative of that agent's state of mind. Of course, the assertedly comparable evidence must reflect discrimination under similar circumstances to be admissible on the question whether the particular plaintiff was also the victim of unlawful discrimination.

These modes of intentional discrimination are designed to ferret out and penalize only employer conduct that adversely differentiates on the basis of one or more of Title VII's prohibited grounds; they are not designed to assure workplace norms or mores that are fair in other respects. Thus, any reason for the employer's challenged decision deemed not "because of" race, gender, religion, or national origin (or a proxy for one of those grounds) is likely to be viewed as legitimate, even if the trier of fact also considers that reason unfair, unreasonable, or unenlightened. In particular, courts express great reluctance to substitute their own judgment for the standards of proficiency or competence assertedly relied on by academic employers.

Where an employer offers more than one "legitimate, non-discriminatory reason" in response to a plaintiff's *McDonnell Douglas* prima facie case, the circuits are divided on whether the plaintiff, to raise a permissible inference of unlawful discrimination, must negate each such reason. See L. Rosenthal, *Motions for Summary Judgment When Employers Offer Multiple Justifications for Adverse Employment Actions: Why The Exceptions Should Swallow The Rule*, 2002 UTAH L. REV. 335 (collecting cases).

     ii.   Pleading Sufficiency

The Supreme Court has held that a plaintiff relying on the *McDonnell Douglas* proof mode need not allege the prima facie or other elements of that case, but instead need only allege the ultimate fact of unlawful discrimination on a ground prohibited by Title VII. *Swierkiewicz v. Soreman N.A.*, 534 U.S. 506 (2002). Subsequently, however, the Court ruled in a civil rights case that any federal civil plaintiff must plead facts that make his claim facially "plausible," and while plausible does not equate to "probable," it does require enough pleading detail to enable the court to conclude that liability is more than a mere possibility. In particular, merely pleading facts that are consistent with liability falls short of pleading the required plausibility of the plaintiff's entitlement to relief. *Ashcroft v. Iqbal*, ___ U.S. ___, ___, 129 S.Ct. 1937, 1949 (2009). Yet the opinion appears to view *Swierkiewicz* as undisturbed. The cases can be reconciled by requiring a Title VII plaintiff to plead facts sufficient to make "plausible" each element of a claim of unlawful discrimination or discriminatory employer reliance on a prohibited ground, resulting in the denial of an employment benefit to or the imposition of an employment detriment on the plaintiff without requiring the plaintiff to plead the particular elements of any particular trial proof mode, e.g., *McDonnell Douglas*.

iii. Supervisors: Special Evidentiary and Employer Liability Problems

a. "Me, Too" Evidence

Under what circumstances should a court admit evidence offered by an individual disparate treatment plaintiff alleging a discriminatory act by his own supervisor that one or more coworkers' supervisors (who did not supervise the plaintiff) discriminated against those coworkers on the same ground? In *Sprint/United Management Co. v. Mendelsohn*, 552 U.S. 379 (2008), the Supreme Court held that neither the preliminary relevance question under Federal Rule of Evidence 401, nor the probable value/prejudicial effect balancing inquiry mandated by Rule 403, should be resolved by per se rules. If, for example, there are common company policies respecting discrimination that all supervisors must follow, or other evidence shows work-related or personal interaction between the supervisors in question, the scale would tilt toward admission of the evidence concerning supervisors who do not supervise the plaintiff.

b.   Employer Liability in "Cat's Paw" Cases

Suppose the plaintiff can prove an unlawful discriminatory motive on the part of his supervisor, who then recommends discipline or discharge to his supervisor, who in turn exercises the ultimate authority on behalf of the employer to discipline or discharge the plaintiff. May the employer in such a "Cat's Paw" case be liable for intentional discrimination tracing to the proven unlawful animus of the subordinate supervisor where there is no separate evidence of unlawful bias on the part of the ultimate decision-maker? Again declining to issue per se rules, the Supreme Court has held, in a case under the Uniformed Services Employment and Reemployment Rights Act, Pub. L. 103–353, 108 Stat. 3149 (1994) ("USERRA"), that if a plaintiff can prove that the biased, subordinate supervisor's action was intended to cause an adverse employment action and was a proximate cause thereof, the employer will be liable. *Staub v. Proctor Hospital*, ___ U.S. ___, 131 S.Ct. 1186 (2011). In so holding, the Court specifically rejected two hard-and-fast rules proposed by the employer: that the ultimate decision-maker's exercise of independent judgment, or his independent investigation and rejection of the allegations of discriminatory animus by the recommending subordinate supervisor, should negate the earlier subordinate agent's animus and responsibility for the adverse action.

Although the decision was under USERRA, it will almost inevitably be applied to Title VII cases because both statutes' texts impose liability when a prohibited ground is a "motivating factor" in the adverse employment action, and because the opinion is supported in part by reference to Title VII precedents.

iv. The Problem of "Mixed Motives"

The classic evidentiary structure erected by *McDonnell Douglas* and *Burdine*, while furnishing a workable matrix for inferentially ferreting out intentional discrimination, does not fully come to grips with the complexities of many cases because it assumes that an employer's motivation was grounded entirely on a prohibited reason or a legitimate one. In fact, employers commonly advance more than one asserted legitimate reason for a challenged employment decision, and courts often conclude that an employer relied on one or more of those reasons and a ground of discrimination condemned by Title VII. As a practical matter, the vast majority of intentional discrimination cases involve mixed motives: The plaintiff must prove the employer acted, at least in part, for an unlawful reason, and employers respond to the plaintiff's prima facie case by offering evidence of one or more "legitimate nondiscriminatory reasons" for their action. So it is vitally important in the great bulk of Title VII cases to know whether plaintiffs can prevail, and if so what remedies they may receive, where the evidence shows both lawful and unlawful reasons.

In *Price Waterhouse v. Hopkins*, 490 U.S. 228 (1989), a Supreme Court plurality concluded that when an employer undertakes a challenged employment decision for more than one reason, and the reason that is unlawful under Title VII is a "motivating" or "substantial motivating" factor in the employer's decision, liability will attach unless the employer can prove by a preponderance of the evidence that it would have reached the same decision for one or more independent, lawful reasons. If an employer carries that persuasion burden, the plurality wrote, it should be found not to have committed an unlawful employment practice, despite the evidence of partial unlawful motive. *Id.* at 244 n.10. If, on the other hand, the employer cannot carry by a preponderance of the evidence the "same-decision" showing, it will be liable.

But a critical fifth vote assigning the employer the burden of persuasion on this "same decision" issue was cast by Justice O'Connor, and she would have imposed that burden only where the plaintiff proffers "direct evidence" that the discriminatory factor played a substantial role in the employer's decision. *Id.* at 276 (O'Connor, J., concurring). Subsequently, Congress enacted Section 107 of the Civil Rights Act of 1991, codified as new Title VII section 703(m). It declares simply that an unlawful employment practice is established when the plaintiff demonstrates that employer reliance on protected group status was a "motivating factor" for "any" employment practice, "even though other factors also motivated the practice." In 2003, the Supreme Court resolved a longstanding circuit split arising from Justice O'Connor's crucial fifth vote in *Price Waterhouse*: whether a plaintiff could establish a violation under section 703(m), in mixed-motive cases, and therefore receive the limited remedies afforded by section 706(g)(2)(B), when her proof that race, sex, religion, or national origin was a motivating factor in the employer's decision was not "direct" but solely under *McDonnell Douglas*. In *Desert Palace, Inc. v. Costa*, 539 U.S. 90 (2003), a unanimous court concluded that after the 1991 amendments to Title VII, the plaintiff need not offer "direct" evidence—only persuasive evidence, direct or indirect—that race, sex, religion, or national origin was a "motivating" factor in an employer's adverse employment decision in order to obtain a "mixed-motive" or "same-decision" instruction requiring the employer to demonstrate that it would have made the same employment decision wholly apart from its consideration of one of those unlawful grounds.

The Supreme Court, speaking through Justice Thomas, concluded that the words of section 703(m) were unambiguous; that the section "does not mention, much less require, that a plaintiff make a heightened showing through direct

evidence" and accordingly that Congress abrogated the "direct
evidence" requirement of Justice O'Connor's *Price Waterhouse* concurrence. *Id.* at 98–99. Congress did define the
quantum of evidence a plaintiff must develop to show a
partial, unlawful motivating factor (and the quantum of evidence a defendant must produce to make a same-decision
showing) by providing in a different section of the 1991 Act
that "demonstrates," as used in sections 703(m) and 706(g),
means meeting "the burdens of production and persuasion."
Id. at 99. But it did not define the nature of the evidence
plaintiff must use to show an unlawful motivating factor—the
showing that establishes a violation under section 703(m) and
triggers the production and persuasion burden the defendant
must carry with respect to the same-decision issue if it wishes
to avail itself of the limited affirmative defense of section
706(g)(2)(B). For that purpose, the Court observed, circumstantial evidence not only suffices but may sometimes be more
persuasive than direct evidence. *Id.* at 99–101. As observed
above, a lower federal court consensus concludes that *Desert
Palace* does not replace the highly indirect *McDonnell Doug-
las/Reeves* mode of proving individual disparate treatment. So
long as a plaintiff presents sufficient evidence for a "reasonable jury" to find by a preponderance that race, sex, religion,
or national origin was a motivating factor (which in most
circuits means "played some part") in the challenged employment decision, the plaintiff is eligible to establish a violation
pursuant to section 703(m) and is entitled to the same-
decision instruction imposing the persuasion burden on defendant respecting the limited affirmative defense of section
706(g)(2)(B)—even, apparently, over the defendant's objection.

To avoid monetary liability once the plaintiff has demonstrated through any combination of "direct" or circumstantial
evidence that the employer relied at least in part on an
unlawful ground, the employer must demonstrate "that [it]

would have taken the same action in the absence of the impermissible motivating factor"—even if there is evidence that at the time of the adverse employment action the employer knew that the employee had disobeyed work rules or lied. Section 107(b) (amending Title VII § 706(g), 42 U.S.C.A. § 2000e–5(g) (West 2010)); *Stacks v. Southwestern Bell Yellow Pages, Inc.*, 27 F.3d 1316 (8th Cir. 1994). The Act codifies the *Price Waterhouse* view that the required employer "demonstration," once triggered, extends to the burden of persuasion as well as production on this question. Section 104 (adding subsection 701(m) to Title VII, 42 U.S.C.A. § 2000e-m (West 2010)).

The legislation goes somewhat beyond the *Price Waterhouse* plurality in providing that even the defendant who does make the required demonstration remains liable, but not for hire or reinstatement orders, back pay, or other monetary remedies. If unlawful discrimination was a "motivating" factor in the challenged employment decision, the employer has committed a law violation; but if it carries the "same decision" showing, the violation is remediable only by prospective relief and attorney's fees. Section 107(b)(3) (adding paragraph (2)(B) to Title VII § 706(g), 42 U.S.C.A. § 2000e–5(g) (West 2010)).

The addition to Title VII of sections 703(m) and 706(g)(2)(B), and, in contrast, their omission from the ADEA, is significant in practice. First, thanks to section 703(m), the plaintiff's ultimate burden in establishing Title VII liability is only to demonstrate that an unlawful ground motivated, rather than determined, the imposition of an employment detriment or denial of an employment benefit. Where the Title VII plaintiff attempts to meet this burden through the indirect *McDonnell Douglas* formula, judges ruling on summary judgment and Federal Rule of Civil Procedure 50 motions will apply the *Reeves* requirements for demonstrating "pretext." Second, a Title VII plaintiff who takes the *McDonnell Douglas* path and presents evidence sufficient under *Reeves* to survive a Rule 50 motion at the close of all the evidence will, like the Title VII plaintiff who uses "direct" evidence, be entitled to a section 703(m) instruction imposing on the employer the burden of demonstrating that it would have reached the same decision independent of the unlawful reason. Third, under section 706(g)(2)(B), the Title VII defendant who carries the "same-decision" showing is nevertheless liable and subject to limited declaratory and injunctive relief and attorney's fees. The ADEA plaintiff, in contrast, must show not just that age was a "motivating" factor but that it was a "determinative" or "but for" factor in the challenged decision. If he does, the defendant is liable for all ADEA remedies; if he does not, there is no ADEA liability. Either way, the ADEA defendant is never required to make a "same decision" showing. *Gross v. FBL Fin. Servs.*, ___ U.S. ___, 129 S.Ct. 2343 (2009).

v.　"After–Acquired Evidence": A Limitation of Employer Liability

Suppose an employer produces evidence—discovered during a post-termination investigation or litigation—of the plaintiff's misconduct during employment that would have led the employer to take the same adverse action. Should the employer be relieved of liability altogether, enjoy a limitation on liability, or be subject to full relief?

In *McKennon v. Nashville Banner Publishing Co.*, 513 U.S. 352 (1995), the Court steered a middle course among these alternatives. To capitalize on employee misconduct discovered only after the employer discriminatorily imposed an employment detriment, the employer bears the burden of proving "that the wrongdoing was of such severity that the employee *in fact would* have been *terminated* on those grounds alone if the employer had known of it at the time of the discharge." *Id.* at 362–63 (emphasis added). It is unnecessary for the court to agree with the employer's assessment that the employee's misconduct is "serious" or "pervasive" so long as the employer can prove that under its established rules, applied without discrimination, it would have discharged the employee had it known of such conduct when it occurred.

Still, the employer demonstration of such misconduct serves only to limit liability, not as a complete defense. The Supreme Court observed that under ADEA as well as Title VII, remedies serve the twin objectives of deterring violations and compensating past injuries. The plaintiff advances those objectives, the Court wrote, by demonstrating the employer's discrimination. Allowing after-acquired evidence to serve as a complete bar to liability would unjustifiably undermine the statutes' remedial goals. In reaching this conclusion, the Court specifically distinguished mixed-motive situations; after-acquired evidence does not even figure in the decisional calculus until the factfinder has determined that the employer's sole or motivating basis for the challenged employment decision was unlawful (and that the employer would not have reached the same decision independent of its pure or partial unlawful motivation). *Id.* at 359.

But the Court was equally insistent that the employer's wrongdoing could not simply be disregarded in the formulation of an appropriate remedy. In this connection, the Court read ADEA's authorization of legal or equitable relief as a mandate for the trial court to take the employee's wrongdoing into account as a way of recognizing the significant managerial prerogatives that ADEA, like Title VII, preserves to the employer. While acknowledging that the relevant equitable considerations will vary from case to case, the Court nevertheless concluded that here, and as a general rule in cases of this type, neither reinstatement nor front pay is an appropriate remedy.

Declining to formulate an across-the-board rule for back pay, the Court concluded that the "beginning point in the trial court's formulation of a [monetary] remedy should be calculation of backpay from the date of the unlawful discharge to the date the new information was discovered." *Id.* at 362. Unlike the "mixed-motive" employer who establishes that it would have taken the challenged action at the time even absent reliance on a motivating factor forbidden by Title VII, the employer who carries the persuasion burden on after-acquired evidence will almost surely sustain some monetary liability, even if that liability terminates as of the date of discovery of employee wrongdoing. This is because after-acquired evidence presupposes that the employer committed an unlawful employment practice; the tardily discovered legitimate reason was not any part of its motivation when it demoted or terminated the plaintiff.

The EEOC and at least one circuit court have since opined that Title VII compensatory and punitive damages and ADEA liquidated damages are available notwithstanding after-acquired evidence. *Russell v. Microdyne*, 65 F.3d 1229 (4th Cir. 1995). Further, the EEOC does not view the *McKennon* concern of protecting the employer's interest in severing the employment relationship as a warrant to place a time limit on compensatory damages for emotional harm. Rather, the after-acquired showing limits only those out-of-pocket losses that are analogous to back pay. Nor does the EEOC see in *McKennon* a ban or limitation on punitive damages, provided the plaintiff proves the employer's malice or reckless indifference. If this view prevails in the courts, the employer who can prove that it would have made the same decision adverse to the plaintiff based on a legitimate nondiscriminatory reason known to it at the time gets greater relief from monetary remedies than the employer who discovers such evidence only after the fact.

(3) Systemic Disparate Treatment

Intentional discriminatory treatment may also be demonstrated in the aggregate. "Systemic disparate treatment" proof depends primarily upon statistical evidence of gross disparities between the actual and expected representation of the plaintiff's group in one or more levels of an employer's workforce. According to the underlying theory, articulated in *International Brotherhood of Teamsters v. United States*, 431 U.S. 324 (1977), an employer that does not routinely discriminate should over time achieve within its employee complement an incidence of protected group representation not significantly less than the group's representation in an available pool of qualified applicants.

Systemic disparate treatment, the residue of a number of individually discriminatory decisions, is evidenced by a significant workforce underrepresentation of a protected group relative to the incidence one would expect based on its members' interest, availability, and qualifications. Unlike the impact case, it is predicated on a showing of intentional discrimination. Further, the systemic treatment case is typically brought by several joined plaintiffs or a plaintiff class, and endeavors to prove that the defendant, as the result of an unspecified variety of policies, practices, and individual decisions by employer agents, discriminated against members of the protected group in general. In the systemic treatment case, all members of the protected group denied hire or promotion to the job level during the period when the protected group was found to be grossly underrepresented are presumptively entitled to remedies, regardless of which particular employer policies or decisions by employer agents led to their rejection. *Franks v. Bowman Transp. Co.*, 424 U.S. 747 (1976). By contrast, relief in the "impact" case is limited to those plaintiffs, sometimes as few as one, who suffered an employment detriment as the result of a particular practice shown to have had disproportionate adverse impact on the plaintiff's group.

Occasionally, an employer's policy will on its face draw a distinction on the basis of a prohibited characteristic; a group of plaintiffs suing as a class or joined under Federal Rule of Civil Procedure 20 could then establish systemic disparate treatment on the basis of the policy alone. More typically, the plaintiffs will offer statistical evidence in an attempt to show a raw, substantial underrepresentation of their protected group relative to the numbers of their members that might have been expected had the employer hired or promoted randomly. This prima facie statistical case of systemic disparate treatment compares the employer's actual or "observed" number of protected group members hired for or promoted to the job in question against a hypothetical number of protected group members that an employer who hired or promoted randomly might have been "expected" to select. The theoretical underpinning of statistically-premised judicial findings of systemic disparate treatment is that, "absent explanation, it is ordinarily to be expected that nondiscriminatory hiring practices will in time result in a work force more or less representative of the racial and ethnic composition of the" relevant pool. *Teamsters*, 431 U.S. at 339 n.20. Although anecdotal evidence of instances of individual disparate treatment certainly fortifies the inference of systemic disparate treatment raised by statistical disparities, the disparities alone may prove intentional discrimination, at least where they are gross. *EEOC v. O & G Spring and Wire Forms Specialty Co.*, 38 F.3d 872 (7th Cir. 1994).

In undertaking a showing of gross underrepresentation of the protected group, the plaintiff must take care to calculate the "expected" number by reference to the relevant pool from which the selection will be made, and that pool must be refined to account for the minimum qualifications, including geographic proximity, requisite for the job in question. In an order that ascends with the complexity of the skill level at issue, this pool may range from general population or workforce statistics within an actual or feasible recruiting zone, to a nationwide pool of candidates with the key educational or experience credentials. In the case of promotions that the employer has historically made exclusively or primarily from within, the pool would consist of lower-level employees in the employer's own workforce who meet the base requirements for promotion.

Defining the pool from which the expected percentage of minority representation should be calculated is often keenly contested. While protected group representation in a recruiting-zone population or local workforce may suffice where the jobs in question are largely unskilled, or from the percentage of protected group members employed by other area employers for jobs that are moderately skilled, the fair measurement of disparities in highly skilled positions demands refinement not just for availability and interest but, above all, for specialized qualifications. Courts have on occasion dispensed with refined evidence of the characteristics of the pool from which applicants are drawn when the disparities presented are extreme. The classic example is where the protected group in question constitutes what has been termed the "inexorable zero"—no representation at all in the employer's workforce.

Whatever comparison is used, the plaintiff must establish a statistically significant "gross" disparity between observed and expected protected group representation. The magnitude of this disparity must be sufficient to show that discrimination was an employer's routine operating procedure such that relief should be granted to the entire underrepresented class. This generally requires expert testimony concerning the statistical technique of binomial distribution and its key measure, standard deviation. The actual and expected numbers of protected group members, together with the total number of persons hired for or promoted to the job during the liability period alleged in the complaint, are fed into the binomial distribution formula, which is designed to gauge the degree to which an "underrepresentation" departs from hypothetical "random" or "chance" hiring or promotion. Statisticians have conventionally ruled out chance as the likely cause of a negative deviation from the norm when the formula shows that the observed number falls more than 1.95 standard deviations below the expected number; this convention holds that there is then less than a 5% chance that the underrepresentation is itself the result of chance. Apparently determined to avoid "false positives"—implicating an innocent employer—the Supreme Court has written somewhat vaguely that unlawful discrimination may be suspected as the cause of an underrepresentation only "if the difference between the expected value and the observed number is 'greater than two or three [negative] standard deviations' "—a level at which statisticians would exclude chance as the explanation with overwhelming confidence. *Hazelwood*, 433 U.S. at 309 n.14.

It is because the law requires an underrepresentation of this magnitude that a court may rely solely on statistical evidence to indict an employer for systemic disparate treatment discrimination in violation of section 703(a) without running afoul of a distinct provision of Title VII § 703(j). Section 703(j) provides that Title VII shall not be:

interpreted to require any employer ... to grant preferential treatment ... because of race, color, religion, sex, or national origin ... on account of an imbalance which may exist with respect to the total number or percentage of persons of any race, color, religion, sex, or national origin employed by any employer ... in comparison with the total number or percentage of persons of such race, color, religion, sex, or national origin in any community . . . or in the available work force in any community.

The Court in *Teamsters* rejected the argument that holding an employer liable for systemic treatment discrimination upon proof of a gross statistical underrepresentation violates section 703(j) by ordering the employer to maintain a work force that mirrors the general population. 431 U.S. at 339 n.20. Many employee complements will fail to mirror the protected group's percentage in a surrounding population or work force without falling short enough to violate the "two or three standard deviation" test or therefore to violate section 703(a).

A more sophisticated statistical technique, multiple regression analysis, will usually be required to establish the requisite disparity when variations in the particular term and condition of employment at issue—for example, compensation—are explainable by reference to a large number of factors. The Court has indicated, however, that a plaintiff's multiple regression analysis need not eliminate all potential nondiscriminatory explanations of disparity, only the most significant. *Bazemore v. Friday*, 478 U.S. 385 (1986).

Once the plaintiff group adduces express or statistical evidence of systemic disparate treatment, the employer has an opportunity to offer what *Teamsters* termed a nondiscriminatory "explanation" by way of rebuttal. Absent a defense, liability will be deemed established and the case moves to a second, bifurcated remedy phase. The employer's principal defense in these cases is to present evidence that casts doubt on the logical, statistical, or legal probative value of the plaintiff's evidence. For example, an employer may avoid the force of evidence of disparity by showing infirmities in the plaintiff-defined pool that exaggerate the availability of qualified members of the protected group, or by challenging the validity of the statistical conclusions drawn by the plaintiff's expert, including objections to insufficient sample size.

In the alternative, the employer may affirmatively present counter-comparative statistics. A more restrictively refined availability pool, for example, may generate negative disparities of a magnitude (less than two or three standard deviations) that judges will deem insignificant to alter the status quo and impose liability on an employer. Indeed, the employer may refute the existence of any negative disparity by offering data suggesting that it hired or promoted a greater number of protected group members than their availability in the employer-advocated pool would predict; in that instance, the standard deviation would be positive. Most powerfully, an employer that has maintained records differentiating its applicants by race, national origin, or gender may be able to offer "applicant-flow" statistics to establish that it hired at least as great a percentage of protected group members as of others. See *Hazelwood*, 433 at U.S. 208 n.13. Such evidence tends to show the particular defendant's comparative treatment of actual members of the protected group and others who had the requisite interest to offer themselves for hire or promotion. Applicant-flow evidence is therefore generally credited with greater probative value than standard deviation evidence drawn from the number of hires or promotions that might theoretically have been expected based on protected group availability in an appropriately defined pool of persons, none of whom may have actually sought employment with the defendant.

In the face of a showing of gross underrepresentation of the protected group, as evidenced by substantially unimpeached standard deviation data, applicant-flow data could nevertheless exonerate the employer when it treated a relatively small number of protected group applicants fairly or even favorably. But why did so few protected group members apply, given their significant representation in the underlying pool? Employers will contend the explanation is a self-selected lack of interest in the particular employment, despite presumptive minimum qualifications and availability. See, e.g., *EEOC v. Sears, Roebuck & Co.*, 839 F.2d 302 (7th Cir. 1988). That argument appears to have lesser force when the court views the statistical underrepresentation as overwhelming. And the plaintiff class's contrary explanation for the under-application by the protected group will be a long-standing, notorious employer reputation for discrimination against the group in question, a reputation so extreme as to render it "futile" for a member of that group to apply. If the plaintiffs can prove that more protected group members would have applied during the period of the alleged discrimination but for the employer's discriminatory practices, they may persuade a court to disregard or discount the employer's applicant flow evidence.

An employer unable to impeach or counter a finding of gross statistical underrepresentation must nevertheless be permitted to attempt to offer some other nondiscriminatory "explanation" for the disparity. *Teamsters*, 431 U.S. at 340 n.20. A protected group's apparent lack of interest in seeking the positions in question is one such explanation. Alternatively, an employer may explain a prima facie gross statistical underrepresentation by evidence demonstrating that one of its own neutral practices had disproportionate adverse impact on the protected group. This puts the employer in the odd position of becoming its own accuser, since such a practice may independently give rise to Title VII neutral practice liability even as it avoids liability for a practice motivated by discriminatory intent. In effect, the employer argues that an unlawful employment practice (a facially neutral test or experience requirement that disproportionately affects the protected group) explains the significant bottom-line underrepresentation of the protected group in the job level for which the test or experience requirement screens. See, e.g., *Griffin v. Carlin*, 755 F.2d 1516 (11th Cir. 1985). The employer would then be liable at most to those members of the protected group who were personally affected by the neutral practice rather than to all protected group members who applied for the position in question. Further, even to that reduced number of remedy-eligible plaintiffs, the employer will be liable only for back pay and not for the compensatory and punitive damages available since 1991 for intentional discrimination. An even better outcome for the employer results if it can persuade the court that its neutral practice that accounted for the underrepresentation is justified because it is "job related for the position in question and consistent with business necessity" within the meaning of section 703(k)(1)(A)(i), added by section 105(a) of the Civil Rights Act of 1991. In that event, the employer would not be liable to anyone for anything.

An amendment to Title VII, also added by § 105(a) of the Civil Rights Act of 1991, provides, "A demonstration that an employment practice is required by business necessity may not be used as a defense against a claim of intentional discrimination under this title." Title VII § 703(k)(2). At a minimum, this provision confirms the Supreme Court's position in *International Union, UAW v. Johnson Controls, Inc.*, 499 U.S. 187 (1991), that a facially discriminatory practice may be excused, if at all, only under the stringent BFOQ defense, and not merely by a showing of job relatedness and business necessity. Read broadly, however, the new section 703(k)(2) could also be applied to cases where the prima facie evidence of intentional discrimination consists of gross statistical disparities sufficient to establish systemic disparate treatment of the plaintiff class. If so, section 703(k)(2) would appear to deny the employer the last-chance defense discussed in *Griffin*. More likely, however, new section 703(k)(2) will be limited to the context that gave rise to its enactment: individual plaintiff evidence of express

or facial evidence, as contrasted to statistically proven systemic disparate treatment.

(4) The Relief Stage of the Bifurcated Systemic Disparate Treatment Action

Systemic treatment trials are conducted in distinct liability
and remedial phases. First, from evidence of a facially discriminatory policy, statistics alone, anecdotal evidence, or some
combination of the above, the court determines whether the
employer has intentionally discriminated against the plaintiff's protected group. If so, individual members of the plaintiff
class who reapply (or, in certain cases, apply for the first time)
for a position or promotion at this stage of the action may
thus become eligible to receive the full panoply of all otherwise
appropriate Title VII remedies: not only declaratory and injunctive relief but reinstatement, back pay, retroactive seniority, and, since the violation involves intentional discrimination,
the capped compensatory and punitive damages made available by the Civil Rights Act of 1991.

The Supreme Court has substantially eased the individual
plaintiff's burden of demonstrating entitlement to relief at the
remedy stage of the systemic treatment case. Even if the
prima facie case consists only of statistical evidence, that
evidence, if believed by the factfinder and not successfully
rebutted with a nondiscriminatory explanation, gives rise to a
presumption that each plaintiff who unsuccessfully sought
hire, promotion, or retention during the established liability
period was rejected because of her protected group status.
Franks v. Bowman Transp. Co., 424 U.S. 747 (1976). So long
as the individual applied for the position in question during
the established liability period, she need not even produce
evidence of her minimum qualifications. Proof of a broad-
based policy of unlawful discrimination, in other words, generates "reasonable grounds to infer that individual hiring deci-

sions were made in pursuit of the discriminatory policy and to require the employer to come forth with evidence dispelling that inference." *Teamsters*, 431 U.S. at 359. Although the prima facie case does not "conclusively demonstrate that all of the employer's decisions were part of the proven discriminatory pattern and practice," it creates "a greater likelihood that any single decision was a component of the overall pattern." *Id.* at 359 n.45.

To rebut the presumption, the employer may avoid liability to individual plaintiffs or plaintiff class members by persuading a court that they were not in fact victims of discrimination. For example, the employer may demonstrate that there were no vacancies in the pertinent position at the time a particular class member applied, that the plaintiff lacked minimum qualifications that the employer insisted upon at the time of the plaintiff's rejection, or that a successful applicant was better qualified. *Id.*; *Franks*, 424 U.S. at 773 n.32. Even class members who did not apply for a position during the proven liability period may sometimes receive individual relief, but they carry the heavy burden of persuading the court that it was futile for them to apply because of an employer's notorious reputation for egregious discrimination against their protected group and that they would have applied otherwise. *Teamsters*, 431 U.S. at 365. It does not suffice for non-applicants to show that they are interested in obtaining a job only at the time of judgment; further, unlike "applicant" plaintiff class members, they bear the burden of showing their own minimum qualifications at the time that, but for futility, prove they would have applied. *Id.* at 369 n.53.

(5) HOW THE INDIVIDUAL AND SYSTEMIC DISPARATE TREATMENT CASES INTERRELATE

Given the relative ease of establishing a prima facie case of individual disparate treatment under *McDonnell Doug-*

las/Burdine, and the expense and difficulty of gathering and analyzing the data necessary to establish a case of systemic disparate treatment, solo plaintiffs usually proceed with "direct" or inferential evidence alone. Nevertheless, there is a complementary relationship between evidence of individual and systemic disparate treatment. A well-financed individual plaintiff may fortify the individual disparate treatment case with evidence of statistically discriminatory patterns. Similarly, a plaintiff class may, and as a practical matter is well advised, to bolster a case of systemic discriminatory treatment with anecdotal evidence of discrimination against its individual members.

On the other hand, the failure of a systemic treatment class action—or of the government plaintiff equivalent, a "pattern or practice" action by the U.S. Attorney General under section 707—does not imply lack of merit to the individual disparate treatment case of any particular member of the plaintiff class. *Cooper v. Federal Reserve Bank of Richmond*, 467 U.S. 867 (1984).

(6) Neutral Practices With Disproportionate Adverse Impact

The federal courts have at times struggled to clarify the evidentiary frameworks for proving individual and systemic disparate treatment, but there has been no real question that such intentional conduct constitutes unlawful discrimination. By contrast, neutral employer practices that in operation fall with disproportionate adverse impact on the plaintiff's protected group have proven far more troublesome.

Initially, a strong judicial consensus emerged that Congress intended to eradicate such practices on much the same terms as intentional acts of discrimination. Writing for a unanimous Court in *Griggs v. Duke Power Co.*, 401 U.S. 424 (1971), Chief Justice Burger wrote that practices fair in form but discriminatory in effect may violate Title VII even though the employer's motivation in adopting the practice is neutral or benign. The early cases developing this theory considered the lawfulness of "objective" (really, specific or concrete or readily identifiable) employer practices such as educational requirements or standardized aptitude or psychological tests. The classic example is a labor union's requirement that an applicant for membership had to be sponsored by one of the existing members, all of whom were white. When none of the thirty members admitted under this policy during a six-year period were African–American or Hispanic, the plaintiff had proven prima facie that this "neutral" practice had a disproportionate adverse impact on members of the protected group. *EEOC v. Steamship Clerks Union, Local 1066*, 48 F.3d 594 (1st Cir. 1995).

Occasionally, however, disproportionate adverse impact analysis was applied to a "subjective" employer process, such as the unstructured evaluation of black employees by white foremen. *Rowe v. General Motors Corp.*, 457 F.2d 348 (5th Cir. 1972). The Supreme Court approved the use of impact analysis to scrutinize these "subjective" promotion decisions in *Watson v. Fort Worth Bank & Trust*, 487 U.S. 977 (1988), a decision not addressed and therefore apparently left undisturbed by the Civil Rights Act of 1991. Even a single employer practice—for example, a one-time layoff—may trigger disproportionate adverse impact analysis; the practice need not be a repeated or customary method of operation to be subject to impact scrutiny. *Council 31, Am. Fed'n of State, County and Mun. Emps. v. Ward*, 978 F.2d 373 (7th Cir. 1992). Yet even after the 1991 Act, there are decisions ruling out the use of disparate impact proof when, in the court's view, the plaintiff fails to specify a particular aspect of an employer's subjective decision-making process that is allegedly responsible for an underrepresentation of the plaintiff class. A court has held that an employer's reliance on interviews to screen subjectively for such traits as empathy and caring in the selection of social workers does not in and of itself reflect gender bias, even if those traits are disproportionately evident in women, because one may assume the traits are present in all candidates for the position of social worker. *Scott v. Parkview Mem'l Hosp.*, 175 F.3d 523 (7th Cir. 1999).

In *Connecticut v. Teal*, 457 U.S. 440 (1982), the Supreme Court clarified that a single component of an employer's multi-stage selection process may have unlawfully discriminatory adverse impact on the particular protected group members it screens out, even if the protected group as a whole fares better than a non-minority group in the overall process. The Court explained that the "principal focus" of Title VII is "the protection of the individual employee," rather than of minority groups. *Id.* at 453. It rooted the disproportionate adverse impact theory in the language of section 703(a)(2): Even though a plaintiff is not "discriminated against" in the disparate treatment sense intended by section 703(a)(1), neutral practices may, in the language of section 703(a)(2), "deprive or tend to deprive [the] individual of employment opportunities." *Id.* at 456. Section 703(a)(2) is accordingly not concerned solely with how the plaintiff's group fares at the statistical "bottom line" of jobs or promotions, but also with "limitations" or "classifications" that deprive individual members of that group of the chance to advance. *Id.* at 448. In sum, a racially balanced workforce—even one that results from affirmative action in favor of the plaintiff's protected group—does not immunize an employer from liability for a specific act of discrimination, whether intentional or neutral.

How to measure whether an employer's neutral practice has a "disproportionate" adverse impact on a protected group is a question that is addressed only vaguely by the Court's cases and remains unresolved by the 1991 Act. Some courts have adopted as a measure of disproportion the "80% rule" from

the EEOC's Uniform Guidelines on Employee Selection Procedures. *In re Employment Discrimination Litigation Against
the State of Alabama*, 198 F.3d 1305, 1312 (11th Cir. 1999);
Smith v. Xerox Corp., 196 F.3d 358, 365 (2d Cir. 1999). These
provide that a protected group's selection rate that is less than
80% of the rate for the group with the greatest success will be
regarded by the Commission for enforcement purposes as
evidence of adverse impact. 29 C.F.R. § 1607.4 (2010).

But the 80% rule has come under increasing attack from
academic and court critics alike. It does not take sample size
into account and thus may fail to detect statistically significant adverse impact on large samples, and its comparison of
group pass rates may not measure the magnitude (as opposed
to mere statistical significance) of a disparity as well as other
techniques. D. BALDUS & J. COLE, STATISTICAL PROOF OF DISCRIMI-
NATION (1989). Justice O'Connor, writing for a plurality in
Watson v. Fort Worth Bank & Trust, 487 U.S. 977 (1988),
observed that the EEOC's 80% test, while perhaps appropriate
as a rough administrative guide for allocating agency prosecutorial resources, was not binding on judges. Insisting that the
plaintiff should have to produce evidence that the challenged
practice had a "significantly discriminatory impact," Justice
O'Connor alluded to the need for a more rigorous and reliable
measure of intergroup disparity. *Id.* at 995. Justice O'Connor
hinted that a better measure of whether a practice has legally
and not just statistically significant adverse impact is the
binomial distribution analysis approved by the Court for cases
of systemic disparate treatment.

A year later, a majority of the Court in *Wards Cove Packing
Co. v. Atonio*, 490 U.S. 642, 657 (1989), appeared to agree with
this approach when it required a prima facie demonstration
that the challenged practice has a "significantly disparate
impact" on the protected group. Further, the Court in *Wards
Cove* appeared to demand prima facie evidence virtually indis-

tinguishable from the statistical showing it had required for systemic treatment cases. Regardless of the particular measure of the magnitude of disparate impact created by an employer's neutral practice, the disparity will have no significance unless it is based on a fair and logical comparison. Thus, "what the plaintiff must attempt to do is show that there is a legally significant disparity between (a) the racial composition, caused by the challenged employment practice, of the pool of those enjoying a job or benefit; and (b) the racial composition of the qualified applicant pool." *In re Employment Discrimination Litigation Against the State of Alabama*, 198 F.3d at 1312.

The amendments to Title VII made by the Civil Rights Act of 1991 unequivocally declare that the employer's justification to a prima facie case is an affirmative defense on which the employer bears the burden of persuasion. In most other respects, though, the Act reflects Congress's inability to reach agreement about any of the three previously described stages of the disproportionate adverse impact case. It fails to clarify the magnitude of the required prima facie case of disproportionate impact; it procedurally complicates the prima facie showing by requiring that the plaintiff ordinarily disentangle the effects of bundled employer practices; it declares that the defense consists of separate elements of job relatedness and business necessity, but offers only a calculatedly ambiguous understanding of what business necessity means; and it carries forward an unworkable *Wards Cove* innovation that the employer may avoid liability by adopting, perhaps even at the eleventh hour in the middle of a trial, an alternative, less discriminatory practice proposed by the plaintiff. On balance, the legislation falls well short of restoring the impact case to its pre-*Wards Cove* state.

The central provision, section 703(k)(1)(A), declares that an impact-based unlawful employment practice is proved when:

(i) a complaining party demonstrates that a respondent uses a particular employment practice that causes a disparate impact on the basis of race, color, religion, sex, or national origin and the respondent fails to demonstrate that the challenged practice is job related for the position in question and consistent with business necessity; or

(ii) the complaining party makes the demonstration described in subparagraph (C) with respect to an alternative employment practice and the respondent refuses to adopt such alternative employment practice.

The legislation sheds no light on the required magnitude of the plaintiff's prima facie showing that the challenged practice had disproportionate adverse impact. New section 701(k)(1)(B)(i) does relieve the plaintiff who is attempting to demonstrate adverse impact under section 703(k)(1)(A)(i) from having to disentangle bundled practices, but only if she can "demonstrate" (again a burden of persuasion as well as production) "that the elements of a respondent's decision-making process [a 'process' is apparently a package of 'practices'] are not capable of separation for analysis." Section 105(a) (adding Title VII § 703(k)(1)(B)(i)). Otherwise, she must show that "each particular challenged employment practice causes a disparate impact." *Id.* These provisions invite satellite litigation over the extent to which the plaintiff has taken advantage of discovery and the employer has forthrightly responded. Employer-initiated motions on the issue are more than a remote possibility.

A related provision, section 703(k)(1)(B)(ii), is apparently intended to apply when the plaintiff has been allowed, by virtue of section 703(*l*), to attack an entire selection process without demonstrating the adverse impact of each particular component practice. Subdivision (ii) relieves the employer of showing the business necessity of any particular practice that it can demonstrate does not cause a disparate impact on plaintiff's group. In tandem, subdivisions (i) and (ii) of section 703(k)(1)(B) seem to assume that sometimes the employer will be able to disentangle the effects of bundled practices even after the plaintiff has satisfied the court that, after discovery, she cannot.

Once the plaintiff demonstrates that a specific practice causes a disparate impact, the employer must, after the effective date of the 1991 Act, "demonstrate that the challenged practice is job-related for the position in question and consistent with business necessity." Section 105(a) (adding Title VII § 703(k)(1)(A)(i), 42 U.S.C.A. § 2000e–2(k)(1)(A)(i) (West 2010)). The obligation to "demonstrate" these elements imposes on the employer the burden of persuasion. The employer bears the compound burden of proving that a neutral practice is necessary for the business and is "related to" the particular position it is designed to screen for. Requiring the employer to link its practice to requirements of the job, and not just to unspecified "legitimate goals" of the business as a whole, seems to place the plaintiff in a somewhat better posture than she was in after *Wards Cove*. But what do job-relatedness and business necessity now mean? Congress tell us in a preliminary provision on legislative purpose, Section 3, that it seeks to codify those concepts as they were defined by *Griggs* and in subsequent Supreme Court disparate impact decisions before *Wards Cove*. In an unusual attempt to control the judicial interpretive process in advance, Congress adds in section 105(b) that only one specified interpretive memorandum may be "relied upon in any way as legislative history in construing or applying ... any provision of this Act that relates to *Wards Cove*—Business necessity/cumulation/alternate business practice." Unfortunately, the referenced memorandum, dated October 25, 1991, rather unhelpfully repeats virtually verbatim section 3's statement that the business necessity and job relatedness concepts in the Act are akin to those developed by the Supreme Court before *Wards Cove*.

This apparently calculated Congressional ambiguity leads to confusing lower court decisions. Compare *Lanning v. SEPTA*, 181 F.3d 478 (3d Cir. 1999) (adopting a strict test requiring defendant to show that its aerobic capacity requirement was necessary to predict minimum job performance), with *Lanning v. SEPTA*, 308 F.3d 286 (3d Cir. 2002) (loosely applying that test to permit the defendant to use that hiring criterion for improving workforce capability beyond minimum levels, even respecting tasks applicants would seldom encounter on the job). See also *International Brotherhood of Electrical Workers, AFL–CIO, Local Unions Nos. 605 & 985 v. Mississippi Power & Light Co.*, 442 F.3d 313 (5th Cir. 2006) (permitting employer to raise a cutoff score in order to marginally increase the chance that an applicant meeting the higher score would do better than average work).

Leaving the definition of the defense for decision by the federal bench could result in a formulation markedly less stringent than the consensus approach of the intermediate appellate courts during the years preceding *Wards Cove*. There is even some possibility that the Supreme Court will return to a definition that approximates the lax *Wards Cove* standard: whether the challenged practice serves to some unspecified degree unspecified general business goals. The Court's latitude to do so arises from the opposing directions, pointed to by its pre-*Wards Cove* decisions, the new benchmark mandated by the 1991 Act.

Two decisions subsequent to the 1991 Act, in reaching different conclusions about the validity of a no-beard rule, illustrate how application of the new job relatedness and business necessity defense may vary depending upon the requirements of the job. *Bradley v. Pizzaco of Neb., Inc.*, 7 F.3d

795 (8th Cir. 1993) (no beard rule for pizza delivery men struck down); *Fitzpatrick v. City of Atlanta*, 2 F.3d 1112 (11th Cir. 1993) (fire department beard ban for black males upheld).

The Act responds to the *Wards Cove* requirement that an alternative, less discriminatory practice proposed by the plaintiff be "equally effective" by returning to "the law as it existed on June 4, 1989 [the day before the *Wards Cove* decision], with respect to the concept of 'alternative employment practice.'" Section 105(a) (adding subparagraph (k)(1)(C) to section 703 of Title VII, 42 U.S.C.A. § 2000e–2 (West 2010)). This leaves the possibility that the courts will continue to adhere to the *Wards Cove* insistence on equal effectiveness, with its focus on avoiding additional cost to the employer, because that notion had surfaced previously in the plurality opinion in *Watson*. Perhaps, however, the Act will be construed to allow the plaintiff to rebut the defendant's job relatedness/business necessity showing with a somewhat less effective, somewhat more expensive, but less discriminatory alternative practice.

But that rebuttal may ultimately fail because the Act also carries forward another innovation of *Wards Cove* that first surfaced in *Watson*: There will be no law violation unless in addition "the respondent refuses to adopt such alternative employment practice." Section 105(a)(ii) (adding subsection (k)(1)(A)(ii) to Title VII § 703, 42 U.S.C.A. § 2000e–2 (West 2010)). Section 703(k)(1)(A)(ii) provides that an unlawful employment practice is established if the plaintiff "makes the demonstration described in subparagraph (C) with respect to an alternative employment practice [the subparagraph that returns to the pre-*Wards Cove* law] and the respondent refuses to adopt such alternative practice." This implies that an employer may defeat the plaintiff's newly relaxed showing of a lesser discriminatory alternative as late as the latter stages of a trial on the merits. That construction is supported by the present-tense verbs in section 703(k)(1)(A)(ii): The violation is established if the respondent "refuses to adopt" an alternative practice, but that happens only after the complaining party "makes the demonstration" of such a practice. A "demonstration," in turn, probably cannot be made until judicial trial; "demonstrates" is defined by new § 701(m) to refer to satisfying burdens of production and persuasion.

By subjecting the plaintiff's prima facie case to the vagaries of discovery to disentangle the effects of compound employer practices, as well as to ad hoc judicial rulings about the required magnitude of disproportionate adverse impact; by describing a defensive standard only questionably more rigorous than that declared by *Wards Cove*; and by not reinstating the pre-*Wards Cove* version of the plaintiff's rebuttal, the Civil Rights Act of 1991 fails to restore the neutral practice case as a viable alternative to claims of intentional discrimination.

(7) How the Neutral Practice and Systemic Disparate Treatment Cases Interrelate

A particular employer's neutral practice may disproportionately adversely impact those members of the plaintiff group who encounter it even though the group as a whole fares well at the "bottom line" of all the employer policies, practices, and decisions that compose an entire selection process. *Connecticut v. Teal*, 457 U.S. 440 (1982). Thus, the failure of a systemic disparate treatment class action on behalf of the plaintiff's protected group does not negate the employer's potential liability to an individual member of a plaintiff class for harm caused by a neutral employment practice.

The Supreme Court has identified another intersection of these two prima facie cases, ruling that an employer may be liable for unlawful disparate treatment against whites (or, presumably, males) by refusing to certify them as eligible for promotion on the basis of their scores on neutral tests that had a disproportionate adverse impact on minority group members (or, presumably, women). The Court classified an employer's refusal to certify the plaintiffs for promotion as disparate treatment based solely on evidence that the refusal was prompted by its awareness of the disproportionate adverse impact of the test results. And it ruled such a refusal unlawful unless an employer had a "strong basis in evidence" that it would have been liable to the minority group test takers for the disparate impact of those tests. That, in turn, would have required the defendant employer to present strong evidence that its test was NOT job-related for the position in question, was NOT justified by business necessity, and that there were no available alternative selection practices that would have had less discriminatory impact on minorities yet still served the employer's business goals almost as well and cheaply. *Ricci v. DeStefano*, ___ U.S. ___, 129 S.Ct. 2658 (2009).

(8) ADMINISTRATIVE PREREQUISITES AND PROCEDURES

i. In General

Title VII sets out federal and state agency prerequisites to suit. In general, the private sector applicant or employee need only comply with two such prerequisites: (1) timely filing of a charge with the EEOC, either in the first instance or, in the majority of states that have parallel state or local antidiscrimination legislation and agencies, after filing with those agencies; and (2) timely filing of a federal or state court action within 90 days after receipt from the EEOC of a "notice of right to sue." Failure to follow the specified procedures and meet the charge-filing and suit-commencement deadlines usually results in dismissal of the administrative charge or ensuing judicial action.

Although 1972 amendments to Title VII gave the EEOC the right to seek judicial relief in the first instance, most judicial

action takes the form of private suits in federal district court.
The path to court is strewn with a series of intricate and time-
consuming administrative procedures at the state and federal
levels. These requirements are designed to give state or local
antidiscrimination agencies and the EEOC opportunities to
obtain voluntary resolution of discrimination disputes, as well
as to promote federal-state comity.

The complainant must first file a written charge with the
EEOC, "sufficiently precise to identify the parties and to
describe generally the action or practice complained of." 29
C.F.R. § 1601.12 (2010). Charge forms meet this standard if
they identify the charging party, charged employer, the
ground of discrimination (e.g., race, sex, national origin, religion, or retaliation), the term or condition of employment
affected by the alleged discrimination, and the time and place
of the challenged employer conduct. Less formal EEOC intake
questionnaires or even letters to the EEOC will suffice if in
addition they appear to ask the Agency to take some remedial
action. *Federal Exp. Corp. v. Holowecki*, 552 U.S. 389 (2008).

Title VII requires prior "deferral" to a state or local agency
where local law prohibits the unlawful employment practice
alleged and establishes an agency with authority to grant or
seek relief concerning that practice. In the few states that do
not have such fair employment practices legislation and enforcement agencies, or where the local law does not provide its
authority jurisdiction over a particular violation, a charge
must be filed with the EEOC within 180 days of an alleged
unlawful employment practice. In the great majority of states
that do have such laws and agencies, the charge must be filed
with EEOC within the earlier of 300 days of the alleged
violation, or 30 days after the charging party receives notice
that the state or local antidiscrimination agency has terminated proceedings under state or local law. But unless it dismisses a charge earlier, this state or local "deferral" agency must

be given 60 days in which to attempt to resolve the dispute before the EEOC may proceed. This latter requirement suggests not only that the filing under state law must ordinarily precede a filing with the EEOC, but also (if one subtracts 60 from 300) that the charge must ordinarily be filed with the state or local "deferral" agency within 240 days of the alleged unlawful employment practice. *Mohasco Corp. v. Silver*, 447 U.S. 807 (1980). However, a state or local filing later than 240 but still within 300 days of the alleged unlawful practice will be considered timely if the state or local agency terminates its proceedings before day 300. Moreover, the plaintiff gets the benefit of the 300–day period for filing with EEOC, and may use the 240–day "plus" schedule approved by *Mohasco* for filing with the state or local agency, even if the latter filing is untimely under the state or local antidiscrimination law.

A "single-filing" rule recognized by most federal circuits outside the class-action context permits plaintiffs who have not filed their own EEOC charge, or in some circuits, plaintiffs who have filed an invalid charge, to piggyback on a charge or charges filed by co-plaintiffs. The plaintiffs are relieved of filing their own valid charges if the claims of all parties are based on a common employer practice or practices during the same rough time frame and the filed charge or charges timely and adequately alerted the employer to the alleged illegality of all the practices ultimately challenged in court. It is not a prerequisite to single filing that the foundation claim allege class-wide discrimination. The rule has also been applied to permit the plaintiff who has not filed an EEOC charge to intervene in an action brought by the plaintiff who has, or to join that action as co-plaintiff after an unsuccessful attempt at intervention.

Another requirement, that the action be brought against the respondent named in the charge, has sometimes been construed to authorize jurisdiction over a successor employer or even over a defendant improperly named, or not formally named in the charge at all, if its identity is sufficiently revealed in the substance of the charge or if that employer is closely related to a named respondent. In some circuits, the civil action has even been allowed to reach defendants not likely to have received notice of the original EEOC charge if the agency's investigation, reasonably confined to the facts alleged in the charge, would have focused on them.

The foregoing time limitations specified by statute refer to filing directly "with" the state or local agency and then "with" the EEOC. In fact, informal administrative agreements between the EEOC and many state and local deferral agencies, now sanctioned by the Supreme Court, *Love v. Pullman Co.*, 404 U.S. 522 (1972), have altered these requirement so that a filing with one can constitute a filing with the other; the EEOC filing may even precede the local one. For example, the state or local administrative filing will be considered adequate even where the complainant has filed a charge only or initially with the EEOC, if the EEOC itself refers the charge to the local agency and suspends its proceedings for the required 60 days or until local proceedings terminate. Conversely, a "worksharing" agreement may specify that where the complainant files first with a state or local agency, that agency becomes the EEOC's agent for receiving the charge even if it never forwards the charge to the EEOC.

Where a state or local agency waives the right to process the charge initially, or to proceed if the charge is filed more than a specified time after the occurrence of the alleged unlawful employment practice, the circuit courts have extended the Supreme Court's approval of work-sharing agreements by holding that the state's waiver is a "termination" of state or local proceedings that authorizes the EEOC to begin its investigation without waiting 60 days. In such a jurisdiction, the complainant need never file with a state or local agency and need file a charge with the EEOC only within 300 days of the alleged unlawful employment practice, instead of the 240 days that would govern if there were no work-sharing agreement. The state or local agency may retain jurisdiction, however, to process the charge thereafter if it chooses. Where the state or local agency has made a prior determination, the statute directs the EEOC to give its findings "substantial weight" in determining whether there is reasonable cause to support the charge. Nevertheless, it is not a prerequisite to suit that the EEOC find reasonable cause to believe the Act violated, and even an EEOC determination to the contrary will not bar suit in court.

The 180–day or 300–day charge-filing deadline periods are triggered only when the alleged unlawful employment practice is complete and when the applicant or employee knows or should know of the facts that support a claim under the statute. For this purpose, the date of an alleged unlawful employment practice is usually the date on which the complaining applicant or employee should be aware of the consequences and unlawfulness of employer conduct, not when those consequences are later felt. This approach can cut both ways: to start the charge-filing clock well before a termination is consummated, or to stop the clock from running until, after termination, the employee learns the facts that suggest the termination was unlawful. Pursuing a grievance under a collective bargaining agreement will not toll the time to file a charge with the EEOC. But the 180–day and 300–day EEOC charge-filing deadlines, although critical, are not technically jurisdictional. Rather, they are procedural preconditions to suit, analogous to statutes of limitation, and thus may be waived, estopped, or equitably tolled.

Tolling does not necessarily require positive misconduct on the part of the employer. Some courts have equitably tolled the 300–day EEOC filing deadline when an unrepresented claimant receives misleading advice about filing from a state deferral agency, even when the advice is only ambiguous rather than false. But equitable tolling will not save the untimely filing of a claimant who simply waits until others similarly situated complete a successful challenge to the policy affecting them all. Further, there is no general doctrine that allegations of constructive discharge will equitably toll the relevant deadlines.

ii. Continuing Violations

The judicially-created continuing violations doctrine aids attacks on discriminatory acts that occurred "outside," that is, before the beginning of, the applicable Title VII charge-filing deadline. Because that deadline is 180 or at most 300 days, but the Act permits back pay to accrue as far back as two years (i.e., roughly 730 days) before the filing of an EEOC charge, Congress may have envisioned continuing remediable violations that existed prior to the running of the period. The courts, however, have generally limited the employer's liability to discriminatory acts that occur within the charge-filing period. Adverse effects of pre-period discriminatory conduct do not ordinarily revive the statute on that conduct even when those effects are felt within the period. *United Air Lines, Inc. v. Evans*, 431 U.S. 553 (1977). Rather, the present consequence of a one-time violation does not extend the period, and so the EEOC charge must be filed within 300 (or 180) days of that discrete act. See *EEOC v. Westinghouse Electric Corp.*, 725 F.2d 211, 219 (3d Cir. 1983).

The relatively permissive use of the continuing violation doctrine under the Equal Pay Act is explained by the fact that the sole EPA violation, discrimination in compensation, is an ongoing practice. A 2009 amendment to Title VII affords similar temporal liberality in asserting such claims under that statute. It provides that an unlawful practice respecting wages or salaries occurs not only when the practice is adopted, but also, perhaps years later, when the particular plaintiff becomes subject to that practice and even, later still, when she suffers adverse effects therefrom in the form of reduced paychecks. Lilly Ledbetter Fair Pay Act of 2009, Pub. L. No. 111–2, 123 Stat. 5 (2009), codified in sections of 29 U.S.C.A. and 42 U.S.C.A. (West 2010).

Title VII, by contrast, also reaches a variety of employer decisions that may be deemed complete at one moment in time. For example, the Supreme Court, rejecting a simple "last day of work" rule, held that a college professor's claim of discriminatory discharge accrued when he was notified of the employer's decision to deny him tenure, not later when his appeals or grievances were denied or his contract expired. *Delaware State Coll. v. Ricks*, 449 U.S. 250 (1980). It is clear, however, that some Title VII violations are subject to the continuing violations doctrine. In *Bazemore v. Friday*, 478 U.S. 385 (1986), plaintiffs challenged a public employer's pay system as racially discriminatory. The employer argued that the statute's charge filing period should run from the dates it adopted and first applied the system, but the Court held that "[e]ach week's paycheck that delivers less to a black than to a similarly situated white is a wrong actionable under Title VII." *Id.* at 394–95. The Court also observed that even where the doctrine is inapplicable, evidence of past, out-of-time discrimination may be admissible because it "might in some circumstances support the inference that such discrimination continued [into the 180–day or 300–day charge-filing period], particularly where relevant aspects of the decisionmaking process had undergone little change." *Id.* at 402.

Aside from salary discrimination, continuing violations have been found respecting some ongoing denials of promotion and racial or sexual harassment that consists not of one dramatic or "discrete" episode but of a series of less aggravated acts that in the aggregate alter the plaintiff's conditions of employment or create a hostile or abusive work environment. Provided that at least one alleged act of harassment occurred within the charge-filing period, courts will admit related evidence, antedating the beginning of that period, that constitutes part of the same general pattern of conduct. The Supreme Court has approved a generous continuing violation approach to hostile work environment, that is, non-"discrete" sexual (or racial) harassment, upholding the timeliness of an entire claim provided any one incident forming part of the pattern occurred within the applicable charge-filing period. *National R.R. Passenger Corp. v. Morgan*, 536 U.S. 101 (2002).

The Civil Rights Act of 1991 has made resort to the continuing violation doctrine unnecessary with respect to Title VII violations caused by the unlawful adverse impact of unlawful, non-bona-fide seniority systems. Overruling a Supreme Court decision, the Act provides that such violations occur not only when the system is adopted, but subsequently when a person is injured by it. Title VII § 706(e)(2). Thus, claims alleging that an employer's neutral practice has unlawful discriminatory impact do not even accrue until the plaintiff's protected group experiences adverse effects and the plaintiff herself is denied an employment benefit through the implementation of that practice.

It is often difficult to distinguish between an ongoing unlawful practice and the delayed consequence of a single discriminatory act that took place more than 180 or 300 days before an EEOC charge was filed. The circuits are split, for example, on when the limitations period begins to run on challenges to hiring lists compiled from discriminatory test results. Compare *Bouman v. Block*, 940 F.2d 1211 (9th Cir. 1991), with *Bronze Shields, Inc. v. New Jersey Dep't of Civil Serv.*, 667 F.2d 1074 (3d Cir. 1981). While a challenge to a subjective employment evaluation has been held timely if filed within a limitations period running from the date the evaluation resulted in adverse effect, another court deems the limitations period triggered by a denial of training, not the subsequent layoff resulting from the lack of training. See, respectively, *Johnson v. General Elec.*, 840 F.2d 132 (1st Cir. 1988), and *Hamilton v. Komatsu Dresser Indus., Inc.*, 964 F.2d 600 (7th Cir. 1992).

iii. Charge–Filing Procedure

EEOC regulations provide that certain amendments to charges may relate back to the filing date of the original charge, and if so would be deemed timely although the amendment was not made until after the applicable 180–or 300–day deadline. Under the regulations, an amendment, to be eligible for relation back, must correct technical defects or omissions, clarify or amplify the allegations in the original charge, or add new allegations "related to or growing out of the subject matter of the original charge." 29 C.F.R. § 1601.12(b) (2010).

Regardless of who files a charge, the EEOC is required to serve a notice of the charge on the respondent or respondents, setting forth the "date, place and circumstances of the alleged unlawful employment practice," within 10 days after its filing. 29 C.F.R. § 1691.5(a) (2010). The statute protects the confidentiality of Commission proceedings by stipulating criminal penalties if a Commission employee, prior to the institution of a judicial proceeding, makes public information obtained by the Commission. This prohibition, however, does not apply to the charging party. To protect the Commission's role as a guardian of the public interest, courts have regularly invalidated private agreements, usually entered into to settle an ongoing dispute, whereby an employee or former employee agrees not to file a charge with the EEOC or not to assist in an EEOC investigation.

Recognizing the Agency's public function, the Supreme Court has declined to limit the EEOC's ability, after investigation, to seek judicial enforcement in its own name to the 180–day period in which it alone, to the exclusion of a private party, may file suit. *Occidental Life Ins. Co. v. EEOC*, 432 U.S. 355 (1977).

iv.   From the EEOC to Federal or State Court

The EEOC investigation ultimately arrives at one of two basic conclusions. After investigation, the Agency may find "reasonable cause" to believe that the Act has been violated, and must then undertake conciliation. Alternatively, the EEOC may find "no reasonable cause" and issue a notice of dismissal. 42 U.S.C.A. § 2000e–5 (West 2010). In either event, a complainant is entitled upon demand to receive a "right-to-sue" letter from the EEOC no later than 180 days after the effective date of the filing of a charge with the agency. Since the EEOC frequently takes years to process charges, the question has arisen how long a prospective Title VII plaintiff may wait beyond 180 days before demanding a right-to-sue letter. Courts have occasionally barred Title VII actions in these circumstances on grounds of laches, when a delay of several years in demanding a suit letter was deemed unreasonable and caused tangible prejudice to the defendant. On the other hand, if the EEOC is willing to issue the right-to-sue notice before the end of its 180–day period of presumptive exclusive jurisdiction, the plaintiff may proceed to court, provided she files within 90 days of receiving the notice. *Sims v. Trus Joist MacMillan*, 22 F.3d 1059 (11th Cir. 1994).

Title VII affords plaintiffs a liberal federal venue choice among the districts where the alleged unlawful employment practice occurred; where records pertaining to the practice are maintained; or where the plaintiff allegedly would have worked but for the unlawful practice. Title VII § 706(f)(3), 42

U.S.C.A. § 2000e–5(f)(3) (West 2010). When the prospective defendant cannot be "found" in any of the above districts, the statute provides as a default the district where it has its principal office. The text also indicates that each of these districts is a suitable place for the action to be transferred under 28 U.S.C.A. §§ 1404 and 1406 (West 2010). It has been held that in considering a motion for transfer under Title VII, the court should apply the same considerations of party and witness convenience that ordinarily apply under those sections, rejecting the argument that the special Title VII venue choices are intended to give plaintiff the last word on forum selection. *Ross v. Buckeye Cellulose Corp.*, 980 F.2d 648, 655 (11th Cir. 1993).

Although the vast majority of Title VII actions are brought in federal court, state courts have concurrent jurisdiction. *Yellow Freight v. Donnelly*, 494 U.S. 820 (1990). A complainant who wishes to sue in either state or federal court must commence an action by filing a complaint within 90 days after receipt of the EEOC right-to-sue letter or notice of dismissal. That deadline is generally strictly enforced, although it, like the administrative charge-filing deadline, is apparently amenable to equitable tolling, estoppel, or waiver. See *Baldwin Cnty. Welcome Ctr. v. Brown*, 466 U.S. 147 (1984). Related actions under the Reconstruction Civil Rights Acts, notably § 1981, may be commenced even before Title VII charges have been administratively processed, but the limitations periods and administrative deadlines of the respective statutes must be satisfied independently. *Johnson v. Railway Express Agency, Inc.*, 421 U.S. 454 (1975).

The right to bring a judicial lawsuit does not turn on the EEOC's evaluation of the probable merits of a charge. The judicial action may be commenced even if the EEOC concludes that there is no reasonable cause to believe that the employer has violated Title VII. The case may proceed even if the EEOC believes that an employer offer of settlement affords the charging party full relief. An EEOC determination of no reasonable cause to believe that race discrimination allegations are true may be admissible under the public record exception to the hearsay rule in a private action for employment discrimination. *Barfield v. Orange Cnty.*, 911 F.2d 644 (11th Cir. 1990). Similarly, an EEOC or state agency determination that there is reasonable cause is also presumptively admissible, at least, in a jury trial, if the court gives a cautionary instruction advising about the non-adjudicatory nature of an EEOC determination. *Goldsmith v. Bagby Elevator Co., Inc.*, 513 F.3d 1261 (11th Cir. 2008); *Heyne v. Caruso*, 69 F.3d 1475 (9th Cir. 1995); *Gilchrist v. Jim Slemons Imps.*, 803 F.2d 1488, 1500 (9th Cir. 1986). In any event, the Agency's determination of "reasonable cause" or "no reasonable cause" will be given only such weight at trial as the federal court believes it deserves. If EEOC certifies to the court that a case initiated by a private party is of "general public importance," it may intervene as of right in the proceeding. Section 706(f)(1), 42 U.S.C.A. § 2000e–5(f)(1) (West 2010).

v.   Arbitration

Until 1991, it was settled that a putative plaintiff's resort to a grievance or arbitration procedure, prosecuted by her union, would not bar her later judicial action under Title VII, even after an unfavorable arbitral disposition. That was the message of *Alexander v. Gardner–Denver Co.*, 415 U.S. 36 (1974). Today, however, the judicial avenue of redress may be altogether foreclosed to an uncertain number of potential plaintiffs who, individually or perhaps even through their union's agreement in collective bargaining, have agreed to arbitrate claims of employment discrimination.

In 1991, the Supreme Court considered an arbitration requirement contained in a securities exchange's rules that a

brokerage house employee agreed to abide by in his application with a member firm. The Court ruled that an employee
who made such an individual agreement could be compelled to
arbitrate his statutory discrimination claim—there, under the
ADEA—by virtue of the Federal Arbitration Act, 9 U.S.C.A.
§§ 1–14 (West 2010) ("FAA"). *Gilmer v. Interstate/Johnson
Lane Corp.*, 500 U.S. 20 (1991). The Court also strongly
implied, although it did not hold, that an adverse arbitration
award would bar the plaintiff's subsequent ADEA action—
although not, as it later held in *EEOC v. Waffle House*, 534
U.S. 279 (2002), a class-wide enforcement action by the
EEOC. In so suggesting, the Court distinguished *Gardner–
Denver* as a case where the agreement to arbitrate (1) was
collectively bargained and (2) required arbitration only of
claims concerning the interpretation and application of the
terms of the union contract, rather than claims of statutory
employment discrimination.

For individually-bargained employment contracts—that is,
outside the collective bargaining context—federal appellate
courts have extended *Gilmer* beyond the ADEA by enforcing
individual employees' agreements to arbitrate claims arising
under Title VII. The Supreme Court has indirectly supported
these rulings. For example, it has narrowly construed an
exception contained in FAA section 1 that excludes from the
FAA's reach arbitration agreements in "contracts of employment of seamen, railroad employees, or any other class of
workers engaged in foreign or interstate commerce." In line
with the eleven circuit courts that embraced the narrow,
"transportation-only" interpretation of section 1, the Court in
Circuit City Stores, Inc. v. Adams, 532 U.S. 105 (2001), held
that only employment contracts of transportation workers
were exempted from the FAA.

While the Civil Rights Act of 1991 is silent about *Gilmer*,
section 118 provides additional impetus for the arbitration of

several kinds of statutory discrimination claims. Section 118 provides:

Where appropriate and to the extent authorized by law, the use of alternative means of dispute resolution, including settlement negotiations, conciliation, facilitation, mediation, fact-finding, mini-trials, and arbitration, is encouraged to resolve disputes arising under the Acts or provisions of Federal law amended by this title [including Title VII, ADEA, § 1981, and ADA].

Plaintiffs have argued that because the Civil Rights Act of 1991 was enacted to expand employees' rights and section 118 encourages "voluntary" alternative dispute resolution, the 1991 amendments implicitly prohibit employers from requiring their employees, as a condition of employment, to agree to arbitrate Title VII claims. But the circuit courts are now in agreement that the FAA permits compulsory enforcement of pre-dispute agreements to arbitrate statutory discrimination claims even though those agreements were extracted as a condition of initial employment. See, e.g., *EEOC v. Luce, Forward, Hamilton & Scripps*, 345 F.3d 742 (9th Cir. 2003) (en banc). Similarly, while the Older Workers Benefit Protection Act, Pub. L. No. 101–433, 104 Stat. 978 (1990) ("OWBPA"), which amends ADEA, requires that any waiver of ADEA "rights or claims" be "knowing and voluntary," the federal courts to consider the issue have uniformly held that the OWBPA does not undermine the holding of *Gilmer*.

Where a union-negotiated waiver of members' rights to sue in a judicial forum for the alleged violation of federal employment discrimination statutes was "clear and unmistakable," the Supreme Court subsequently distinguished *Gardner–Denver* and held the waiver enforceable. 14 Penn Plaza LLC v. Pyett, 556 U.S. 247 (2009). The opinion observed without comment that *Gardner–Denver* had denied preclusive effect to an arbitral decision because the collective bargaining agreement there authorized arbitration only of contract, not statutory claims. A recent circuit decision seizes on that distinction, holding that merely because collectively bargained rights are contractually defined as coterminous with federal statutory rights does not suffice to clearly and unmistakably confer arbitral authority to resolve statutory claims; accordingly, *Gardner–Denver* rather than *14 Penn Plaza* controlled and the award did not preclude the plaintiffs' claims under federal employment discrimination statutes. *Mathews v. Denver Newspaper Agency*, 2011 WL 892752 (10th Cir. 2011). The Supreme Court has not directly disturbed the actual holding of *Gardner–Denver* that permits Title VII or ADEA plaintiffs to pursue their statutory discrimination claims in court after an adverse arbitration award determines their contractual rights under a collective bargaining agreement. Nor has it decided whether *Gardner–Denver* permits a court to entertain a Title VII claim following confirmation of an arbitral award in state court.

vi.   Pattern or Practice Suits by EEOC

The EEOC has an option other than issuing a determination of reasonable or no reasonable cause, followed by a notice of right to sue. It may initiate suit in its own name against private employers. See Title VII §§ 706(f)(1) and 707, 42 U.S.C.A. §§ 2000e–5(f)(1) and 2000e–6 (West 2010). The EEOC's authority to bring such "pattern or practice" suits on behalf of a class affected by a systemic unlawful employment practice enables it to assert claims on behalf of large numbers of employees whose diverse claims might not withstand a typicality or representativeness attack under Federal Rule 23 in a private class action. *EEOC v. Mitsubishi Motor Mfg. of America, Inc.*, 990 F.Supp. 1059 (C.D. Ill. 1998).

Unlike individual plaintiffs, the agency faces no fixed deadlines within which it must file suit. There is even authority that it may commence an action based on a charge filed by an employee whose own judicial action was dismissed as untimely. See *EEOC v. Harris Chernin, Inc.*, 10 F.3d 1286 (7th Cir. 1993). Thus, only a delay long enough to invoke the defense of laches serves as a check on the EEOC's promptness in bringing suit. See *Occidental Life Ins. Co. of Cal. v. EEOC*, 432 U.S. 355 (1977).

If the EEOC files suit before one can be commenced by a private charging party, the private party is limited to intervention in the EEOC's action and may not file her own. See *Behlar v. Smith*, 719 F.2d 950 (8th Cir. 1983). If, however, the charging party commences an action under Title VII before the EEOC does, the EEOC may only exercise its statutory right to intervene. *Johnson v. Nekoosa–Edwards Paper Co.*, 558 F.2d 841 (8th Cir. 1977). There is authority under the ADEA, however, that the EEOC may either intervene or commence an independent action even if the complainant has filed first. *EEOC v. G–K–G, Inc.*, 39 F.3d 740 (7th Cir. 1994).

vii.   Plaintiff Joinder and Class Actions

Title VII actions in federal court are limited by statutory requirements concerning parties and allegations. The EEOC charge that forms the predicate for a Title VII action may be filed either "by or on behalf of" a person who is "aggrieved." Thus, named plaintiffs who have filed charges may prosecute the action on behalf of class members in a Federal Rule of Civil Procedure 23 class action, and those class members need not themselves have filed individual EEOC or state agency charges if the class is certified.

Rule 23(a), applicable also to class actions under the ADA and § 1981, has the following four threshold requirements:

(1) a sufficient number of class members that ordinary joinder under Rule 20 would be impracticable ("numerosity");

(2) questions of law or fact common to the class ("commonality");

(3) claims (or, in a defendant class action, defenses) of the representative parties that are "typical" of those of the class as a whole ("typicality"); and

(4) a likelihood that the representative parties will fairly and adequately protect the interests of the class ("adequacy").

The first two requirements are usually easily met in employment discrimination class actions, which characteristically involve a plaintiff class. Numerosity is seldom a problem, with classes containing as few as eighteen members having been certified. So long as the named plaintiffs assert that disparate treatment on a prohibited ground is class-wide, or that one or more neutral practices has class-wide impact on a protected group, the commonality requirement is also rarely a barrier. Employment discrimination by its very nature partakes of class-wide discrimination.

The third and fourth factors, typicality and adequacy, have proven most difficult to surmount. The Supreme Court, with its decision in *General Telephone Co. of the Southwest v. Falcon*, 457 U.S. 147 (1982), has applied these Rule 23(a) requirements for class certification strictly. For a putative class to comply with Rule 23's requirement that the claims of the named plaintiffs be "typical" of those of the class, *Falcon* insists that in most cases the complement of named plaintiffs in a private Title VII class action include at least one representative who complains not only on the same prohibited ground of discrimination (e.g., race or sex) as the putative class, but also of each particular discriminatory practice the class proposes to attack. In a famous footnote 15, the court recognized an exception that permits certification—despite diversity in the practices challenged by the representative plaintiffs and class members—where those practices are the product of a common device (e.g., a test) or common decision-maker applying the same subjective criteria. Defendants have argued that *Falcon* also demands that at least one of the named plaintiffs must have allegedly suffered the same detrimental term or condition of employment—failure to hire, unequal pay or discipline, non-promotion, on-the-job harassment, or discharge—as the members of each class or subclass sought to be represented. Thus, unless the named plaintiff or plaintiffs who originally retained class counsel happen to embody all the characteristics of the putative class members, share all their same grievances, and suffer their same injuries, *Falcon* effectively compels class counsel to try to assemble a wider group of named plaintiffs. Then members of the wider group, perhaps sorted as representatives of "subclasses," can assert that they, as applicants or employees, were aggrieved by the particular employment practices, and affected in the same terms and conditions of employment, as other members of the class they seek to represent.

Falcon has had at least two distinct consequences. First, by effectively requiring the formation of a large and diverse plaintiff group, it has more sharply put into focus the ethical concerns associated with the solicitation of additional named plaintiffs. The Court has been rather lenient about permitting plaintiff class counsel, directly or through the original clients, to encourage others similarly situated to join the named plaintiff group, particularly when the class action is serving a "private attorney general" function in combating race discrimination. But there are limits to solicitation even after *Falcon*. For example, the Eleventh Circuit vacated two class communications and a certification order because plaintiffs' counsel's efforts to communicate with class members caused serious irreparable injury to the defendant.

Second, defendants have been resourceful in responding to the larger named plaintiff complements that *Falcon* in effect compels. *Falcon* has spurred more elaborate and expensive motion practice about the propriety of class certification and limitations on precertification discovery. Defendants commonly assert, frequently with success, that the resulting diverse named plaintiff group—representing, for example, applicants, employees, and former employees; subordinates and superiors; unsuccessful test takers and victims of discriminatory discipline; women sexually harassed or suffering unequal pay; persons discharged; and persons not promoted—is rife with internal conflicts, so that, in Rule 23's terms, the named plaintiffs are not fairly "representative" of the class members whose fate will ride with them if the class is certified. To alleviate such conflicts, plaintiffs or district courts have sometimes proposed that the class be subdivided into "subclasses" that one or more of the named plaintiffs can fairly represent. On occasion, however, the result of forming subclasses is that each is fewer than the approximately 30 or so that the courts have generally required before a plaintiff group is sufficiently numerous to warrant class action certification. In this way, a defendant's Rule 23 objections snowball: A challenge to typicality generates a challenge to adequacy that in turn generates a challenge to numerosity. By their nature, these challenges invite early consideration of the merits of the class members' claims, although the court is formally prohibited from considering those merits in determining whether to certify.

A class action may be maintained if all four Rule 23(a) requirements are satisfied and if the case fits any of three circumstances described by Rule 23(b):

(1) prosecuting separate actions by or against individual class members would create a risk of: (A) inconsistent or varying adjudications with respect to individual members of the class that would establish incompatible standards of conduct for the party opposing the class; or (B) adjudications with respect to individual class members that, as a practical matter, would be dispositive of the interest of the other members not parties to the individual adjudications or would substantially impair or impede their ability to protect their interests;

(2) the party opposing the class has acted or refused to act on grounds that apply generally to the class, so that final injunctive relief or corresponding declaratory relief is appropriate respecting the class as a whole; or

(3) the court finds that the questions of law or fact common to the class members predominate over any questions affecting only individual members, and that a class action is superior to other available methods for the fair and efficient adjudication of the controversy.

Rule 23(b)(1) creates a mandatory class and is most appropriate where there is a limited fund that must be distributed "ratably." Rule 23(b)(1) is not generally used by plaintiffs in discrimination class actions. Employment discrimination plaintiffs usually seek certification under Rule 23(b)(2) or occasionally under Rule 23(b)(3).

Rule 23(b)(2) permits class certification where "the party opposing the class has acted or refused to act on grounds generally applicable to the class, thereby making appropriate final injunctive relief or corresponding declaratory relief with respect to the class as a whole." This Rule creates a mandatory class with no opt-out rights, but a court may exercise discretionary authority arising from Rule 23(d)(2) to require notice and opt-out rights, particularly when substantial monetary awards are involved. The Supreme Court has noted that "[c]ivil rights cases against parties charged with unlawful, class-based discrimination are prime examples" of Rule 23(b)(2) class actions. *Amchem Prods., Inc. v. Windsor*, 521 U.S. 591, 614 (1997). A Rule 23(b)(2) class should have more cohesiveness underlying the factual and legal claims of each class member than a Rule 23(b)(3) class. Certification under Rule 23(b)(2) is appropriate only where equitable relief is the predominant remedy sought. This has been interpreted to mean that certification under Rule 23(b)(2) is precluded where monetary relief is sought, unless such monetary relief is in some uncertain sense merely incidental to the requested injunctive or declaratory relief.

To qualify for certification under Rule 23(b)(3), a class must meet two requirements beyond the Rule 23(a) prerequisites: Common questions must "predominate over any questions affecting only individual members"; and class resolution must be "superior to other available methods for the fair and efficient adjudication of the controversy." Fed. R. Civ. P. 23(b)(3). The Rule 23(b)(3) "predominance" inquiry focuses on the legal and factual questions surrounding each potential class member's claims and is "far more demanding" than Rule 23(a)'s commonality requirement. In order to predominate, common issues must constitute a significant part of the individual claims. Courts will generally find that individual issues predominate over common ones where it appears that the class action will devolve into a series of individual mini-trials on issues peculiar to each plaintiff. For example, plaintiffs seeking to certify disparate treatment class actions under the inferential proof mode of *McDonnell Douglas* may face significant certification problems. Defendants can defeat such claims by articulating nondiscriminatory, non-pretextual reasons for the adverse employment actions—an inquiry that courts view as highly individualized. Moreover, claims for emotional distress and punitive damages are also highly variable from plaintiff to plaintiff, also undercutting the commonality and typicality necessary for certification. Still, the need for some individualized proof will not necessarily preclude certification under Rule 23(b)(3). The superiority requirement is satisfied where the advantages of a class action—increased fairness and efficiency—outweigh any problems of case manageability. Considerations relevant to manageability include the potential difficulties in notifying class members of the suit, determining individual injury, calculating individual damages, and distributing damages.

In *Wal–Mart Stores, Inc. v. Dukes*, ___ U.S. ___, 131 S.Ct. 2541 (2011), a five-member majority of the Supreme Court clarified and sharply limited the availability of the federal court class action to challenge intentionally discriminatory practices on a nationwide or perhaps even greater than store-wide basis. The plaintiff class sought injunctive and declaratory relief as well as backpay and punitive damages on behalf of a nationwide class of about 1.5 million current and former employees challenging disparate treatment discrimination in pay and promotions. The Supreme Court observed that the only significant evidence of an across-the-board corporate policy shown in support of class certification was Wal–Mart's committing pay and promotion decisions to the largely subjective discretion of local managers of its 3,400 stores, resulting in a statistically significant national underrepresentation of women promoted into management positions relative to their representation in the minimally qualified available pool of entry-level employees. The Court found no evidence, however, of a specific practice in the exercise of that delegation that united all 1.5 million claims. It held that the evidence that delegating discretion to individual store managers had produced overall sex-based disparities was insufficient to show questions of law or fact common to the class, as required by

Federal Rule of Civil Procedure 23(a)(2), because disparities at a national or even regional level do not demonstrate disparities at individual stores, a premise of the class certification approved by the Ninth Circuit and reversed by the Supreme Court.

Perhaps holding out some hope for less sweeping classes, the majority seemingly reaffirmed the footnoted suggestions of *Falcon* that Rule 23(a)(2) commonality could be shown (a) if every class member had been subjected to the same specific practice, like an intentionally biased test or a facially neutral and neutrally applied test that nevertheless had disproportionate adverse impact on members of the protected group represented by the class; or (b) if the class offered "significant proof" that a central corporate policy (like unguided delegation of managerial discretion) manifested itself in discriminatory hiring or promotion (or presumably pay) decisions "in the same general fashion." There was no evidence of such a test in *Wal-Mart*. Further, the Court concluded that the plaintiff class' sociological expert's testimony that Wal-Mart's corporate culture rendered it vulnerable to gender bias failed the second *Falcon* route, because the expert was unable testify how frequently sex stereotyping had played a part in Wal-Mart's employment decisions. Evidence of Wal-Mart's common corporate policy of delegated discretion also fell short of demonstrating a general policy applied in a general fashion: Not "every" employee will suffer intentional discrimination—the premise of the request for nationwide certification—from subjective discretionary decision-making by individual store managers, because some managers would exercise that discretion by using neutral selection criteria rather than by intentionally discriminating against women. Finally, the Court concluded that 120 individual affidavits fell short of the *Falcon* "general policy" approach given the scope of the requested class, as they recounted the experiences of only 1 of every

12,500 class members and related to only about 235 of 3,400 Wal–Mart stores.

Lack of Rule 23(a)(2) commonality would have sufficed for reversal of the lower court's approval of class certification. But the Supreme Court also held that claims for monetary relief may not be certified under Rule 23(b)(2), despite that subsection's application to discrimination cases, "at least where (as here) the monetary relief is not incidental to the injunctive or declaratory relief." In reaching that conclusion, the Court stressed that at the remedy stage of a policy-or statistically-based Title VII pattern or practice case, the defendant has a right to prove that particular members of a class that has demonstrated the employer's liability for systemic disparate treatment were nevertheless not in fact victims of that discrimination. Rule 23(b)(2) "does not authorize class certification when each class member would be entitled to an individualized award of monetary damages." For the most part, then, Title VII class actions seeking monetary relief that varies by class member will henceforth probably have to be certified under Rule 23(b)(3), with its requirements that class members receive individual notice of proposed certification and the opportunity to opt out of the class and thus avoid its potential binding effects. And given the Court's stringent view of Rule 23(a)(2) commonality, those classes must now also be limited to claims of discrimination turning on "an issue that is central to the validity of each one of the claims in one stroke."

ADEA suits are not subject to Rule 23. Instead, these "collective actions" are governed under section 216 of the Fair Labor Standards Act, 29 U.S.C.A. §§ 201–219 (West 2010) ("FLSA"). There are some substantial differences between the ADEA collective action and a Rule 23 class action. First, the only prerequisite for a section 216 action is that all putative class members must be "similarly situated." This is, of course, a fact-based inquiry, but courts have held that the standard is lower than that imposed by Rule 23(a). Second, all ADEA section 216 actions are opt-in actions; that is, no potential plaintiff is part of the collective action unless that plaintiff affirmatively consents in writing to be part of the action. Third, plaintiffs who do opt-in to an ADEA collective action are granted full party status.

The rejection on the merits of class claims of systemic treatment does not bar the claims of individual class members alleging disparate treatment. Moreover, when a court denies class-action certification, the claims of individual class members who have not filed a charge with the EEOC or commenced a judicial action may still be timely. This is because the filing of a class action has been held to toll, until the denial of certification, both the 90–day period for filing suit and the applicable deadline (180 or 300 days) for filing a charge with the EEOC. *Crown, Cork & Seal Co. v. Parker*, 462 U.S. 345 (1983). Even when a class was decertified because no class representative had standing to assert the claim subsequently brought by individual plaintiffs, those plaintiffs have been allowed to "piggyback" on the timely filed EEOC charges of the class-action plaintiffs. But rejection of class claims on the merits has preclusive effect under federal common law in subsequent actions asserting the same pattern claims. And the pendency of a class action in which class status was denied or a class decertified does not toll the charge-filing or action-commencement deadlines for class members who bring a subsequent class action—otherwise, there would be "endless rounds of litigation . . . over the adequacy of successive named plaintiffs to serve as class representatives." *Griffin v. Singletary*, 17 F.3d 356, 359 (11th Cir. 1994).

viii.   Relation of Federal Lawsuit to EEOC Investigation

Since the EEOC charge is the necessary foundation for a Title VII action, the issues that may be litigated in federal court will be tied to some degree to the contents of the charge. But recognizing that EEOC charges are often drafted by unrepresented employees ill-equipped to craft them with care, courts following the leading case of *Sanchez v. Standard Brands, Inc.*, 431 F.2d 455, 466 (5th Cir. 1970), have permitted Title VII plaintiffs to try claims "like or related to allegations contained in the charge and growing out of such allegations during the pendency of the case before the Commission."

The widespread adoption of the Sanchez rule puts a premium on defendants' efforts to limit the scope of EEOC proceedings. Generalizations about the meaning of "like or related" are particularly hazardous, but it may be ventured that allegations in a Title VII judicial complaint that add a new ground of discrimination (race or sex, for instance) are less likely to be entertained than are allegations that touch on additional terms or conditions of employment or implicate other potential plaintiffs in different departments or divisions. Even then, plaintiffs whose administrative charges complained of adverse treatment respecting limited terms and conditions of employment will be permitted to target in court only those other terms and conditions of employment that the EEOC could reasonably have been expected to investigate based on the charge. The Seventh Circuit has sometimes applied an alternative, and apparently stricter, standard: whether the claims in the judicial action are "fairly encompassed" within or "implied" by the charge the plaintiff filed with the EEOC. E.g., *Vela v. Village of Sauk Village*, 218 F.3d 661 (7th Cir. 2000).

An especially liberal application of the charge-filing requirement generally permits a plaintiff to press a retaliation claim under section 704 of Title VII without first filing a separate EEOC charge of retaliation, where that claim grows out of a properly and timely-filed predicate charge of discrimination under section 703. But that liberality is usually extended only when the underlying charge of primary discrimination was itself administratively exhausted and timely, or added by an amendment to the original charge that the court permits to relate back to the original. Some circuits have limited the federal court's ancillary jurisdiction in such cases to charges of alleged retaliation occurring after, and not before, the filing of the underlying charge; this position is consistent with the applicable EEOC regulations, discussed above, that require the filing of an original charge within the applicable 180–or 300–day period after a claim accrues.

ix. Employer Recordkeeping Requirements

Pursuant to section 709(c), the EEOC has promulgated regulations requiring employers to maintain records pertinent to a wide range of employment decisions. These require employers to retain all personnel records for six months after they are created and, when a charge is filed, to retain all records relevant to that charge "until final disposition of the charge or the action." 29 C.F.R. § 1602.14 (2010). In employment discrimination actions, the employer has custody of virtually all records critical to resolution of the disputed claim; hence, in the reported decisions, it is the employer that allegedly violated the Title VII recordkeeping requirements.

But judicial enforcement of employer recordkeeping violations has generally been conspicuously lenient. Sometimes, the courts of appeals that have found employers to have destroyed documents in violation of the EEOC regulation give the plaintiff the benefit of a "presumption that the destroyed documents would have bolstered her case." See, e.g., *Favors v. Fisher*, 13 F.3d 1235, 1239 (8th Cir. 1994). But then they may either assume or conclude that the presumption was "overcome"—the evidence for which may simply be an innocent explanation by an authorized employer agent, coupled with his assertion that he had not been instructed to preserve records in accordance with the government regulation. And sanctions have typically been mild: requiring the defendant to bear the costs of record reconstruction; limiting its production of evidence on the matters reflected in the destroyed documents; or invoking the presumption that the records would have supported the plaintiff's case. See *EEOC v. Jacksonville Shipyards, Inc.*, 690 F.Supp. 995, 998–99 (M.D. Fla. 1988).

(9) TITLE VII REMEDIES

i. Reinstatement and Back Pay

The range of judicial remedial authority is prescribed by section 706(g). This section provides for injunctions and "such affirmative action as may be appropriate," including orders directing reinstatement or hire, back pay, and other equitable relief. It also "limits" a defendant's back pay liability retrospectively to no earlier than two years before the filing of a charge with the EEOC. "Limits" is placed in quotation marks because the statute's deadlines for filing a charge with the EEOC are only 180 days, in the handful of states that do not have their own local antidiscrimination laws and agencies, or 300 days in the majority of states that do. Thus, in effect, the two-year "limit" on back pay authorizes its award earlier than the "trigger" date that starts the running of Title VII's administrative charge-filing deadlines.

Prevailing plaintiffs are routinely awarded injunctions against ongoing violations, and, where disparate treatment has been proved, reinstatement or, if there is no position available at the time of judgment, priority in filling vacancies. As with the systemic disparate treatment case, discussed above, reinstatement may be denied where the discriminatee, although qualified when unlawfully rejected, is no longer qualified for the position in question at the time of judgment.

Back pay is also awarded almost as a matter of course. This is because, as the Supreme Court has explained, back pay serves both of the Act's remedial goals: to restore discrimination victims to the approximate status they would have enjoyed absent discrimination (the "make whole" purpose), and to deter employer violations. Accordingly, the Court, while recognizing that federal judges enjoy some discretion to withhold any Title VII remedy in particular circumstances, held in *Albemarle Paper Co. v. Moody*, 422 U.S. 405 (1975), that back pay may be denied only for unusual reasons which, if applied generally, would not impede those remedial objectives. For example, the "neutral practice/disproportionate adverse impact" case dispenses with evidence of discriminatory intent, and a general good-faith exception to back pay liability would therefore seriously erode the advantages of that mode of proof. The Court has consequently rejected such an exception. It has also suggested that the ordinary Eleventh Amendment immunity of states from federal court monetary awards is overridden in Title VII actions because Congress enacted the statute in at least partial reliance on its powers under the Fourteenth Amendment to enforce the Equal Protection Clause. It has not directly decided, however, if Congress exceeded those powers in enacting the state liability provisions of Title VII.

Back pay is defined as the total compensation the employee would have earned absent the unlawful conduct, reduced by any compensation the employee actually received and any additional amount the employee would have received through reasonable efforts to mitigate the damages. It is awarded only for a period in which plaintiff is "available and willing to accept substantially equivalent employment," with periods of disability usually excluded from the award. The employer bears the burden of proof on the issue of mitigation, which is itself a jury issue. An employer's "unconditional" offer of reinstatement that is refused by the plaintiff ends the defendant's ongoing responsibility for back pay.

Rejected applicants seeking back pay are not required to prove they would have been hired absent the unlawful discrimination, but any plaintiff seeking back pay must have made reasonable efforts to mitigate her losses. Back pay awards are reduced by amounts the plaintiff earned, or with reasonable diligence could have earned, since the date of a discharge or failure or refusal to hire, but a failure to mitigate may not absolutely forfeit the right to recovery for back pay. In those courts where an employer is relieved of the burden to prove there was comparable work available after it proves that the employee made no reasonable efforts to seek subsequent work, the employee must prove that comparable compensation was not available to save any part of a back pay award. Several circuits have held that self-employment is an acceptable form of mitigation for this purpose. The back pay clock should stop when "the sting" of discriminatory conduct has ended. There is considerable division in the circuit opinions as to whether "collateral sources" of income may be deducted from the back pay award, and if so which ones.

Title VII authorizes the award of back pay to a date as early as two years before the filing of the required EEOC charge— as distinct from the later date on which the complaint is filed in a judicial action. In states without their own anti-discrimination laws and agencies, the EEOC may immediately assert jurisdiction over a plaintiff's initial charge, and any charging party may demand a notice of right to sue from EEOC after it has exercised that jurisdiction for 180 days. Even in the majority of states, where the charging party must, at least in theory, exhaust administrative remedies before state or local "deferral" agencies, the plaintiff may be able to invoke the EEOC's jurisdiction promptly if the state or local agency waives its right to proceed either in the individual case or by a "work-sharing" agreement with the EEOC. And at the outside, the plaintiff has 300 days from the latest alleged unlawful employment practice to file with the EEOC, which then can be compelled to authorize suit 180 days later. Thus, as a practical matter, most Title VII judicial actions will be commenced well before two years have expired after the filing of the EEOC charge. The two-year back pay accrual rule nevertheless permits back pay for violations that occurred up to two years before that charge was filed. That is to say, back pay may be recovered for "continuing violations" that began before the last event that triggers the running of Title VII's "statute of limitations."

The 1991 Act adds compensatory and punitive damages as "legal" remedies to the Title VII plaintiff's arsenal, but it does not change the "equitable" character of the pre-existing remedies like back pay or restoration of lost pension benefits. Determination of eligibility for back pay, although virtually automatic under the *Albemarle* presumption, is therefore formally for the court, not the jury, as is the critical calculation of the back pay amount. Yet, at least one circuit has held that "the issue of reasonable mitigation is ultimately a question of fact for the jury."

Front pay is a discretionary remedy granted by the court as a substitute for reinstatement if reinstatement is impossible, impracticable, or inequitable. It may be the only feasible way to make a victim of discrimination whole where there is no available position in which to reinstate her, or where, as in a constructive discharge or other harassment case, reinstatement would be unsuccessful or unproductive because of the workplace hostility that either prompted the claim or resulted from its prosecution. It is awarded in an amount that estimates the total future salary, pension, and other benefits the plaintiff, absent an unlawful discriminatory discharge, would have earned with the employer from the date of judgment until the probable loss of job or date of retirement; prospective losses of post-retirement benefits may be measured until the actuarially predicted date of death. Because it is awarded and calculated on the basis of highly speculative assumptions about the health of the business, the health of the plaintiff, and the plaintiff's future satisfactory work performance and prospects for advancement, front pay is devilishly difficult to measure. That difficulty suggests that front pay may be a form of future non-pecuniary, rather than pecuniary, loss. Yet, there is an irreducible element of speculation in almost every front pay award—e.g., trying to determine if the plaintiff, after termination, would have survived a subsequent reduction in force and otherwise performed well enough to resist termination—and speculation alone should not render front pay unavailable, unless it is excessive.

The lower federal courts have come to presume the front pay award appropriate where reinstatement is infeasible or ill advised. Most but not all circuit courts, in decisions before the 1991 Act, held front pay available under Title VII. The principal argument against front pay revolved around the fact that all Title VII remedies were then equitable, and some judges characterized front pay as "legal." Now that the 1991 Act adds legal remedies to the menu of relief under Title VII, the Supreme Court, in dictum, has noted the availability of front pay with approval.

Front pay leaves the incumbent in place and, beginning as of final judgment, orders the employer to pay the discriminatee an amount equivalent to what he would earn if actually reinstated. Because of the uncertain duration of the period during which the victim of discrimination would have remained employed after judgment, or at what level and pay, the front pay remedy is fraught with computational difficulties. Given its purpose to restore an injured party to the position she would have occupied absent the employer's unlawful discrimination, determining the appropriateness, duration, and amount of front pay is an exercise that entails "predicting the future": Such an exercise involves an attempt to determine the degree to which a plaintiff possesses qualities that would make the plaintiff successful in attaining career advancement. For advancements that come simply with longevity, courts have uniformly assumed that such advancement would occur, in the absence of specific disqualifying information; on the other hand, courts will not automatically assume that a person discriminated against possesses characteristics so sterling as to receive every advancement not made illegal or logically impossible under the employer's rules.

The circuit opinions grapple with a host of circumstances governing the appropriateness and duration of front pay awards. The award will not necessarily terminate when plaintiff quits subsequent, substitute employment; on the other hand, in recognition of the duty to mitigate, the employer need only pay such a plaintiff the difference between the amount she would have received had she remained employed (or secured substantially equivalent employment) and the amount she could have continued to receive in the lesser-paying substitute job that she quit. Almost invariably when front pay is awarded, there are numerous considerations counseling the reduction or termination of the award, including mitigation, unclean hands, speculation about the duration of the plaintiff's position or personal retention, collateral sources, and the kinds and amounts of other relief awarded for the unlawful discrimination. Because front pay awards are replacing anticipated compensation after judgment that is not yet due, they must be discounted to present value, and there are numerous other technical issues that must be faced in calculating the award. All that can be said with confidence is that purely arbitrary limits on front pay may be overturned as an abuse of the trial court's discretion. The Supreme Court has held that front pay is not subject to the 1991 Act's caps on "damages," as discussed below.

Because each species of Title VII relief before the 1991 Civil Rights Act was considered equitable, jury trials were not available unless a Title VII claim was joined with a claim for legal relief—for instance, a claim under § 1981. Although the Supreme Court strongly suggested that there was no right to jury trial under Title VII, it never actually ruled on the question. Section 102 of the Civil Rights Act of 1991, codified at 42 U.S.C.A. § 1981a (West 2010), now specifically authorizes jury trials for claimants alleging intentional discrimination in actions under, among other statutes, Title VII and the ADA. In addition, there is clearly a jury trial right under § 1981, and where an action presents claims under both statutes, the right to jury trial under § 1981 may not be estopped by the prior bench trial of an equitable claim. Rather, prior jury determinations of facts reached in deciding the legal, § 1981 claims should be adopted by the trial court when it later determines any equitable claims under Title VII.

The "equity" characterization has also limited the available monetary relief under Title VII (before the 1991 amendments) to an award of back pay, precluding more generous measures such as compensation for emotional distress or punitive damages. The equitable nature of all Title VII awards before the new Act also led some courts to deny nominal damages, viewing them as compensatory in nature. While nominal damages now appear available, some courts insist that the plaintiff demand them as early as the Federal Rule of Civil Procedure 16 pretrial order; under that view, a plaintiff could not wait until after the verdict, or even shortly before, to seek nominal damages as a way of obtaining at least the minimal economic recovery that may be needed to support an award of punitive damages. But prejudgment, as well as the standard post-judgment, interest is an ordinary item of compensation integrally related to back pay, routinely awarded in Title VII actions. It may even be an abuse of discretion to deny it, absent unusual reasons.

Any prevailing party, plaintiff or defendant, is of course eligible for an award of "costs" under Federal Rule of Civil Procedure 54(d). These are limited, however, to items specified by 28 U.S.C.A. § 1920 (West 2010): clerk and marshal fees, fees by court reporters for transcripts "necessarily obtained for use in the case", printing disbursements and witness fees, specified docket fees, and fees for court-appointed experts and certain interpreters. Most importantly, "costs" as used in Rule 54(d) do not include the prevailing party's attorney's fees. This is consistent with the ordinary "American rule," which, absent express statutory authorization, calls for each side to pay its own attorney's fees. Section 706(k) of Title VII is one such statute. It provides that a prevailing party may recover a reasonable attorney's fee as part of "costs." For purposes of calculating the post-judgment interest allowed by 28 U.S.C.A. § 1961 (West 2010) "on any money judgment in a civil case recovered in a district court," these statutorily shifted attorney's fees shall be included as part of the judgment.

Section 113 of the Act authorizes the court to include the fees of experts, without a specific cap, as part of the award of attorney's fees to prevailing Title VII plaintiffs, contrary to the thrust of two recent decisions of the Court. This change facilitates the neutral practice case as well as the case of intentional discrimination. But the Act's authorization of prospective relief, and hence attorney's fees, despite the defendant's discharge of the "same decision" burden in the intentional "mixed motive" situation, affords greater relative inducement to bring intentional discrimination claims.

ii. Compensatory and Punitive Damages for Title VII and Americans With Disabilities Act Violations After November 20, 1991

Section 102 of the Civil Rights Act of 1991, codified at 42 U.S.C.A. § 1981a (West 2010), authorizes jury trials and compensatory and punitive damages for claimants alleging intentional discrimination in actions under, among other statutes, Title VII and the ADA. These remedies are "in addition to any relief authorized by" section 706(g) of Title VII, and the compensatory portion of an award "shall not include back pay, interest on back pay, or any other type of relief authorized under" section 706(g) of Title VII—in other words, the equitable relief available before the Civil Rights Act of 1991. But compensatory and punitive damages are available only if the "complaining party cannot recover under 42 U.S.C.A. § 1981." Citing applicable legislative history, however, the EEOC has interpreted the latter restriction only to bar double recovery under Title VII and § 1981, not to interfere with administrative or judicial processing of claims under either statute prior to judgment.

The Act expressly denies either form of damages—compensatory or punitive—to challengers of facially neutral practices. Title VII plaintiffs who prevail only by demonstrating the disproportionate adverse impact of neutral practices, or ADA plaintiffs who demonstrate only a failure to reasonably accommodate by an employer who "demonstrates good faith efforts," are still limited to the traditional, equitable Title VII remedies of prospective relief and back pay. Perhaps more than any other, these provisions manifest the congressional view that intentional discrimination deserves more serious legal sanctions.

Section 1981a also makes compensatory, but not punitive, damages available to plaintiffs who prosecute intentional discrimination claims successfully against a government agency or subdivision. The Supreme Court held in *West v. Gibson*, 527 U.S. 212 (1999), that the EEOC may award compensatory damages to federal employees for intentional discrimination during the federal administrative complaints process.

Punitive damages are authorized against nongovernmental defendants who are proven to have engaged in an unlawful discriminatory practice "with malice or with reckless indifference to the federally protected rights of an aggrieved individual." Although the precise standards governing jury awards of punitive damages will require considerable case law explication by analogy to punitive damages in tort, it has already been held that, as under §§ 1981 and 1983, compensatory damages are not a prerequisite to a punitive award. This is particularly important in environmental harassment claims, as victims may not incur always compensatory damages.

Section 1981a(b)(3) places dollar caps that vary with employer size on the sum of compensatory and punitive damages "for each complaining party." For this purpose, compensatory damages are defined by § 1981a(b)(2) to include monetary relief for "future pecuniary losses, emotional pain, suffering, inconvenience, mental anguish, loss of enjoyment of life, and other non-pecuniary losses." These caps are set at $50,000 for businesses that employ between 15 and 100 persons; $100,000 where the employer has between 101 and 200 employees; $200,000 where the employer has between 201 and 500 employees; and $300,000 for all employers with 501 or more employees. Because these damages are "in addition to" traditional, pre-November 1991 Title VII equitable relief, complaining parties' recoveries of back pay, interest on back pay, and other relief formerly available under Title VII before the 1991 amendments are not restricted by the caps. Moreover, despite the somewhat uncertain status of front pay under the pre–1991 Act case law, the EEOC considers it a type of relief previously authorized by Title VII and hence excluded from the § 1981a(b)(2) definition of compensatory damages, and in turn, not subject to a § 1981a(b)(3) cap. In any event, a plaintiff with a state law claim that authorizes unlimited damages may avoid the Title VII and ADA damages caps altogether, and in some circumstances may assert that claim in the same federal court action.

In *Pollard v. E.I. DuPont de Nemours Co.*, 532 U.S. 843 (2001), the Supreme Court held that front pay is not subject to the caps of § 1981a. Acknowledging that front pay is often awarded in lieu of reinstatement, the Court reasoned that because front pay is a remedy authorized under section 706(g), Congress did not limit the availability of such awards in § 1981a. Instead, Congress sought to expand the available remedies by permitting the recovery of compensatory and punitive damages in addition to previously available remedies, such as front pay.

An EEOC guidance on damages concludes that the caps apply to the sum of the damages received by each plaintiff on all claims on which that plaintiff prevailed, and most circuit decisions have followed this approach.

Left unanswered by the text of the damages provision and the EEOC's Damages Guidance is whether the plaintiff who joins in one action claims under both Title VII and the ADA for distinct, independently unlawful employer practices may recover more than the applicable cap pertaining to each statute alone. One reading would limit the plaintiff's recovery concerning the conduct violative of Title VII to the Title VII cap referenced in § 1977A(a)(1), and his recovery for the conduct violative of ADA to the cap of the same amount referenced in § 1977A(a)(2)—subject, of course, to standard instructions forbidding the jury from authorizing greater damages for the combination of these unlawful employment practices than plaintiff actually suffered.

The Commission also assumes that, as with back and front pay, the complaining party has a duty to mitigate pecuniary losses, with the burden of proof on the employer to demonstrate a failure to exercise reasonable diligence. On claims for non-pecuniary loss, such as emotional distress, it expects the complainant to bear the usual burdens developed by tort law concerning causation. Thus, the claim will be seriously undermined if the onset of symptoms preceded the discrimination; but the fact that an unusually sensitive complainant resembles the classical "eggshell plaintiff" of tort law will not absolve the respondent from responsibility for the greater emotional harm. Expert testimony that stress resulted from discriminatory working conditions is an adequate basis for an award, and sometimes even the plaintiff's own testimony about loss of sleep, marital strain, humiliation, and the like will suffice. Defense motions to compel a mental examination have not been successful, but a plaintiff alleging emotional distress damages probably waives her psychotherapist-patient privilege.

Most circuit decisions addressing the question conclude that an emotional distress award is adequately supported by the plaintiff's own testimony standing alone, although a few require corroboration by witnesses like family and friends, or even by medical experts.

In cases of intentional Title VII and ADA violations against non-governmental defendants, 42 U.S.C.A. § 1981a(b)(1) (West 2010) authorizes punitive damages where the plaintiff also shows the defendant acted with "malice or with reckless indifference to the federally protected rights of an aggrieved individual."

In *Kolstad v. American Dental Ass'n*, 527 U.S. 526 (1999), the Court held that the statutory requirements of "malice" or "reckless indifference" focus solely on the defendant's state of mind. Accordingly, while evidence of an employer's egregious conduct may enable the plaintiff to persuade a judge or jury that the defendant, through its agent or agents, acted with the requisite "malice" or "reckless indifference," § 1981a(b)(1) "does not require a showing of egregious or outrageous discrimination independent of the employer's state of mind." *Kolstad*, 527 U.S. at 535. Accordingly, if the employer's agents could be shown on remand to have acted with malice or reckless indifference to the plaintiff's rights, and the employer shown to be responsible for their actions undertaken with that state of mind, the employer might be liable for punitive damages even if its agents' conduct could not be characterized as "egregious" or "outrageous."

The Court summarized on this point that § 1981a(a)(1) requires proof of an intentional violation to subject the defendant to the possibility of compensatory or punitive damages; § 1981a(b)(1) further qualifies the availability of punitive damages, limiting them to situations where the employer has carried out intentional discrimination with " 'malice or with reckless indifference to [the plaintiff's] federally protected rights.' "

Kolstad creates a three-part framework for determining whether an award of punitive damages is proper. First, a plaintiff must demonstrate that the employer acted with the requisite mental state, i.e., the employer must have acted with knowledge that its actions may have violated federal law. Second, the plaintiff must establish a basis for imputing liability to the employer. Third, the employer may avoid liability for punitive damages if it can show that it engaged in good faith efforts to implement an antidiscrimination policy.

Courts have particularly struggled with establishing reasonable limits on the amount of a punitive award. In general, the award should "bear some relation" to the nature of defendant's conduct and the harm it caused; and taking defendant's resources into account, it should "sting" rather than "destroy." But the EEOC takes the position that in general, punitive awards under Title VII and the ADA should rarely be grossly excessive, either under the statute or the Due Process Clause, because the sum of punitive damages together with future pecuniary losses and all non-pecuniary losses must stay within the caps of § 1981a(b)(3).

iii.   Tax Treatment of Settlement or Judgment Proceeds in Employment Discrimination Cases

Plaintiffs are, of course, more inclined to settle for less if they are persuaded that the proceeds of a settlement will not be taxed. Until August 20, 1996, when President Clinton signed the Small Business Job Protection Act of 1996, Pub. L. No. 104–188, 110 Stat. 1755, Section 104(a)(2) of the Internal Revenue Code, 26 U.S.C.A. § 104(a)(2), excluded from gross income "the amount of any damages received (whether by suit or agreement ...) on account of personal injuries or sickness...."

The "personal injuries or sickness" requirement was acutely raised by employment discrimination, and to a lesser degree civil rights, claims. In most such cases, the plaintiff's immediate injuries, while arguably "personal," and commonly resulting in emotional distress that is sometimes medically treated, are nonphysical. In 1995, the Supreme Court held that in the typical, nonphysical situation, neither the back pay nor the liquidated damages recoverable in an action under the ADEA could ordinarily be considered "damages" on account of "personal injuries." That decision rested uncomfortably with the Court's strong suggestion three years earlier that the back pay and emotional distress damages recoverable under Title VII, as amended by the 1991 Civil Rights Acts, would be excludable from the plaintiff's income under section 104(a)(2). At the same time, text added to section 104 in 1989 rendered punitive damages, available since November 1991 in Title VII actions, non-excludable in a case—like most employment discrimination and many civil rights cases—that did "not involv[e] physical injury or physical sickness." (The Supreme Court has since rejected the negative pregnant that punitive damages were excludable in cases that did involve physical injury or sickness.)

Section 104(a)(2) provides that gross income does not include "the amount of any damages (other than punitive damages) received (whether by suit or agreement ...) on account of personal physical injuries or physical sickness." An addendum to Section 104(a) explains that for "purposes of paragraph (2), emotional distress shall not be treated as a physical injury or physical sickness. The preceding sentence shall not apply to an amount of damages not in excess of the amount paid for medical care ... attributable to emotional distress."

In sum, this means that physical injury is a precondition for excludability from income under section 104(a)(2). So in the usual Title VII or ADEA case, where the employer's conduct does not result in "physical" injury or sickness, no recovery in a judgment or settlement for back or front pay will be eligible for exclusion under section 104(a)(2). Second, because the first sentence of the addendum excludes emotional distress from the section 104(a)(2) definition of "physical" injury or sickness, the part of any settlement or judgment representing recovery for the intangible harms of emotional distress will also be non-excludable in non-physical cases. Third, however, where a civil rights (or, more rarely, employment discrimination) plaintiff does suffer some actual "physical" injury as the result of the defendant's conduct—police abuse cases may be the paradigm, with the rape and invasive touching variants of sexual harassment strong possibilities—she may exclude "any damages" (other than punitive) received in respect of those injuries. Fourth, because of the "other than punitive damages" language, punitive damages will now almost never be eligible for exclusion, even when they are awarded in cases of physical injury. It therefore may be important in non-physical injury cases where the plaintiff incurred medical expenses related to emotional distress for the plaintiff to seek settlement agreements that label as "compensatory" rather than "punitive" as much of the total monetary recovery as may plausibly be so characterized consistent with the underlying facts and the allegations of any previously asserted demand letters, pleadings, and subsequent litigation documents. A recent Tax Court decision, warns, however, that an allocation negotiated by the parties will not be respected if they never bargained over the allocation before arriving at an overall settlement or if an allocation is "patently inconsistent" with the underlying claims.

The essence of these changes, as applicable to claimants under federal employment discrimination and civil rights laws, may be summarized as follows: (1) At least some "physical" (probably bodily) injury or sickness is necessary for the taxpayer to exclude from gross income any settlement or judgment proceeds, except the relatively minor portion representing reimbursement for medical expenses attributable to emotional distress and except for attorneys' fees, discussed immediately below; (2) where the settlement or judgment resolves a claim involving some "physical" injury or sickness, the taxpayer may exclude all back pay, front pay, or compensatory damages that are received "on account of" that injury or sickness, including all emotional distress damages, not just those that reimburse for medical expenses; but (3), even in cases of actual physical injury or sickness, punitive damages will not be excludable.

Even more fundamentally troublesome for plaintiffs than ending up in a higher tax bracket as a result of the compensatory and punitive component. A lump sum award was the dominant judicial view that attorneys' fees must be included in the plaintiff's own gross income, not just the attorney's, and then treated as a miscellaneous itemized deduction that was available only to the extent the fees exceeded 2% of a plaintiff's adjusted gross income. Congress overturned this double taxation of attorneys' fees awarded under Title VII, the ADEA, and the ADA, among other statutes, with respect to fees and costs paid after October 22, 2004 in the American Jobs Creation Act, Pub. L. No. 108–357, 118 Stat. 1418 (2004). Henceforth, plaintiffs may deduct all attorneys' fees and costs received by judgment or settlement as an above-the-line deduction. But Congress declined to amend or reject the 1996 provisions that made back pay, emotional distress damages, and punitive damages non-excludable, except in physical injury cases.

(10) RETROACTIVE SENIORITY FOR PROVEN VICTIMS OF DISCRIMINATION: A FIRST LOOK AT THE PROBLEM OF "REVERSE DISCRIMINATION"

More complex and controversial than the availability of back pay in Title VII actions are awards of retroactive "remedial" seniority to victorious discriminatees who secure orders directing their hire, promotion, or reinstatement. These are awards of seniority that enhance the measure of employer-paid compensation or benefits. Because remedial seniority restores discriminatees to their "rightful place"—the rung on the ladder to which they likely would have climbed between the date of discrimination and date of judgment—and produces benefits that are paid by the adjudicated wrongdoer (the employer), it serves both Title VII remedial objectives, deterrence as well as compensation. Accordingly, in *Franks v. Bowman Transportation Co.*, 424 U.S. 747 (1976), the Supreme Court held that retroactive remedial seniority for those benefit purposes is presumptively available on the same terms as back pay. In doing so, the Court rejected the argument that section 703(h)—which insulates bona fide seniority systems from being declared unlawful, and therefore protects them from wholesale dismantling by injunction—also prohibits the incremental adjustment of places on the seniority ladder that results when judges award discriminatees fictional, retroactive seniority as a remedy for an underlying discrimination in hiring, assignment, or promotions.

On the other hand, retroactive seniority also serves an alternative or additional purpose: improving the discriminatee's position relative to other employees in competing for scarce job resources like better-paying positions, more favorable hours, or, most critically, protection against demotion or layoff. Unlike seniority for benefits purposes, retroactive "competitive" seniority furthers only the goal of compensation, not employer deterrence. In *Franks*, the Court recognized that such protection is necessary to make a proven victim of discrimination whole; without it, she is vulnerable to layoff, termination, or simply poorer job assignments without any of the seniority protection that she would almost surely have earned absent the employer's unlawful conduct. It therefore held, following *Albemarle Paper Co. v. Moody*, 422 U.S. 405 (1975), that the "competitive" as well as the "benefits" brand of retroactive fictional seniority is presumptively available. *Franks*, 424 U.S. at 779.

A year later, in *International Brotherhood of Teamsters v. United States*, 431 U.S. 324 (1977), the Court also agreed that an award of retroactive seniority, because it is essential to redress proven discrimination, is also not a "preference" prohibited by section 703(j). But there, in contrast to the situation in *Franks*, immediate implementation of retroactive seniority for competitive purposes would have visited highly visible harm on incumbent employees already out on layoff: Restoring the discriminatees to "their" rung on the seniority ladder would have delayed the incumbents' day of recall. On those facts, the Court drew back from authorizing the automatic or immediate implementation of retroactive seniority for competitive purposes. Rather, to decide "when" and "the rate at which" discriminatees may be made whole by such awards, it directed the district courts to exercise their "qualities of mercy and practicality" in balancing several unweighted equities. These include the number of protected group and non-protected group persons interested in the scarce resource, the number of current vacancies, and the economic prospects of the industry. *Teamsters* left undisturbed the *Franks* holding that seniority for benefits purposes should be implemented presumptively, unequivocally, and immediately after issuance of a judgment.

Although the Supreme Court has implied that section 706(g) provides limited discretion to "bump" an incumbent employee in order to reinstate a proven victim or "discriminatee," lower courts have displayed great reluctance to do so, even when the order protects the displaced employee's former level of compensation. They have instead sometimes awarded the discriminatee "front pay."

(11) AFFIRMATIVE ACTION BY "VOLUNTARY" PROGRAMS AND JUDICIAL DECREES

"Voluntary," "benign" employer affirmative action, and reverse discriminatory remedies imposed by court order or consent decree, raise similar yet legally distinct questions of fairness as between minority and majority group employees. Employer affirmative action in the form of self-imposed quotas or goals does not really implicate the judiciary's remedial authority under section 706(g) at all. An employer simply institutes racial or gender preferences, without court compulsion, typically to avoid lawsuits by the group benefitting from the preference or to preserve federal contracts that require affirmative action. Rather, such a plan is unlawful, if at all, because it operates to prefer members of defined minority groups (or women), rather than individual minority members or women proven to have suffered discrimination at the hands of the defendant employer. As a result, these preferences are suspect under section 703 as ordinary unlawful employment practices directed against any majority group members or males who are denied employment opportunities by the plan.

In a landmark 1979 opinion, *United Steelworkers of America v. Weber*, 443 U.S. 193 (1979), that expressly elevated a supposed legislative "spirit" over statutory text, the Supreme Court gave qualified approval to "voluntary," "benign" racial preferences. A majority held that the employer there had lawfully taken race into account in preferring black employees as a group for admission to an on-the-job training program—a preference that on its face violated the specific terms of section 703(d). The Court acknowledged that the white race of Brian Weber was the factor that resulted in his denial of the employment benefit, in apparent violation of that section.

The *Weber* majority listed a number of sanitizing factors to circumscribe the scope of lawful "benign" discrimination. It observed that the employer plan before it did not require white employees to be discharged and therefore did not "unnecessarily trammel" their interests; that it did not absolutely bar white employees from the skilled positions, but merely limited their numbers; and that it was a temporary measure, intended not to maintain a racial balance but to eliminate a manifest imbalance in the skilled job categories. The Court satisfied itself on these points again in *Johnson v. Transporta-*

tion Agency of Santa Clara County, 480 U.S. 616 (1987), when it extended the *Weber* principle by upholding an explicit gender preference for promotions, this time in the face of the apparently plain prohibition of section 703(a).

Affirmative action plans by government employers are subject to constitutional norms, including equal protection. In *City of Richmond v. J.A. Croson Co.* 488 U.S. 469 (1989), the Court struck down a municipal program to set aside a minimum amount of subcontracting work for minority business enterprises. The Court insisted that the Equal Protection Clause is violated whenever government takes race into account unless (1) it has a compelling justification and (2) the means adopted are narrowly tailored to go only so far as that justification requires. *Croson*, then, supplies the framework for evaluating the constitutionality of a current plan.

In public contracting and employment settings, it is not a sufficiently compelling justification for the government to offer a purportedly "benign" preference designed to redress general societal or historical discrimination against African–Americans; in general, race has been accepted as a lawful factor in doling out benefits only to redress the governmental unit's own prior discrimination, and only as long as and to the extent necessary to remedy the discriminatory injury the government inflicted. No formal, judicial determination of past discrimination by the governmental unit in question is necessary to show the requisite compelling governmental interest. Still, the evidence of such discrimination must be "strong" or "convincing."

Unlike "voluntary" affirmative action, judgments directing preferential treatment for a minority or gender group, issued after litigated findings of discrimination or upon the parties' consent, squarely test the limits of a court's remedial authority under section 706(g) to "order such affirmative action as may be appropriate." In the case of public employers, these judgments may also deny the disfavored racial or gender groups equal protection. The justices have been deeply divided over the equitable propriety under section 706(g) of consent judgments that afford relief to minority group members who are not themselves proven victims of discrimination. The degree of "trammelling" appears important.

(12) Procedures and Remedies in Affirmative Action Challenges

The Title VII plaintiff may assert that a failure to hire or promote was caused by an unlawful affirmative action plan, or the employer may raise the plan as a defense. The Court has held that the private employer may defend simply by producing evidence that its challenged decision was made pursuant to an affirmative action plan; in contrast to the BFOQ defense to express discrimination, the employer does not bear the burden of persuasion in defending an individual employment decision made pursuant to a valid affirmative action plan. Rather, the plaintiff must prove either that the decision was not made pursuant to the plan, or that the plan is invalid. *Johnson*.

But when race-conscious government action is challenged under the Equal Protection Clause, the Court has placed the burden on the defendant to show the affirmative action plan can survive the compelling justification and narrow tailoring requirements of strict scrutiny. See *Bass v. Board of Cnty. Comm'rs, Orange Cnty., Fla.*, 256 F.3d 1095 (11th Cir. 2001). This asymmetry means that an equal protection challenge to a government employer's decision based on an affirmative action plan is easier to sustain than a Title VII challenge to a similar decision by a private employer for both a substantive reason—it is easier to show that a plan fails strict scrutiny than that it violates the *Weber/Johnson* factors—and a procedural reason—Title VII plaintiffs bear the burden of showing a plan's invalidity, whereas § 1983/equal protection government defendants bear the burden of showing a plan's validity.

4. AGE DISCRIMINATION IN EMPLOYMENT ACT OF 1967 (ADEA)

a. *Coverage*

The ADEA prohibits age discrimination against employees or job applicants who are 40 years of age or older. It is therefore clear that while the plaintiff must be 40 at the time of the alleged unlawful employment practice, she need not show that she was replaced by someone younger than forty, *O'Connor v. Consolidated Coin Caterers Corp.*, 517 U.S. 308 (1996), only by someone younger than the plaintiff. *General Dynamics Land Sys., Inc. v. Cline*, 540 U.S. 581 (2004). Prima facie, she need only produce evidence from which it may be inferred that the employer relied on the comparator's younger age in making the challenged decision, but "such an inference cannot be drawn from the replacement of one worker with another worker insignificantly younger."

The ADEA was amended in 1986 to remove the then current upper-age limitation, 70, for the vast majority of covered employees. Thus, in general, the ADEA prohibits mandatory retirement because of age at any age for covered employers. The most important surviving exception authorizes the mandatory retirement at age 65 of a highly compensated person "employed in a bona fide executive or a high policy making position" who has an "immediate, nonforfeitable annual retirement benefit" aggregating $44,000. ADEA § 12(c)(1), 29 U.S.C.A. § 631(c)(1) (West 2010). But to be "entitled" to that nonforfeitable benefit within the meaning of the exemption, and hence denied protection, it may not suffice that the executive is actually receiving in excess of $44,000.

Other exceptions formerly permitted the mandatory retirement of tenured college-and university-level professors and law enforcement officers and firefighters. They were subject to involuntary retirement at age 70 (professors) or, in the case of public safety officers, younger, at the local governments' discretion. But those exceptions expired December 31, 1993. Legislation re-established a retirement exemption with respect to the public safety officers. ADEA § 4(j), 29 U.S.C.A. § 623(j) (West 2010), as reenacted and amended by the Age Discrimination in Employment Amendments of 1996, Pub. L. No. 104–208, 110 Stat. 3009. Similarly, in October 1998, a "safe harbor" provision was added to the ADEA under which institutions of higher education, subject to certain conditions, may offer to tenured faculty members, upon their voluntary retirement, supplemental benefits that are reduced or eliminated as employees age. Higher Education Amendments of 1998, Pub. L. No. 105–244 § 941, 112 Stat. 1581.

The ADEA covers "employers" who have 20 or more employees for each working day in each of 20 weeks in the current or preceding calendar year; labor unions having 25 members; and employment agencies. *Hoekel v. Plumbing Planning Corp.*, 20 F.3d 839 (8th Cir. 1994). As of July 1994, the numerical coverage threshold under the ADA has been coextensive with that under Title VII, namely 15 employees; this will mean that fewer persons will be protected from age than from the other major forms of discrimination, an irony given the previously broader scope of the prohibition against age discrimination. The Older American Act Amendments of 1984, Pub. L. No. 98–459, 98 Stat. 1767, specifically protect U.S. citizens "employed by an employer in a workplace in a foreign country." At a minimum, this covers overseas employees of American corporations, and may also cover employees working at U.S. branches of foreign employers with more than 20 workers worldwide. State and local governments were included in the term "employer" by amendments in 1974, but the Supreme Court has since held that Congress lacked the authority under § 5 of the Fourteenth Amendment to abrogate the states' Eleventh Amendment immunity from the ADEA suits in federal court. *Kimel v. Florida Bd. of Regents*, 528 U.S. 62 (2000).

Elected officers of state and local government are excluded from the "employee" definitions and thus enjoy no protection under Title VII or the ADEA. Moreover, until recently, these definitions also excluded from protection members of such officers' personal staffs, immediate advisors, and other appointees responsible for setting policy, unless they were subject to state or local civil service laws. The Civil Rights Act of 1991 generally protects previously exempt appointees of elected officials by extending to them all "rights" and "protections" of both Title VII and the ADEA, together with the "remedies" that would ordinarily be available in actions against state or local government—that is, all but punitive damages. But unlike other state or local government (or private) employees, whose charges are simply investigated and perhaps conciliated by the EEOC and who are therefore entitled to a de novo hearing in state or federal court, these newly-covered government appointees are remitted to an adjudicatory hearing before the EEOC, subject only to limited judicial review. Section 321(c) and (d).

Although the Act does not include the federal government within the definition of "employer," a separate provision requires that personnel actions affecting most federal employees 40 or older shall be made "free from any discrimination based on age." ADEA § 15, 29 U.S.C.A. § 633a (West 2010). Specific provisions in other statutes authorize mandatory separation of federal air traffic controllers, law enforcement officers, and firefighters at various specified ages, and it appears that only civilian members of the military departments are covered. *Helm v. California*, 722 F.2d 507 (9th Cir. 1983). The EEOC has adjudicatory authority to resolve federal employees' age discrimination complaints. In contrast to federal employee complaints under Title VII, the age discrimination complainant may bypass any process available from his employing agency as well as from the EEOC and proceed directly to federal court for a de novo hearing. A complainant making this choice need only give the EEOC, within 180 days after the alleged unlawful employment practice, 30 days' notice of its intent to sue. ADEA § 15(c), (d), 29 U.S.C.A. § 633a(c), (d) (West 2010). The federal age discrimination complainant who chooses to initiate administrative review of the challenged decision will be deemed to have exhausted those remedies if the employing agency or the EEOC has taken no action on a charge within 180 days of its filing. Alternatively, if the agency or the EEOC reaches a decision, the complainant has 90 days within which to file a judicial action.

The ADEA forbids age discrimination in hiring, firing, or classifying employees or job applicants and in other "terms, conditions, or privileges of employment." 29 U.S.C.A. § 623(a)(1) (West 2010). It also bars age-related bias in employment advertisements or referrals.

b. Proof Modes

The prima facie theories of liability under the ADEA parallel those of Title VII, from which its language was derived. Many cases involve express or direct evidence, such as statements attributed to management agents that the employer needs "new blood," strives to become "young, lean, and mean," or needs to purge itself of "old farts" or "dead wood." A supervisor's reference in the context of plaintiff's termination to cutting down "old, big trees so the little trees underneath can grow" qualified as direct evidence despite its metaphorical nature.

Liability may not be predicated on such statements when they are merely "stray remarks in the workplace," by which courts usually mean that they are uttered by co-employees or low-level supervisors or are divorced from the decisional process affecting the particular plaintiff. Express statements reflecting preference for youth or animus toward age lose their "stray" character and become actionable when announced by top executives, incorporated into official company planning documents, or uttered by a representative of management with decision-making authority with respect to the plaintiff. The fact that such comments were made over a long period of time argues for rather than against their admissibility; while any particular comment may be remote in time from the alleged violation, as a whole, the comments may show a pattern of age-based animus.

One argument that seems to have particular potency in ADEA claims, perhaps even more than in actions under Title VII, is the "same actor" doctrine, which applies where the supervisor who imposed the employment detriment (e.g., firing) on the plaintiff is the same person who had hired him. Thus, it may be difficult to believe that the employer developed a certain aversion to older people only two years after hiring one. *Rand v. CF Indus., Inc.*, 42 F.3d 1139 (7th Cir. 1994). In such circumstances, the plaintiff must show that this proffered justification is a pretext for age discrimination. *Roper v. Peabody Coal Co.*, 47 F.3d 925 (7th Cir. 1995). Similarly, if the decision-maker is also a member of the protected group, an inference of age discrimination is weakened.

An employer does not intentionally discriminate in violation of the ADEA simply by making a decision based on a factor other than age—e.g., the fact that the plaintiff is nearing pension eligibility—even if that factor strongly correlates with age. *Hazen Paper Co. v. Biggins*, 507 U.S. 604 (1993). Thus, firing an older worker to reduce high current salaries or future benefits, *Dilla v. West*, 179 F.3d 1348 (11th Cir. 1999); *Broaddus v. Florida Power Corp.*, 145 F.3d 1283, 1287 (11th Cir. 1998); *Anderson v. Baxter Healthcare Corp.*, 13 F.3d 1120 (7th Cir. 1994), making employment decisions based on employees' bad backs, *Beith v. Nitrogen Products, Inc.*, 7 F.3d 701, 703 (8th Cir. 1993), choosing an older worker for termination because his eligibility for a pension would lessen the blow of the termination, *Cruz–Ramos v. Puerto Rico Sun Oil Co.*, 202 F.3d 381 (1st Cir. 2000), or distinguishing on the basis of seniority, *Williams v. General Motors Corp.*, 656 F.2d 120, 130 n.17 (5th Cir. 1981), do not violate the Act even though in each case the distinguishing neutral feature may be more prevalent in older workers.

The plaintiff's ultimate burden in an ADEA disparate treatment case, critical where the evidence shows a mixture of lawful and unlawful motives, is to demonstrate that the employer's reliance on age had a "determinative" influence on the challenged decision, a requirement more onerous than the Title VII plaintiff's burden, after the 1991 amendments, to show that race, sex, religion, or national origin was a "motivating factor." *Hazen*, 507 U.S. 604 (1993).

A common mode of proof individual disparate treatment proof under the ADEA tracks *McDonnell Douglas*, the proof mode that also predominates under Title VII. In a key ADEA case, *Reeves v. Sanderson Plumbing Products, Inc.*, 530 U.S. 133 (2000), discussed at length above in connection with its extension to Title VII actions, the Supreme Court held that a jury verdict finding liability may be legally sufficient even if it is based solely on two kinds of evidence: (1) evidence establishing the modest *McDonnell Douglas* prima facie case of age discrimination (see the discussion of the *McDonnell Douglas* proof mode in the Title VII materials above); and (2) "sufficient" evidence that the employer's asserted legitimate nondiscriminatory explanation is false. But it added that the jury may properly find liability on such evidence only if, upon proper instructions, it makes the dual findings (1) that the reason or reasons the employer offered for taking adverse action against the plaintiff were not its real reasons (i.e., "pretext") and (2) the unlawful ground was in fact the employer's real reason.

One common legitimate nondiscriminatory reason the employer may advance to rebut the *McDonnell Douglas* prima facie case is that plaintiff's layoff or termination took place as part of a comprehensive, economically motivated reduction in force ("RIF"). Because such a force reduction is itself a legitimate reason for termination, courts typically require plaintiffs discharged in those circumstances to produce "plus" evidence beyond the prima facie case tending to show that age was a factor in the challenged termination. In appellate decisions, one plaintiff carried that burden by offering evidence of two age-related comments by company officials in connection with the transfer of two younger employees into the department from which the plaintiff had been downsized. Another succeeded by showing half-hearted efforts to place him in alternative positions for which he was qualified. *Cronin v. Aetna Life Ins. Co.*, 46 F.3d 196 (2d Cir. 1995). In the latter case, the company's statistical evidence tending to show that the organization as a whole was not age-discriminatory failed to conclusively negate the inference the plaintiff's evidence raised that he individually had been treated unfavorably because of his age. If the plaintiff makes that showing, the employer must then come forward with an age-neutral justification for the discharge of the particular plaintiff—a neutral justification, that is, separate and apart from the fact that the termination took place as part of a reduction in force. *Viola v. Philips Med. Sys. of N. Am.*, 42 F.3d 712 (2d Cir. 1994).

The RIFFed plaintiff must often show that one or more similarly situated persons below the age of 40, or at least younger than herself, were retained or hired shortly after the plaintiff's layoff, while she was dismissed despite having met the employer's legitimate performance expectations. Even then, the employer can avoid liability by offering evidence of a legitimate, nondiscriminatory reason for retaining the younger workers, thereby casting on the plaintiff the final burden of demonstrating the pretextual nature of that justification. When an employer reduces its force for economic reasons, it generally incurs no duty to transfer laid-off workers to other positions. However, if a job is currently available for which the plaintiff is qualified and the employer fills that job with a person outside the protected group, an inference of discrimination is permitted. Similarly, the inconsistent application of RIF criteria can suffice to show pretext. One circuit court has stressed that in analyzing RIF cases, "the similarity of the jobs held by an older and younger employee is the touchstone for determining whether a lay-off of the older may be found to be an ADEA violation by a trier of fact." *Burger v. New York Inst. of Tech.*, 94 F.3d 830, 833 (2d Cir. 1996). That same circuit delineates two types of actionable RIFs: cases that center on "who took the place of the covered employee," and those that center on whether the selection of RIFFed employees was influenced by an impermissible ground. *Danzer v. Norden Sys., Inc.*, 151 F.3d 50, 55 (2d Cir. 1998).

c.   *Mixed Motives in ADEA Disparate Treatment Cases*

Where the evidence shows lawful as well as unlawful factors for the employer's conduct, ADEA plaintiffs must show that age was a "determinative" factor in the challenged employment decision. *Hazen*, 507 U.S. 604 (1993). The Supreme

Court has now clarified that demonstrating age was "determinative" equates with "but for" causation. *Gross v. FBL Fin. Servs.*, ___ U.S. ___, 129 S.Ct. 2343 (2009). If the ADEA plaintiff must show prima facie that age was a "determinative" factor in the sense that "but-for" the employer's reliance on age it would not have taken the challenged action, then a "same-decision" defense in an ADEA case would be illogical: To carry that defense, the employer would have to negate exactly what the plaintiff had just proved!

Moreover, the 1991 Civil Rights Act provisions that relaxed the Title VII plaintiff's burden from "but-for" to "motivating factor" causation did not amend the ADEA. For these reasons, the Supreme Court has concluded that the ADEA defendant is never required to make a "same decision" showing. If the plaintiff proves age was a "determinative" factor, the employer could not carry that defense; if the plaintiff fails to make that showing, the employer needs no defense. *Id*.

The individual disparate treatment evidence of age discrimination may be buttressed, as under Title VII, by statistical or anecdotal evidence, or both, that the employer systemically discriminates on a widespread, routine basis. See *EEOC v. Western Elec. Co., Inc.*, 713 F.2d 1011 (4th Cir. 1983).

d. A Diluted "Neutral Practice/Adverse Impact" Theory Survives Under the ADEA

The neutral practice theory derived from the *Griggs v. Duke Power* interpretation of Title VII remains available to prove claims under the ADEA. *Smith v. City of Jackson*, 544 U.S. 228 (2005). But an employer may defeat the prima facie showing that a specific neutral practice causes disproportionate adverse impact on a group over forty years of age under the relaxed *Wards Cove* version of the Title VII "business necessity" defense, simply by showing that the challenged practice significantly serves any business goal. Alternatively, the employer may defend the neutral practice that has age-discriminatory effect by relying on the ADEA "reasonable factor other than age" defense, *Smith*, 544 U.S. 228 (2005); and reliance on factors that clearly correlate with age like rank and seniority (which in turn correlates with costs savings) are nevertheless "reasonable factors." *Meacham v. Knolls Atomic Power Lab.*, 554 U.S. 84 (2008).

e. Retaliation

Title 29, U.S.C.A. § 623(d) (West 2010) provides protection against retaliation for employees of covered private employers in the same terms as section 704(a) of Title VII. Former employees, in particular those who have been discharged, are among the "employees" shielded by section 623(d). *Passer v. American Chem. Soc'y*, 935 F.2d 322, 330–31 (D.C. Cir. 1991); *EEOC v. Cosmair, Inc.*, 821 F.2d 1085, 1088–89 (5th Cir. 1987). The ADEA provision, like the Title VII counterpart, has been construed to shield a wide range of on-the-job "opposition" in addition to formal participation in ADEA proceedings. Although the ADEA, unlike Title VII, does not textually prohibit retaliation against federal sector employees, the Supreme Court has recognized such a claim as fairly implied. *Gomez–Perez v. Potter*, 553 U.S. 474 (2008).

f. The Older Workers Benefit Protection Act (OWBPA)

Prior to the 1990 enactment of the OWBPA, section 4(f)(2) of the ADEA exempted employers from liability for "a bona fide employee benefit plan such as retirement, pension, or insurance plan, which is not a subterfuge to evade the purpose of [the ADEA]." 29 U.S.C.A. § 623(f)(2) (West 2010). The EEOC had interpreted this exemption to require a cost justification for any age discriminatory provision in an employee benefit plan: Any reduction in fringe benefits for older employees would be lawful only if the employer's actual cost of providing that benefit was higher for older employees than younger ones. Overruling an intervening Supreme Court decision, the OWBPA, enacted October 16, 1990, repeals the section 4(f)(2) exemption, reinstates the EEOC cost justification rule, and declares that employee benefit plans are covered by the ADEA's general prohibition against age discrimination. Specifically, the Act requires that "for each benefit or benefit package, the actual amount of payment made or cost incurred on behalf of an older worker [shall be] no less than that made or incurred on behalf of a younger worker."

The OWBPA also expressly permits employers to follow the terms of a bona fide seniority system, provide for the attainment of a specified age as a condition of eligibility for a pension plan, and provide bona fide voluntary early retirement incentive plans. Such a voluntary plan is bona fide if it does not confer more valuable benefits on younger workers.

g. Waiver of Rights or Claims Under the ADEA After the OWBPA

Some employers have required employees to sign a release waiving all rights and claims, if any, under the ADEA as a condition to receiving severance benefits. Prior to the enactment of the OWBPA, the ADEA did not state whether an employee could release her rights under the ADEA without supervision by the EEOC. Courts of appeals, however, generally have upheld the validity of private releases so long as a waiver is "knowing and voluntary."

The OWBPA resolves this question by specifically permitting unsupervised releases (those not approved by EEOC), provided that: (1) the waiver is in writing and written in terms likely to be understood by the average individual eligible to participate in the plan (or by the individual herself); (2) the waiver specifically refers to the rights or claims arising under the ADEA; (3) the individual does not waive rights or claims that may arise after the waiver is executed (see *Adams v. Philip Morris, Inc.*, 67 F.3d 580 (6th Cir. 1995)); (4) the individual waives rights or claims only in exchange for additional consideration (that is, consideration in addition to anything of value the individual is already entitled to receive); (5) the individual is advised in writing to consult with an attorney prior to executing the waiver; (6) the individual is given at least twenty-one days in which to consider the agreement (the individual must be given 45 days if the waiver is requested in connection with an exit incentive or group termination program); (7) the agreement provides for a period of at least seven days following execution to revoke the agreement and does not become effective until this period has expired; and (8) if the waiver is requested as part of an exit incentive or group termination program, the employer must inform the individual in writing (in understandable language) of: (a) any class or group of individuals covered by the program and any eligibility factors and time limits for the program; and (b) the job titles and ages of all individual eligible or selected for the program and those within the same job classification or organization unit not eligible or selected for the program.

Waivers are subject to attack as not "knowing and voluntary." See *Griffin v. Kraft Gen. Foods, Inc.*, 62 F.3d 368 (11th Cir. 1995). No waiver or settlement of an EEOC or court action is considered "knowing or voluntary" unless the above requirements have been met and the individual is given a "reasonable period" in which to consider the settlement. The OWBPA imposes the burden of proof upon the proponent of the release to prove that the minimum statutory requirements for ADEA releases have been satisfied. No waiver agreement affects the EEOC's ability to enforce the ADEA or an individual's right to file a charge or participate in an EEOC investigation or proceeding.

The Supreme Court has held that an employee's release that fails to comply with the OWBPA does not bar an action under the ADEA. The plaintiff's retention of consideration received for a waiver agreement does not ratify the waiver, and the employee need not tender back that consideration as a prerequisite to suit. *Oubre v. Entergy Operations, Inc.*, 522 U.S. 422 (1998). The EEOC has subsequently issued regulations on waiver of rights and claims under the ADEA. 29 C.F.R. pt. 1625 (2010).

Employer policies that require terminated employees to sign a general release of all claims to be eligible for enhanced severance benefits do not discriminate expressly, even though they may put pressure only on members of the over–40 protected group to waive rights under the ADEA. The bundle of accrued claims that an over–40 employee would be required to release would not necessarily be worth more than the bundle released by any particular employee under 40.

h. *ADEA Procedures*

The EEOC is charged with enforcement of the Act, and the ADEA provides criminal penalties for intentional or willful interference with its processes. It investigates claims of age discrimination, attempts conciliation, and has the power to file civil actions. But individual actions are the major means of enforcement, and many ADEA procedures and remedies are borrowed from the FLSA. See, e.g., *EEOC v. Tire Kingdom, Inc.*, 80 F.3d 449 (11th Cir. 1996).

The standards for administrative charge filing under the ADEA are more relaxed than those under Title VII. The major superficial similarities are the twin requirements that a complainant file a charge of discrimination (1) with the EEOC, within 180 days of an alleged violation, or within 300 days in a deferral state; and (2) with an appropriately empowered state agency, if one exists. But the EEOC itself is given only 60 days of deferral, in contrast to the 180 days specified by Title VII. ADEA plaintiffs may then proceed to federal court without demanding or receiving a "right to sue" letter from that agency. But if the charging party awaits an EEOC dismissal or other termination of the proceedings, the Civil Rights Act of 1991, section 115, requires the EEOC to notify the charging party, who then may (and must) bring a private action against the respondent within 90 days of receipt of that notice.

In addition, the Supreme Court has leniently construed the ADEA not to require the state or local filing to precede either the filing of a charge with the EEOC or ever the filing of an ADEA action in court. A complainant's failure to file a state agency charge before commencing a federal action is not fatal; the federal court will simply stay its proceedings until a state charge is filed and the state deferral period elapses. *Oscar Mayer & Co. v. Evans*, 441 U.S. 750 (1979). For this reason, lower courts in ADEA cases have also not followed the approach taken by the Supreme Court's *Mohasco* decision under Title VII, which subtracts the 60–day state deferral period from the 300–day EEOC filing deadline and thus effectively requires a state filing by day 240; the 300 days that the ADEA gives complainants in "deferral" states to file with the EEOC is a true 300 days, rather than 240 days. *Thelen v. Marc's Big Boy Corp.*, 64 F.3d 264 (7th Cir. 1995).

Paralleling the practice followed under Title VII, most circuit courts have adopted a "single-filing" rule that rather liberally permits would-be ADEA complainants who have not filed timely charges with the EEOC to piggyback on the timely-filed charges of their co-joined individual plaintiffs or "representatives." See, e.g., *Grayson v. K Mart Corp.*, 79 F.3d 1086 (11th Cir. 1996); *Howlett v. Holiday Inns, Inc.*, 49 F.3d 189 (6th Cir. 1995). But see *Whalen v. W.R. Grace & Co.*, 56 F.3d 504 (3d Cir. 1995).

The ADEA may be somewhat more restrictive than Title VII in one procedural respect, although probably largely in form. No ADEA class action may be maintained under Federal Rule of Civil Procedure 23, which in appropriate circumstances permits class members to be bound without their specific consent. But multiple plaintiffs may join together under Federal Rule 20; and "representative" actions are permitted under ADEA section 7(b), which incorporates by reference section 16(b) of the FLSA, 29 U.S.C.A. § 216(b) (West 2010). The class representatives must frame their court complaint so as to notify the employer that it will have to defend an opt-in representative action, and the statute allows a would-be "class member" who has not filed a charge affirmatively to "opt in" the action by giving a written consent to joinder as a party plaintiff. The Supreme Court has authorized district courts to facilitate this process by ordering employers to produce the names and addresses of employees similarly situated to the representative and to issue a consent document approved in form by the court itself. *Hoffmann–La Roche Inc. v. Sperling*, 493 U.S. 165 (1989). And the required degree of similarity between the allegations of the putative joiner and those of the named plaintiff is less than is required for Rule 20(a) permissive joinder. *K–Mart Corp. v. Helton*, 894 S.W.2d 630 (Ky. 1995).

i. ADEA Remedies

An individual may be awarded injunctive relief, back wages, statutory "liquidated" damages equal to the amount of back wages, attorney's fees, and costs. 29 U.S.C.A. § 626(b) (West 2010), incorporating by reference the remedies authorized under the FLSA, *id.* §§ 216–217. Although, as under Title VII, back pay is routinely available as a remedy for a proven ADEA violation, similar limitations on its scope apply. For example, back pay will be denied for the period beginning after an employer eliminates the position from which plaintiff was terminated, provided it has not created a comparable position. *Bartek v. Urban Redevelopment Auth. of Pittsburgh*, 882 F.2d 739, 746–47 (3d Cir. 1989).

The circuits generally approve front pay as an ADEA remedy that is almost routinely available when needed. See, e.g., *McKnight v. General Motors Corp.*, 908 F.2d 104, 117 (7th Cir. 1990). But see *Wells v. New Cherokee Corp.*, 58 F.3d 233 (6th Cir. 1995); *Blum* v. Witco, 829 F.2d 367, 375–76 (3d Cir. 1987). Its duration extends until the plaintiff fails to make reasonable efforts to secure substantially equivalent employment or until he obtains or is offered such employment, or until a date the court determines his job would no longer be available, or plaintiff would have quit. See *Dominic v. Consolidated Edison Co. of N.Y., Inc.*, 822 F.2d 1249 (2d Cir. 1987).

Since the age seventy cap on the class protected by the ADEA was removed effective January 1, 1987, it is theoretically possible for front pay to continue indefinitely, or at least for the duration of an employee's lifetime as predicted by a standard mortality table. But an employer's normal retirement age may well serve as a practical cap on the duration of what would otherwise be an astronomical total amount of front pay. *Olitsky v. Spencer Gifts, Inc.*, 964 F.2d 1471 (5th Cir. 1992).

Liquidated damages equal to the compensatory back pay award are available under the ADEA in the same circumstances as they are available under the EPA, i.e., when the violation is "willful" within the meaning of the FLSA. This means that the double award is available only if the employer knows that its employment practice violates the ADEA or recklessly disregards whether its conduct will violate the Act; it is not enough that the employer knows that the Act is potentially applicable to the practice in question. *Trans World*

Airlines, Inc. v. Thurston, 469 U.S. 111 (1985). Employer conduct must be more than merely voluntary and negligent to constitute a willful violation, but need not involve the kind of egregiousness or malice that most circuits require for punitive damages under Title VII or the ADA. The Supreme Court specifically rejects these additional requirements. *Hazen Paper Co. v. Biggins*, 507 U.S. 604 (1993).

Hazen also made it clear that the *Thurston* definition of willfulness applies to cases concerning alleged ad hoc disparate treatment against individual employees, as well as to alleged disparate treatment resulting from the kind of formal policy at issue in *Thurston*. But the Court also wrote that an employer "who knowingly relies on age" does not "invariably" commit a knowing or reckless violation of the ADEA. This is because the Court's test finds willfulness only when the employer knows that or recklessly disregards whether it is violating the prohibitions of the statute, not simply when it knowingly takes age into account. Specifically, the Court in *Hazen* sought to preserve "two tiers of liability" in ADEA cases by finding liability for back pay whenever an intentional violation is established, but denying liquidated damages even for intentional violations when "an employer incorrectly but in good faith and nonrecklessly" believes that its conduct is not prohibited or is affirmatively authorized by the statute.

Consequently, while conduct constituting a constructive discharge is by its nature serious, aggravated, and almost surely intentional, it does not follow that every such violation is willful. *Peterson v. Insurance Co. of N. Am.*, 40 F.3d 26 (2d Cir. 1994). Some violations, however—unlawful retaliation is an example—may inherently involve knowledge or reckless disregard of the prohibitions of the statute, so liquidated damages should follow as a matter of course from a finding of liability. Compare *Edwards v. Board of Regents*, 2 F.3d 382, 383–84 (11th Cir. 1993), with *Starceski v. Westinghouse Elec.*

Co., 54 F.3d 1089 (3d Cir. 1995), and *Grant v. Hazelett Strip–Casting Corp.*, 880 F.2d 1564 (2d Cir. 1989).

Although a 1978 amendment clarifies that jury trials are available on liquidated damages claims as well as on claims for lost wages, there are unresolved legal questions about the computation of the liquidated damages award. The major issue is whether the doubling should be based on the full compensatory award, including front pay, replacement of lost pension income, and other fringe benefits, or, as one circuit has held, should be limited to the amount of back pay. Compare *Bruno v. W.B. Saunders Co.*, 882 F.2d 760 (3d Cir. 1989), with *Blim v. Western Electric Co.*, 731 F.2d 1473 (10th Cir. 1984).

The circuits also disagree whether, when liquidated damages are awarded, the court may additionally award front pay. See *Walther v. Lone Star Gas Co.*, 952 F.2d 119 (5th Cir. 1992). A similar debate surrounds prejudgment interest. Courts that, despite *Thurston*, view liquidated damages as at least partly compensatory reject prejudgment interest, holding that the plaintiff who receives both would be overcompensated. See *McCann v. Texas City Refining, Inc.*, 984 F.2d 667 (5th Cir. 1993). Courts that consider liquidated damages as the ADEA's substitute for punitive damages allow prejudgment interest in addition. *Starceski*, 54 F.3d 1089 (3d Cir. 1995); *Reichman v. Bonsignore, Brignati & Mazzotta*, 818 F.2d 278 (2d Cir. 1987). The latter view is fortified by the Supreme Court's reaffirmation that ADEA liquidated damages are designed to be punitive. *Commissioner v. Schleier*, 513 U.S. 998 (1994).

Despite *Hazen*'s confirmation that the ADEA authorizes "legal remedies," the Civil Rights Act of 1991 gives Title VII plaintiffs alleging disparate treatment important remedies that the circuit courts have uniformly held unavailable under the ADEA: compensatory and punitive damages. See *Moskow-*

itz v. Trustees of Purdue Univ., 5 F.3d 279 (7th Cir. 1993). But state law claims authorizing compensatory or punitive damages may often be joined with ADEA claims. See *Sanchez v. Puerto Rico Oil Co.*, 37 F.3d 712 (1st Cir. 1994).

Accordingly, while it could be said categorically before the 1991 Act that an ADEA plaintiff was remedially better situated than a claimant under Title VII, that is no longer necessarily true. To be awarded more than back and, with luck, front pay, the ADEA plaintiff must prove willfulness; and even then, she is likely to receive an award that is only twice the amount of back and front pay combined. By contrast, the Title VII plaintiff, by showing no more than an intentional violation, may now recover not just back and front pay but compensatory damages, although those will be capped in amounts that vary with the size of the defendant's employee complement. Only when she seeks punitive damages must the Title VII plaintiff show something akin to ADEA willfulness. On the other hand, the 1991 Act caps the sum of compensatory and punitive damages available under Title VII, while there is no absolute cap on the size of ADEA liquidated damages. An ADEA plaintiff who recovers a very large award of back pay, front pay, or both may accordingly still find that his liquidated damages exceed the capped amount a Title VII counterpart could recover by way of compensatory and punitive damages.

The 1991 Act denies successful ADEA plaintiffs, unlike their Title VII counterparts, more than a nominal recovery at the statutory rate for the fees of expert witnesses. *James v. Sears, Roebuck & Co.*, 21 F.3d 989 (10th Cir. 1994). In contrast to section 706(k) of Title VII, the ADEA, per the FLSA, authorizes attorneys' fees only to "plaintiffs," not "prevailing parties." Thus, even a prevailing ADEA defendant who can make the extraordinary showing of frivolousness demanded by the *Christiansburg Garment* interpretation of section 706(k) of

Title VII may not be entitled to an award of attorneys' fees from the plaintiff.

5. EQUAL PAY ACT OF 1963 (EPA)

The Equal Pay Act of 1963, 29 U.S.C.A. § 206(d) (West 2010) ("EPA"), requires "equal pay for equal work" within the same establishment, regardless of sex. The concept of "equal work" lies at the heart of the Act. General comparisons between two jobs carrying unequal pay will not suffice to establish that work is "equal"; rather, demonstrating an EPA violation demands specific showings of equivalent skill, effort, and responsibility, as well as performance under similar working conditions. Once an inequality is found, however, it cannot be remedied by reducing the wages of the higher-paid member of the other sex.

The EPA contains four affirmative defenses. It permits exceptions to the equal pay for equal work principle when differentials are pursuant to: (1) seniority systems, (2) merit systems, (3) systems which measure earnings by quantity or quality of production (incentive systems), or (4) factors other than sex.

a. EPA Coverage, the Prima Facie Case, and Affirmative Defenses

(1) COVERAGE

Why would a plaintiff resort to the EPA when Title VII proscribes sex discrimination in all terms and conditions of employment, not just for compensation between persons of different genders holding "equal" jobs? For starters, it may be the only game in town. The EPA looks primarily to the FLSA, to which it is an amendment, for provisions on coverage and enforcement. In sharp contrast to Title VII, the EPA has no coverage threshold defined in terms of the employer's number of employees. Instead, it covers most employers of any size, unless the employer is in one of several specifically exempted industries. 29 U.S.C.A. § 213 (West 2010). These industries include certain fishing and agricultural businesses as well as small local newspapers.

An employee not in an exempted industry may assert an FLSA, and therefore an EPA, claim if she has some contact with interstate commerce. This contact may be established by satisfying one of two requirements. The first concerns the nature of the work implicated by the plaintiff's claim. If the employee is "engaged in commerce" or produces "goods for commerce," the work is covered, no matter what the employer's size.

An alternative FLSA avenue protects employees who, though not themselves engaged in or producing goods for interstate commerce, work for nonexempt businesses that are. This alternative measure of FLSA coverage extends the EPA's protection to persons employed by "enterprises" engaged in commerce or producing goods for commerce. Such enterprises will be deemed to meet the interstate commerce test if they (1) achieved certain sales volumes or (2) were part of certain industries specifically mentioned in the FLSA.

A third approach, based on text unique to the EPA, arguably reaches more broadly than the FLSA alternatives. It focuses on the relation between other employees' production and interstate commerce, without regard to the commerce involvement of the plaintiff or the defendant employer. The EPA prohibits employers that have "employees subject to" the EPA from engaging in unequal pay discrimination against [other] "employees." 29 U.S.C.A. § 206(d)(1) (West 2010). Read literally, the EPA would therefore appear to protect all employees of employers that have at least two employees of different genders who are engaged in or producing goods for commerce, even if those employers are not FLSA "enterprises."

The Act defines an employer as "any person acting directly or indirectly in the interest of an employer in relation to an employee." *Id.* § 203(d). Notwithstanding this definition, claims against supervisors or managers in their individual as distinct from official capacities are likely to be dismissed because in an individual capacity a defendant lacks control over the plaintiff's terms of employment. See *Welch v. Laney*, 57 F.3d 1004 (11th Cir. 1995).

(2) EQUAL WORK

The first step in the plaintiff's prima facie case is to establish that the plaintiff performed work equal to that of another of the opposite sex. Job equivalence, as measured by skill, effort, responsibility, and working conditions, need not be precise, only substantial. *Corning Glass Works v. Brennan*, 417 U.S. 188 (1974). The issue in *Corning Glass* was whether the employer violated the EPA by paying a higher base wage to male night shift inspectors than it paid to female day shift inspectors. Historically, Corning had paid higher wages to the night inspectors, who were then all male. After the enactment of the EPA, Corning opened both jobs to men and women, but a collective-bargaining agreement perpetuated the differential in favor of the night jobs. The Court defined "working conditions" to refer to a job's "hazards" and "surroundings," but not time of day, which the Court concluded did not render substantially equal working conditions unequal. Accordingly, Corning had prima facie violated the EPA by paying women who worked days less than men who worked nights for equal work.

The circuit courts have similarly disregarded minor differences between jobs to find work "equal." See, e.g., *Hein v. Oregon Coll. of Edu.*, 718 F.2d 910 (9th Cir. 1983). But when a plaintiff of one gender is not responsible for tasks important to the enterprise that are assigned to a comparator of the other gender, she does not perform equal work and therefore has no right to equal pay.

(3) UNEQUAL PAY

Another element of the plaintiff's prima facie case is a showing that the plaintiff is paid less than another of the opposite sex. First, the plaintiff must be paid a lesser "rate" of pay. Second, this rate must be compared with that of an individual of the opposite sex performing substantially similar work.

i. Equal "Rate" of Pay

Commissions worth less per sale to female than to male employees who provide the same total service to an employer's clientele violate the EPA because they yield women a lesser "rate." *Bence v. Detroit Health Corp.*, 712 F.2d 1024 (6th Cir. 1983).

ii. The Necessity of a "Comparator" Within a Single "Establishment"

In order to show unequal pay, there must be some comparison between the complaining individual and one of the opposite sex in a substantially similar position. The plaintiff, therefore, must demonstrate that an individual of the opposite sex received greater compensation for substantially the same job. This task is accomplished through the use of a comparator. The comparator may be one who held the job before the plaintiff, who replaced the plaintiff, or who held a substantially similar position contemporaneously with the plaintiff. See *Brinkley–Obu v. Hughes Training, Inc.*, 36 F.3d 336 (4th Cir. 1994). Finally, the comparator must also be employed in the same establishment as the plaintiff. These requirements may be subdivided into four components.

First, the comparator may not be hypothetical, but rather, must be a specific, identifiable, and better-paid individual performing a job of substantially equal skill, effort, and responsibility. *EEOC v. Liggett & Myers Inc.*, 690 F.2d 1072, 1076–78 (4th Cir. 1982). Where a plaintiff identified her male comparators in general terms as "any men who got any higher salary increases than [the plaintiff] did," the plaintiff failed to carry a prima facie case. *Houck v. Virginia Polytechnic Inst. and State Univ.*, 10 F.3d 204, 206 (4th Cir. 1993).

Second, the comparator must perform a substantially similar job. The court analyzes the job, not the qualification or performance characteristics of individual employees holding the job, and only the skill and qualifications actually needed to perform the job in question are considered. *Miranda v. B & B Cash Grocery Store, Inc.*, 975 F.2d 1518 (11th Cir. 1992). Additionally, the examination rests on the primary, not the incidental or insubstantial, job duties. Where the plaintiff performs substantially similar tasks but the comparator also has significant additional primary duties, the prima facie case fails. *Mulhall v. Advance Sec., Inc.*, 19 F.3d 586, 593 (11th Cir. 1994).

Third, the comparator may be a past, present, or future employee in a substantially similar position. There can be a valid comparison between the plaintiff, a former "Vice–President, Administration," and a current "Vice–President, Controller" because financial concerns were essential to both jobs. *Id.* But if the plaintiff cannot establish that the plaintiff's predecessor, successor, or contemporary was paid more for the same responsibilities, the plaintiff has failed to make a prima facie showing. *Weiss v. Coca–Cola Bottling Co. of Chicago*, 990 F.2d 333, 337–38 (7th Cir. 1993).

Finally, the comparator must be an employee of the same "establishment" as the plaintiff. The Secretary of Labor has defined "establishment" to mean "a distinct physical place of business rather than ... an entire business or 'enterprise' which may include several separate places of business." 29 C.F.R. § 1620.9(a) (2010). In "unusual circumstances," however, a single establishment can include more than one physical location. *Id.* § 1620.9(b).

When there is centralized control and administration, some courts have been willing to find a single EPA establishment despite several physical locations. See, e.g., *Brennan v. Goose Creek Consol. Indep. Sch. Dist.*, 519 F.2d 53 (5th Cir. 1975). By contrast, other circuits have restricted the comparison of salaries to employees in one physical location when the local office where plaintiff worked made the ultimate hiring decision and, within a broad range determined by the central office, set specific salaries, *Meeks v. Computer Associates Int'l*, 15 F.3d 1013, 1017 (11th Cir. 1994), or where the employer conferred independent personnel decision-making authority on managers at the plaintiff's facility. *Foster v. Arcata Associates, Inc.*, 772 F.2d 1453, 1464 (9th Cir. 1985).

(4) THE EMPLOYER'S DEFENSES

Once a plaintiff has established a prima facie case, the employer bears the burden of producing evidence and persuading that the employment practice fits within one or more of the EPA's four affirmative defenses. "Unequal pay" for equal work is permitted when the payment is made pursuant to (i) a seniority system, (ii) a merit system, (iii) a system measures earnings by quantity or quality of production, or (iv) a differential based on any factor other than sex. 29 U.S.C.A. § 206(d)(1) (West 2010).

The burden of establishing one of the four affirmative defenses is "a heavy one," because the statutory exemptions are "narrowly construed." Indeed, a recent circuit opinion demonstrates that the employer's burden in EPA cases is heavier than that in a Title VII case, and, in at least one sense, the plaintiff's burden is lighter. Unlike in Title VII, once the employer proffers one of the four affirmative defenses, the burden to prove the defense remains with the employer. Compare this to the burden shifting scheme of Title VII pretext inferential proof cases, where the plaintiff must persuade that the defendant's proffered legitimate, nondiscriminatory reason for the adverse term or condition of employment is but a pretext for intentional discrimination. Moreover, under the EPA, the employer must submit evidence from which a reasonable factfinder could conclude not merely that the employer's proffered reasons could explain the wage disparity (as under the Title VII burden-shifting paradigm), but that the proffered reasons do in fact explain the wage disparity.

In *Ryduchowski v. Port Authority of New York and New Jersey*, 203 F.3d 135 (2d Cir. 2000), the Court reversed a grant of judgment as a matter of law after a plaintiff's verdict on her EPA claim. The appellate court found that the jury could have reasonably concluded that the defendant failed to meet its burden to establish that a valid merit system was in place and systematically administered.

Affirmative defenses (i)–(iii) are rarely used. These three defenses specifically require a "system"; it need not be formalized or structured, but employees must know about it nonetheless. A defendant asserting a seniority system affirmative defense must "be able to identify standards for measuring seniority which are systematically applied and observed." *Irby v. Bittick*, 44 F.3d 949, 954 (11th Cir. 1995). Further, the system must be operated in good faith and not used as a way to maintain sex-based wage differences. The third defense, a system based on quality or quantity of production, has little independent vitality. First, if employees are paid the same "rate" for their work based on production, there is no EPA violation. Second, a quality or quantity system is so closely related to a merit system that it may have no separate significance. The majority of litigation in the area of affirmative defenses, therefore, has centered around the rather ambiguous defense (iv), "any factor other than sex."

Examples of "factors other than sex" include salary retention policies, prior salary, and economic benefit to the employer. See, e.g., *Kouba v. Allstate Ins. Co.*, 691 F.2d 873 (9th Cir. 1982). Another circuit has allowed reliance on prior salary only when other business considerations—such as the selectee's greater amount of experience in a closely related job— reasonably explain its utilization. *Irby*, 44 F.3d 949 (11th Cir. 1995). A comparator's greater experience in similar positions remains a neutral, nondiscriminatory reason, even if the plaintiff has greater total service. See *Lindale v. Tokheim Corp.*, 145 F.3d 953 (7th Cir. 1998). But regardless of other factors, where sex is even a "but for" cause, the EPA is violated. See *Peters v. City of Shreveport*, 818 F.2d 1148 (5th Cir. 1987).

Another factor that has been approved as something "other than sex" is reliance on differential economic benefit to the employer of otherwise equal "male" and "female" jobs. *Byrd v. Ronayne*, 61 F.3d 1026 (1st Cir. 1995) (alternative holding). A clothier could pay its salesmen more than its saleswomen, a controversial decision holds, where the men produced greater benefit to the employer because the men's clothing department generated higher profit margins and revenues. *Hodgson v. Robert Hall Clothes, Inc.*, 473 F.2d 589 (3d Cir. 1973). But compensation disparities keyed solely to gender-based actuarial differences are not saved by the "other than sex" exception. *City of Los Angeles, Dep't of Water & Power v. Manhart*, 435 U.S. 702 (1978). The Supreme Court has also rejected time of day as an "other than sex" defense. *Corning Glass*, 417 U.S. 188 (1974).

(5) Retaliation

The FLSA anti-retaliation provision, applicable by reference to EPA, prohibits retaliation in language more cramped than section 704 of Title VII. By offering protection against reprisal only to those who have "filed any complaint" or "instituted any proceeding," it does not in terms protect those who have made an informal on-the-job protest. But the federal judiciary views access to available avenues of protest of such importance that at least five circuit courts have nevertheless extended such protection to informal protesters. See *EEOC v. Romeo Cmty. Schs.*, 976 F.2d 985, 989 (6th Cir. 1992). But see *Lambert v. Genesee Hosp.*, 10 F.3d 46 (2d Cir. 1993). Consistent with the tradition under the FLSA, it has been held that the EPA authorizes compensatory and punitive damages for unlawful retaliation. *Travis v. Gary Cmty. Mental Health Ctr., Inc.*, 921 F.2d 108, 112 (7th Cir. 1990).

b. Enforcement, Limitations, and Remedies

(1) Enforcement

Although the EEOC has enforcement responsibility and may file civil actions under the EPA, a private plaintiff need not exhaust state or federal administrative remedies before proceeding to court. Under provisions of the FLSA that the EPA incorporates by reference, the action may be brought in state or federal court against a private or public employer. 29 U.S.C.A. § 216(b) (West 2010). A suit may be brought under the EPA by an employee or the EEOC. The EPA grants authority to the Secretary of Labor to initiate suit against an employer for monetary damages or injunctive relief. The courts have upheld the constitutionality of a 1978 Presidential transfer of this authority to the EEOC. See, e.g., *EEOC v. Hernando Bank, Inc.*, 724 F.2d 1188 (5th Cir. 1984).

While under Title VII the EEOC must try to eliminate an unlawful practice through informal methods of conciliation, the EPA contains no similar provision. The EPA, unlike Title VII, has no requirement of filing administrative complaints or awaiting administrative conciliation or determination. *County of Washington v. Gunther*, 452 U.S. 161, 175 n.14 (1981). Accordingly, courts have found no requirement of prior administrative filing or informal conciliation. See *Hernando Bank*, 724 F.2d 1188 (5th Cir. 1984).

An employee may initiate suit seeking monetary damages up until the point the EEOC files a complaint against the employer. If the EEOC files an action, the employee's right to sue or become a party to an action brought by other employees is terminated. The EEOC's suit is deemed to commence from the date a complaint is filed that names the EEOC as a party plaintiff, or from the date the EEOC's name is added as a party plaintiff.

Suit may be brought individually or on behalf of a class. As under the ADEA, if the suit is brought as a class action, each class member must consent in writing to become a party and the consent must be filed with the court. 29 U.S.C.A. § 216(b) (West 2010). Under either the ADEA or the EPA, therefore, a class action may not be pursued under Federal Rule of Civil Procedure 23. See *Lachapelle v. Owens–Illinois, Inc.*, 513 F.2d 286 (5th Cir. 1975).

(2) LIMITATIONS

The FLSA provides a two-year statute of limitations for filing an EPA action, three years in the case of a "willful" violation. These statutes of limitations compare favorably from the plaintiff's perspective with the 180–day or 300–day administrative filing deadlines of Title VII, now also made applicable to the ADEA.

The three-year limitations period for willful violations is available when an employer knows that, or recklessly disregards whether, its conduct violates the statute. See *McLaughlin v. Richland Shoe Co.*, 486 U.S. 128, 133 (1988). Willfulness under the FLSA refers to conduct that is more than merely negligent, yet the requisite willfulness for purposes of limitations may be found not just when the employer believes its conduct violates the statute, but also when the employer was merely indifferent to whether its conduct constituted a violation. *Trans World Airlines, Inc. v. Thurston*, 469 U.S. 111, 125–29 (1985); *Walton v. United Consumers Club, Inc.*, 786 F.2d 303, 310–11 (7th Cir. 1986).

(3) Continuing Violations

The judicially-created "continuing violations" doctrine provides certain plaintiffs an escape from the statute of limitations. The doctrine allows a court to take jurisdiction over a cause of action, or impose liability, for a discrete EPA violation that occurred outside the limitations period. Plaintiffs have invoked the doctrine under both the EPA and Title VII, but the courts have afforded it a wider sweep in EPA cases. This is probably because of the nature of the sole EPA violation, which is predicated on unequal compensation, a practice that continues from paycheck to paycheck. *Brinkley–Obu v. Hughes Training, Inc.*, 36 F.3d 336 (4th Cir. 1994).

Because "each unequal paycheck is considered a separate violation of the Equal Pay Act, a cause of action may be brought for any or all violations occurring within the limitations period...." *Gandy v. Sullivan Cnty.*, 24 F.3d 861, 865 (6th Cir. 1994). The plaintiff took a position at a pay rate below that of her predecessor and was paid unequally for nine years before she filed suit. The defendant argued that the statute tolled three years after the first unequal paycheck. The court concluded that the action was not time-barred as long as at least one discriminatory act occurred within the limitations period. A majority of circuits concur with *Gandy* that an actionable EPA violation occurs each time an employee receives an "unequal" paycheck, not just when the first such paycheck is issued. See, e.g., *Ashley v. Boyle's Famous Corned Beef Co.*, 66 F.3d 164 (8th Cir. 1995).

(4) REMEDIES

EPA remedies are governed by two provisions of the FLSA, 29 U.S.C.A. §§ 216 and 217 (West 2010). These sections authorize recovery not only of unlawfully withheld wages, but also of an equal amount denominated "liquidated damages." An employee plaintiff may then recover unlawfully withheld wages, liquidated damages, and attorney fees plus costs. Unlawfully withheld wages accrue from no earlier than two years prior to the filing of the complaint and continue until a court order. The accrual period begins three years prior to the filing of a complaint if the employer is found to have acted "willfully."

After the passage of the Portal-to-Portal Act of 1947, 29 U.S.C.A. §§ 251–262 (West 2010), the imposition of liquidated damages in FLSA cases became discretionary with the trial judge. *Id.* § 260. She may not award liquidated damages when the employer proves "to the satisfaction of the court" that it acted in good faith and had a reasonable belief that its conduct did not violate the FLSA. The burden is on the employer to show that it acted in the sincere and reasonable belief that its conduct was lawful.

c. Gender–Based Compensation Discrimination Outside the Reach of the EPA but Prohibited by Title VII

In *County of Washington v. Gunther*, 452 U.S. 161 (1981), the plaintiff challenged the employer's practice of intentionally setting the wage scale for female, but not male, guards at a level substantially lower than recommended by its survey of outside markets. That decision was actionable, if at all, only under Title VII; the EPA was not implicated because the male and female comparator jobs did not involve substantially equal work. Yet whether Title VII applied was doubtful in view of that part of section 703(h), 42 U.S.C.A. § 2000e–2(h) (West 2010), known as the Bennett Amendment, which removes from Title VII's reach practices "authorized" by the EPA. The Supreme Court held, however, that Title VII may regulate an intentionally discriminatory gender-based compensation practice that the EPA does not prohibit—as well as the "unequal pay for equal work" claim that the EPA does prohibit. In other words, the only compensation practices affirmatively "authorized" by the EPA, and therefore beyond the reach of Title VII by virtue of the Bennett Amendment, are those insulated by the EPA's four affirmative defenses. This holding provides a remedy for intentional, gender-based compensation discrimination to a woman who holds a unique position and therefore cannot invoke the EPA for lack of a male comparator.

Gunther provides little guidance, however, on key related questions about the scope of Title VII respecting gender-based compensation discrimination. May Title VII ban pay practices not prohibited by the EPA where an employer intent to discriminate can be proved only inferentially, à la *McDonnell Douglas/Burdine*? Can Title VII reach compensation practices neutral on their face that have discriminatory gender impact? Or what if the employer has dual intentions, one intentionally discriminatory and another benign, as in *Price Waterhouse*, the landmark Title VII "mixed motives" decision?

d. *Comparable Worth*

The comparable worth theory would mandate upward adjustment in the wage rates of all men and women holding jobs traditionally held predominantly by women, even absent wage discrimination between male and female employees whose work is "equal" or evidence of intentional discrimination based on gender. Plaintiffs would prove simply that a "woman's" job was of similar "worth" to the employer as a "man's" job, yet commanded lesser compensation. The revised wage level is supposed to represent a court's or legislature's evaluation of the job's "worth" to the employer.

The EPA affords no relief for a comparable worth claim, because by hypothesis the plaintiff and the higher-paid employee are performing non-"equal" jobs. The similarity is only in the "worth" of the respective jobs to the employer. The difficulty with a comparable worth challenge under Title VII is that the differences between the comparison jobs preclude the plaintiff from proving that she suffered intentional disparate treatment. Attempts to secure judicial recognition of the comparable worth theory by challenging the employer's pay system as a neutral practice with adverse impact on women have also been conspicuously unsuccessful. See *American Fed'n of State, Cnty., & Mun. Emps. v. Washington*, 770 F.2d 1401 (9th Cir. 1985).

The Supreme Court has not addressed the issue of comparable worth, but in *Gunther*, 452 U.S. at 180–81, the Court specifically noted that allowing the intentional disparate treatment claim there did not require it to make its own subjective assessment of the value of the male and female guard jobs.

Comparable worth claims will therefore probably still fail. Even if the plaintiff may base a prima facie case on the adverse impact of the "subjective" pay practice in question, the employer can assert a market-related justification that is likely to be adjudged a matter of business necessity. In the face of the pre–1991 case law that consistently rejected comparable worth claims, the silence of the Civil Rights Act of 1991 on the subject is a significant indication that Congress hews to the relatively narrow yardstick of nondiscrimination, eschewing gender-based minimum standards. Comparable worth has been endorsed by a few state legislatures, but most states continue to reject the notion that market-driven job wage rates equate to discrimination based on gender.

e. Claims Covered by Title VII and the EPA

Assume a case is covered by both statutes, one involving "equal pay for equal work." Why would some plaintiffs resort to the EPA, with its narrow proscription of only one kind of sex-based wage discrimination, when Title VII also prohibits other forms of sex-based wage discrimination and sex discrimination affecting other terms and conditions of employment? The answer lies in varying proof requirements and differences in enforcement and remedial schemes.

In an unequal pay for equal work situation, there are three potentially available ways of proving a Title VII claim. A plaintiff may offer "direct" evidence of gender discriminatory intent, evidence from which such discriminatory intent may be inferred, or evidence that establishes an EPA violation. The federal circuit decisions are divided over which of these proof modes is permissible or indispensable. Some courts require direct or express evidence of discriminatory intent to show an "equal pay" violation of Title VII. See *EEOC v. Sears, Roebuck & Co.*, 839 F.2d 302, 340–42 (7th Cir. 1988); *Plemer v. Parsons–Gilbane*, 713 F.2d 1127, 1133–34 (5th Cir. 1983). But see *Fallon v. Illinois*, 882 F.2d 1206, 1213–17 (7th Cir. 1989). For these courts, then, the *Gunther* facts represent the outer limit of Title VII liability for gender-based discrimination in compensation.

On the other hand, several circuits have decided that the *McDonnell Douglas/Burdine* inferential evidence approach may be used to prove a Title VII violation of unequal pay for equal work. See, e.g., *Miranda v. B & B Cash Grocery Store, Inc.*, 975 F.2d 1518, 1530–31 (11th Cir. 1992). These circuits, however, divide over whether the traditional Title VII allocation of burdens of proof, or the very different framework established by the EPA, controls. A slim majority consider Title VII and EPA claims completely independent; these courts require proof for each alleged violation that tracks the distinct elements and burden shifts of each statute. See *Meeks v. Computer Associates Int'l*, 15 F.3d 1013, 1021 (11th Cir. 1994). Other circuits, however, hold that a violation of the EPA is ipso facto a violation of Title VII; this means that the Title VII claim requires no independent evidence of intent, direct or indirect. See *Korte v. Diemer*, 909 F.2d 954, 959 (6th Cir. 1990). Regulations promulgated by the EEOC support the latter view. 29 C.F.R. § 1620.27(a) (2010).

The difference between these approaches can substantially affect outcome. The prima facie case for an EPA claim is simply that the employer pays different wages to employees of the opposite sex for "equal work"—work requiring substantially equal skill, effort, and responsibility and performed under similar working conditions. Once the plaintiff has made this showing, the defendant bears the burden of establishing one of the affirmative defenses. There is no separate requirement under the EPA that the plaintiff offer evidence of intent to discriminate; in this sense, the EPA is a "strict liability" statute. See *Meeks v. Computer Associates Int'l*, 15 F.3d 1013 (11th Cir. 1994).

By contrast, the standard, inferential prima facie evidence required to establish a Title VII individual disparate treatment claim begins with a showing that the plaintiff occupies a job similar to that of a higher-paid member of the opposite sex. The defendant must then produce evidence of a legitimate, nondiscriminatory reason for paying less. If the defendant does so, the plaintiff may prevail only by proving in a variety of ways that the employer intended to discriminate based on gender—the *Burdine/McDonnell Douglas* approach. In sharp contrast to the EPA, employer intent is critical, and the Title VII plaintiff throughout the case bears the risk of non-persuasion on the "ultimate" question of intentional disparate treatment because of sex. *St. Mary's Honor Ctr. v. Hicks*, 509 U.S. 502 (1993).

Until the 1991 Civil Rights Act amendments, these different approaches to the required elements of unequal pay for equal work claims under Title VII and the EPA had minimal practical importance. The remedies under the EPA were more congenial to the plaintiff than the remedies under Title VII because the EPA afforded the possibility of liquidated damages, while Title VII remitted the plaintiff to back pay done. So the plaintiff with only an unequal pay for equal work claim usually took the EPA route, which was also easier to establish. But the 1991 amendments expanded the remedies under Title VII to include compensatory and punitive damages for intentional or "disparate treatment" violations, and most EPA violations fit that description, even if no direct evidence of intent is required. In circuits that equate the eased EPA proof standards with the more stringent Title VII standards, the plaintiff can now recover Title VII's potentially more generous remedies (compensation and punitive damages in addition to back and front pay) by carrying the lighter EPA burden.

6. TITLE IX, EDUCATIONAL AMENDMENTS OF 1972

Title IX of the Civil Rights Act of 1964 redresses sex discrimination in employment, as well as in admissions and general educational activities, by federally-funded education programs. *North Haven Bd. of Educ. v. Bell*, 456 U.S. 512, 520–35 (1982). Title VI of that Act prohibits discrimination based on race, color, or national origin in federally-funded programs or activities. 42 U.S.C.A. §§ 2000d–2000d–4a (West 2010). But Title VI does not reach employment practices except where a primary objective of the federal assistance is to provide employment. *Id.* § 2000d–3. Accordingly, even though many judicially-developed liability and remedy standards are used interchangeably in cases under both Titles, discussion here will be limited to Title IX.

Title IX's primary prohibition provides that "[n]o person in the United States shall, on the basis of sex, be excluded from participation in, be denied the benefit of, or be subjected to discrimination under any education program or activity receiving Federal financial assistance." 20 U.S.C.A. § 1681 (West 2010). See also *id.* § 1684 (prohibiting discrimination because of blindness or severe visual impairment).

Federal assistance includes grants, loans, or contracts other than those of insurance or guaranty. *Id.* § 1682; see *id.* § 1685 (contracts of insurance or guaranty). One holding of *Grove City College v. Bell*, 465 U.S. 555 (1984), that federal assistance funneled directly to students constitutes "assistance" to the students' educational institutions, thus triggering Title IX regulation of programs or of the institution itself, appears undisturbed either by subsequent decisions or by the 1987 Civil Rights Restoration Act discussed immediately below.

a. Covered Programs or Activities

Lower courts had held that discrimination in any Title IX "program or activity" within an institution receiving federal assistance was a violation of Title IX, even if the particular discriminatory program was not the subject of the assistance. But in *Grove City College*, the Supreme Court interpreted the phrase "program or activity" narrowly, holding that Title IX prohibited discrimination only in the particular educational program or activity receiving the federal assistance, not in all the educational programs and activities conducted by the institution receiving such assistance. The Civil Rights Restoration Act of 1987, Pub. L. No. 100–259, 102 Stat. 28, overturned this holding by defining the "program or activity" covered by Title IX to include "all" of a recipient's operations. 20 U.S.C.A. § 1687 (West 2010).

So where federal aid is extended to any program within a college, university, or other public system of elementary, secondary, or higher education, the entire institution or system is covered by the prohibitions of Title IX. 42 U.S.C.A. § 1687(2)(B) (West 2010); see *Yusuf v. Vassar College*, 35 F.3d 709 (2d Cir. 1994). Where a state and local government department (or agency) other than a school receives federal aid for an educational program or activity, and the funds stay within that particular department, only that department is subject to Title IX sanctions, but if the aid is distributed to other departments or agencies, all entities that receive it are covered. 42 U.S.C.A. § 1687(1)(B) (West 2010). Finally, a private corporation that receives aid as a whole or that provides a public service would fall under Title IX, but the entire corporation may not be covered if the federal funds are extended to only a geographically separate facility. *Id.* § 1687(3)(B).

b. *Exemptions*

Title IX redresses sex discrimination in employment by federally-funded education institutions. See *North Haven Bd. of Educ.*, 456 U.S. 512 (1982). The Restoration Act exempts entities controlled by religious organizations from Title IX coverage if the application of Title IX's ban on sex discrimination would conflict with the organization's religious tenets. 20 U.S.C.A. § 1687(4) (West 2010).

c.   *Elements of a Private Action Under Title IX*

The Supreme Court has implied a private right of action under Title IX. *Cannon v. University of Chicago*, 441 U.S. 677 (1979). The right of action appears to extend to claims of sex discrimination in employment—for example, claims by teachers against school districts. See *Preston v. Virginia*, 31 F.3d 203 (4th Cir. 1994). The preceding statement must be qualified, however, because a Supreme Court decision holding Title IX applicable to employment practices did not specifically consider whether a violation would give rise to a private right of action. See *North Haven Bd. of Educ.*, 456 U.S. 512 (1982). Thus, circuit decisions differ over whether the existence of a detailed judicial remedy for employment discrimination under Title VII of the 1964 Civil Rights Act (amended as of 1991 to permit compensatory and punitive damages subject to statutory caps) forecloses a judicially-implied remedy for employment discrimination under Title IX with respect to gender-discriminatory practices of federally-funded education institutions that are actionable under Title VII. Compare *Lakoski v. James*, 66 F.3d 751 (5th Cir. 1995), with *Lipsett v. University of Puerto Rico*, 864 F.2d 881, 896–97 (1st Cir. 1988). It is clear, though, that the implied Title IX claim is not sufficiently comprehensive to foreclose an express § 1983 claim on the same facts for a violation of equal protection, especially given the coverage differences between equal protection and Title IX and their varying proof requirements. *Fitzgerald v. Barnstable Sch. Comm.*, 555 U.S. 246 (2009).

Even if a school district is subject to a private damages action under Title IX for gender-discriminatory employment practices, the scope of such liability is unclear. The Supreme Court held in a case involving a teacher's sexual abuse of a student that no damages remedy lies against the education entity unless an official with authority to end the discrimination had actual knowledge of the unlawful discrimination and failed adequately to respond. *Gebser v. Lago Vista Ind. Sch. Dist.*, 524 U.S. 274 (1998). Presumably, some teachers with gender-based employment discrimination claims could meet this strict standard, but only if the harassment was committed by, or came to the attention of, a principal or other high-ranking administrative official. Liability would be considerably broader, and could more readily reach coworker harassment of teachers, if the stringent *Gebser* actual knowledge standard is limited to the student-plaintiff context. Then employee plaintiffs might be able to utilize the broader standards of entity liability developed under Title VII.

The administrative regulations promulgated under Title IX, like those under Title VI, prohibit discrimination resulting from facially neutral policies that have gender-discriminatory effect as well as intentional discrimination based on gender. See 34 C.F.R. § 106.21(b)(2) (2010). Lower courts have applied the impact principle to Title IX actions when the plaintiff distinctly pleads a violation of the applicable implementing regulations, as distinct from the statute alone. See, e.g., *Mabry v. State Bd. of Cmty. Colls. & Occupational Educ.*, 813 F.2d 311, 317 n.6 (10th Cir. 1987).

d. Damages

The Supreme Court has held that a successful Title IX plaintiff is eligible for all traditional legal and equitable relief that may be appropriate, damages as well as back pay and prospective relief. *Franklin v. Gwinnett Cnty. Pub. Schs.*, 503 U.S. 60 (1992). Further, the Civil Rights Remedies Equalization Amendment of 1986 permits federal courts to award retrospective relief under, among other statutes, Titles VI and IX, against a state or state agency, expressly abrogating their Eleventh Amendment immunity. 42 U.S.C.A. § 2000d–7(b) (West 2010). Because *Franklin* concerned intentional discrimination, it is unclear what the effect of its broad language may be on damages in Title IX cases challenging neutral practices. *Franklin* has been limited, however, by a Supreme Court decision barring punitive damages under Title IX, *Barnes v. Gorman*, 536 U.S. 181 (2002).

7. CIVIL RIGHTS ATTORNEY'S FEES AWARDS ACT OF 1976

a. Recovering Costs of Suit: Fed. R. Civ. P. 54(d)

Unlike attorney's fees under Title VII or § 1988, which as we shall see are ordinarily awardable only to prevailing plaintiffs, either side that prevails is presumptively entitled to costs under Federal Rule of Civil Procedure 54(d). The Rule 54(d) "costs" recoverable by any prevailing party are limited, however, to items specified by a separate federal statute, 28 U.S.C.A. § 1920 (West 2010). These include clerk and marshal fees, fees by court reporters for transcripts "necessarily obtained for use in the case;" printing disbursements and witness fees; specified docket fees; and fees for court-appointed experts and certain interpreters.

b. Attorney's Fees for Prevailing Parties: The Civil Rights Attorney's Fees Awards Act

The Civil Rights Attorney's Fees Awards Act, Pub. L. No. 94–559, 90 Stat. 2641 (1976) (the "Act"), an amendment to 42 U.S.C.A. § 1988 (West 2010), permits a discretionary award of attorney's fees, in a "reasonable" amount, as part of the costs recoverable by prevailing parties, other than the United States, in any action or proceeding pursuant to 42 U.S.C.A. §§ 1981, 1982, 1983, 1985, and 1986, as well as Titles VI and IX. The purpose of the award is to enable plaintiffs to attract competent legal counsel; perhaps that is why fees have been denied for lawyers' public relations efforts on behalf of their clients. *Halderman v. Pennhurst State Sch. & Hosp.*, 49 F.3d

939 (3d Cir. 1995). The Act parallels separate statutory authority to award attorney's fees to prevailing parties in actions under the ADEA, the Clean Water Act, the Equal Pay Act, the FLSA, the Rehabilitation Act of 1973, and under Title VII. In fact, over 100 separate statutes allow for court-awarded attorney's fees. The principles governing eligibility for and computation of awards are largely interchangeable among these statutes.

Although a plaintiff must receive at least some relief on the merits in order to become a "prevailing party" eligible for fees, success on a "significant issue," even if it is not a "central" one, will suffice. But opinion is divided as to whether fee eligibility depends upon the plaintiff's having prevailed on a claim under one of the § 1988–referenced federal statutes, rather than a related claim under state law. A plaintiff adjudged to be a prevailing party should ordinarily receive a fee award absent "special circumstances," such as the plaintiff's egregious misconduct, e.g., *Patricia P. v. Board of Educ. of Oak Park*, 203 F.3d 462 (7th Cir. 2000). These circumstances are rarely found. But pro se plaintiffs who also happen to be attorneys have been ruled ineligible for a fee award. *Kay v. Ehrler*, 499 U.S. 432 (1991). A plaintiff who recovers only nominal damages, although a prevailing party, may be entitled to no fee award if those damages represent only a slight degree of success achieved in the litigation. *Farrar v. Hobby*, 506 U.S. 103 (1992).

To achieve success on a "significant issue" and thus "prevail" so as to be eligible for fees, the plaintiff need only obtain some relief that changes his legal relationship with the defendant and is more than merely technical or de minimis. *Hewitt v. Helms*, 459 U.S. 460 (1983). In general, if the relief plaintiff initially seeks is "of the same general type" as the relief eventually obtained, plaintiff may be considered a prevailing party. *Lyte v. Sara Lee Corp.*, 950 F.2d 101 (2d Cir. 1991). An injunction requiring a company to correct a racially intimidating work atmosphere, for example, has sufficed as the predicate for a fee award to a plaintiff who lost on most of his individual claims of race discrimination. *Ruffin v. Great Dane Trailers*, 969 F.2d 989 (11th Cir. 1992). But in applying this standard, courts have sometimes resorted to a highly subjective appraisal of the plaintiff's original objective in bringing suit, denying fees where that objective was not obtained.

A finding of a violation under § 1983 may lead to an award of nominal damages where the predicate constitutional violation is "absolute," that is, not dependent upon the merits of the plaintiff's substantive assertions or the magnitude of injury resulting from a violation. Such damages may now be available under Title VII, which provides for certain kinds of legal relief since its amendment by the Civil Rights Act of 1991. Whether such nominal damages can serve as a springboard for § 1988 attorney's fees was the subject of conflict among the circuits.

In *Farrar v. Hobby*, 506 U.S. 103 (1992), the Supreme Court attempted to resolve this conflict, but did so somewhat oddly. It formally conferred prevailing party status on plaintiffs who recover only nominal damages, but did so under standards that fix the amount of a reasonable attorney's fee at zero when their degree of success is slight. The Court confirmed that "a plaintiff 'prevails' when actual relief on the merits of his claim materially alters the legal relationship between the parties by modifying the defendant's behavior in a way that directly benefits the plaintiff"; and it acknowledged that even a judgment for only nominal damages "modifies the defendant's behavior for the plaintiff's benefit by forcing the defendant to pay an amount of money he otherwise would not pay." *Id.* at 111–13. But it then drained this conclusion of practical significance under most circumstances by adding that when a plaintiff, having failed to prove an essential element of a claim for monetary relief, recovers only nominal damages, "the only reasonable fee is usually no fee at all." *Id.* at 115.

In *Carey v. Piphus*, 435 U.S. 247, 266 (1978), the Court had found that nominal damages must be available for deprivations of "absolute" rights like procedural due process because of "the importance to organized society that those rights be scrupulously observed." After *Farrar*, however, it is difficult to understand how, where there is little or no actual economic or emotional injury, the Court contemplates that such rights will be enforced if attorney's fees are only theoretically and not practically available to plaintiffs who successfully prosecute suits for their violation. One possibility is that lower courts will limit *Farrar* to its facts: no jury specification of the constitutional right violated and no specific jury finding that the defendant's conduct caused the plaintiff's (nominal) damages. In one case, for example, a jury specifically found that a municipality's policy regarding excessive police force resulted in $1 of harm to an otherwise unsympathetic plaintiff, and the city disciplined an officer and modified its policy during the litigation. Upholding a fee award of $66,535, the appellate court distinguished *Farrar*, concluding that the finding benefitted the department and the community and might have collateral estoppel effect in subsequent litigation. *Wilcox v. City of Reno*, 42 F.3d 550 (9th Cir. 1994). These distinctions, however, seem a thin evasion of *Farrar*. Plaintiffs could create them routinely by requesting special interrogatories concerning the right violated and causation, and the jury would presumably find causation whenever it awarded damages, even nominal ones. Another evasive tactic has been specifically rebuffed: If the plaintiff's lawyer first asks for nominal damages at the end of trial, when things look bleak for his client, the plaintiff who then recovers $1, while technically prevailing, will fail to recover fees by virtue of *Farrar*. *Romberg v. Nichols*, 48 F.3d 453 (9th Cir. 1995).

But a small damages award is not necessarily conclusive on the issue of fees. Because there is no federal small-claims court and no amount in controversy requirement in civil rights cases, the Seventh Circuit instructs courts to determine whether the plaintiff aimed high and fell short, in which case *Farrar* may deprive the prevailing plaintiff of a fee, *Cole v. Wodziak*, 169 F.3d 486 (7th Cir. 1999), or whether it was simply a small claim and was tried accordingly, *Hyde v. Small*, 123 F.3d 583 (7th Cir. 1997). Other courts resist a literal adherence to *Farrar*, awarding fees even where plaintiff's monetary recovery falls many multiples short of what she sought. *Brandau v. Kansas*, 168 F.3d 1179 (10th Cir. 1999). These courts follow Justice O'Connor's *Farrar* concurrence in weighing the difference between the judgment sought and that obtained, the significance of the legal issue on which plaintiff prevailed, and the lawsuit's public purpose. Other lower courts, at the opposite end of the spectrum, indulge a virtually insuperable presumption that the only reasonable fee to the prevailing party is zero where plaintiff recovers nominal damages alone after having sought compensatory or punitive damages initially. E.g., *Pouillon v. Little*, 326 F.3d 713 (6th Cir. 2003); *Johnson v. City of Aiken*, 278 F.3d 333 (4th Cir. 2002).

The recovery of nominal damages may permit the § 1983 plaintiff to recover punitive damages otherwise warranted by a malicious or aggravated violation of procedural due process. If a plaintiff from the outset seeks no compensatory or punitive damages, but gains declaratory relief or an injunction, he has probably then achieved substantial success on the merits. In cases of multiple claims, a plaintiff's recovery of compensatory damages on fewer than all claims not only makes him technically prevailing but also entitles him to attorney's fees, although only with respect to the hours reasonably expended in pursuit of the successful claim or claims. *Blum v. Stenson*, 465 U.S. 886 (1984).

Farrar left unresolved a related question: Can one become a prevailing party without having obtained a "consent decree, enforceable judgment or settlement," *Baumgartner v. Harrisburg Hous. Auth.*, 21 F.3d 541 (3d Cir. 1994) (citing *Farrar*), but rather simply because the filing of a lawsuit proved to be the "catalyst" that brought about some of the lawsuit's objectives? This theory would require the plaintiff to prove that the legal action is causally linked to the relief obtained by settlement or defendant's unilateral action, and that the defendant's change in position was required by law and not merely gratuitous. In a 5–4 decision, the Supreme Court held in *Buckhannon Board & Care Home, Inc. v. West Virginia Department of Health & Human Resources*, 532 U.S. 598 (2001), that even a plaintiff who demonstrates that his suit for injunctive relief was the "catalyst" for the defendant's "voluntary" mid-suit abandonment or modification of a challenged practice is not a "prevailing party" within the meaning of federal fee-shifting statutes, and so is ineligible for court-ordered attorneys' fees, unless he is awarded some judicial relief.

The majority ruled that the plaintiff must receive a "judgment" or "some relief by the court" to fit within the statutory term "prevailing party." *Id.* at 603. Although the holding technically extends only to actions under the Fair Housing Amendments Act and the Americans With Disabilities Act, circuit courts, consistent with language in *Buckhannon*, have extended the *Buckhannon* holding to actions under any of the Reconstruction Civil Rights Acts, notably § 1983, under which prevailing parties are eligible for fees pursuant to the Civil Rights Attorneys' Fees Act of 1976, 42 U.S.C.A. § 1988 (West 2010), as well as to the contemporary employment discrimination statutes.

The majority of circuits did agree that settlements enforced through consent decrees, as well as formal determinations of liability on the merits, will count as judicial relief qualifying the plaintiff for prevailing party status, because each effects a court-ordered change in the legal relationship between the parties. *Cody v. Hillard*, 304 F.3d 767 (8th Cir. 2002). Absent those formal judicial rulings, circuit courts are somewhat at sea as to what judicial involvement is necessary.

Recoverability of fees for services performed in a preliminary administrative proceeding depends in part on whether the proceeding is optional or mandatory. If the state or local administrative proceeding is mandated, as it is under Title VII, fees for legal services performed in that hearing can be recovered in an independent Title VII action. This is because the state or local administrative proceedings in a deferral state, and the EEOC proceedings in any state, qualify as a "proceeding under this subchapter" within the meaning of section 706(k) of Title VII. *New York Gaslight Club, Inc. v. Carey*, 447 U.S. 54 (1980). If the prior administrative hearing is optional, however, fees are generally not awarded because such a hearing is not considered an "action or proceeding to enforce" civil rights under the language of § 1988. For example, because a plaintiff is not required to exhaust his administrative remedies before bringing a § 1983 action, *Patsy v. Board of Regents of Fla.*, 457 U.S. 496 (1982), services performed in administrative proceedings on § 1983 claims are not compensable under § 1988. *Webb v. Board of Educ. of Dyer Cnty., Tenn*, 471 U.S. 234 (1985). Sometimes, however, where the administrative work is "useful and of a type ordinarily necessary to advance the civil rights litigation," fees may be awarded. *Id.* at 243. In *Pennsylvania v. Delaware Valley Citizens' Council for Clean Air*, 478 U.S. 546 (1986) ("*Delaware I*"), the Court applied this exception so as to allow fees. The *Delaware I* Court found that post-judgment administrative proceedings, held to enforce a consent decree, were "crucial to the vindication of [the plaintiff's] rights," and concluded that the attorney's services performed for those proceedings were compensable. *Id.* at 561.

But it remains unsettled whether, or under what circumstances, a plaintiff who achieves complete merits relief through settlement or decision in pre-litigation administrative proceedings may pursue a judicial action seeking only compensation for the attorney's fees she incurred in the pre-suit proceedings. After all, in the leading case upholding an action for fees incurred in prior administrative proceedings under Title VII, *New York Gaslight Club, Inc. v. Carey*, 447 U.S. 54 (1980), the plaintiff's action for fees was coupled with a claim on the merits. Yet the Eighth Circuit subsequently extended *Carey* to encompass Title VII actions brought solely to recover fees incurred in prior administrative proceedings. In *Jones v. American State Bank*, 857 F.2d 494 (8th Cir. 1988), the parties settled plaintiff's pregnancy discrimination claim during the administrative proceedings, but the state deferral agency denied attorney's fees as unavailable under state law. The Eighth Circuit affirmed the federal district court's award of fees under section 706(k). It reasoned that because, as the Supreme Court stressed repeatedly in *Carey*, the state deferral agency proceeding was mandated by Title VII and complementary to the federal statutory scheme, the administrative proceeding constituted an "action or proceeding" for which fees might be awarded within the meaning of section 706(k).

Attorney's fees may be awarded for services necessary to implement or enforce a consent decree that resulted from earlier, successful litigation. *Eirhart v. Libbey–Owens Ford Co.*, 996 F.2d 837 (7th Cir. 1993). A prevailing party may also recover, to the degree of her success, fees for services rendered in an unsuccessful judicial action if she ultimately prevails in a subsequent related judicial action. *Cabrales v. County of Los Angeles*, 935 F.2d 1050 (9th Cir. 1991).

To calculate the amount of a "reasonable" award of attorney's fees, the court must arrive first at a "lodestar" figure that represents a reasonable hourly rate multiplied by the number of hours reasonably expended on matters on which the plaintiff prevailed. *Blum v. Stenson*, 465 U.S. 886 (1984); *Hensley v. Eckerhart*, 461 U.S. 424 (1983). Both the reasonable hours and reasonable rates questions are committed to the discretion of the district courts, *Zuchel v. City & Cnty. of Denver*, 997 F.2d 730 (10th Cir. 1993), although elements of legal analysis integral to their decisions are reviewable de novo. *Oviatt v. Pearce*, 954 F.2d 1470 (9th Cir. 1992). Fees sought by the plaintiff that are attributable to attorney time clearly devoted only to unsuccessful claims will be deducted from the overall request. *Green v. Torres*, 361 F.3d 96 (2d Cir. 2004). And a high number of hours in a case with a relatively modest claim for compensatory damages has been sharply reduced. *Gumbhir v. Curators of Univ. of Missouri*, 157 F.3d 1141 (8th Cir. 1998). But where a party prevails on only one of multiple legal claims rooted in the same factual nucleus, fees should not be reduced automatically. *Roberts v. Roadway Exp., Inc.*, 149 F.3d 1098 (10th Cir. 1998). Instead, so long as the plaintiff has obtained "excellent" relief, he should recover a fully compensatory fee encompassing all hours reasonably expended on the litigation, *Villano v. City of Boynton Beach*, 254 F.3d 1302 (11th Cir. 2001); less than "excellent" but still "substantial" relief may warrant a fee reduction in proportion to plaintiff's overall degree of success, *Hensley*, 461 U.S. 424 (1983). By not reducing the fee award simply because the plaintiff fails to prevail on every contention, this approach encourages plaintiff's counsel to advance alternative grounds for relief as authorized by Federal Rule of Civil Procedure 8(e). Similarly, time should not be deducted for unsuccessful but reasonable arguments made in support of a successful claim. *Jaffee v. Redmond*, 518 U.S. 1 (7th Cir. 1998).

Time spent in establishing the prevailing party's entitlement to a fee award under § 1988 is itself compensable. But such requests for "fees-on-fees" are themselves subject to reduction in proportion to the degree by which the "merits fees" award was discounted, as a percentage of merits fees claimed. For example, where plaintiffs recovered 87.2% of the fees claimed for work related to the underlying merits of the action, a reduction of 12.8%, their lodestar award for the fees incurred in petitioning for those fees was also disallowed by 12.8%. *Thompson v. Gomez*, 45 F.3d 1365 (9th Cir. 1995).

Even with respect to claims on which the plaintiff prevailed, fees may not be awarded for hours that are "excessive, redundant, or otherwise unnecessary." *Hensley*, 461 U.S. at 434. The court will carefully scrutinize plaintiff's counsel's time records in the post-judgment hearing, if any, on attorney's fees to determine which hours were reasonably necessary to the outcome on successful claims. *Miller v. Woodharbor Molding & Millworks, Inc.*, 174 F.3d 948 (8th Cir. 1999).

The Court in *Blum v. Stenson*, 465 U.S. 886 (1984), held that the lodestar is based on market rates in the relevant community, and therefore fees awardable to nonprofit legal services organizations may not be limited to actual costs. Similarly, fee awards may compensate for the work of law clerks and paralegals, again at market rates. *Missouri v. Jenkins*, 491 U.S. 274 (1989). To say that the lodestar rate is based on rates prevailing in the relevant community masks two difficult sub issues: which lawyer's rate in a diverse legal community where lawyers of differing experience, special skills, and reputation enjoy different degrees of market power; and which community's rate where a lawyer from one community performs services in another with a significantly different prevailing market average. *Blum* seems to rest on the premise that the appropriate market rate for § 1988 purposes is "the opportunity cost of that time, the income foregone by [the lawyer in] representing this plaintiff." *Gusman v. Unisys Corp.*, 986 F.2d 1146, 1149 (7th Cir. 1993). It follows that an established billing rate of the prevailing party's lawyer deserves significant weight. Thus, a district court erred in compensating the prevailing plaintiff's counsel in an excessive force case at the lower rate that the defendant city paid lawyers to defend those cases. *Trevino v. Gates*, 99 F.3d 911 (9th Cir. 1996).

Another difficult task facing a court in calculating a lodestar is to identify the issues on which the plaintiff prevailed and in turn the number of hours counsel reasonably expended on those issues. In this sense, degree of success is a critical component of the ultimate fee award. But a lodestar-based fee award need not be proportionate to the amount of damages a plaintiff recovers with respect to a successful issue. *City of Riverside v. Rivera*, 477 U.S. 561 (1986).

There is a strong presumption that the lodestar represents a reasonable fee, and any upward or downward adjustments may take into account only those factors not used in arriving at the lodestar. *Hensley*, 461 U.S. at 437. In any event, the lodestar may not be adjusted upward by a "multiplier" to compensate for an attorney's risk of loss, or "contingency"— as distinct from the loss caused by delay—unless, perhaps, evidence is produced to show that the possibility of an enhanced fee was required in order to attract counsel. *Pennsylvania v. Delaware Citizens' Council for Clean Air*, 483 U.S. 711 (1987) (*"Delaware II"*). Attorney's fees may be augmented to compensate for delay in payment (as distinct from risk of nonpayment or "contingency," to be discussed below). Risk of delay is compensated "either by basing the award on current rates or by adjusting the fee based on historical rates to reflect its present value." *Jenkins*, 491 U.S. at 282.

Additional adjustment factors to the lodestar include the novelty and difficulty of the questions presented, the extent to which the demands of the case preclude other legal employment, the undesirability of the case, awards in similar cases, and the experience, reputation, and ability of the attorneys. The Supreme Court has reaffirmed a "strong presumption" against enhancement of the lodestar, in particular for superior attorney performance. *Perdue v. Kenny A.*, ___ U.S. ___, ___ – ___, 130 S.Ct. 1662, 1673–75 (2010). Enhancements should not be awarded without specific evidence that the lodestar fee would not have been adequate to attract competent counsel. *Id.* at 1674.

What if a putative plaintiff cannot attract counsel? Section 706(f)(1)(B) of Title VII authorizes the court, upon application and under such circumstances as it deems just, to "appoint an attorney" for a complainant and authorize commencement of the action without fees, costs, or security. And what if the court is unable, after diligent effort, to locate a lawyer willing to take the case without up-front compensation? There is authority that section 706(f)(1)(B) may be read to require the coercive appointment of counsel. *Scott v. Tyson Foods, Inc.*, 943 F.2d 17 (8th Cir. 1991); *Bradshaw v. United States Dist. Ct. for S. Dist. Cal.*, 742 F.2d 515 (9th Cir. 1984); *Bradshaw v. Zoological Soc. of San Diego*, 662 F.2d 1301 (9th Cir. 1981).

Circuit courts have been reluctant to approve reduction in the amount of an award below the lodestar because of erroneous "billing judgment" by a plaintiff's lawyer in spending considerable time pursuing a claim that a district court considered relatively simple. *Quaratino v. Tiffany & Co.*, 166 F.3d 422 (2d Cir. 1999); *Robinson v. City of Edmond*, 68 F.3d 1226 (10th Cir. 1995). These adjustment factors may refine but cannot substitute for the basic multiplication of a reasonable billing rate by the number of hours reasonably expended on successful claims. Similarly, the attorney's fee award may not be limited by a contingent-fee arrangement that yields a lesser sum than the lodestar. *Blanchard v. Bergeron*, 489 U.S. 87 (1989).

In *Evans v. Jeff D.*, 475 U.S. 717 (1986), the Court approved the practice of compulsory waiver of attorney's fees by settlement. Federal Rule of Civil Procedure 23 requires district court approval of class action settlements. Parties are free to negotiate the terms of a settlement and may waive statutorily authorized attorney's fees. The Court held that § 1988 does not interfere with that freedom, and the Civil Rights Act of 1991 leaves *Evans* intact. The Court in *Evans* did, however, leave open the possibility that a defendant's insistence that the plaintiff waive an attorney's fee award under § 1988, while not violating federal law, might violate local law or ethical prohibitions, and a few jurisdictions have on occasion so held. In addition, it is undecided whether a city or county's uniform policy of insisting on waiver of § 1988 fees as a condition of settling any federal civil rights action unlawfully conflicts with the policies of § 1988.

Venegas v. Mitchell, 495 U.S. 82 (1990), treats the effect of a § 1988 fee award on the plaintiff's contractual arrangement with his own attorney. It holds that § 1988 does not invalidate a contingent fee agreement providing for payments substantially in excess of the reasonable fee recoverable from the defendant. That is, § 1988 controls only the relationship between the losing defendant and the prevailing plaintiff, not between the plaintiff and the plaintiff's own attorney. Although under general § 1988 principles the plaintiff's own portion of a recovery may not include amounts she has agreed to pay her attorney that exceed the "reasonable" amounts recoverable as attorney's fees from the defendant, *Venegas* also reinforces a plaintiff's capacity to secure counsel of her choice by upholding the integrity of the private fee agreement. This decision has been applied to actions under Title VII as well. *Gobert v. Williams*, 323 F.3d 1099 (5th Cir. 2003). On the other hand, the plaintiff's attorney's fee award under § 1988 may not be absolutely limited by a contingent-fee arrangement that calls for a lesser sum than the lodestar. *Blanchard*, 489 U.S. 87 (1989).

Previously, a prevailing plaintiff was not entitled to have its expert witnesses compensated by the losing party, absent contractual or statutory authority stating otherwise. *Crawford Fitting Co. v. J.T. Gibbons*, 482 U.S. 437 (1987). In *West Virginia University Hospitals, Inc. v. Casey*, 499 U.S. 83 (1991), the Court held that § 1988 does not authorize the recovery of expert witness fees. They are limited to the amount designated for all witnesses, $30 per day. *Id.* at 86. The Civil Rights Act of 1991, which includes expert fees as a part of an attorney's fee award under Title VII, reverses *Casey* in part. The Act authorizes expert witness fees in actions or proceedings to enforce provisions of § 1981 and § 1981a, but not § 1983. Of course, the Supreme Court has already included certain related costs, e.g., those for law clerks and paralegals, as part of the attorney's fees recoverable under § 1988. *Jenkins*, 491 U.S. 274 (1989).

Depending on the circuit, post-judgment interest on attorney's fees may begin to accrue either from the date of the judgment that unconditionally entitled the prevailing party to reasonable attorney's fees, *Associated Gen. Contractors of Ohio, Inc. v. Drabik*, 214 F.3d 730 (6th Cir. 2000); *Jenkins v. Missouri*, 931 F.2d 1273 (8th Cir. 1991); *Friend v. Kolodziec-zak*, 72 F.3d 1386 (9th Cir. 1995); *BankAtlantic v. Blythe Eastman Pain Webber, Inc.*, 12 F.3d 1045 (11th Cir. 1994); *Mathis v. Spears*, 857 F.2d 749 (Fed. Cir. 1988); *Copper Liquor, Inc. v. Adolph Coors Co.*, 624 F.2d 575 (5th Cir. 1980), or from the date that the award of attorney's fees is quantified. *Eaves v. County of Cape May*, 239 F.3d 527 (3d Cir.

2001); *MidAmerica Fed. Sav. & Loan Ass'n v. Shearson/American Express, Inc.*, 886 F.2d 1249 (10th Cir. 1989).

While a prevailing plaintiff is ordinarily to be awarded attorney's fees in all but special circumstances, the Supreme Court in *Christiansburg Garment Co. v. EEOC*, 434 U.S. 412, 421 (1978), interpreted section 706(k) to preclude attorney's fees to a prevailing defendant unless the plaintiff's action was "frivolous, unreasonable, or without foundation." This appears to mean that a fee award to a prevailing defendant is unwarranted where the plaintiff's claim, although plainly flawed, is colorable. The plaintiff's failure to establish a prima facie case, the unprecedented nature of a claim, the defendant's offer of a settlement, or the dismissal of an action before trial all figure in determining whether a claim is sufficiently frivolous, unreasonable, or groundless to justify taxing attorney's fees against a plaintiff. E.g., *Bass v. E.I. DuPont de Nemours Co.*, 324 F.3d 761 (4th Cir. 2003). If the defendant can show that a plaintiff asserted a claim in subjective bad faith, the case for awarding the defendant his attorney's fees is stronger. But the circumstances warranting fees to a prevailing defendant must be truly exceptional, so much so that a trial court does not abuse its discretion in denying such fees even if no reason is stated for the denial. *Maag v. Wessler*, 960 F.2d 773 (9th Cir. 1991). Where the EEOC is the plaintiff, it is not even enough for the defendant seeking attorney's fees to show that the EEOC failed to present credible evidence of discrimination. In such a case, the defendant has the even more difficult burden of demonstrating that the EEOC should have "anticipated at the outset that none of its evidence of discriminatory conduct was credible" or unreasonably believed that it had made adequate efforts to conciliate. *EEOC v. Bruno's Restaurant*, 13 F.3d 285, 290 (9th Cir. 1993). It is difficult to imagine a situation in which the defendant could carry that showing.

If the standard for prevailing plaintiffs announced in *Farrar* were the test of whether a defendant is a "prevailing party," the defendant might qualify for fees when the plaintiff voluntarily dismisses her suit with prejudice even before a decision on the merits by motion for summary judgment or at trial. Such a dismissal does, after all, alter the legal relationship between the parties to the benefit of the defendant. To show the frivolousness, unreasonableness, or groundlessness demanded by *Christiansburg*, the defendant must ordinarily have prevailed summarily on the pleadings or on a motion for summary judgment on the merits. E.g., *Le Blanc–Sternberg v. Fletcher*, 143 F.3d 748 (2d Cir. 1998). On the other hand, the granting of a summary judgment motion does not necessarily show the claim was "frivolous" or therefore ensure an award of defendants' fees. *Riddle v. Egensperger*, 266 F.3d 542 (6th Cir. 2001). Yet, a denial of a defendant's summary judgment motion does not necessarily preclude the defendant's recovery of attorney's fees under the *Christiansburg* standard if the plaintiff should have realized, from subsequent pretrial discovery, that his claim was groundless. *Flowers v. Jefferson Hosp. Ass'n*, 49 F.3d 391 (8th Cir. 1995). The prevailing defendant eligible for fees under *Christiansburg* may, like the prevailing plaintiff, also recover the reasonable fees and expenses incurred in proceedings to collect the underlying fee award, should plaintiff decline to pay it. *Vukadinovich v. McCarthy*, 901 F.2d 1439 (7th Cir. 1990).

The *Christiansburg* test has been applied to govern the award of attorney's fees against unsuccessful intervenors. The Supreme Court characterized as "particularly welcome" a union's intervention challenging a proposed settlement of a sex discrimination action in order to protect "the legitimate expectations of . . . [male] employees innocent of any wrongdoing." *Independent Fed'n of Flight Attendants v. Zipes*, 491 U.S. 754, 764 (1989). The decision encouraged intervention by holding that intervenors would be liable for plaintiffs' costs of defending a settlement only when the intervention is "frivolous, unreasonable, or without foundation." *Id.* at 766. In effect, then, intervention becomes per se a "special circumstance" that warrants denial of a fee award to a prevailing plaintiff. The Civil Rights Act of 1991 leaves this approach intact. In actions under the ADEA, several circuits have required prevailing defendants to show not that the plaintiff's claim was objectively frivolous, but that it was brought in bad faith. *Turlington v. Atlanta Gas Light Co.*, 135 F.3d 1428 (11th Cir. 1998).

c. *Rule 68 Offers of Judgment*

Federal Rule of Civil Procedure 68(a) authorizes the defendant, at any time more than fourteen days before trial, to serve an offer allowing judgment on terms specified in the offer, "with the costs then accrued." It then provides that, if the offer is not accepted and a judgment obtained by the plaintiff "is not more favorable than the unaccepted offer, the offeree must pay the costs incurred after the making of the offer." On its face, then, Rule 68 merely relieves a defendant who makes such an offer that is not accepted by the plaintiff and equaled or exceeded by a final judgment from what would otherwise be its liability for the "costs" routinely taxable under Rule 54(d) in favor of prevailing parties in any federal civil action. Such an offer is valid even when it is conditioned upon acceptance of its terms by all plaintiffs, and a settlement agreement counts as a "judgment" that triggers the cost-shifting permitted by Rule 68. An offer not accepted during the fourteen-day period is treated as withdrawn, but the defendant may make a subsequent offer. Fed. R. Civ. P. 68(b).

Rule 54(d) costs, however, are relatively minor, as they are universally understood not to include attorney's fees. The real bite of Rule 68 in civil rights and employment discrimination actions results from the interplay of that Rule with the provisions in Title VII and § 1988 that call for an award of "a reasonable attorney's fee as part of the costs." Importing the italicized language into the word "costs" as it appears in Rule 68, the Supreme Court in *Marek v. Chesny*, 473 U.S. 1 (1985), held that a defendant's offer of judgment in a civil rights action governed by statutory provisions for attorney's fees can shift what would otherwise be the losing defendant's liability for the prevailing plaintiff's attorney's fees, as well as ordinary costs. That is, a plaintiff's judgment failing to exceed an unaccepted Rule 68 offer by the defendant relieves the defendant of liability for the plaintiff's post-offer attorney's fees as well as plaintiff's ordinary costs of litigation. This holding greatly increases the defendant's incentive to make a Rule 68 offer. The Civil Rights Act of 1991 leaves *Marek* intact. The prevailing Title VII plaintiff, for example, who obtains a judgment worth less than or equal to the Rule 68 offer he rejected not only forfeits Rule 54(d) post-offer costs and attorneys' fees awardable under section 706(k), but also must pay the defendant's post-offer costs. In *Lyte v. Sara Lee Corp.*, 950 F.2d 101 (2d Cir. 1991), the court held that attorney's fees are a part of the "costs" shifted by a defendant's offer of judgment under Rule 68 in actions under any statute that allows fee awards as a "part of," rather than "in addition to" "costs," which includes fees under Title VII, but not under ADEA.

The defendant's offer, to avoid liability for costs and fees to the prevailing plaintiff, must, in the words of Rule 68, include the plaintiff's "costs then accrued," that is, up until the time of the offer. The "costs" that must be included in the offer— like the "costs" mentioned in the subsequent phrase of Rule 68 that shifts liability for attorney's fees if the offer is rejected—have been held to include the amount of the plaintiff's attorney's fees accrued at the time of the offer. This is because a prevailing plaintiff would, absent an offer, ordinarily be entitled by judgment to an award of attorney's fees for pre-offer work. Accordingly, those fees, together with ordinary costs, must be added to the judgment to calculate the total received by judgment that the offer must equal or exceed to shift post-offer costs and fees under Rule 68. *Scheeler v. Crane Co.*, 21 F.3d 791 (8th Cir. 1994).

In another case, the offer promised not only "costs then accrued," as prescribed by Rule 68, but also "reasonable attorney fees as determined by the court." *Holland v. Roeser*, 37 F.3d 501 (9th Cir. 1994). The Ninth Circuit construed the language of the offer to authorize a district judge's award of attorney's fees for plaintiffs' counsel's preparation of a fee petition after they accepted the offer, even though under Rule 68 costs, and hence, under *Marek*, fees are halted by a successful offer. The court indicated that if the defendant had offered to pay only the plaintiff's "costs then accrued," the offer would have clearly and unambiguously limited the plaintiff's fees to the full extent that *Marek* and Rule 68 permit. The decision points up the necessity for defendant's counsel to draft tightly-worded offers that meet Rule 68's strictures. A majority of circuits that have confronted the question have held that any waiver of or limitation on attorney's fees in actions under statutes providing for the recovery of fees by prevailing plaintiffs must be "clear and unambiguous." E.g., *Ellis v. University of Kan. Med. Ctr.*, 163 F.3d 1186 (10th Cir. 1998); *Jennings v. Metropolitan Gov't of Nashville*, 715 F.2d 1111 (6th Cir. 1983). Similarly, a circuit court has ruled ineffective a Rule 68 offer that failed to apportion the offer among the multiple plaintiffs. By advising only that the offered sum was "to be divided among all three plaintiffs," the offer failed to give the notice each required to evaluate whether to accept. *Gavoni v. Dobbs House, Inc.*, 164 F.3d 1071 (7th Cir. 1999).

The inclusion of attorney's fees in the Rule 68 post-offer "costs" that the plaintiff may be precluded from recovering assumes that the underlying fee statute includes "attorney's fees" within the definition of "costs." That is the case with most fee statutes, including § 1988, and the principal Title VII fee provision, section 706(k). By contrast, since the "mixed-motive" remedies section of Title VII, section 706(g)(2)(B), refers to "costs" and "attorney's fees" distinctly and separately, attorney's fees will not be counted as part of the post-offer Rule 68 "costs" a plaintiff is barred from recovering where the entitlement to fees flows only from that section. *Sheppard v. Riverview Nursing Ctr., Inc.*, 88 F.3d 1332 (4th Cir. 1996). The same is true under ADEA.

Likewise, at least one circuit has held that attorney's fees are not shifted as part of costs in ADA actions because the text of the ADA does not define attorney's fees as part of costs. *Webb v. James*, 147 F.3d 617 (7th Cir. 1998). In an ADA action, "the court or agency, in its discretion, may allow the prevailing party ... a reasonable attorney's fee, including litigation expenses, and costs." 42 U.S.C.A. § 12205 (West 2010). Under this section, then, Congress did not define costs to include fees for the purposes of the ADA. Therefore, an offer that mentions only "costs" and is silent on the issue of fees cannot relieve the defendant of its statutory liability for fees (*Webb, supra*).

Can Rule 68 be used not just to relieve the defendant of cost and fee liability to a prevailing plaintiff but as the basis for an award of attorney's fees to a prevailing defendant? If so, Rule 68 could serve as the defendant's end run around the *Christiansburg Garment* test applicable to claims under the Reconstruction Acts and employment discrimination statutes. That is, a defendant would become eligible for attorney's fees simply by submitting what proves to be a shrewd offer of judgment in cases where the plaintiff has prevailed and therefore defendant has not shown the groundlessness, frivolousness, or subjective bad faith the Supreme Court has required. But the circuits to have considered the issue have all rejected this argument in civil rights and employment discrimination actions governed by *Christiansburg Garment*'s plaintiff-tilted interpretation of "prevailing party." They confirm that Rule 68, while a one-way street available only to defendants, helps them only if the plaintiff prevails, *Delta Air Lines, Inc. v. August*, 450 U.S. 346 (1981), and then only by relieving them of what would otherwise be their liability for plaintiff's costs and fees, and enabling them to receive costs, not by making them eligible for a fee award themselves, e.g., *Le v. University of Pennsylvania*, 321 F.3d 403 (3d Cir. 2003).

By contrast, there is also complete consensus among the circuits to have decided the issue that where an employment discrimination or civil rights plaintiff's trial recovery (plus court-ordered pre-offer costs and fees) does not exceed the defendant's rejected Rule 68 offer, the defendant is entitled to an award from plaintiff of its post-offer costs, i.e., excluding post-offer fees, e.g., *Pouillon v. Little*, 326 F.3d 713 (6th Cir. 2003); *Crossman v. Marcoccio*, 806 F.2d 329 (1st Cir. 1986). These decisions thus read the Rule 68 requirement that the offeree "pay the costs incurred after the making of the offer" to mean not just that offeree bear its own post-offer costs, but that it be ordered to pay those of the offeror. These courts find no tension between Rule 54(d), which awards presumptive but still discretionary costs only to prevailing parties, and this application of Rule 68, which mandates costs to a non-prevailing defendant that submitted a Rule 68 offer that was successful in the sense that the plaintiff, after rejecting it, could not recover more at trial.

If, however, as the circuits agree, plaintiffs who fail to surpass at trial a Rule 68 offer they rejected must pay post-offer defense costs; and if Rule 68 "costs," per *Marek*, are defined by reference to the underlying statute awarding costs and/or fees to prevailing parties; and if, as is true of § 1988, in the case of civil rights actions, and section 706(k), in the cases of Title VII actions, the underlying statutes authorize the recovery of fees as part of "costs"; then shouldn't Rule 68 also require the plaintiff to pay the defendant's post-offer fees? The circuit decisions summarized above have all rejected this syllogism. They stress the statement in *Marek* that "the term 'costs' in Rule 68 was intended to refer [only] to all costs properly awardable under the relevant substantive statute...." 473 U.S. at 9. And fees to a defendant where Rule 68 is triggered would not be properly awardable under § 1988 or section 706(k) for two reasons. First, those statutes authorize fees only to prevailing parties, whereas Rule 68 is triggered only where the plaintiff, not the defendant, has prevailed. Second, *Christiansburg Garment* interprets those statutes to mean that a defendant can be a prevailing party only where the plaintiff's claim is frivolous, unreasonable, or without foundation, and that will certainly not be the case in the Rule 68 situation under examination, where the plaintiff has to some degree prevailed.

In brief, Rule 68 is triggered when the sum of the plaintiff's trial recovery, plus her pre-offer costs and fees as awarded by the court, fails to exceed the defendant's offer. When the Rule is triggered in civil rights or employment discrimination cases, it denies the plaintiff eligibility for the post-offer costs or fees she would ordinarily be awarded by virtue of the underlying applicable fee-authorizing statute, and it also requires the plaintiff-offeree to pay the defendant-offeror the latter's post-offer costs, but not fees.

Courts have generally held that Rule 68 offers of judgment may not be revoked during the period set by the Rule, e.g., *Webb v. James*, 147 F.3d 617 (7th Cir. 1998); *Richardson v. National R.R. Passenger Corp.*, 49 F.3d 760 (D.C. Cir. 1995).

Moreover, rescission may not be an available remedy for mutual mistakes because the mandatory language of Rule 68, requiring that the clerk "shall enter judgment" upon the filing of an offer, removes discretion from the trial court as to whether to enter judgment upon the filing of the accepted offer. *Webb*, 147 F.3d at 621. Relief from a judgment entered as a result of a Rule 68 offer and acceptance may be available under Rule 60. Rule 60(b) provides in relevant part that

> [o]n motion and upon such terms as are just, the court may relieve a party or a party's legal representative from a final judgment order or proceeding for the following reasons: (1) mistake, inadvertence, surprise, or excusable neglect; . . . (4) the judgment is void; . . . or (6) any other reason justifying relief from the operation of the judgment.

Webb, 147 F.3d at 622 (alterations in original). On the other hand, a defendant who fails to renew an offer of judgment on retrial of an action remains eligible for Rule 68 costs from the plaintiff if on retrial the plaintiff's judgment fails to exceed the amount of the offer. *Pouillon*, 326 F.3d at 718–19.

B. STATE LAWS IN GENERAL

Most of the states have enacted anti-discrimination statutes that supplement the remedies available under federal law by extending protection to persons not federally protected or, in some cases, adding grounds of prohibited discrimination or supplementary remedies. For the most part, state laws prohibiting employment discrimination are called "Fair Employment Practices" laws. But Michigan has a Civil Rights Act, California has a Fair Employment and Housing Act, New Mexico has a Human Rights Act, and New York's employment discrimination prohibitions are part of its Executive Law. See generally CCH EMPLOYMENT PRACTICES GUIDE.

The federal laws, standards, and programs do not generally preempt these state efforts unless a state law purports to permit conduct that would be federally prohibited or would in practice undermine the enforcement of a federal law.

The state legislation usually forbids discrimination based upon race, religion, color, ancestry, national origin, sex, age, or marital status. Still, there is considerable variation in prohibited grounds. Alabama, for example, has very little in the way of fair employment laws regulating private employment, while California has enacted laws specifically covering race, age, sex, national origin, religious, arrest record, and blindness discrimination. California also regulates equal pay, pregnancy benefits, and employee records, as well as the employment uses of lie detector tests and voice stress analyzers. A few states regulate the use of credit reports. A growing minority of states prohibit discrimination on the basis of sexual orientation, a ground Congress has declined to protect but recurrently reconsiders.

CHAPTER 21

WRONGFUL DISCHARGE

Traditionally, the employment-at-will concept freely allowed the employer or the employee to terminate the employment relationship at any time and for any reason without further obligation. See *Adair v. United States*, 208 U.S. 161 (1908). However, recent litigation and legislation concerning wrongful terminations or unjust discharges have dramatically changed this entire area of the law. See, e.g., Mont. Code Ann. §§ 39–2–901 *et seq.* (2009); *Smith v. Atlas Off–Shore Boat Serv., Inc.*, 653 F.2d 1057 (5th Cir. 1981). See generally J. Castagnera, P. Cihon & A. Morriss, *Termination of Employment* (2002); S. Pepe & S. Dunham, *Avoiding and Defending Wrongful Discharge Claims* (1987); P. Tobias, *Litigating Wrongful Discharge Claims* (1987).

The common-law doctrine of employment-at-will has been the subject of rapid revision by state and federal legislation and judicial decision. Federal and state laws concerning unions, civil service employees, and fair employment give certain classes of workers fairly comprehensive protection from certain types of discharges.

The following theories or laws may provide an employee with a remedy for an unjust discharge or wrongful termination: (1) violation of public policy, see *Sheets v. Teddy's Frosted Foods, Inc.*, 427 A.2d 385 (Conn. 1980) (discussion of illegal act and whistleblowing), (2) breach of an implied contract of employment, usually based upon employment handbooks or oral representations, see *Toussaint v. Blue Cross &*

Blue Shield of Mich., 292 N.W.2d 880 (Mich. 1980) (handbook), *Schipani v. Ford Motor Co.*, 302 N.W.2d 307 (Mich. Ct. App. 1981) (oral representations can override written disclaimers), (3) breach of implied covenant of good faith and fair dealing, see *Wagenseller v. Scottsdale Memorial Hospital*, 710 P.2d 1025 (Ariz. 1985); (4) breach of express employment contract; (5) promissory estoppel, see *Grouse v. Group Health Plan, Inc.*, 306 N.W.2d 114 (Minn. 1981) (job change in reliance on employment offer that was later revoked); (6) common-law tort actions growing out of the discharge, including but not limited to prima facie tort, intentional infliction of emotional distress, fraud, defamation, tortious interference with contract, and invasion of privacy; some jurisdictions recognize a separate tort action for the discharge itself, under the headings of wrongful discharge, retaliatory discharge, abusive discharge, unjust discharge, etc.; and (7) state and federal statutory protections.

In *Kasten v. Saint–Gobain Performance Plastics Corp.*, ___ U.S. ___, 131 S.Ct. 1325 (2011), the Supreme Court held that a worker's oral complaints concerning workplace conditions made to a employer's supervisor are covered by the anti-retaliation provisions of the Fair Labor Standards Act, contained in 29 U.S.C.A. § 215(a)(3). This decision has potential implications for broadening the use of other federal statutory anti-retaliation provisions that can be found in numerous laws.

A non-exclusive list of federal statutory protections against discharge includes the following:

Age Discrimination in Employment Act of 1967 ("ADEA"), 29 U.S.C.A. § 621 *et seq.* (West 2010);

Americans with Disabilities Act ("ADA"), 42 U.S.C.A. § 12203 (West 2010);

Asbestos Hazard Emergency Response Act of 1986, 15 U.S.C.A. § 2651 (West 2010);

Asbestos School Hazard Detection and Control Act of 1980, 20 U.S.C.A. § 3608 (West 2010);

Bankruptcy Reform Act of 1978, 11 U.S.C.A. § 525(a) (West 2010);

Civil Rights of Institutionalized Persons Act, 42 U.S.C.A. § 1997(d) (West 2010);

Civil Rights Statutes, 42 U.S.C.A. §§ 1981, 1983, 1985(3) (West 2010);

Civil Service Reform Act of 1978; 5 U.S.C.A. § 2302 (West 2010);

Civilian Employees of the Armed Forces, 10 U.S.C.A. § 1587 (West 2010);

Clean Air Act, 42 U.S.C.A. § 7622(b)(1) (West 2010);

Comprehensive Environmental Response, Compensation, and Liability Act of 1980 ("Superfund Act"), 42 U.S.C.A. § 9610 (West 2010);

Conspiracy to Obstruct Justice Act, 42 U.S.C.A. § 1985(2) (West 2010);

Consumer Credit Protection Act, 15 U.S.C.A. § 1674 (West 2010);

Contractor Employees of the Armed Forces, 10 U.S.C.A. § 2409 (West 2010);

Education Amendments (Title IX) of 1972, 20 U.S.C.A. § 1681 *et seq.* (West 2010);

Employee Polygraph Protection Act of 1988 ("EPPA"), 29 U.S.C.A. § 2002 (West 2010);

Employment Retirement Income Security Act of 1974 ("ERISA"), 29 U.S.C.A. § 1140 (West 2010);

Energy Reorganization Act of 1974, 42 U.S.C.A. § 5851 (West 2010);

Equal Pay Act of 1963, 29 U.S.C.A. § 206(d) (West 2010);

Fair Labor Standards Act of 1938, 29 U.S.C.A. § 215 (West 2010);

False Claims Act, 31 U.S.C.A. § 3730(h) (West 2010);

Family and Medical Leave Act of 1993 ("FMLA"), 29 U.S.C.A. § 2617 (West 2010);

Federal Antitrust Laws, 15 U.S.C.A. § 15(a) (West 2010);

Federal Coal Mine Health and Safety Act of 1969, 30 U.S.C.A. § 815(c) (West 2010);

Federal Credit Unions, 12 U.S.C.A. § 1790b (West 2010);

Federal Deposit Insurance Act, 12 U.S.C.A. § 1831j(a)(2) (West 2010);

Federal Employers' Liability Act ("FELA"), 45 U.S.C.A. § 60 (West 2010);

Federal Water Pollution Control Act Amendments of 1972, 33 U.S.C.A. § 1367 (West 2010);

Financial Institutions Reform, Recovery, and Enforcement Act of 1989, 12 U.S.C.A. § 1790(b) (West 2010);

Foreign Service Act of 1980, 22 U.S.C.A. § 3905 (West 2010);

Hazardous Materials Transportation Act, 49 U.S.C.A. § 20109 (West 2010);

Immigration Reform and Control Act of 1986 (IRCA); 8 U.S.C.A. § 1324b (West 2010);

International Safe Container Act, 46 U.S.C.A. § 80501 (West 2010);

Juror Protection, 28 U.S.C.A. § 1875 (West 2010);

Landrum–Griffin Act; 29 U.S.C.A. § 411(a)(5) (West 2010);

Lloyd—La Follette Act, 5 U.S.C.A. § 7211 (West 2010);

Longshore and Harbor Workers' Compensation Act ("LHWCA"), 33 U.S.C.A. § 948a (West 2010);

Migrant and Seasonal Agricultural Worker Protection Act, 29 U.S.C.A. § 1855 (West 2010);

Military Whistleblower Protection Act, 10 U.S.C.A. § 1034 (West 2010);

National Labor Relations Act ("NLRA"), 29 U.S.C.A. § 158(a)(4) (West 2010);

Occupational Safety and Health Act of 1970, 29 U.S.C.A. § 660(c) (West 2010);

Racketeer Influenced and Corrupt Organizations Act ("RICO"), 18 U.S.C.A. §§ 1961–1968 (West 2010);

Railway Labor Act, 45 U.S.C.A. §§ 151–188 (West 2010);

Rehabilitation Act of 1973 ("RA"), 29 U.S.C.A. § 701 (West 2010);

Reporting and Recording of Monetary Instruments, 31 U.S.C.A. § 5328 (West 2010);

Safe Drinking Water Act, 42 U.S.C.A. § 300j–9 (West 2010);

Sarbanes–Oxley Act of 2002, 18 U.S.C. § 1514A (West 2010);

Seaman's Protection Act, 46 U.S.C.A. § 2114 (West 2010);

Selective Service Act of 1948, 38 U.S.C.A. § 2021 (West 2010);

Solid Waste Disposal Act, 42 U.S.C.A. § 6972 (West 2010);

Surface Mining Control and Reclamation Act of 1977, 30 U.S.C.A. § 1293 (West 2010);

Surface Transportation Assistance Act, 49 U.S.C.A. § 31105(a)(1)(A) (West 2010);

Title VII of Civil Rights Act of 1964, 42 U.S.C.A. § 2000e–3(a) (West 2010);

Toxic Substances Control Act, 15 U.S.C.A. § 2622 (West 2010);

Uniformed Services Employment and Reemployment Rights Act of 1994 ("USERRA"), 38 U.S.C.A. § 4301 *et seq.* (West 2010);

Vocational Rehabilitation Act, 29 U.S.C.A. § 793 (West 2010);

Whistleblower Protection Act of 1989, 5 U.S.C.A. §§ 1212, 1213, 1214, 1221, 2302 (West 2010).

In a similar fashion, but in a less comprehensive manner, many states have begun to enact protections against discharge. State unjust discharge actions that involve claims by union employees covered by a collective bargaining agreement may be the subject of preemption under § 301 of the Labor Management Relations Act, 1947 ("LMRA"), 29 U.S.C.A. § 185 *et seq.* (West 2010). However, state tort claims, independent of the collective bargaining agreement, are not subject to preemption. *Lingle v. Norge Div. of Magic Chef, Inc.*, 486 U.S. 399 (1988).

The U.S. Department of Labor maintains a website about whistleblower protections at http://www.dol.gov/compliance/laws/comp-whistleblower.htm.

CHAPTER 22

MISCELLANEOUS EMPLOYEE PROTECTION LAWS

A. NATIONAL LABOR RELATIONS ACT

The National Labor Relations Act ("NLRA"), 29 U.S.C.A. §§ 151–169 (West 2010), primarily governs employer-union relations. The act grants employees important rights to create or become members of unions, to choose representatives and to bargain collectively, and to engage in or refrain from "concerted activities" for mutual aid and protection. This concerted activity protection is afforded non-union employees, and the National Labor Relations Board ("N.L.R.B.") frequently intervenes to protect non-union employees so long as their activities are related to wage or working conditions. For example, N.L.R.B. involvement based upon "concerted activity" could arise in an employment situation if an employee solicited additional employee support for a group health insurance plan. *Edward Blankstein, Inc. v. N.L.R.B.*, 623 F.2d 320 (3d Cir. 1980); see *N.L.R.B. v. Washington Aluminum Co.*, 370 U.S. 9 (1962).

Most private-sector employers are covered by the NLRA, but workers in the public sector, domestic and agricultural workers, workers employed by parents or spouses, independent contractors, supervisors, and workers covered under the Railway Labor Act (rail and air carrier workers) are excluded.

In 2011, the NLRB's Office General Counsel issued a complaint against the Boeing Company for deciding to transfer a second airplane production line to a non-union facility in

South Carolina from a union facility in the state of Washington. The complaint has sparked much debate over the NLRB's power and role in employee-employer relations. See http://www.nlrb.gov/boeing-complaint-fact-sheet.

For a more complete summary of the various federal laws regulating unions, management, strikes, boycotts, etc., see generally D. Leslie, *Labor Law in a Nutshell* (5th ed. 2008); L. Modjeska & A. Modjeska, *Federal Labor Law: NLRB Practice* (1994).

The N.L.R.B. maintains a useful website at http://www.nlrb.gov/about_us/overview/national_labor_relations_act.aspx.

B. LABOR MANAGEMENT RELATIONS ACT

The National Labor Relations Board ("N.L.R.B."), in administering the Labor Management Relations Act, 1947 ("LMRA"), 29 U.S.C.A. §§ 141–144, 167, 171–75, 175a, 176–183, 185–187 (West 2010), may encounter unlawful discrimination during union representation campaigns, certifications, fair representation disputes, duty to bargain situations, or other unfair labor practice proceedings. A certified union's duty of fair representation may be enforced by aggrieved black union members or applicants for union membership in private federal damages actions, *Steele v. Louisville & N.R. Co.*, 323 U.S. 192 (1944), and probably in N.L.R.B. unfair labor practice proceedings. See *DelCostello v. International Bhd. of Teamsters*, 462 U.S. 151 (1983). But minority employees are not protected from union discipline when, bypassing their union, they raise employment discrimination grievances directly with an employer. *Emporium Capwell Co. v. Western Addition Cmty. Org.*, 420 U.S. 50 (1975). An employer probably has a duty to bargain over employment discrimination issues, but employer discrimination standing alone will not constitute an unfair labor practice absent a link between the employer's alleged discriminatory conduct and interference with rights conferred by the LMRA. See *Jubilee Mfg. Co.* (1973), *enf'd sub nom. United Steelworkers of Am. v. N.L.R.B.*, 504 F.2d 271 (D.C. Cir. 1974).

Although election results may be overturned if either a union or an employer has appealed directly to race hatred during a campaign, a union is not foreclosed from invoking the election procedures of the LMRA because it has a history of racial discrimination. Compare *Sewell Mfg. Co.*, 138 N.L.R.B. 66 (1962), with *Handy Andy, Inc.*, 228 N.L.R.B. 447 (1977). Some courts of appeals, however, have found that the N.L.R.B. is constitutionally compelled to withhold certification from an illegally discriminating union. See *N.L.R.B. v. Heavy Lift Serv., Inc.*, 607 F.2d 1121 (5th Cir. 1979); *N.L.R.B. v. Mansion House Center Management Corp.*, 473 F.2d 471 (8th Cir. 1973). In any event, the Board may revoke a union's certification if it breaches the duty of fair representation by engaging in discriminatory practices.

See generally D. Leslie, *Labor Law in a Nutshell* (5th ed. 2008); L. Modjeska & A. Modjeska, *Federal Labor Law: NLRB Practice* (1994). The U.S. Department of Labor maintains a relevant website at http://www.dol.gov/dol/topic/labor-relations/index.htm. The NLRB maintains a useful website at http://www.nlrb.gov/index.aspx.

C. FEDERAL CONSTRUCTION PROJECTS

Two important federal laws protect workers employed on federal construction projects. The Miller Act (Public Works Act), 40 U.S.C.A. §§ 3131–3133 (West 2010), contains a performance bond requirement for federal construction contractors on projects in excess of $100,000. The law also permits those supplying labor and materials to sue in federal district court to collect monies owed for unpaid wages or supplies. See generally 15B *Federal Procedure, Lawyers Edition* § 39:1210–12 (1983).

The Copeland Anti–Racketeering Act or "Anti–Kickback" Act, 18 U.S.C.A. § 874 and 40 U.S.C.A. § 3145 (West 2010), 29 C.F.R. pt. 3 (2006), prohibits by criminal penalty any attempt to force or induce workers to pay kickbacks from wages under federal construction contracts. The U.S. Department of Labor, Wage and Hour Division, administers the Act. See generally U.S. Department of Labor website, http://www.dol.gov/compliance/guide/kickback.htm.

D. EXECUTIVE ORDERS

A number of Executive Orders issued under the authority of the President prohibit employment discrimination. These orders usually establish federal policy in a particular area, require affirmative action programs, and specify responsibility for enforcement. No private rights of action are created, and enforcement and implementation are usually left to the executive agency or department involved.

By far, the most important for present purposes is Executive Order 11246. As amended, it prohibits employment discrimination by government contractors on grounds of race, religion, sex, or national origin. It also demands that contractors take "affirmative action" by means of "goals" and "timetables" to boost the representation of protected group members in major job categories to levels that reflect the availability of qualified members of the protected group. There is no specific legislative basis for the Order, but lower courts have followed the lead of the Third Circuit in holding that Congress should be "deemed to have granted" the President the general authority to so protect federal interests. *Contractors Ass'n of E. Pa. v. Secretary of Labor,* 442 F.2d 159 (3rd Cir. 1971). See generally U.S. Department of Labor websites: http://www.dol.gov/compliance/guide/discrim.htm and http://www.dol.gov/compliance/guide/discrcon.htm.

Executive Order 11141 prohibits age discrimination by government contractors and subcontractors; Executive Order 11478 prohibits race, color, religion, sex, national origin, handicap, and age discrimination by the federal government. Other Executive Orders establish coordinated enforcement efforts and special programs for minority and women's enterprises.

A listing of the most important Executive Orders related to employment or discrimination is as follows:

Executive Order 11141 Age Discrimination;

Executive Order 11758 Authority Under Rehabilitation Act of 1973;

Executive Order 11935 Citizenship Requirements for Federal Employment;

Executive Order 12125 Competitive Status for Handicapped Federal Employees;

Executive Order 12067 Coordinating of Equal Employment Opportunity Programs;

Executive Order 13518 Employment of Veterans in the Federal Government Executive;

Executive Order 12250 Enforcement Coordination of Nondiscrimination Laws in Federal Programs;

Executive Order 13279 Equal Protection of the Laws for Faith-based and Community Organizations;

Executive Order 11478 Federal Employees;

Executive Order 13145 Genetic Information Discrimination in the Federal Government;

Executive Order 11246 Government Contractors and Subcontractors;

Executive Order 13488 Granting Reciprocity on Excepted Service and Federal Contractor Employee Fitness and Reinvestigating Individuals in Positions of Public Trust;

Executive Order 13166 Improving Access to Services for Persons with Limited English Proficiency;

Executive Order 13078 Increasing Employment of Adults with Disabilities;

Executive Order 13548 Increasing Federal Employment of Individuals with Disabilities;

Executive Order 13170 Increasing Opportunities and Access for Disadvantaged Businesses;

Executive Order 13157 Increasing Opportunities for Women–Owned Small Businesses;

Executive Order 13515 Increasing Participation of Asian Americans and Pacific Islanders in Federal Programs;

Executive Order 13163 Increasing the Opportunity for Individuals with Disabilities to be Employed in the Federal Government;

Executive Order 11830 Interagency Committee on Handicapped Employees;

Executive Order 11625 National Program for Minority Business Enterprise;

Executive Order 12138 National Program for Women's Business Enterprise;

Executive Order 13160 Nondiscrimination in Federally Conducted Education and Training Programs;

Executive Order 11914 Nondiscrimination with Respect to the Handicapped in Federally Assisted Programs;

Executive Order 13495 Nondisplacement of Qualified Workers Under Service Contracts;

Executive Order 13496 Notification of Employee Rights Under Federal Labor Laws;

Executive Order 12866 Regulatory Planning and Review;

Executive Order 13164 Requiring Federal Agencies to Establish Procedures to Facilitate the Provision of Reasonable Accommodation;

Executive Order 12640 The President's Committee on Employment of People with Disabilities;

Executive Order 13187 The President's Disability Employment Partnership Board;

Executive Order 13465 Use of E–Verify by Federal Contractors;

Executive Order 13502 Use of Project Labor Agreements for Federal Construction Projects.

A website with the Executive Orders is maintained at http:// www.presidency.ucsb.edu/executive_orders.php.

E. FOREIGN BOYCOTT LAWS

The Export Administration Act of 1969, as amended, popularly known as the Anti–Boycott Law, 50 U.S.C.A. App. § 2407 (West 2010), authorizes the President to prohibit the facilitating of discrimination by foreign governments against "any United States person" on the basis of race, religion, sex, or national origin. It also expressly prohibits furnishing racial, religious, gender, or national origin information about any "United States person," or any owner, officer, director, or employee of such person. Violations of the Act or regulations promulgated under it can result in criminal penalties. See generally R. Folsom, *International Business Transactions* § 18.11 Discriminatory actions (3d ed. 2008).

F. FEDERAL CREDIT LAWS

Title III of the Consumer Credit Protection Act ("CCPA"), 15 U.S.C.A. §§ 1671–1677 (West 2010), 29 C.F.R. pt. 870 (2006), prohibits the discharge of an employee because of a garnishment for any one indebtedness. See generally U.S. Department of Labor website, http://www.dol.gov/compliance/guide/garnish.htm.

Title VI of the Consumer Credit Protection Act, called the Fair Credit Reporting Act ("FCRA"), 15 U.S.C.A. §§ 1681–1681t (West 2010), regulates the use of credit reports for employment purposes. It should be noted that state laws frequently regulate garnishments. Additionally, blacklisting, employer statements, and "service letters" relating to former employees are often areas of state regulation. Some states also regulate or prohibit wage assignments. See generally W. Brown, 1 *The Law of Debtors and Creditors* §§ 1:1 *et seq.* (Rev. ed. 2007).

G. JURY SERVICE

The Jury System Improvements Act of 1978, as amended, 28 U.S.C.A. §§ 1363, 1875 (West 2010) protects any employee's job security in the event the employee is called to serve on a federal jury. See *Shea v. County of Rockland*, 810 F.2d 27 (2d Cir. 1987) (damages are limited to economic losses). A number of states have enacted similar employee protection laws for state jury service.

H. DRUGS IN THE WORKPLACE

Public- and private-sector drug testing of employees has generated increased litigation and legislation in recent years. This area of the law involves sensitive issues of employee privacy versus employer concern for safety and health. For example, Congress passed the Drug Free Workplace Act of 1988, 41 U.S.C.A. §§ 701 *et seq.* (West 2010), to force most federal contractors to establish, supervise, and maintain an employee drug program designed to eliminate the use of drugs in the workplace. See also *National Treasury Emps. Union v. Von Raab*, 489 U.S. 656 (1989); *Skinner v. Railway Labor Execs.' Ass'n.*, 489 U.S. 602 (1989). See generally K. Zeese, *Drug Testing Legal Manual* (1988).

The National Labor Relations Board views drug testing as a mandatory subject of bargaining when union represented employees are involved. *Johnson–Bateman Co.*, 295 N.L.R.B. 180 (1989).

The U.S. Department of Labor maintains a website at http://www.dol.gov/asp/programs/drugs/workingpartners/regs/other_fedlaws.htm.

I. POLYGRAPHS

For the most part, the Employee Polygraph Protection Act of 1988 ("EPPA"), 29 U.S.C.A. § 2001 (West 2010), 29 C.F.R. pt. 801 (2006), prohibits the use of polygraphs by employers with regard to job applicants or employees. Limited exceptions are made for some government contractors, some providers of security services, some drug industries, and some instances involving employee crime. The act is administered by the Secretary of Labor, and employees are given a private right of action. See generally S. Pepe & S. Dunham, *Avoiding and Defending Wrongful Discharge Claims* § 2:5—Interviewing prospective employees—Lie detectors (1987).

The U.S. Department of Labor website on the subject is located at http://www.dol.gov/compliance/guide/eppa.htm.

J. NOTICE OF PLANT CLOSINGS

Most layoffs or plant closings by employers with 100 or more employees are subject to the notice requirements of the Worker Adjustment and Retraining Notification Act ("WARN"), 29 U.S.C.A. §§ 2101 *et seq.* (West 2010). Employers must give 60 days' notice to the employees' union, or to the employees in the absence of a union, prior to such actions. Failure to comply with the act can result in employer liability for backpay and benefits to employees, and the imposition of fines. Enforcement actions are to be brought in federal district court. See generally 11 *Employment Coordinator*—Labor Relations § 39:212–:245 (2011).

The U.S. Department of Labor website is located at http://www.doleta.gov/layoff/warn.cfm.

K. MIGRANT FARM WORKERS

The Migrant and Seasonal Agricultural Worker Protection Act, 29 U.S.C.A. §§ 1801 *et seq.* (West 2010), attempts to regulate migrant and seasonal farm labor by requiring farm labor contractor registration; by regulating workers safety, housing, and transportation; and by requiring employers to keep certain records. Enforcement provisions include a private right of action for act violations. See *Barrett v. Adams Fruit Co.*, 867 F.2d 1305 (11th Cir. 1989) (act preempts exclusive remedy provision of Florida's workers' compensation law). See generally 7 *Employment Coordinator*—Employment Practices §§ 92:42, 96:15 (2011).

The U.S. Department of Labor website is located at http://www.dol.gov/compliance/laws/comp-msawpa.htm.

L. UNIFORMED SERVICES PERSONNEL

Congress enacted special legislation for Vietnam veterans (38 U.S.C.A. § 4212 (West 2010)) that requires contractors to use affirmative action plans to hire, promote, and train qualified Vietnam-era veterans. Congress also guaranteed reemployment rights for service members with the Uniformed Services Employment and Reemployment Rights Act of 1994 ("USERRA"), 38 U.S.C.A. § 4301–4335 (West 2010), 20 C.F.R. pt. 1002 (2006), and generally prohibited discrimination against them. In *Staub v. Proctor Hosp.*, ___ U.S. ___, 131 S.Ct. 1186 (2011), it was held that if a supervisor performs act motivated by antimilitary animus that is intended by the supervisor to cause an adverse employment action, and if that act is proximate cause of ultimate employment action, then employer is liable under USERRA pursuant to 38 U.S.C.A. § 4311(c). This is sometimes referred to as "cat's paw" liability because the discriminatory animus of an employee who influenced, but did not make the ultimate adverse employment decision, is involved. See *EEOC v. BCI Coca–Cola Bottling Co.*, 450 F.3d 476, 484 (10th Cir. 2006). See generally 1 *Employment Discrimination Coordinator*—Analysis of Federal Law § 6:83 (2011).

The U.S. Department of Labor maintains a website at http://www.dol.gov/vets/programs/userra/main.htm.

No federal anti-discrimination laws applicable to the private sector have been enacted by Congress to protect homosexuals and lesbians from discrimination. See generally C. Richey, 1 *Manual on Employment Discrimination* §§ 1:64–68 (2d ed. 1994). In 1993, however, there was a federal effort to assist such individuals in the non-disclosure of their preferences upon entry into the military under what was called a "don't ask, don't tell" ("DADT") policy; see 10 U.S.C.A. § 654 (Pub. L. No. 103–160, § 571, 107 Stat. 1670 (1993)). This policy was repealed by the Don't Ask, Don't Tell Repeal Act of 2010, Pub. L. No. 111–321, 124 Stat. 3515. However, the final implementation will go into effect 60 days only after the President and his senior defense advisers certify that lifting the ban would not affect military readiness. This certification has not occurred as of June 1, 2011.

It should be noted that the Servicemembers Civil Relief Act (Soldiers' and Sailors' Civil Relief Act of 1940, as amended), 50 App. U.S.C.A. §§ 501–596 (West 2010), provides important protections to servicemembers from lawsuits and legal process.

M. IMMIGRATION REFORM AND CONTROL ACT OF 1986 (IRCA)

The Immigration Reform and Control Act of 1986 ("IRCA"), 8 U.S.C.A. § 1324a–b (West 2010), prohibits an employer from hiring an illegal alien, but prohibits employment discrimination based upon (1) an individual's national origin, or (2) the citizenship status of a protected individual as defined in the statute. Intimidation or retaliation are also prohibited. The law permits an employer to give preference in hiring to a U.S. citizen over an alien if he is otherwise equally qualified. See generally 1 *Employment Discrimination Coordinator*—Analysis of Federal Law § 4:10 (2011).

State laws attempting to regulate the employment of unauthorized aliens have been challenged by the federal government and others on preemption grounds. In *Chamber of Commerce of the U.S. v. Whiting*, ___ U.S. ___, 131 S. Ct. 1968 (2011), Arizona's unauthorized alien employment law allowing suspension and revocation of business licenses fell within the IRCA savings clause and was not impliedly preempted for conflicting with federal law. But in *United States v. Arizona*, 641 F.3d 339 (9th Cir. 2011), Arizona laws which criminalized work by unauthorized aliens was held preempted. See generally Fragomen, Shannon, and Montalvo, *Immigration Legislation Handbook* § 1:35.

N. TITLE VI, CIVIL RIGHTS ACT OF 1968 AND INTERGOVERNMENTAL PERSONNEL ACT OF 1970

Title VI of the Civil Rights Act of 1964, 42 U.S.C.A. § 2000d (West 2010), states:

No person in the United States shall, on the ground of race, color, or national origin, be excluded from participation in, be denied the benefits of, or be subjected to discrimination under any program or activity receiving Federal financial assistance.

Federal agencies that furnish financial assistance under this statute have regulations and enforcement procedures established under U.S. Department of Justice guidelines. See generally 2 *Employment Discrimination Coordinator*—Analysis of Federal Law § 89:1–:38 (2011). State and local governments receiving federal grants and funds are required to comply with federal requirements that generally prohibit discrimination in employment or require equal employment opportunity pursuant to the Intergovernmental Personnel Act of 1970, 42 U.S.C.A. § 4701–4728 (West 2010).

O. HEALTH INSURANCE PORTABILITY AND ACCOUNTABILITY ACT OF 1996 ("HIPAA")

The Health Insurance Portability and Accountability Act of 1996 ("HIPAA"), Pub. L. 104–191, 110 Stat. 1936, protects workers, individuals, and beneficiaries enrolled in group health plans. It establishes privacy rights and affords protects workers and dependents from discrimination based upon health status. HIPAA also addresses health care portability, preexisting condition exclusions, and enrollment in new health care plans even in situations where COBRA rights have been exhausted. The original law amended five other federal acts: the Internal Revenue Code ("IRC"), the Employee Retirement Income Security Act ("ERISA"), the Public Health Service Act ("PHSA"), the Social Security Act ("SSA"), and the criminal provisions of Title 18 of the U.S. Code. There have been significant amendments since 1996, including the American Recovery and Reinvestment Act of 2009 and the Healthcare Reform Law of 2010 (Patient Protection and Affordable Care Act of 2010 ("PPACA") (Pub. L. No. 111–148, 124 Stat. 119)), as amended by the Health Care and Education Reconciliation Act of 2010 ("HCERA"), Pub. L. No. 111–152, 124 Stat 1029 (together, the Healthcare Reform Law). See generally M. Stember, *Employer's Guide to the Health Insurance Portability and Accountability Act* (2010).

The U.S. Department of Labor website is http://www.dol. gov/dol/topic/health-plans/portability.htm.

P. LILLY LEDBETTER FAIR PAY ACT OF 2009

The Lilly Ledbetter Fair Pay Act of 2009, Pub. L. No. 111–2, 123 Stat. 5, amended Title VII of the Civil Rights Act of 1964 and the Age Discrimination in Employment Act of 1967 ("ADEA"), and modified the operation of the Americans with Disabilities Act of 1990 ("ADA") and the Rehabilitation Act of 1973 ("RA"), to clarify that a discriminatory compensation decision or other practice that is unlawful under such Acts occurs each time compensation is paid pursuant to the discriminatory compensation decision or other practice. The provisions were made retroactive to May 28, 2007. The law legislatively overruled the decision in *Ledbetter v. Goodyear Tire & Rubber Co.*, 550 U.S. 618 (2007), which had held that the statute of limitations for presenting an equal-pay lawsuit began on the date that the employer made the initial discriminatory wage decision, rather than at the date of the most recent paycheck which continued the wage discrimination.

Q. SARBANES–OXLEY ACT OF 2002 AND DODD–FRANK WALL STREET REFORM AND CONSUMER PROTECTION ACT, 2010

The Sarbanes–Oxley Act of 2002, Pub. L. No. 107–204, 116 Stat. 745, as amended by Pub. L. No. 111–203, 124 Stat. 1376 (2010), provides whistleblower protection for employees of publicly-traded companies who provide evidence of fraud; civil actions are authorized to protect against retaliation. 18 U.S.C.A. § 1514A (West 2010). Retaliation against informants is also protected by criminal penalties. 18 U.S.C.A. § 1513 (West 2010). Enacted in 2010, the Dodd–Frank Wall Street Reform and Consumer Protection Act, Pub. L. No. 111–203, 124 Stat. 1376 (2010), which added Sec. 21F to the Securities Exchange Act of 1934, provides further whistleblower protection against retaliation but also prohibits any award if the whistleblower provides false information.

R. GENETIC INFORMATION NONDISCRIMINATION ACT OF 2008

The Genetic Information Nondiscrimination Act of 2008 ("GINA"), 42 U.S.C.A. § 2000ff (West 2010), bans discrimination based on genetic information and makes it an unlawful employment practice for an employer (1) to fail or refuse to hire, or to discharge, any employee, or otherwise to discriminate against any employee with respect to the compensation, terms, conditions, or privileges of employment of the employee, because of genetic information with respect to the employee; or (2) to limit, segregate, or classify the employees of the employer in any way that would deprive or tend to deprive any employee of employment opportunities or otherwise adversely affect the status of the employee as an employee, because of genetic information with respect to the employee. It is also unlawful for an employer to acquire genetic information except in limited circumstances. Workers' health insurance and employment security are the main protection aims of GINA. Title VII remedies are afforded to workers for GINA violations. See generally M. Rothstein, *Occupational Safety and Health Law* § 20:12 (2011 ed.).

The U.S. Department of Labor website is http://www.dol.gov/ebsa/newsroom/fsGINA.html.

S.　TELEWORK ENHANCEMENT ACT OF 2010

The Telework Enhancement Act of 2010, Pub. L. No. 111–292, 124 Stat. 3165, provides increased work-at-home opportunities for federal employees. The U.S. Office of Personnel Management is required to develop teleworking guidelines and federal agencies must designate Telework Managing Officers. The goal is to better integrate teleworking into Continuity of Operations Planning procedures for operations during emergencies.

INDEX

References are to Pages

HEART CASES
Arising out of employment, 117–118

HEAT
Injuries from exposure, 112–114

HERNIA
As accident, 120

HEALTH INSURANCE PORTABILITY AND ACCOUNTABILITY ACT OF 1996 (HIPAA)
Coverage and purpose, 526–527
Exception for workers' compensation, 171–172

HORSEPLAY
Accidents while engaged in, 116–117
During course of employment, 116–117

HOSPITAL EXPENSES
See, Medical Expenses and Rehabilitation

IDIOPATHIC FALL
Accident due to,118–119

ILLEGAL EMPLOYMENT
See also, Minor Employees
Defined, 98–99
Workers' compensation coverage of, 98–99

ILLEGITIMATE CHILD
See, Child

IMMIGRATION REFORM AND CONTROL ACT OF 1986
Purpose, 525–526

INCREASED RISK TEST
See, Risks

INDEMNITY
Employer's obligation to indemnify third party, 184
Third party's right to indemnity against negligent employer, 184

INDEPENDENT CONTRACTOR
See, Contractor–Independent

INDUSTRIAL BARGAIN
Social and economic policies of workers' compensation, 73–78

INDUSTRIAL BURDEN
Social and economic policies of workers' compensation, 73–78

INSURANCE
See, Social Security Insurance Programs, Unemployment Compensation

SUBCONTRACTORS
Defined, 105–106
Liability of negligent subcontractor's employee to principal contractor's employee, 105–106
Third party liability, 105–106, 183
Workers' compensation coverage of, 105–106

SUBROGATION
See, Third Party Liability

SUCCESSIVE EMPLOYERS
See, Employer

SUCCESSIVE INJURY FUNDS
See, Subsequent Injury Funds

SUICIDE
Post-accident, 130–131

SUPPLEMENTAL SECURITY INCOME
See, Social Security Insurance Programs

TELEWORK ENHANCEMENT ACT OF 2010
Purpose, 529

THIRD PARTY ACTIONS AND LIABILITY
Bad faith administration of workers' compensation claims, 84–85, 183
Co-employee as third party, 81–82, 183
Compensation insurer as third party, 83–84, 183
Contractor, independent, as third party, 182–183
Defenses, 184–185
Dual capacity employers, 82–83, 183
Effect of employee's settlement with third party on employer's rights, 185–186
Effect of employer's concurring negligence, 184–185
Employer as third party, 184
Indemnity
    Employer's obligation to indemnify third party, 184
    Employer's right to indemnity, 184–185
Independent contractors
    As third party, 182–183
    Liability of negligent subcontractor's employee to principal contractor's employee, 105–106
    Principal as third party with respect to contractor's employee, 105–106
Inspectors as third party, 83–84, 183
Insurance carrier as third party, 83–86, 183
Physician
    Physician as independent contractor third party, 85–86, 183
    Physician negligently treating employee may be liable as third party, 85–86, 183
Product liability, 85, 183

†